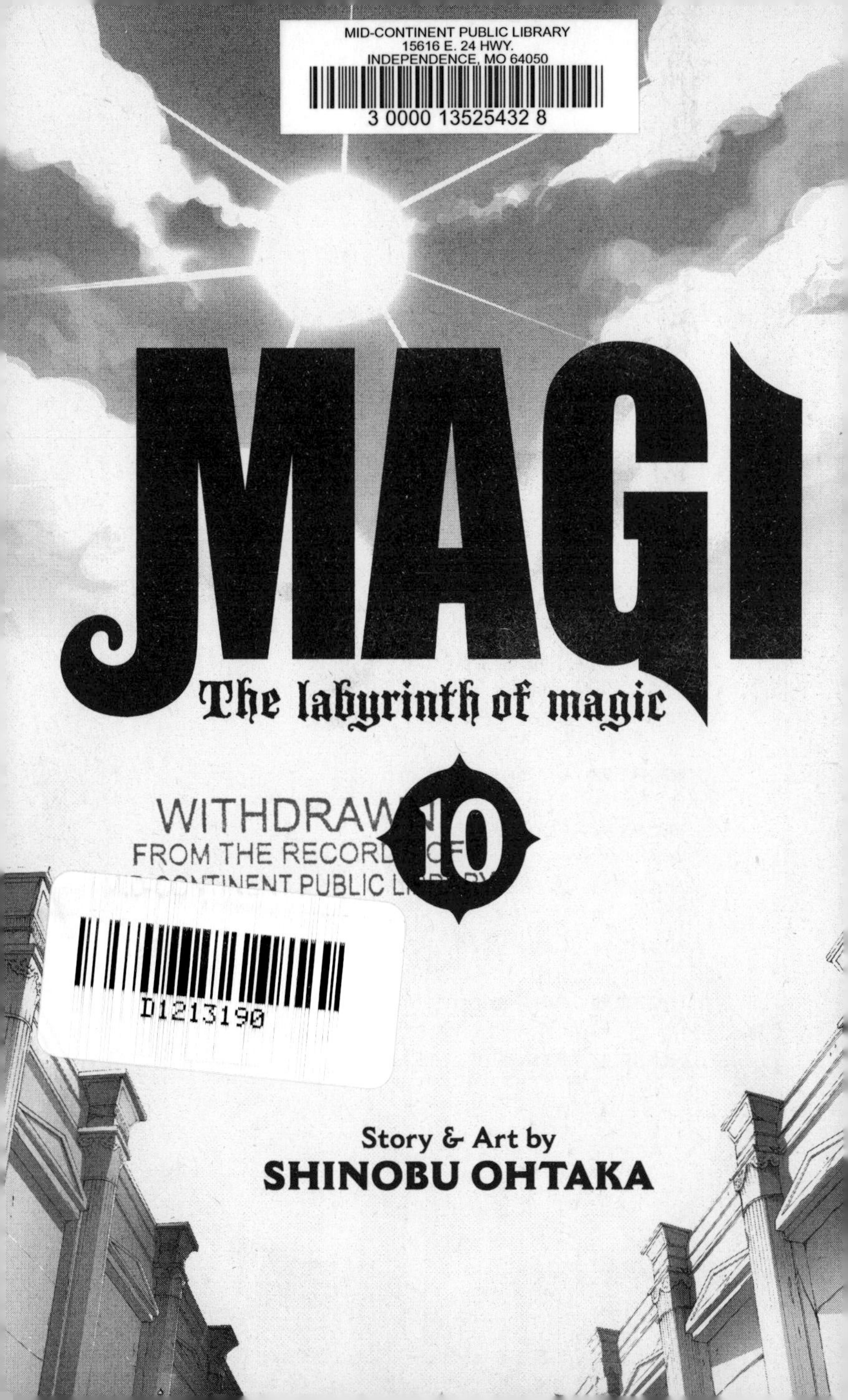
MAGI
The labyrinth of magic
10
Story & Art by
SHINOBU OHTAKA

# MAGI
### The labyrinth of magic
## ⑩

# CONTENTS

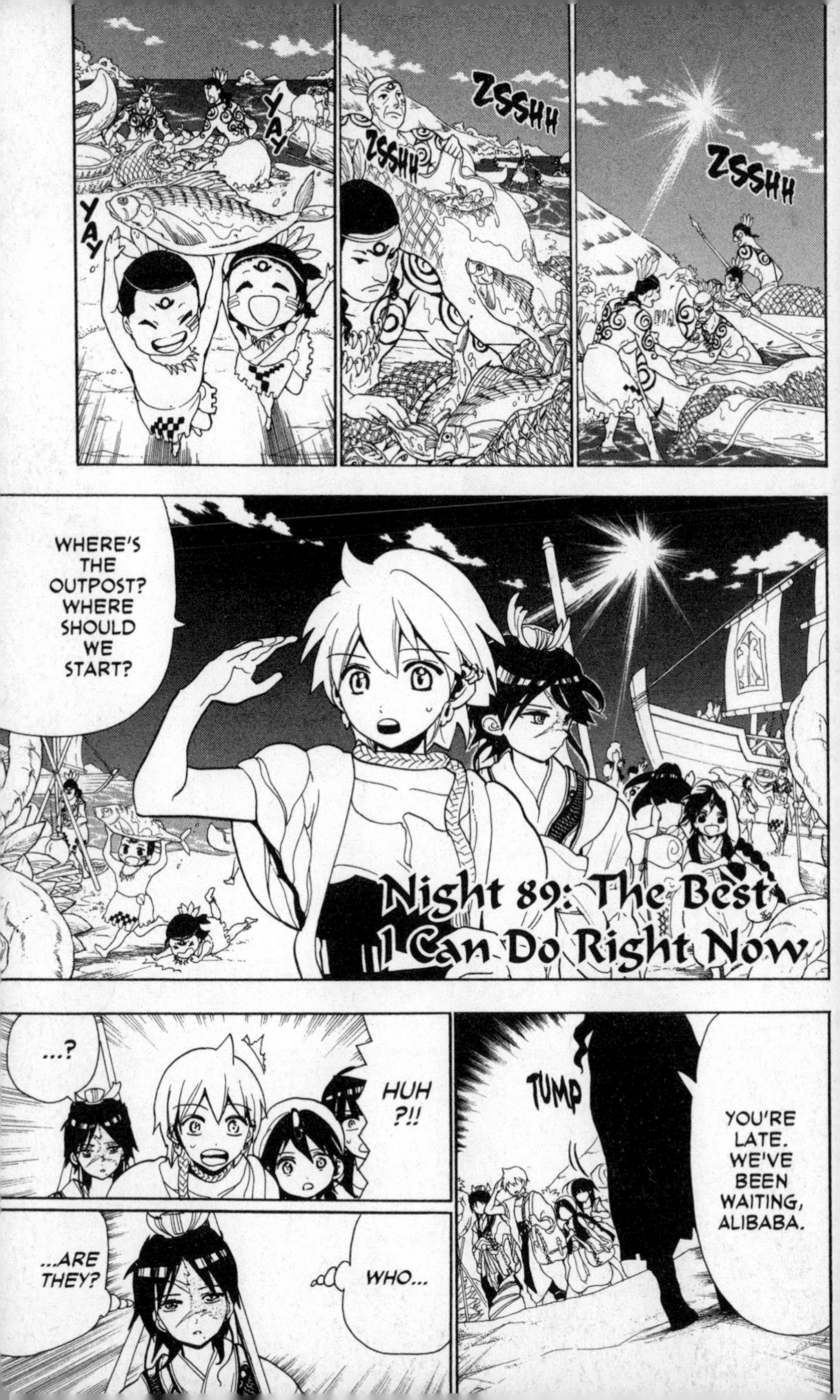
ZSSHH
ZSSHH
ZSSHH
YAY
YAY
WHERE'S THE OUTPOST? WHERE SHOULD WE START?
Night 89: The Best I Can Do Right Now
TUMP
YOU'RE LATE. WE'VE BEEN WAITING, ALIBABA.
HUH?!!
...?
WHO...
...ARE THEY?

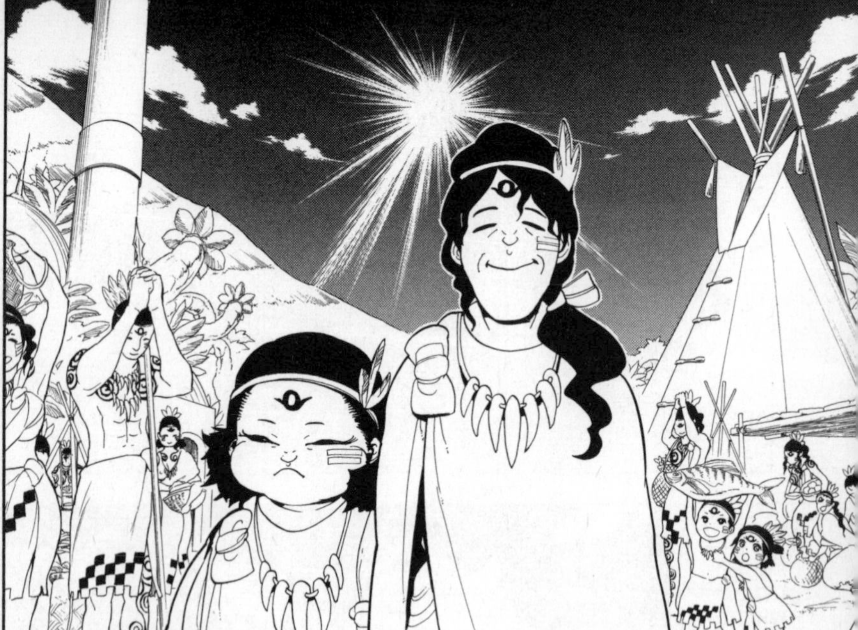
Night 89:
The Best I Can Do Right Now

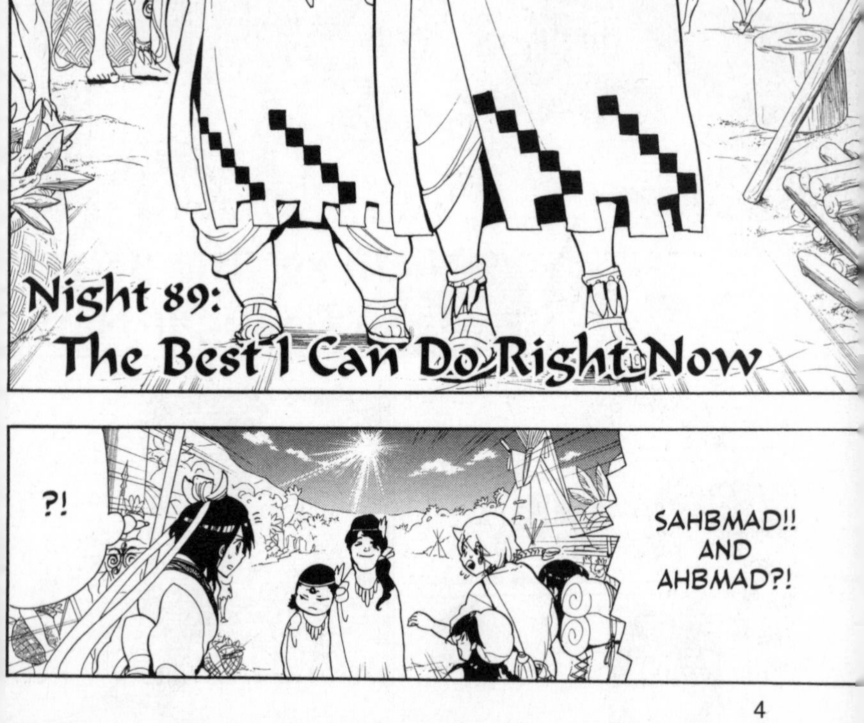
SAHBMAD!! AND AHBMAD?!
?!

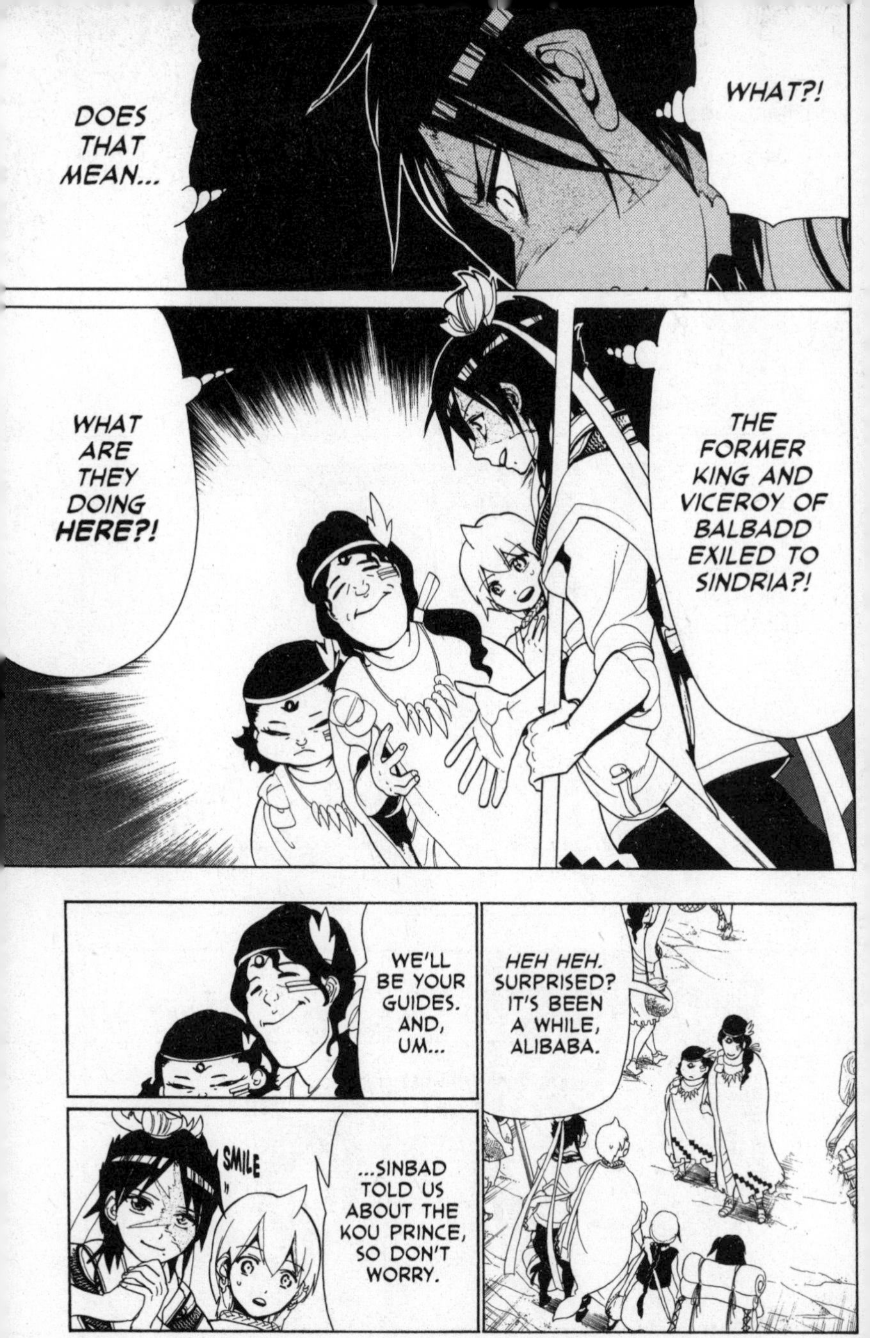
WHAT?!
DOES THAT MEAN...
THE FORMER KING AND VICEROY OF BALBADD EXILED TO SINDRIA?!
WHAT ARE THEY DOING HERE?!
HEH HEH. SURPRISED? IT'S BEEN A WHILE, ALIBABA.
WE'LL BE YOUR GUIDES. AND, UM...
...SINBAD TOLD US ABOUT THE KOU PRINCE, SO DON'T WORRY.
SMILE

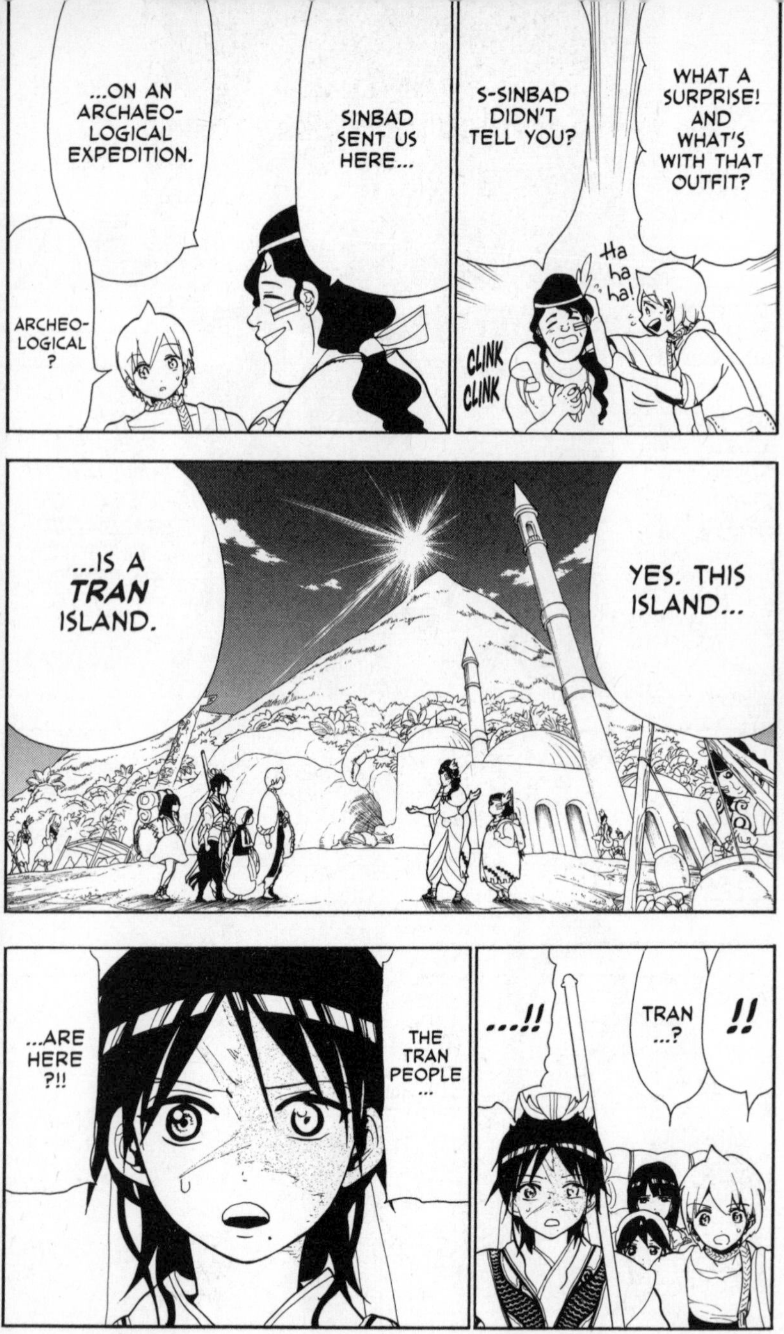
WHAT A SURPRISE! AND WHAT'S WITH THAT OUTFIT?
S-SINBAD DIDN'T TELL YOU?
Ha ha ha!
CLINK CLINK
SINBAD SENT US HERE...
...ON AN ARCHAEO-LOGICAL EXPEDITION.
ARCHEO-LOGICAL ?
YES. THIS ISLAND...
...IS A *TRAN* ISLAND.
!!
TRAN ...?
...!!
THE TRAN PEOPLE ...
...ARE HERE ?!!

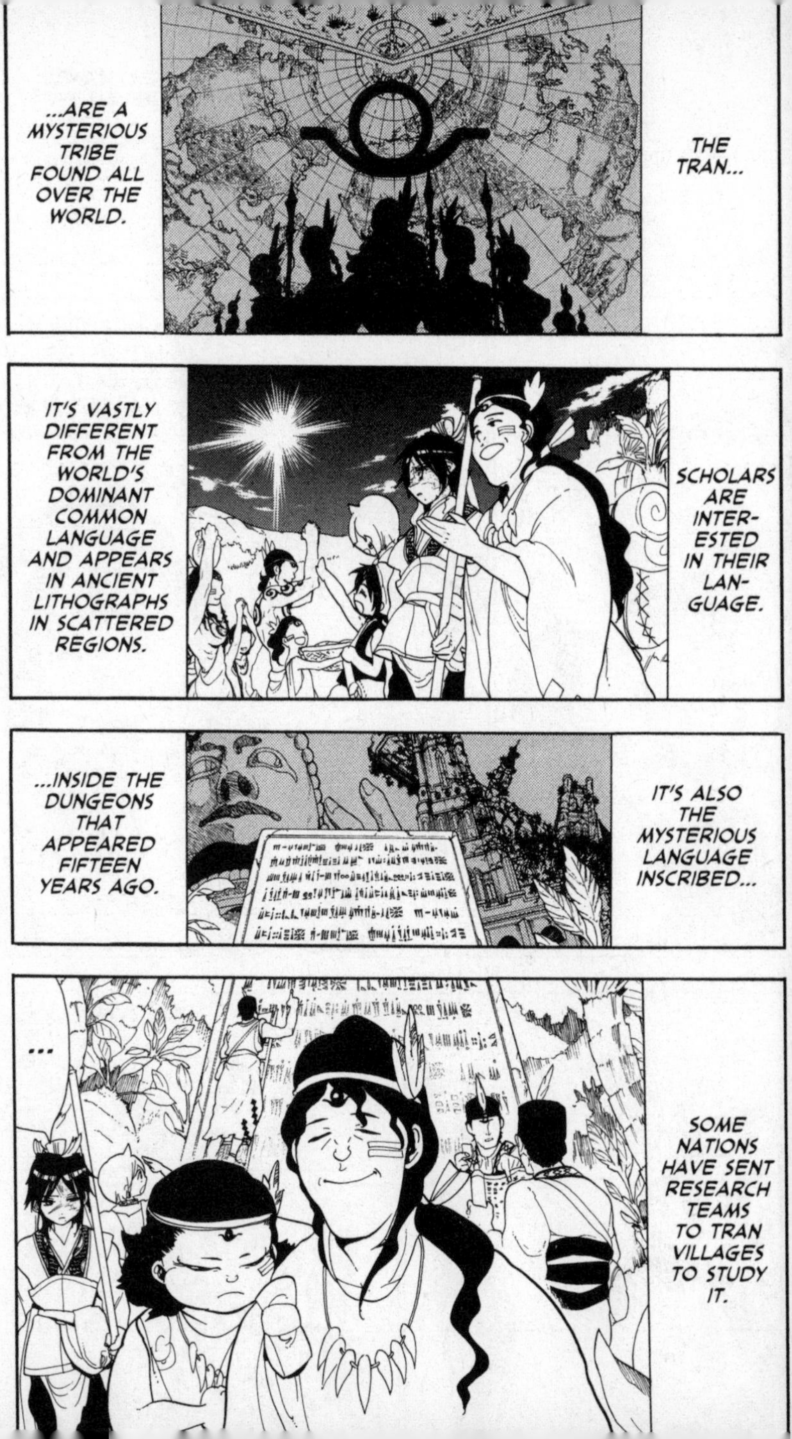
THE TRAN...
...ARE A MYSTERIOUS TRIBE FOUND ALL OVER THE WORLD.
SCHOLARS ARE INTERESTED IN THEIR LANGUAGE.
IT'S VASTLY DIFFERENT FROM THE WORLD'S DOMINANT COMMON LANGUAGE AND APPEARS IN ANCIENT LITHOGRAPHS IN SCATTERED REGIONS.
IT'S ALSO THE MYSTERIOUS LANGUAGE INSCRIBED...
...INSIDE THE DUNGEONS THAT APPEARED FIFTEEN YEARS AGO.
SOME NATIONS HAVE SENT RESEARCH TEAMS TO TRAN VILLAGES TO STUDY IT.
...

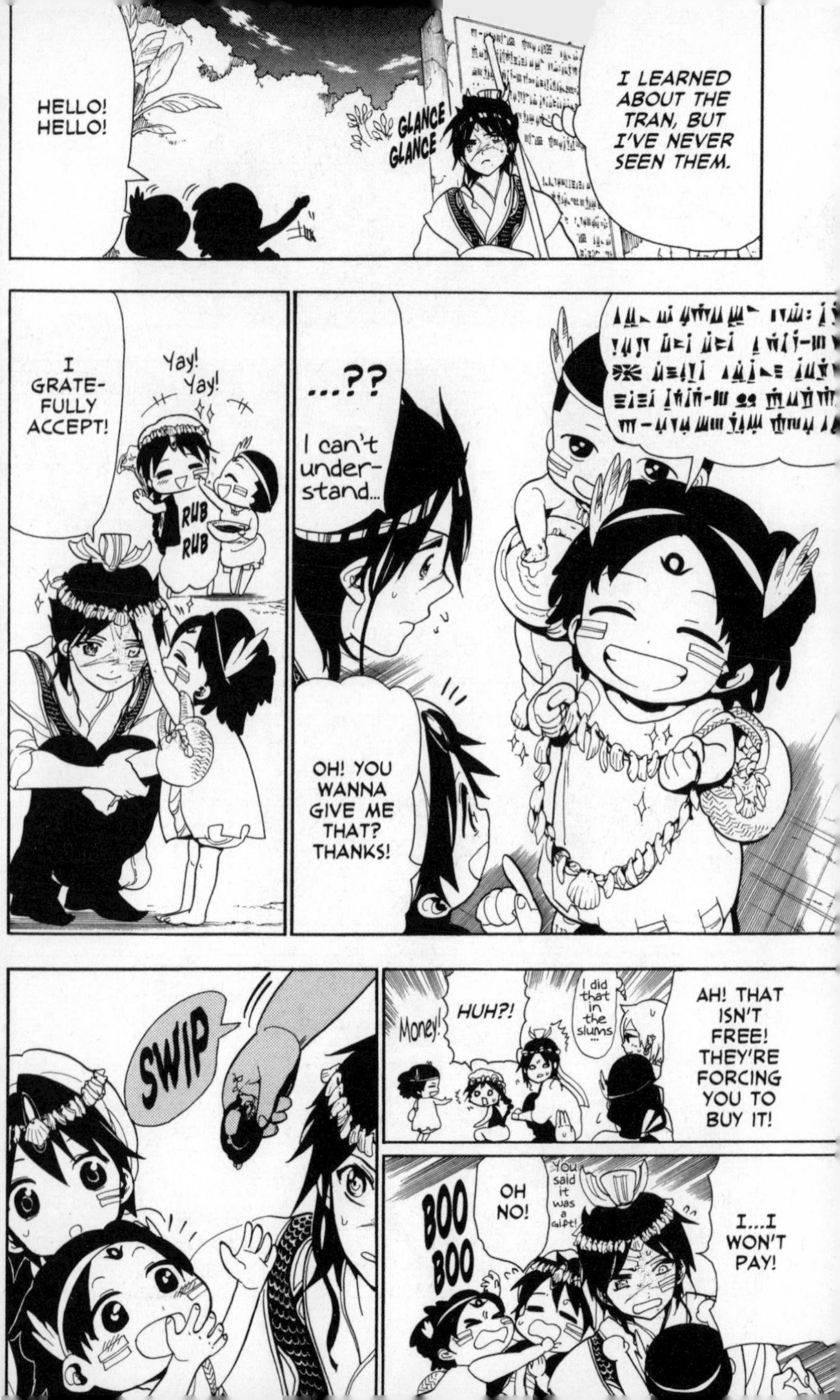

I LEARNED ABOUT THE TRAN, BUT I'VE NEVER SEEN THEM.
GLANCE GLANCE
HELLO! HELLO!
...??
I can't under-stand...
OH! YOU WANNA GIVE ME THAT? THANKS!
Yay! Yay!
I GRATE-FULLY ACCEPT!
RUB RUB
AH! THAT ISN'T FREE! THEY'RE FORCING YOU TO BUY IT!
I did that in the slums...
HUH?!
Money!
I...I WON'T PAY!
You said it was a gift!
OH NO!
BOO BOO
SWIP

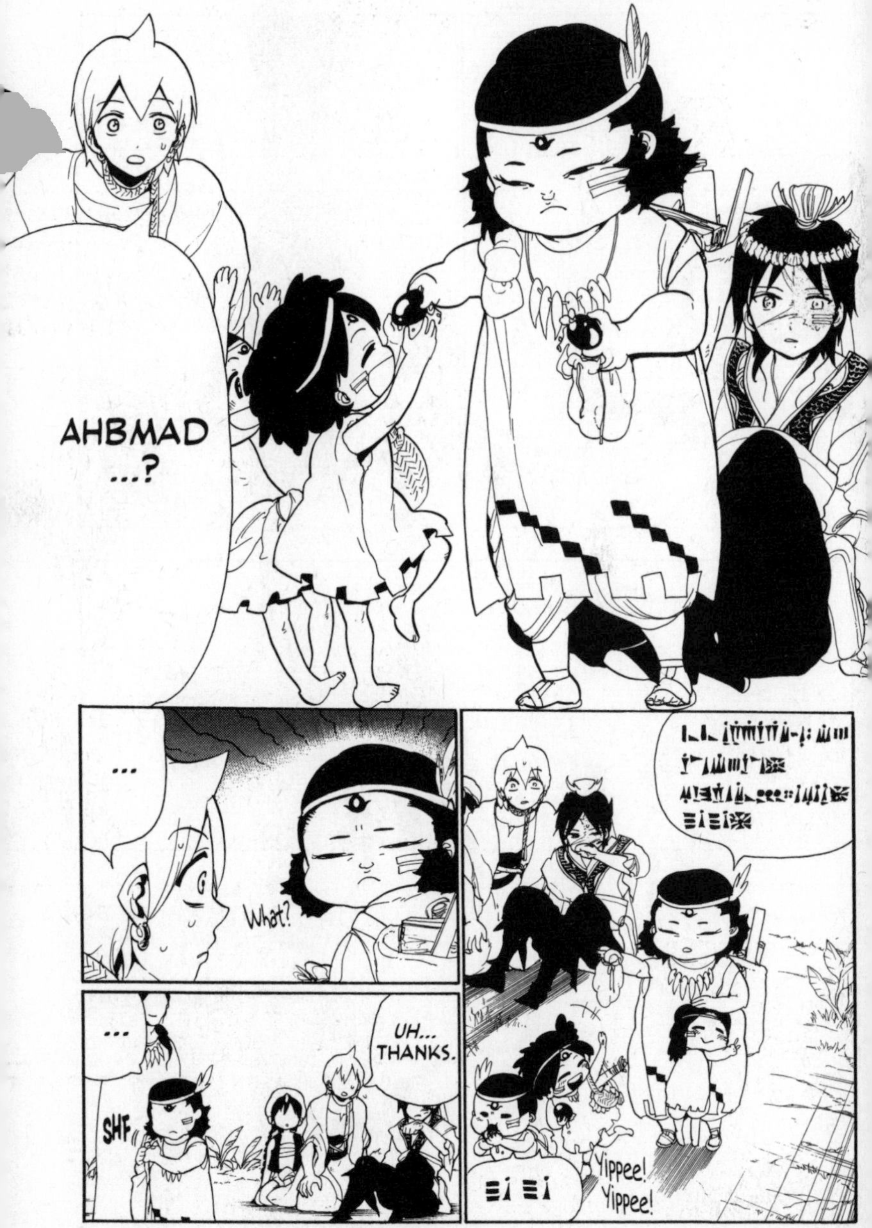
AHBMAD ...?
Yippee! Yippee!
...
What?
...
UH... THANKS.
SHF

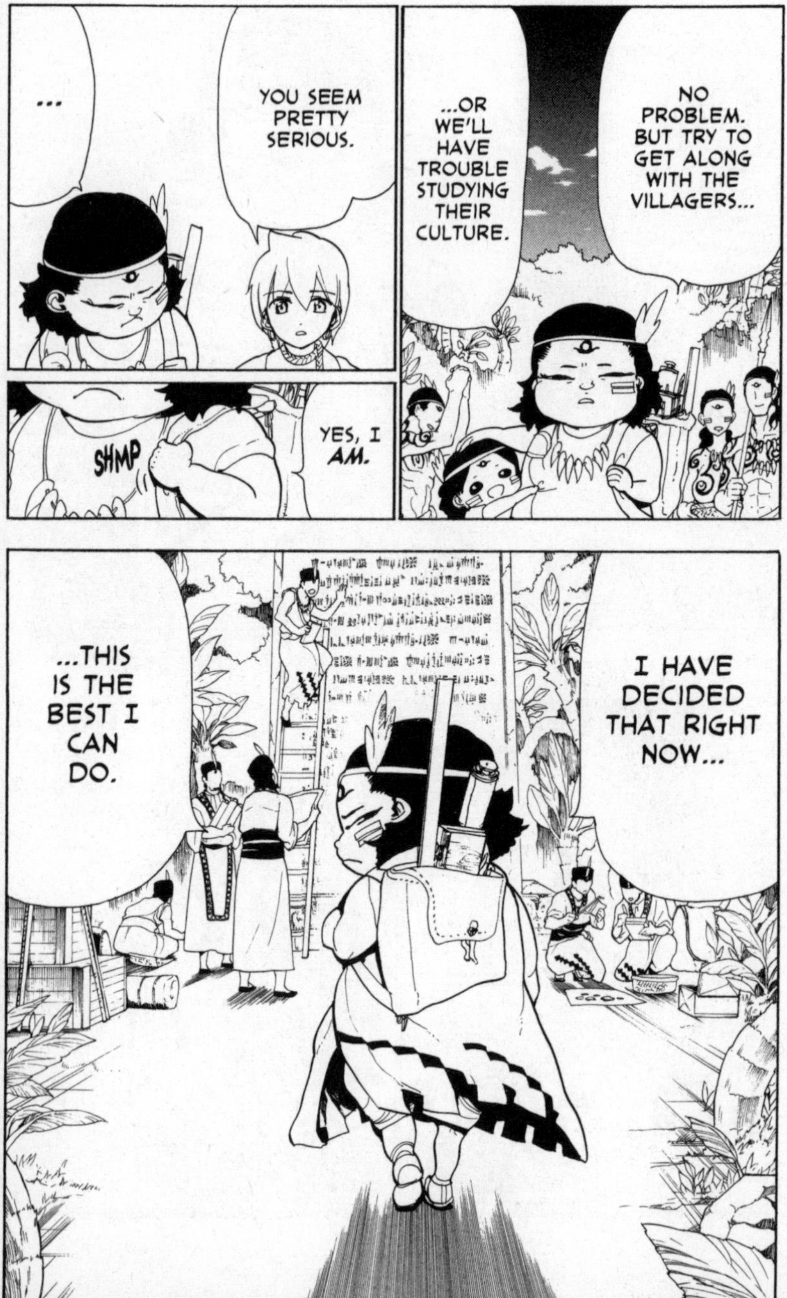
NO PROBLEM. BUT TRY TO GET ALONG WITH THE VILLAGERS...
...OR WE'LL HAVE TROUBLE STUDYING THEIR CULTURE.
YOU SEEM PRETTY SERIOUS.
...
YES, I *AM.*
SHMP
I HAVE DECIDED THAT RIGHT NOW...
...THIS IS THE BEST I CAN DO.

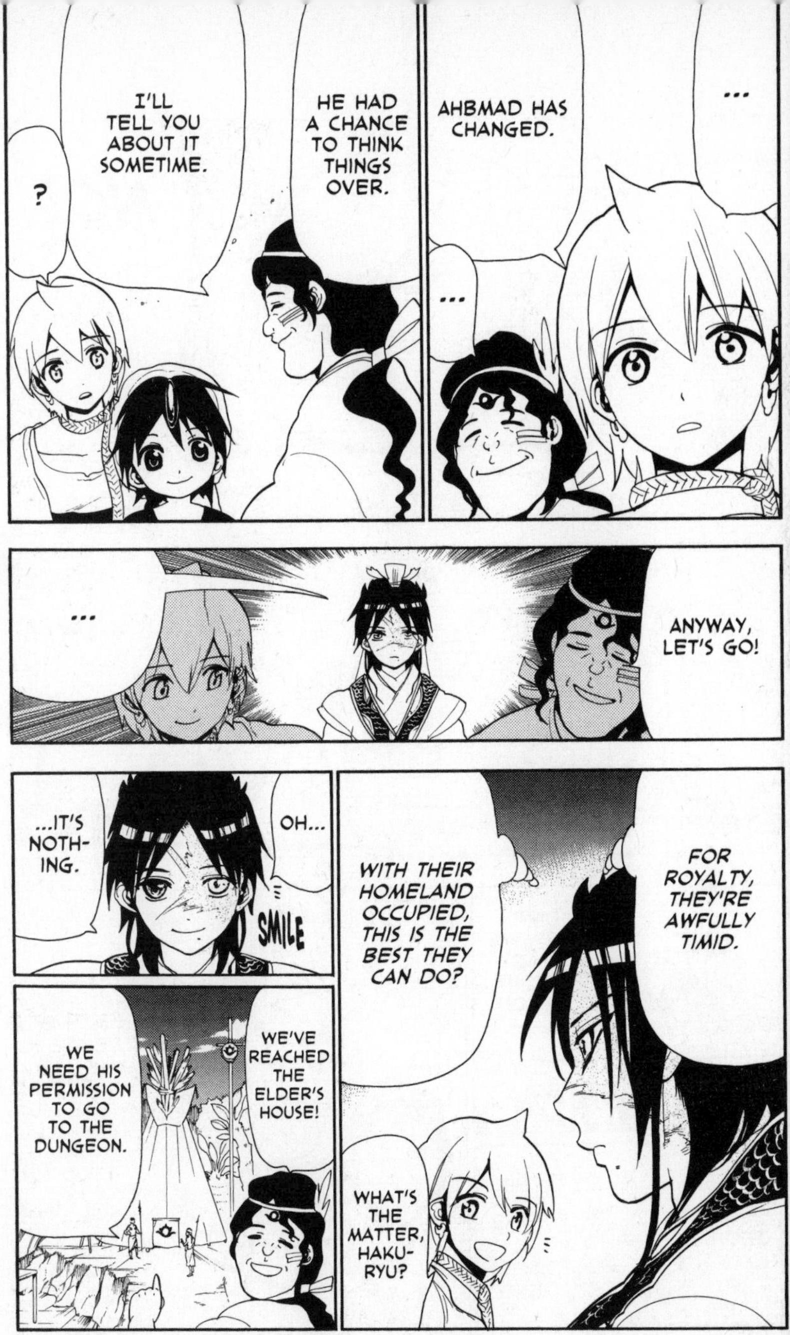
...
AHBMAD HAS CHANGED.
...
HE HAD A CHANCE TO THINK THINGS OVER.
I'LL TELL YOU ABOUT IT SOMETIME.
?
ANYWAY, LET'S GO!
...
FOR ROYALTY, THEY'RE AWFULLY TIMID.
WITH THEIR HOMELAND OCCUPIED, THIS IS THE BEST THEY CAN DO?
WHAT'S THE MATTER, HAKU-RYU?
OH...
...IT'S NOTH-ING.
SMILE
WE'VE REACHED THE ELDER'S HOUSE!
WE NEED HIS PERMISSION TO GO TO THE DUNGEON.

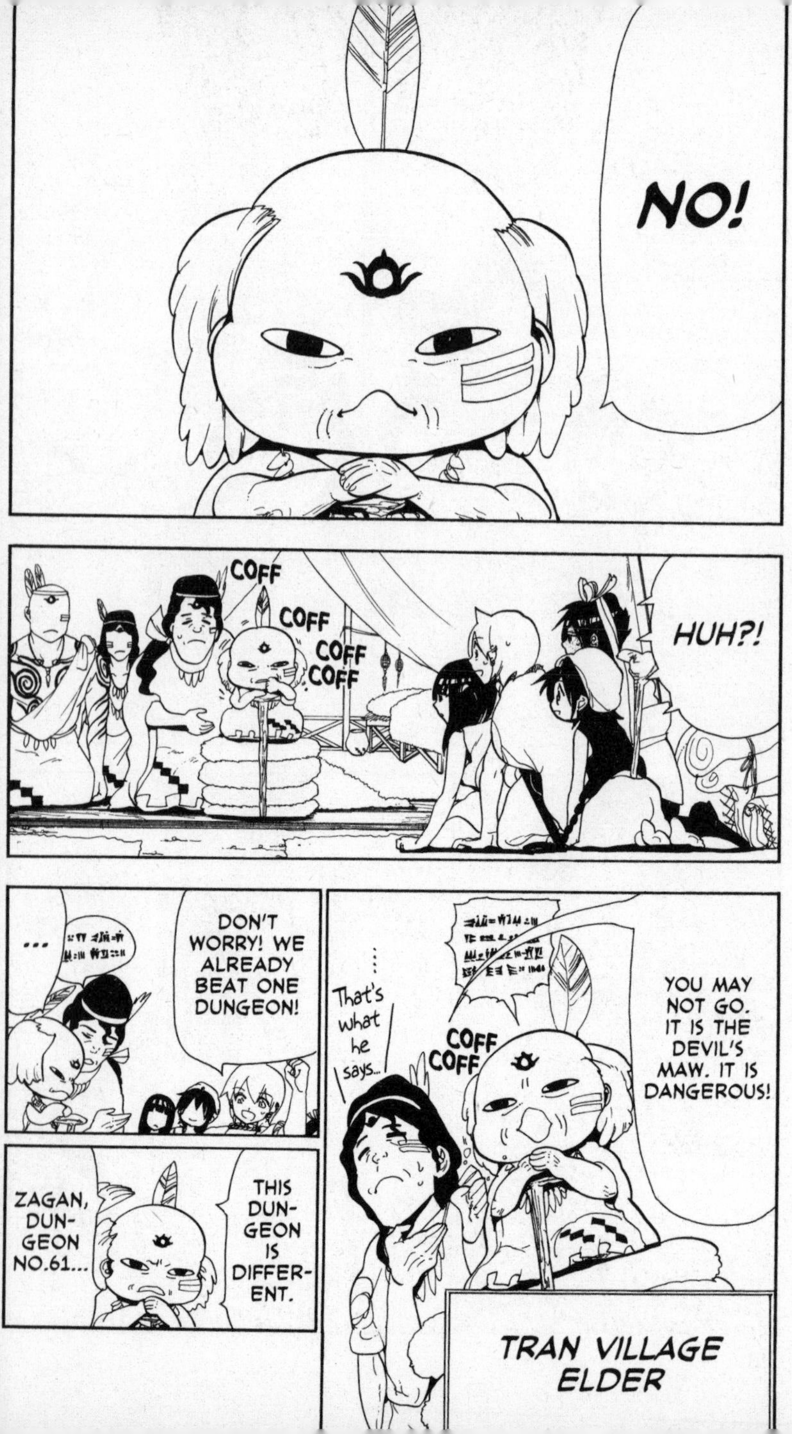
NO!
HUH?!
COFF
COFF
COFF
COFF
YOU MAY NOT GO. IT IS THE DEVIL'S MAW. IT IS DANGEROUS!
...That's what he says...
COFF COFF
TRAN VILLAGE ELDER
DON'T WORRY! WE ALREADY BEAT ONE DUNGEON!
...
THIS DUNGEON IS DIFFERENT.
ZAGAN, DUNGEON NO.61...

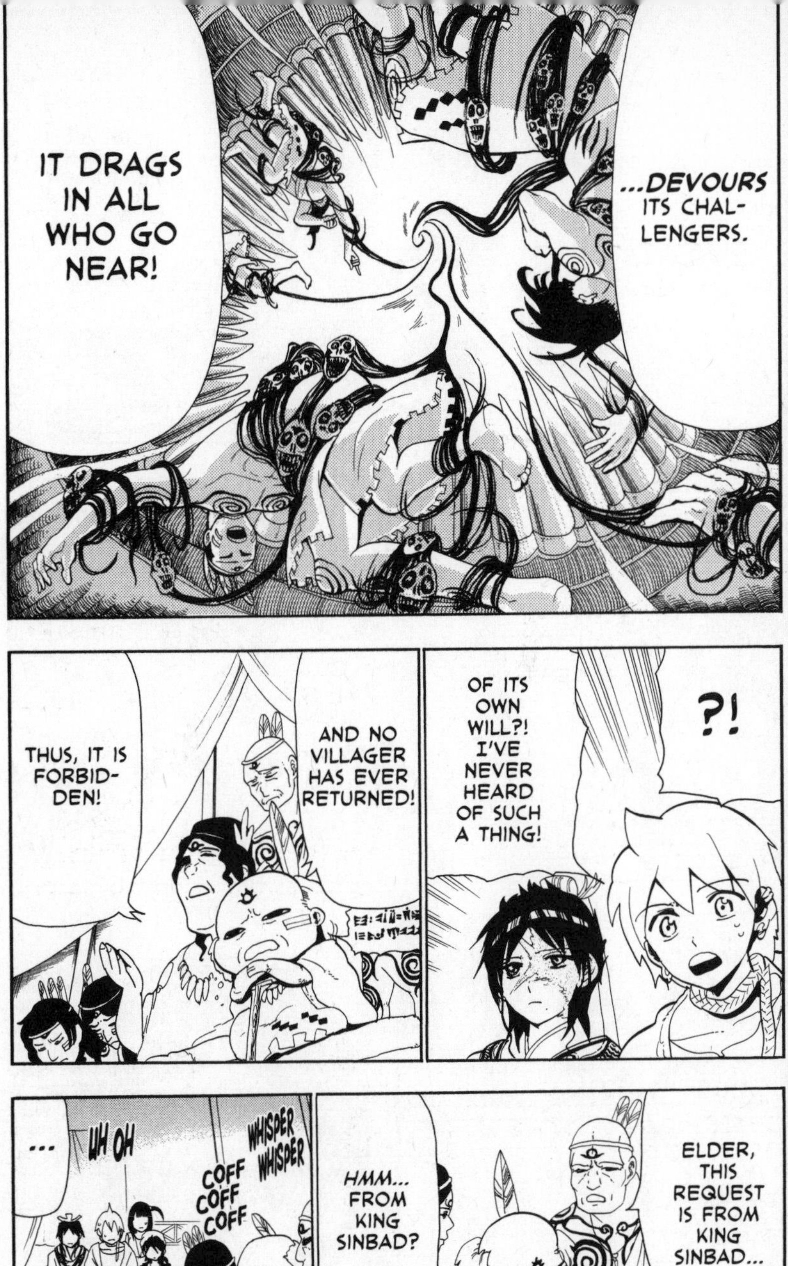
IT DRAGS IN ALL WHO GO NEAR!
...DEVOURS ITS CHALLENGERS.
?!
OF ITS OWN WILL?! I'VE NEVER HEARD OF SUCH A THING!
AND NO VILLAGER HAS EVER RETURNED!
THUS, IT IS FORBIDDEN!
ELDER, THIS REQUEST IS FROM KING SINBAD...
HMM... FROM KING SINBAD?
WHISPER WHISPER
UH OH
...
COFF COFF COFF

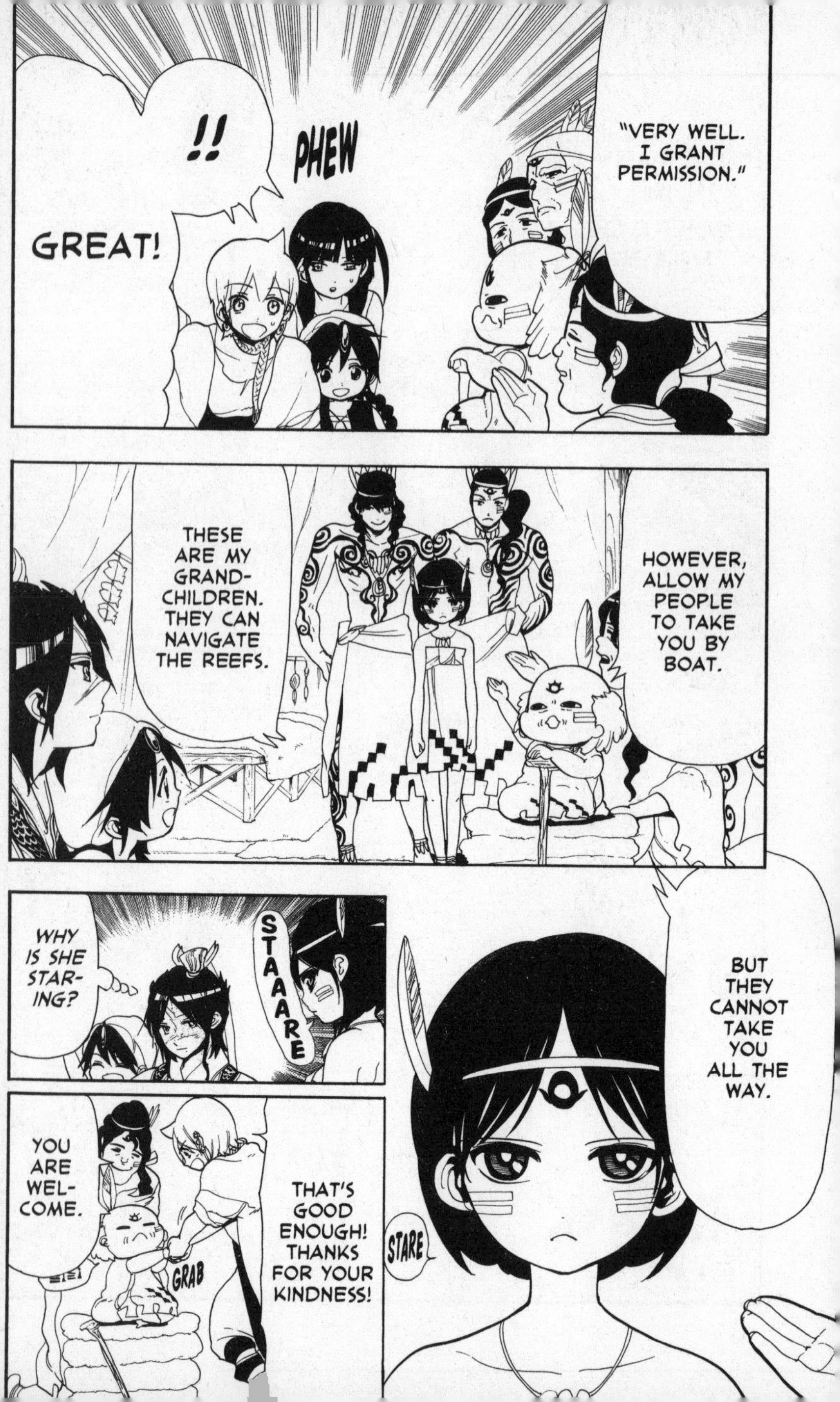
"VERY WELL. I GRANT PERMISSION."
PHEW
!!
GREAT!
HOWEVER, ALLOW MY PEOPLE TO TAKE YOU BY BOAT.
THESE ARE MY GRANDCHILDREN. THEY CAN NAVIGATE THE REEFS.
BUT THEY CANNOT TAKE YOU ALL THE WAY.
STARE
STAAAARE
WHY IS SHE STARING?
THAT'S GOOD ENOUGH! THANKS FOR YOUR KINDNESS!
GRAB
YOU ARE WELCOME.

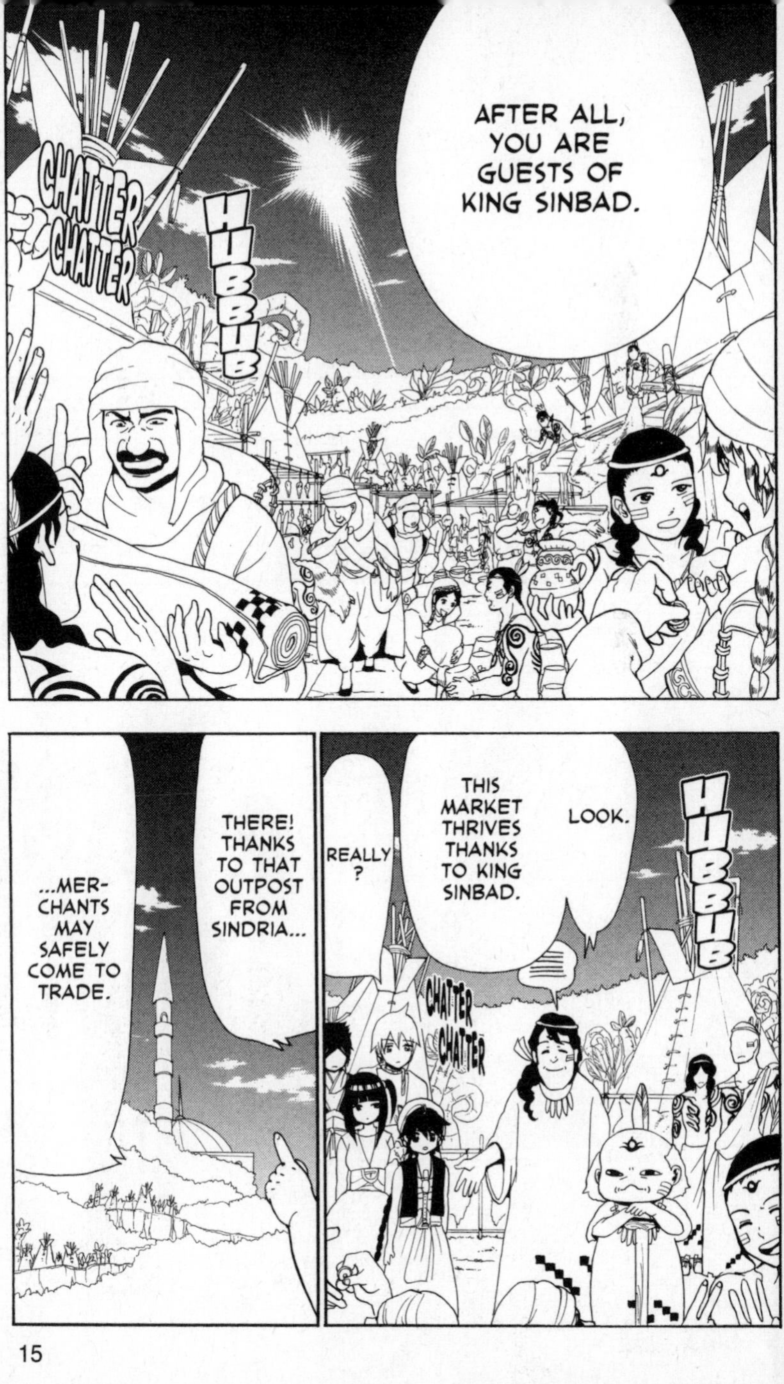
AFTER ALL, YOU ARE GUESTS OF KING SINBAD.
HUBBUB
CHATTER CHATTER
HUBBUB
LOOK.
THIS MARKET THRIVES THANKS TO KING SINBAD.
REALLY?
CHATTER CHATTER
THERE! THANKS TO THAT OUTPOST FROM SINDRIA...
...MER-CHANTS MAY SAFELY COME TO TRADE.

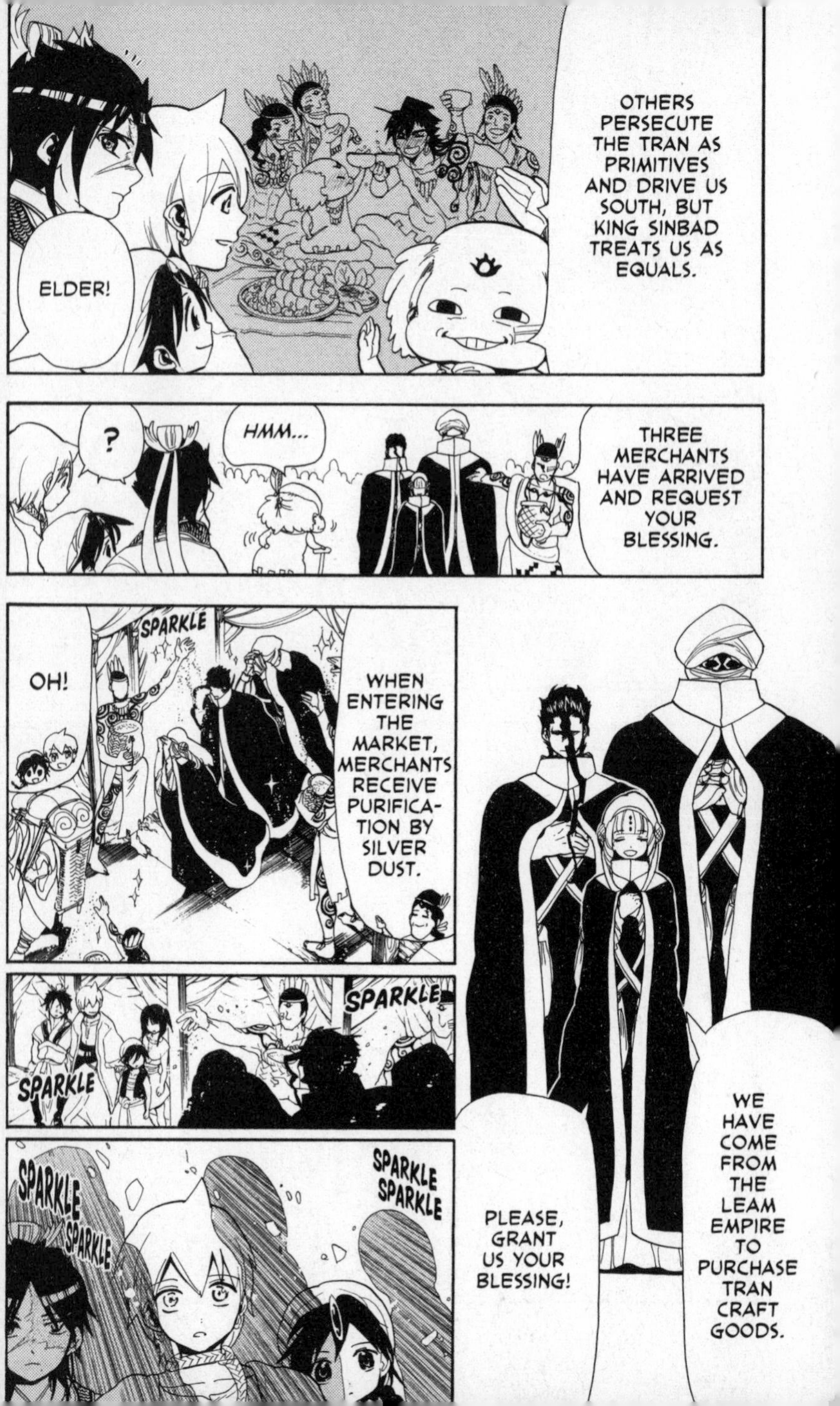
OTHERS PERSECUTE THE TRAN AS PRIMITIVES AND DRIVE US SOUTH, BUT KING SINBAD TREATS US AS EQUALS.
ELDER!
THREE MERCHANTS HAVE ARRIVED AND REQUEST YOUR BLESSING.
HMM...
?
WE HAVE COME FROM THE LEAM EMPIRE TO PURCHASE TRAN CRAFT GOODS.
PLEASE, GRANT US YOUR BLESSING!
WHEN ENTERING THE MARKET, MERCHANTS RECEIVE PURIFICA-TION BY SILVER DUST.
SPARKLE
OH!
SPARKLE
SPARKLE
SPARKLE SPARKLE
SPARKLE SPARKLE

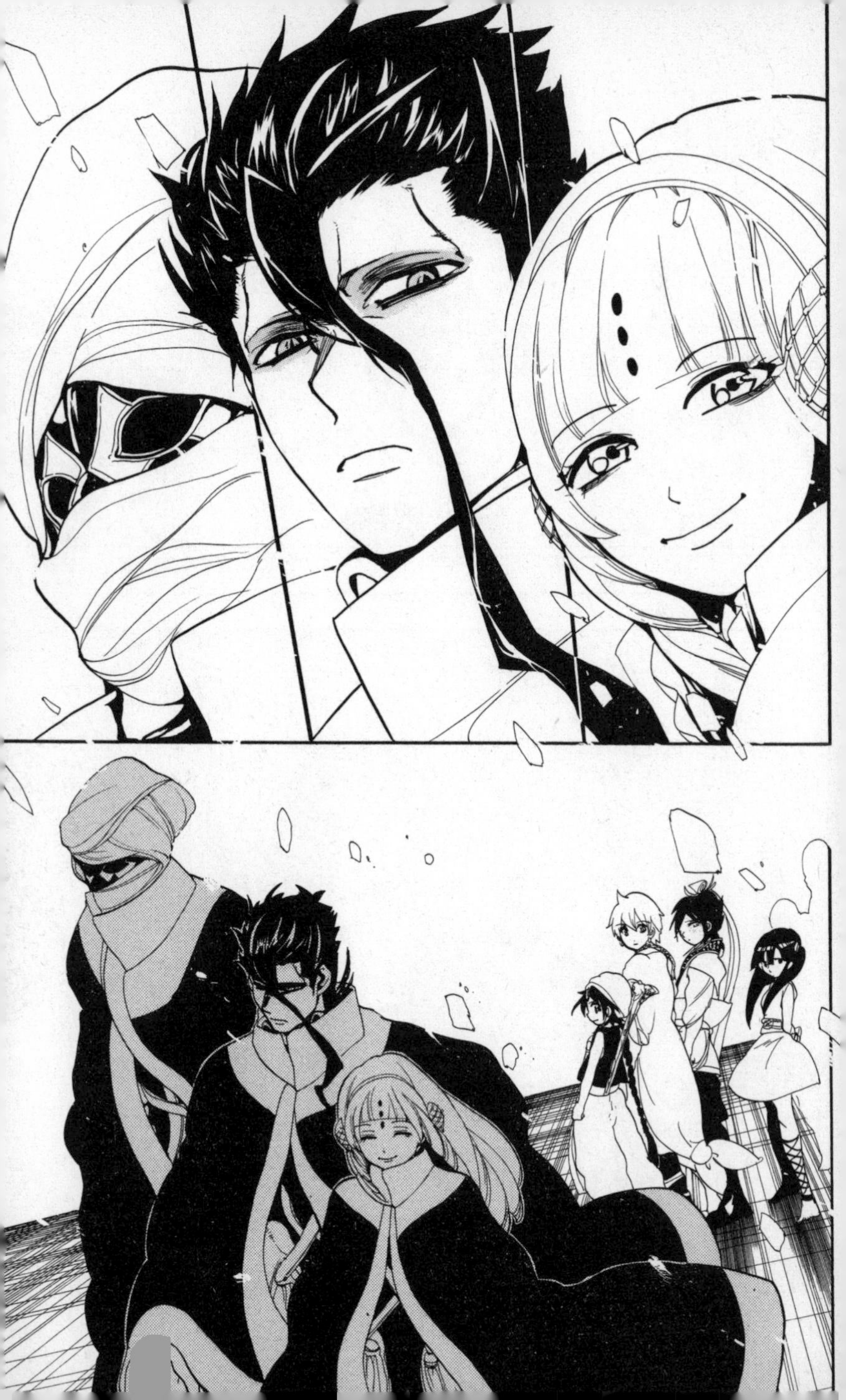

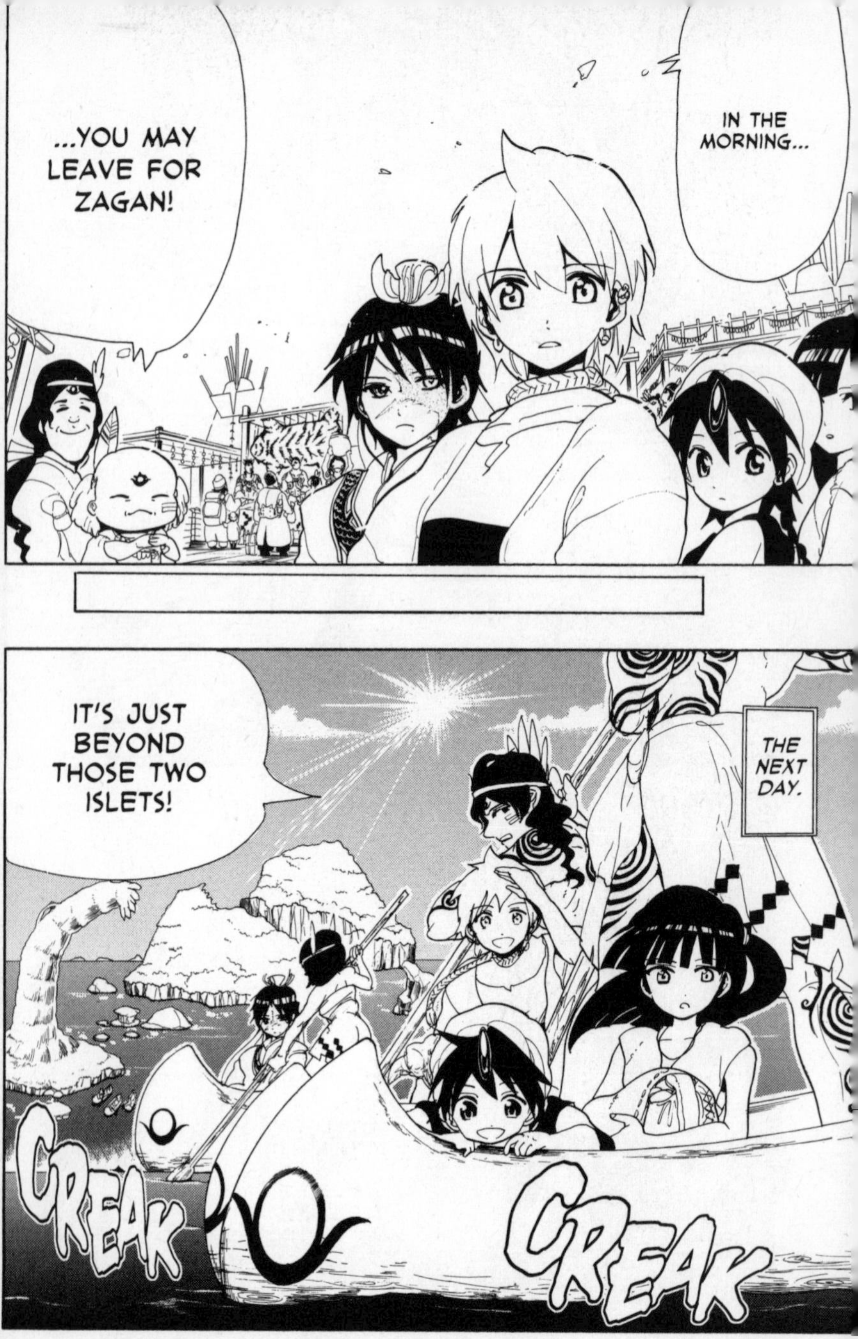
IN THE MORNING...
...YOU MAY LEAVE FOR ZAGAN!
THE NEXT DAY.
IT'S JUST BEYOND THOSE TWO ISLETS!
CREAK
CREAK

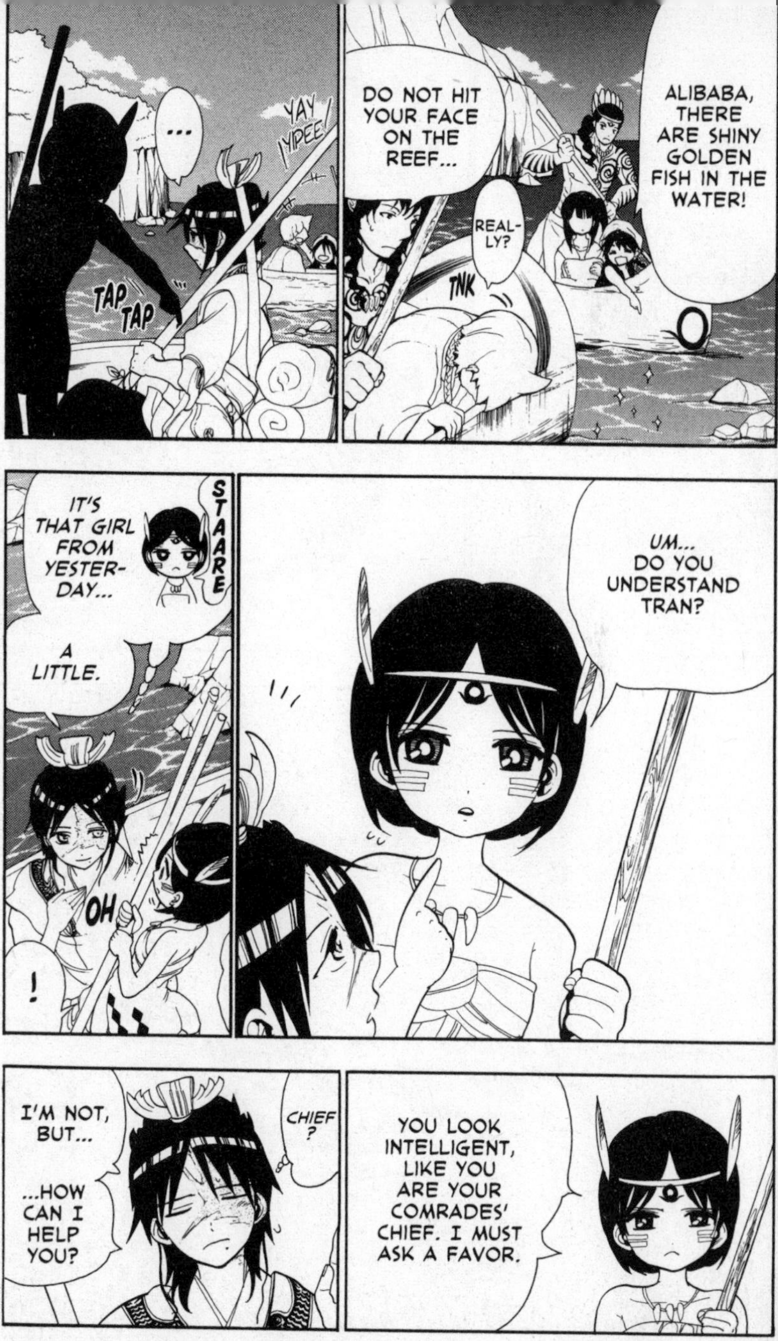
ALIBABA, THERE ARE SHINY GOLDEN FISH IN THE WATER!
DO NOT HIT YOUR FACE ON THE REEF...
REALLY?
TNK
YAY YIPPEE!
...
TAP TAP
UM... DO YOU UNDERSTAND TRAN?
STAARE
IT'S THAT GIRL FROM YESTERDAY...
A LITTLE.
OH
!
YOU LOOK INTELLIGENT, LIKE YOU ARE YOUR COMRADES' CHIEF. I MUST ASK A FAVOR.
CHIEF?
I'M NOT, BUT...
...HOW CAN I HELP YOU?

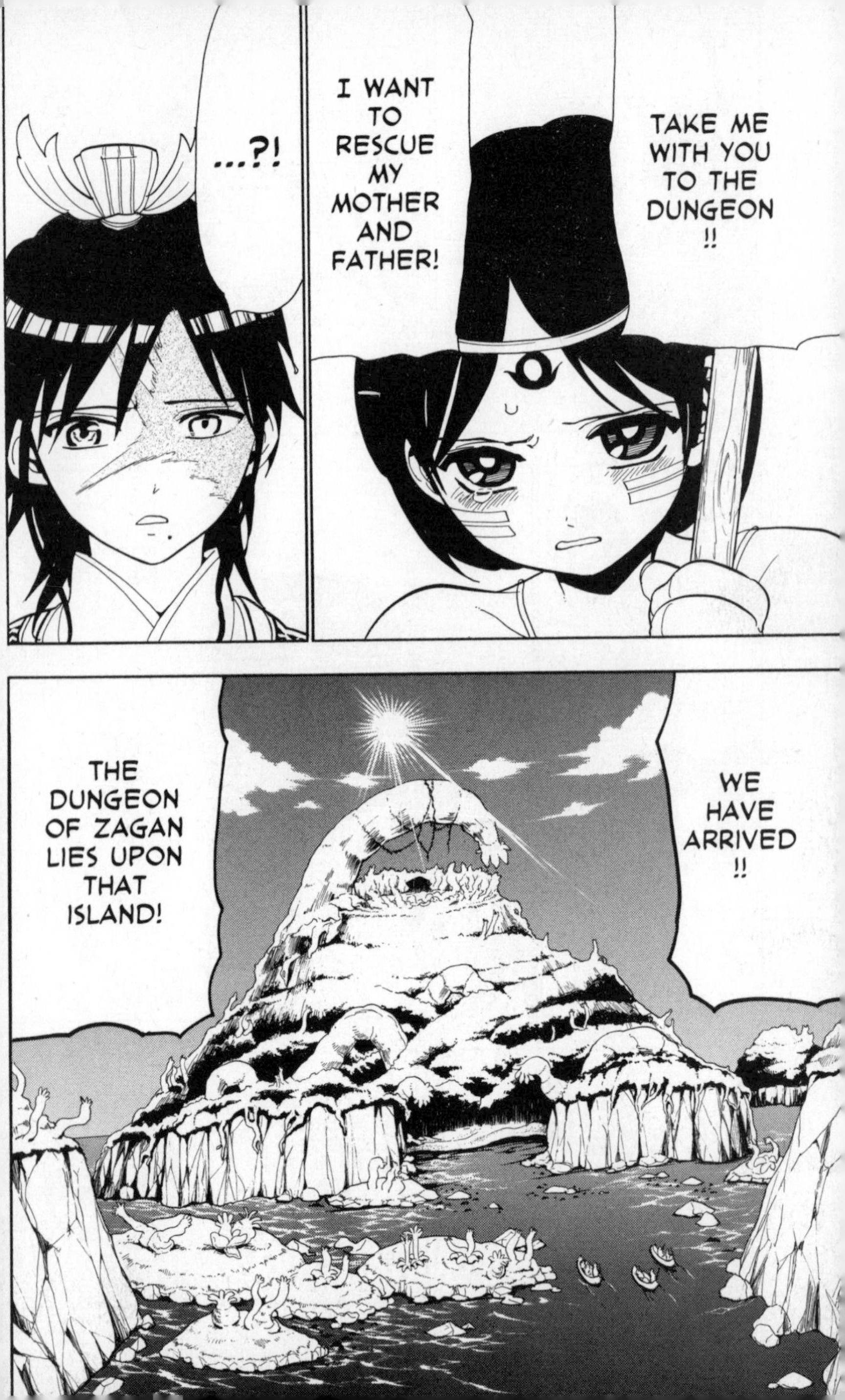
I WANT TO RESCUE MY MOTHER AND FATHER!
TAKE ME WITH YOU TO THE DUNGEON !!
...?!
WE HAVE ARRIVED !!
THE DUNGEON OF ZAGAN LIES UPON THAT ISLAND!

# Night 90: Another Dungeon

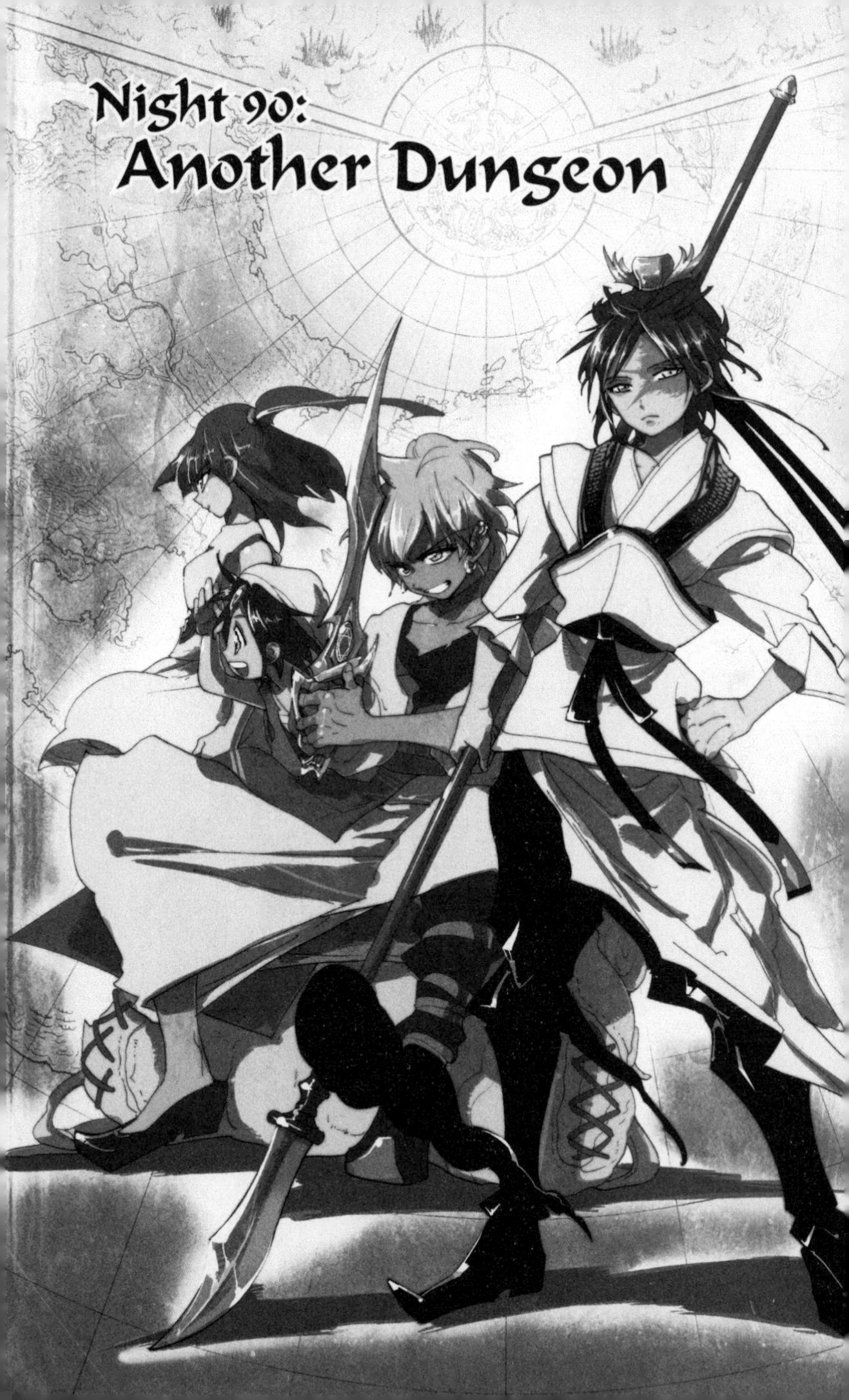

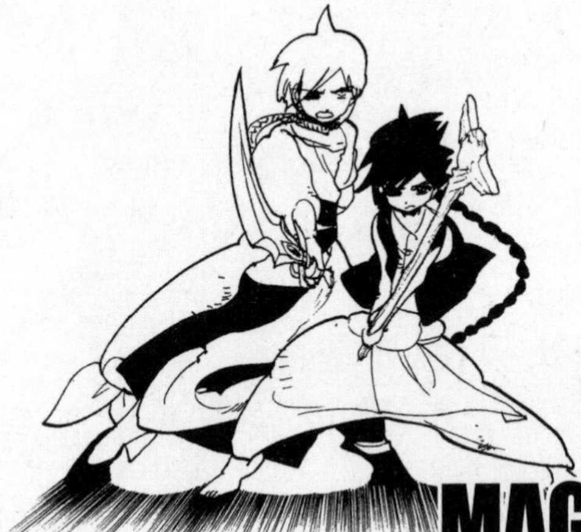

MAGI
The labyrinth of magic

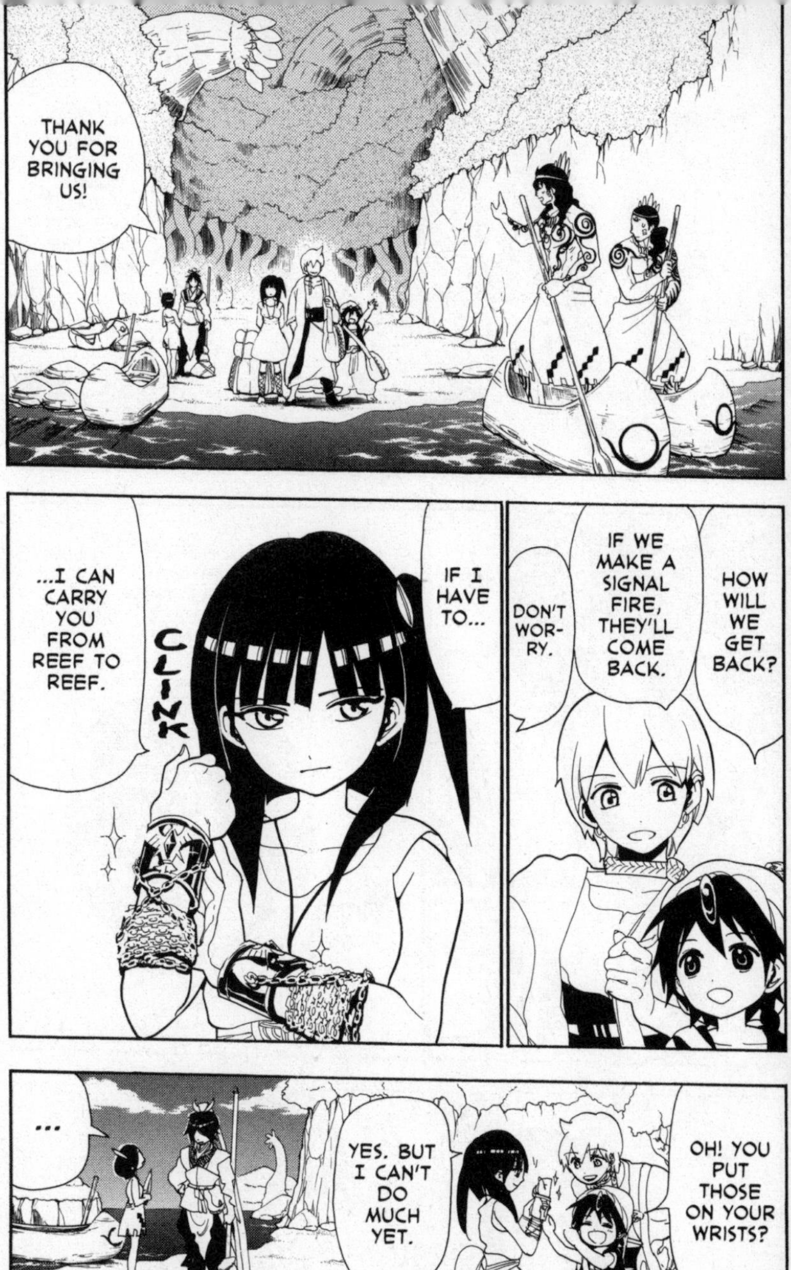
THANK YOU FOR BRINGING US!
HOW WILL WE GET BACK?
IF WE MAKE A SIGNAL FIRE, THEY'LL COME BACK.
DON'T WORRY.
IF I HAVE TO...
CLINK
...I CAN CARRY YOU FROM REEF TO REEF.
OH! YOU PUT THOSE ON YOUR WRISTS?
YES. BUT I CAN'T DO MUCH YET.
...

NO. YOU WOULD SLOW US DOWN. WE CAN'T TAKE YOU INTO THE DUNGEON.

BUT...

...

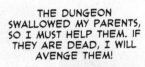

THE DUNGEON SWALLOWED MY PARENTS, SO I MUST HELP THEM. IF THEY ARE DEAD, I WILL AVENGE THEM!

HMPH

...

PERK

I UNDERSTAND.

?!

I WILL DO THAT *FOR* YOU.

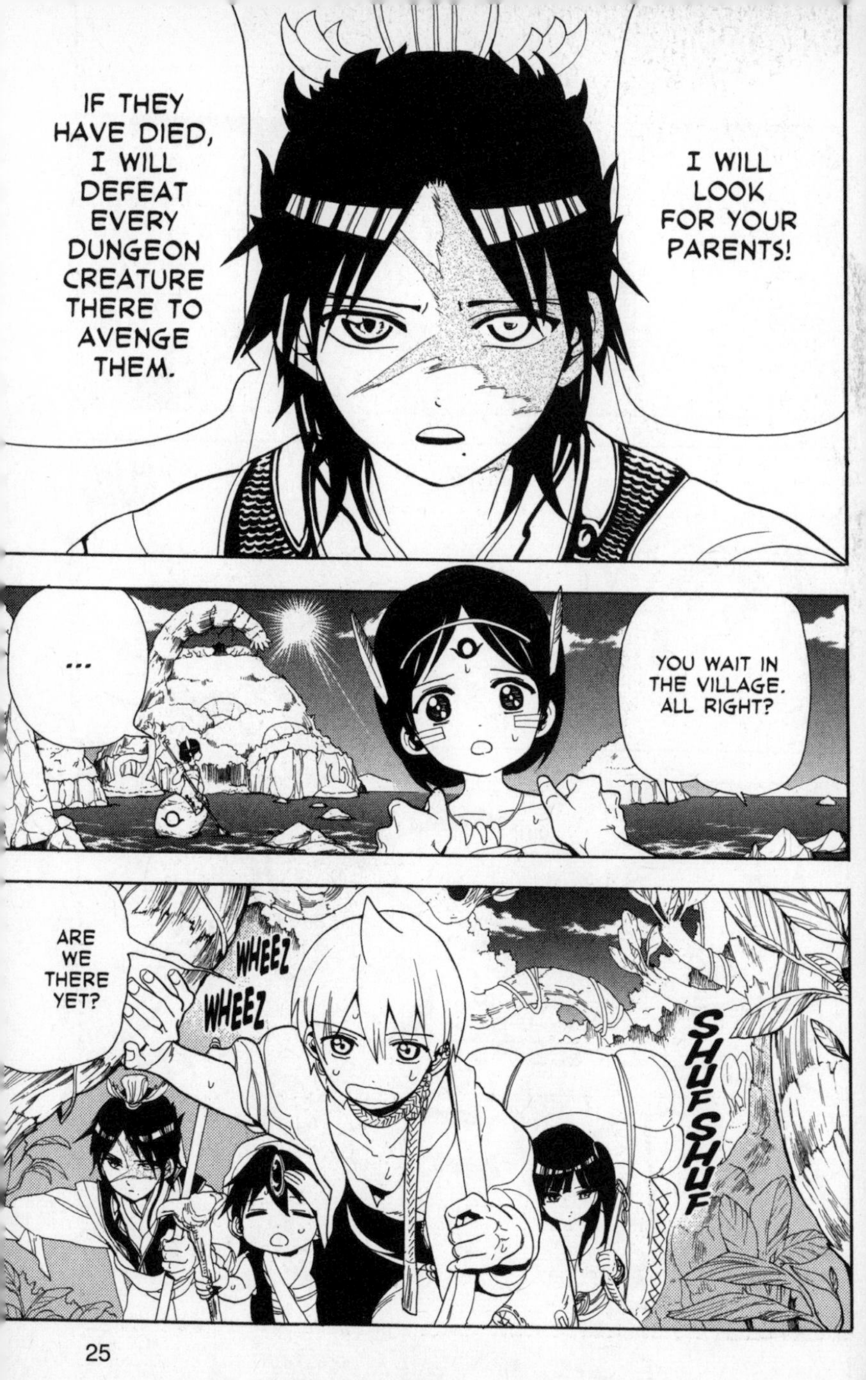
I WILL LOOK FOR YOUR PARENTS!
IF THEY HAVE DIED, I WILL DEFEAT EVERY DUNGEON CREATURE THERE TO AVENGE THEM.
YOU WAIT IN THE VILLAGE. ALL RIGHT?
...
SHUF SHUF
WHEEZ
WHEEZ
ARE WE THERE YET?

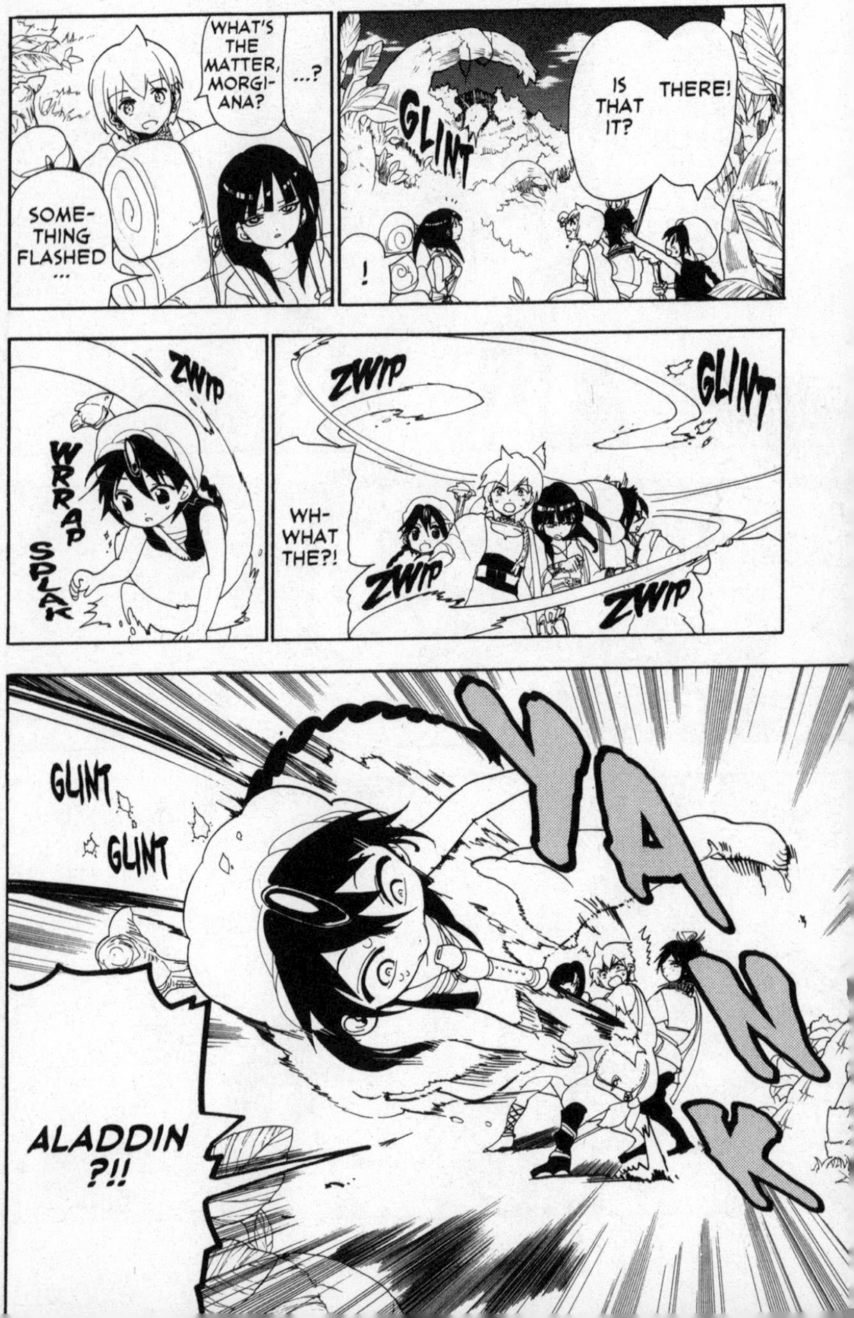
THERE!
IS THAT IT?
GLINT
!
WHAT'S THE MATTER, MORGIANA?
...?
SOME-THING FLASHED...
GLINT
ZWIP
WH-WHAT THE?!
ZWIP
ZWIP
ZWIP
WRRAP
SPLAK
YANK
GLINT
GLINT
ALADDIN?!!

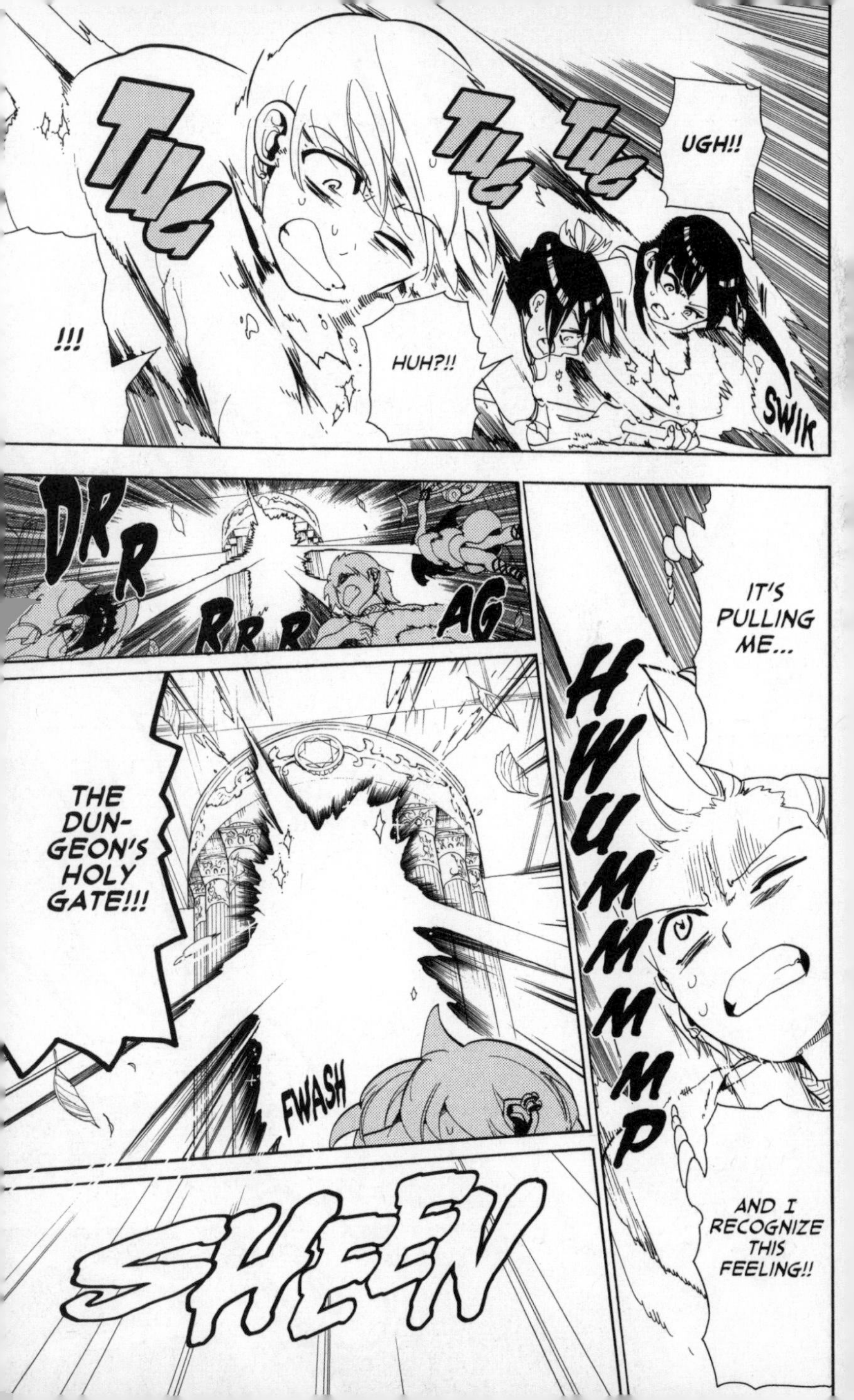
UGH!!
TUG
TUG
SWIK
TUG
HUH?!!
!!!
IT'S PULLING ME...
HWUMMMMMP
AND I RECOGNIZE THIS FEELING!!
AG
DRRRRR
THE DUN-GEON'S HOLY GATE!!!
FWASH
SHEEN

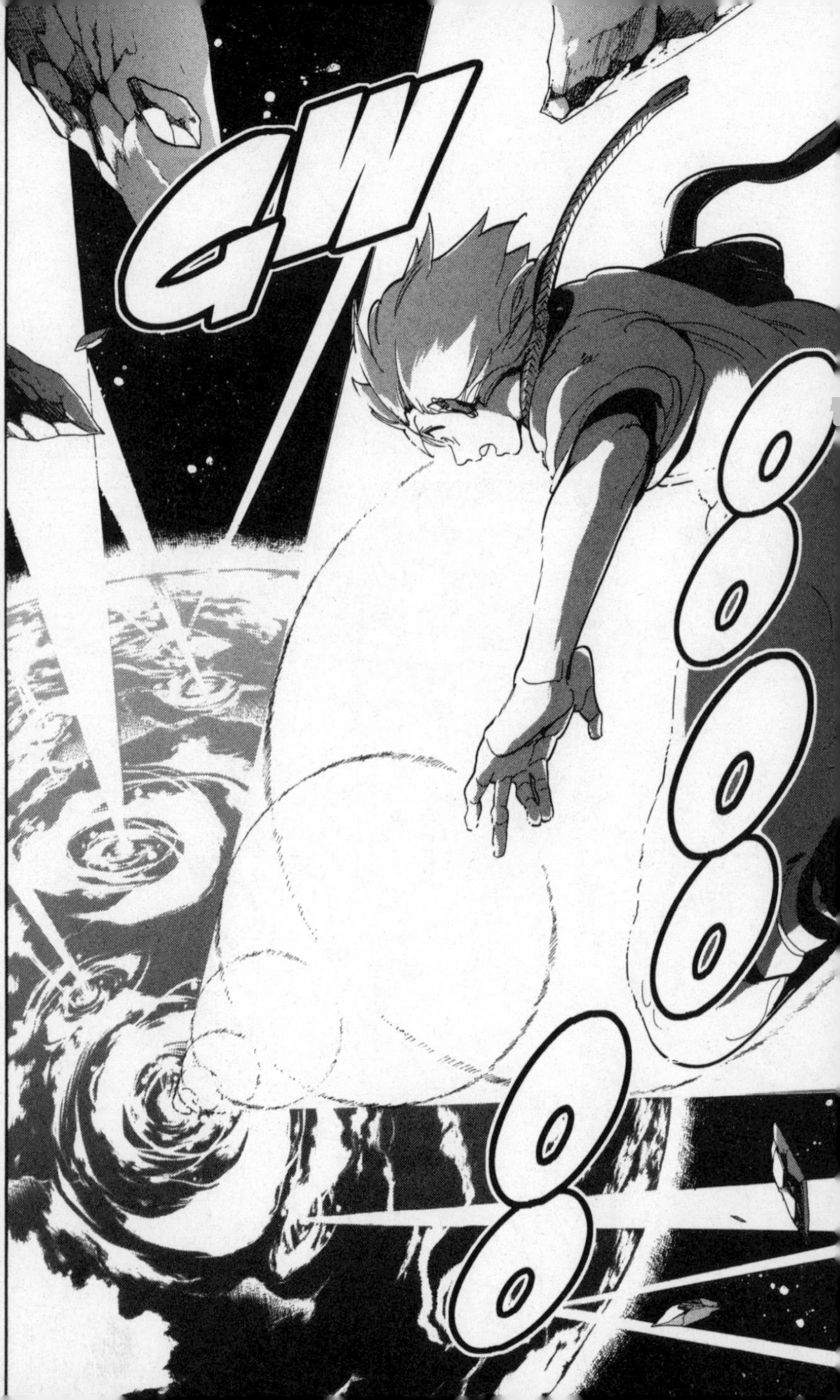
GHOOOOOOO

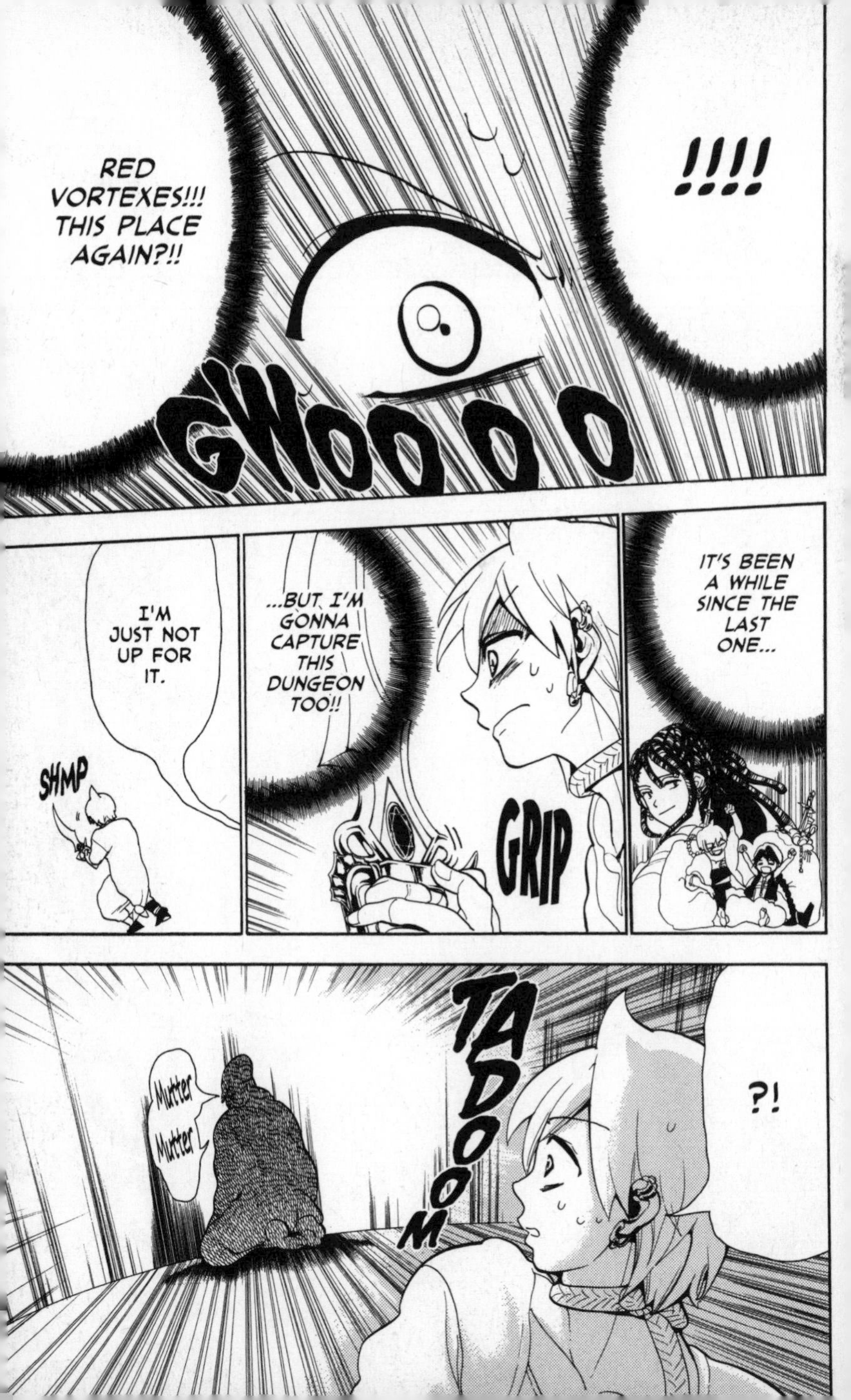
!!!!
RED VORTEXES!!! THIS PLACE AGAIN?!!
GWOOOOO
IT'S BEEN A WHILE SINCE THE LAST ONE...
...BUT I'M GONNA CAPTURE THIS DUNGEON TOO!!
GRIP
I'M JUST NOT UP FOR IT.
SHMP
?!
TADOOOM
Mutter Mutter

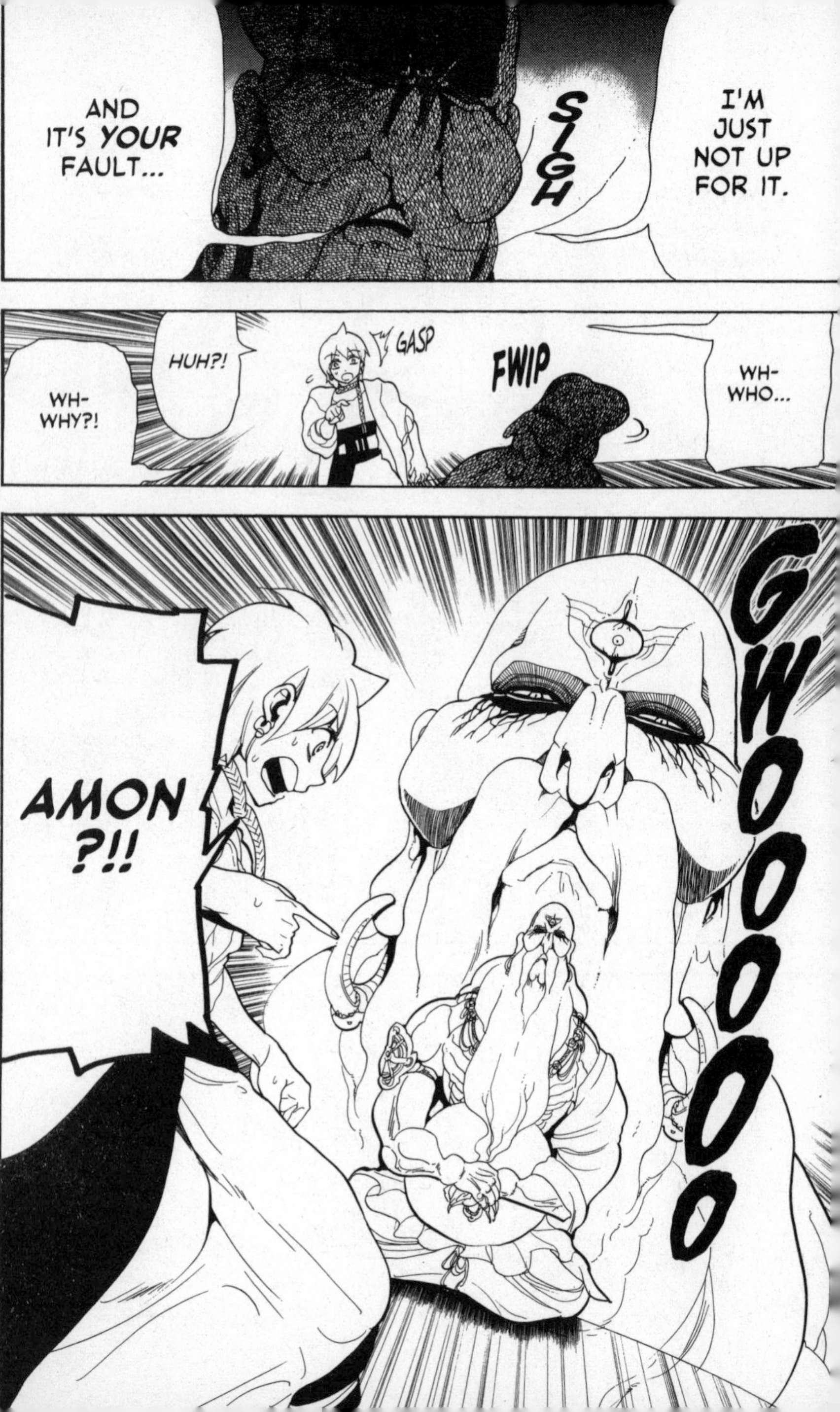
I'M JUST NOT UP FOR IT.
SIGH
AND IT'S *YOUR* FAULT...
WH- WHO...
FWIP
GASP
HUH?!
WH- WHY?!
GWOOOOOOO
AMON ?!!

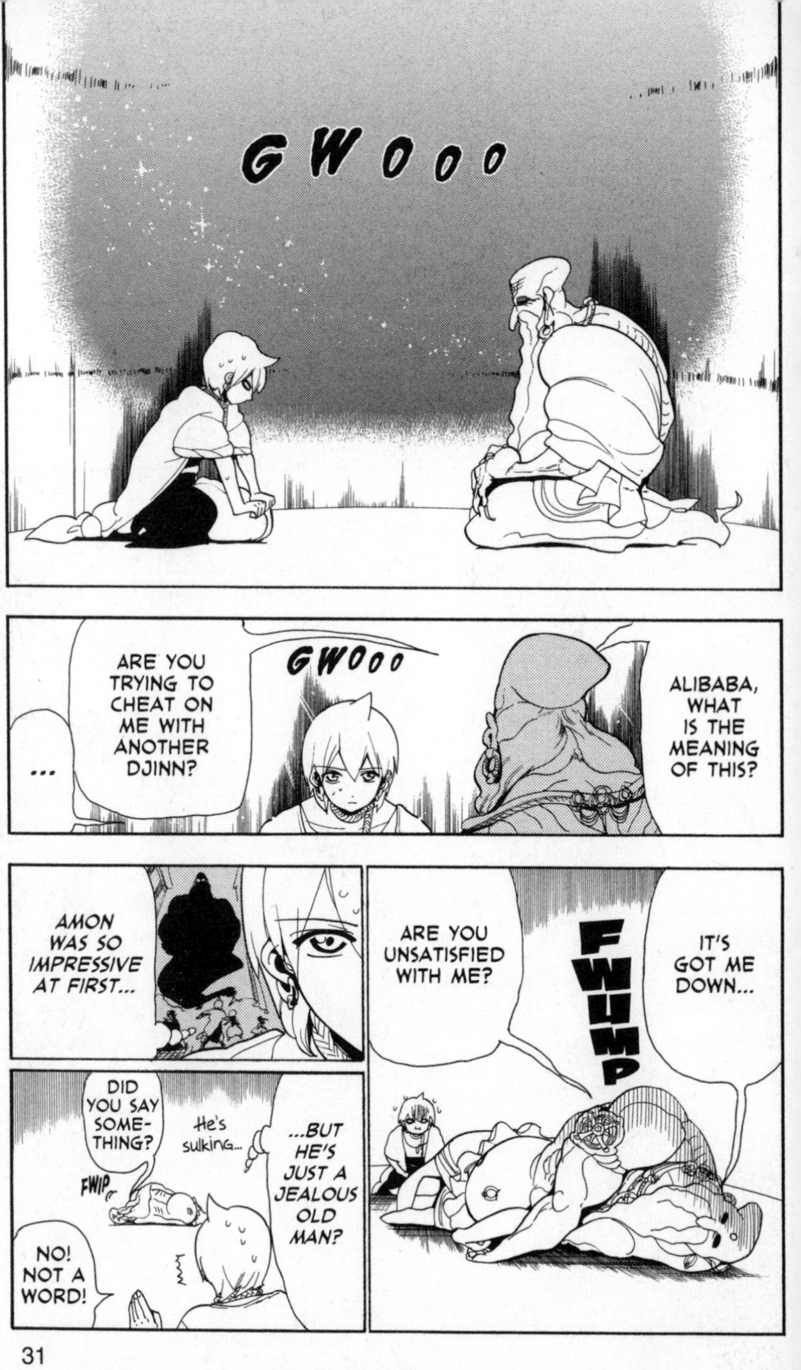
GWOOO
ALIBABA, WHAT IS THE MEANING OF THIS?
GWOOO
ARE YOU TRYING TO CHEAT ON ME WITH ANOTHER DJINN?
...
IT'S GOT ME DOWN...
FWUMP
ARE YOU UNSATISFIED WITH ME?
AMON WAS SO IMPRESSIVE AT FIRST...
...BUT HE'S JUST A JEALOUS OLD MAN?
He's sulking...
DID YOU SAY SOME-THING?
FWIP
NO! NOT A WORD!

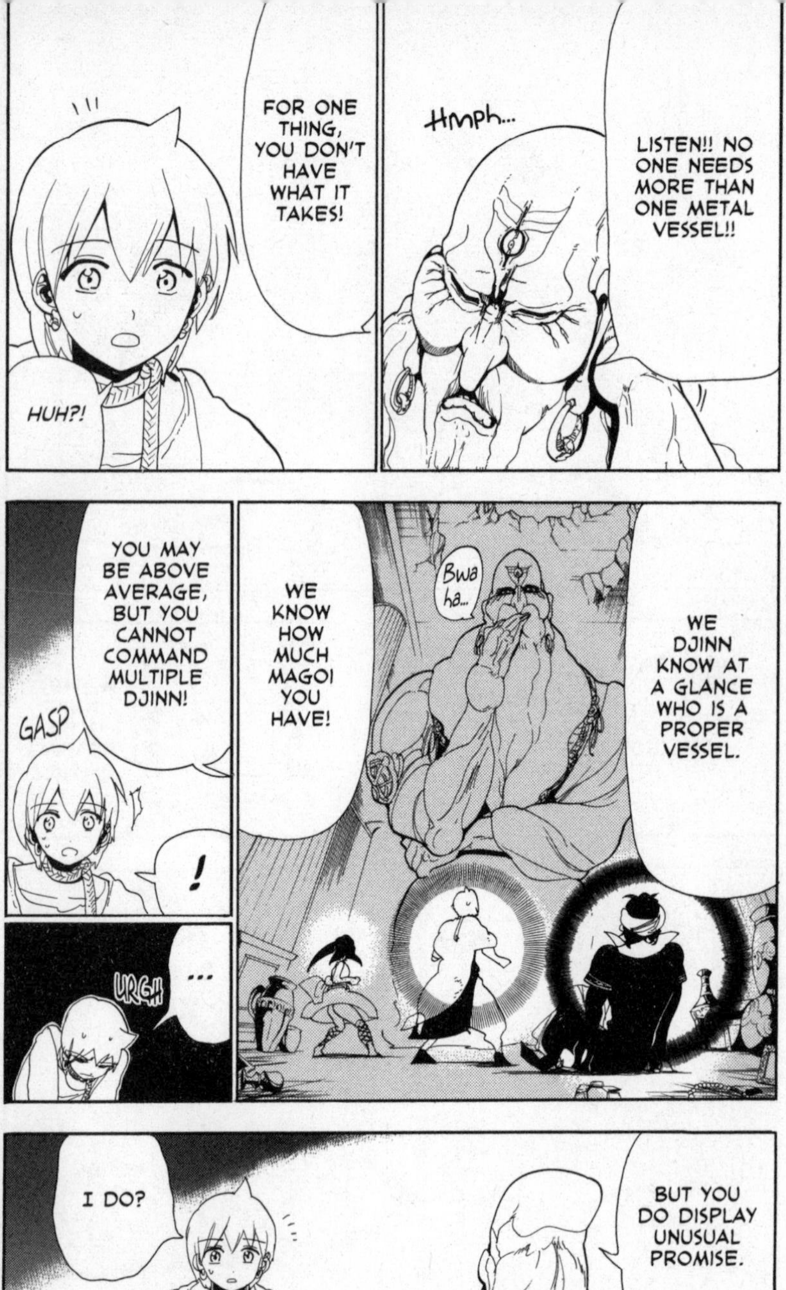
LISTEN!! NO ONE NEEDS MORE THAN ONE METAL VESSEL!!
Hmph...
FOR ONE THING, YOU DON'T HAVE WHAT IT TAKES!
HUH?!
WE DJINN KNOW AT A GLANCE WHO IS A PROPER VESSEL.
Bwa ha...
WE KNOW HOW MUCH MAGOI YOU HAVE!
YOU MAY BE ABOVE AVERAGE, BUT YOU CANNOT COMMAND MULTIPLE DJINN!
GASP
!
...
URGH
BUT YOU DO DISPLAY UNUSUAL PROMISE.
I DO?

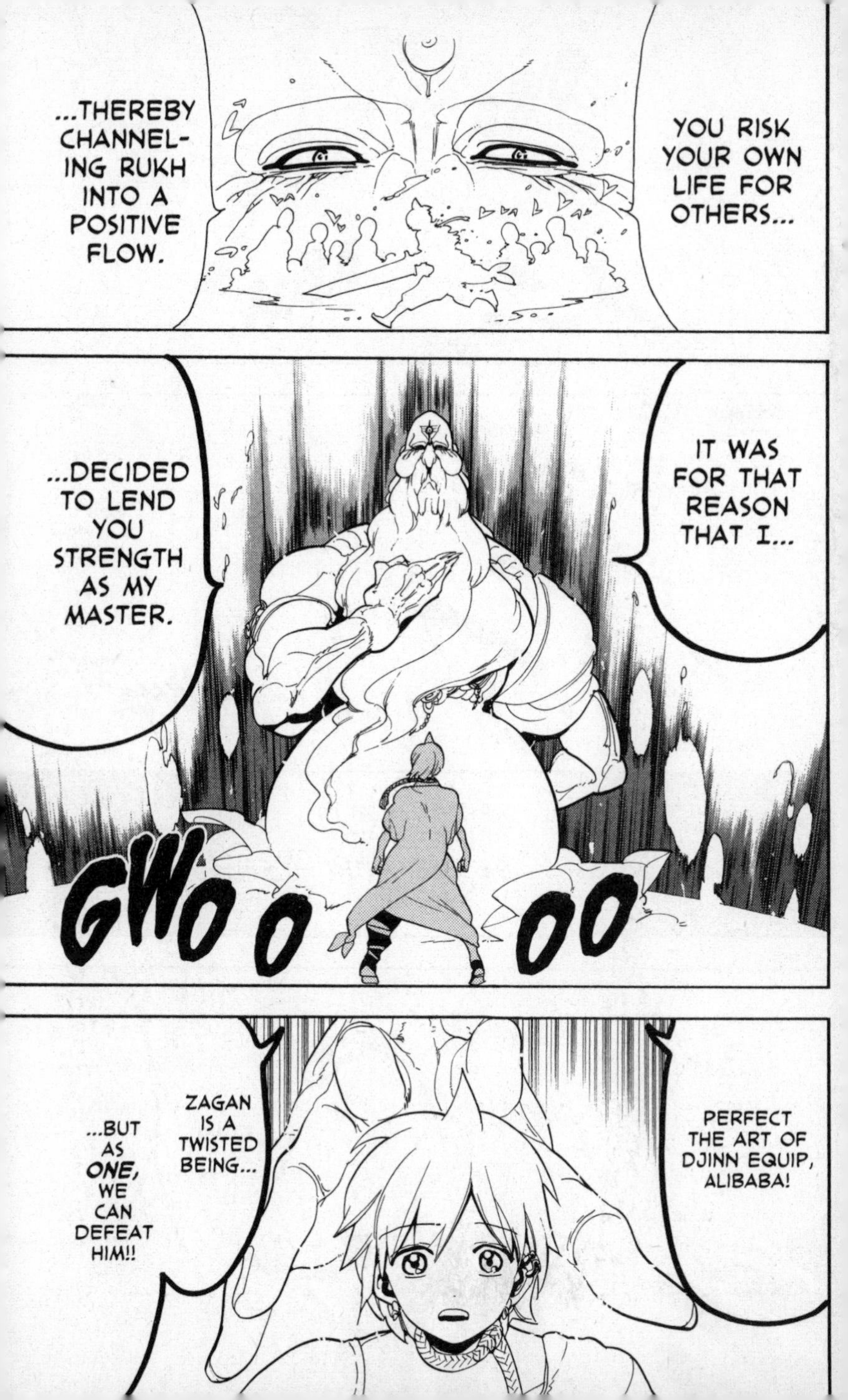
YOU RISK YOUR OWN LIFE FOR OTHERS...
...THEREBY CHANNEL-ING RUKH INTO A POSITIVE FLOW.
IT WAS FOR THAT REASON THAT I...
...DECIDED TO LEND YOU STRENGTH AS MY MASTER.
GWOOOOO
PERFECT THE ART OF DJINN EQUIP, ALIBABA!
ZAGAN IS A TWISTED BEING...
...BUT AS *ONE,* WE CAN DEFEAT HIM!!

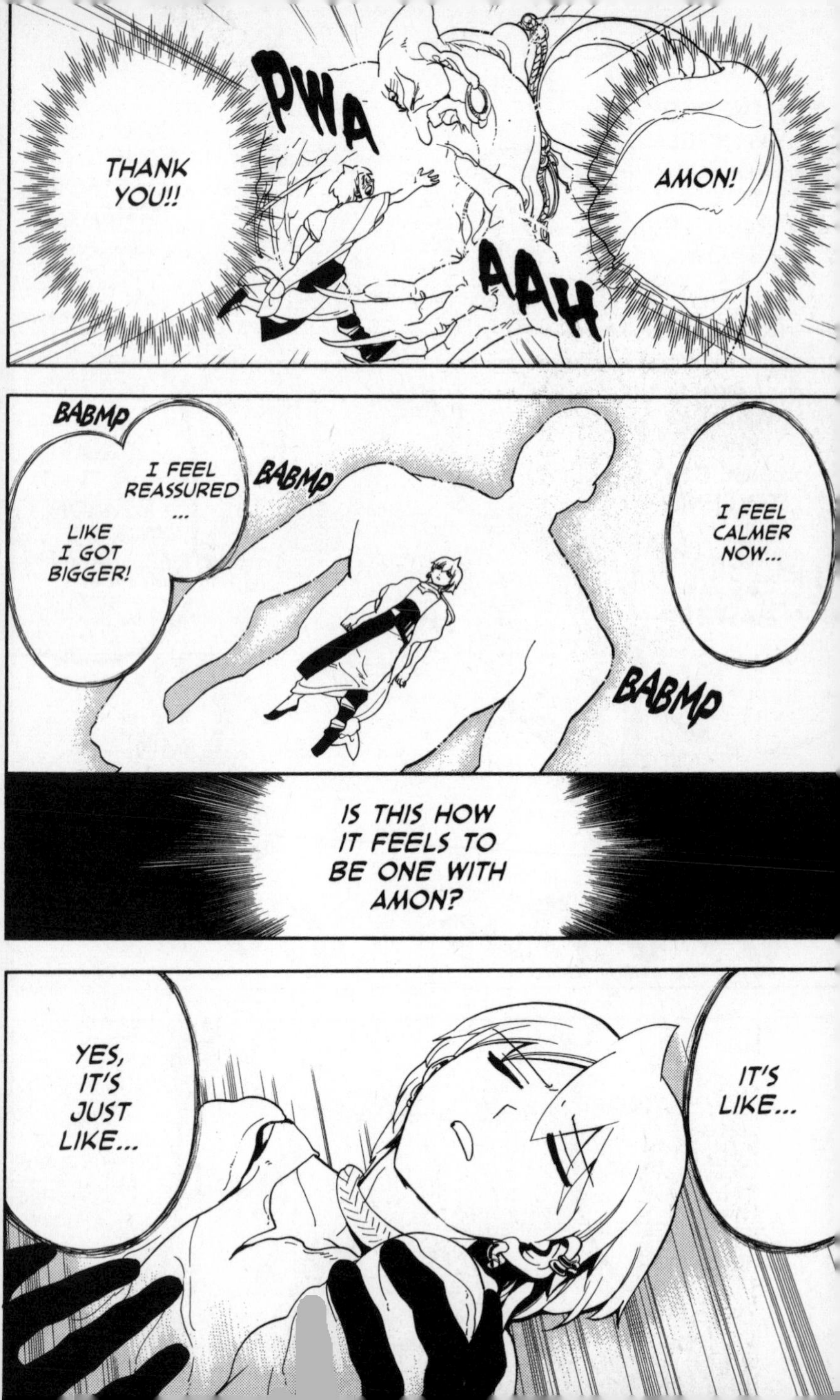
AMON!
PWA
AAH
THANK YOU!!
I FEEL CALMER NOW...
BABMP
BABMP
BABMP
I FEEL REASSURED ... LIKE I GOT BIGGER!
IS THIS HOW IT FEELS TO BE ONE WITH AMON?
IT'S LIKE...
YES, IT'S JUST LIKE...

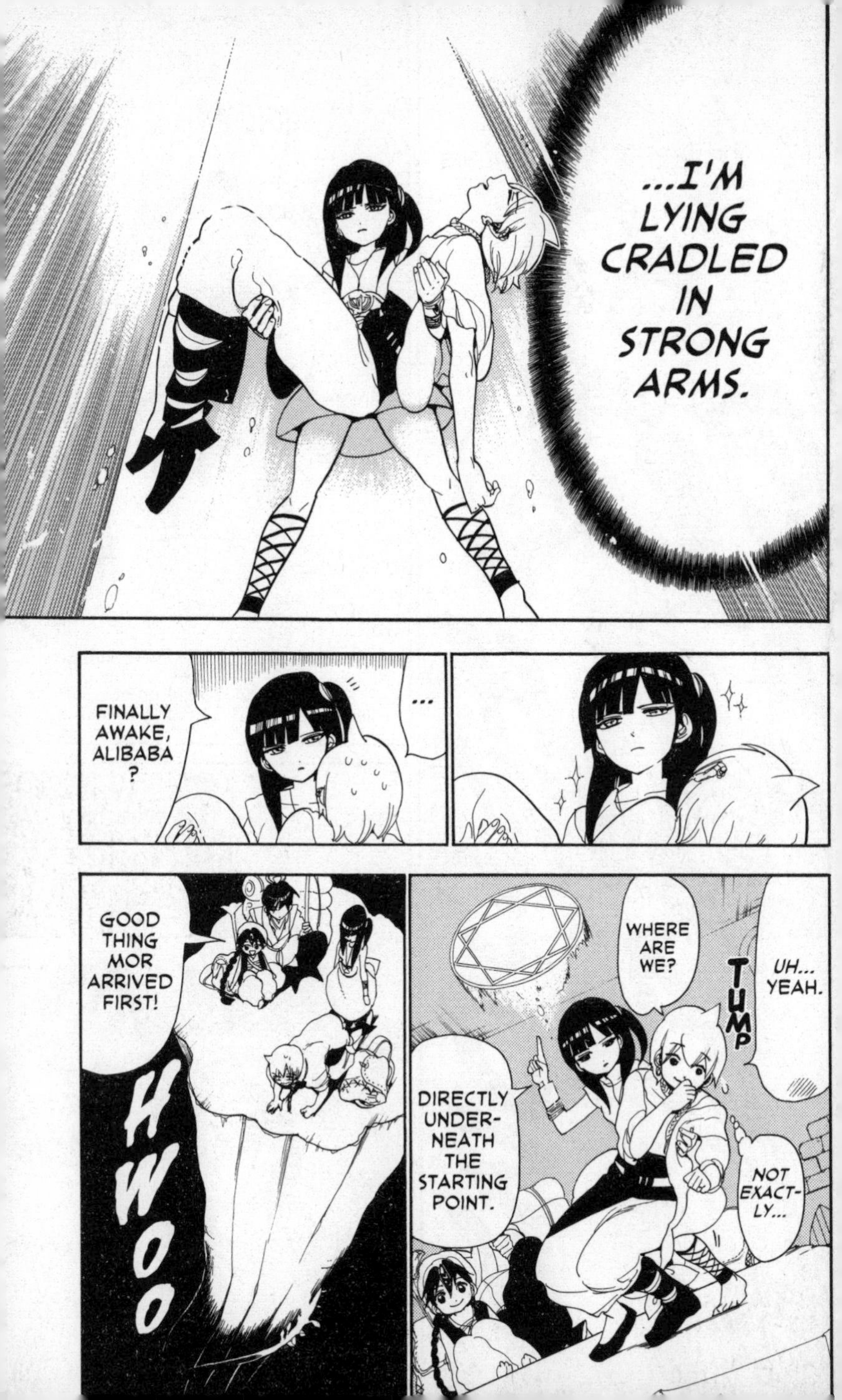
...I'M LYING CRADLED IN STRONG ARMS.
FINALLY AWAKE, ALIBABA?
...
UH... YEAH.
WHERE ARE WE?
TUMP
DIRECTLY UNDERNEATH THE STARTING POINT.
NOT EXACTLY...
GOOD THING MOR ARRIVED FIRST!
HWOOO

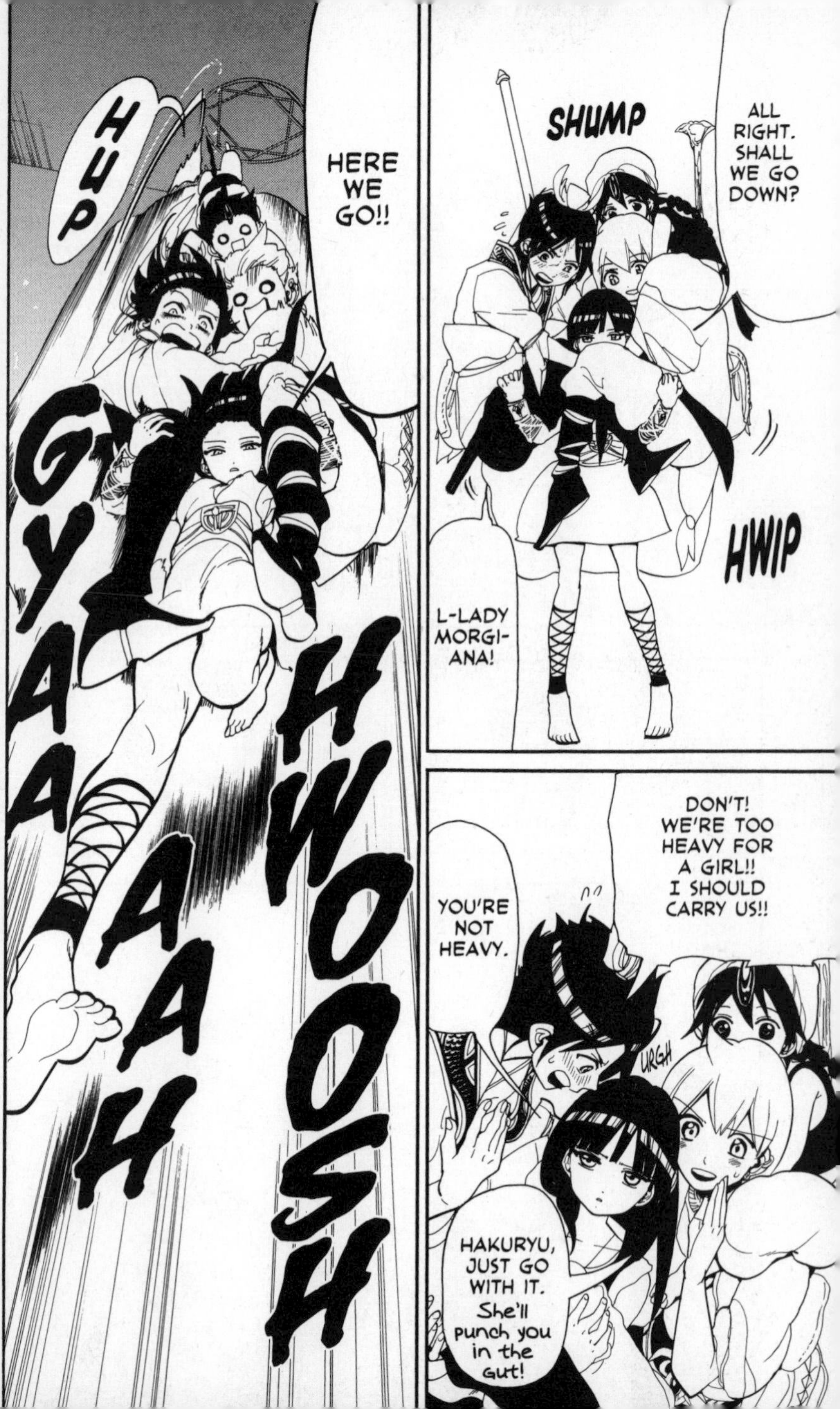
ALL RIGHT. SHALL WE GO DOWN?
SHUMP
HWIP
L-LADY MORGIANA!
DON'T! WE'RE TOO HEAVY FOR A GIRL!! I SHOULD CARRY US!!
YOU'RE NOT HEAVY.
URGH
HAKURYU, JUST GO WITH IT. She'll punch you in the Gut!
HERE WE GO!!
HUP
GYAAAAAH
WHOOSH

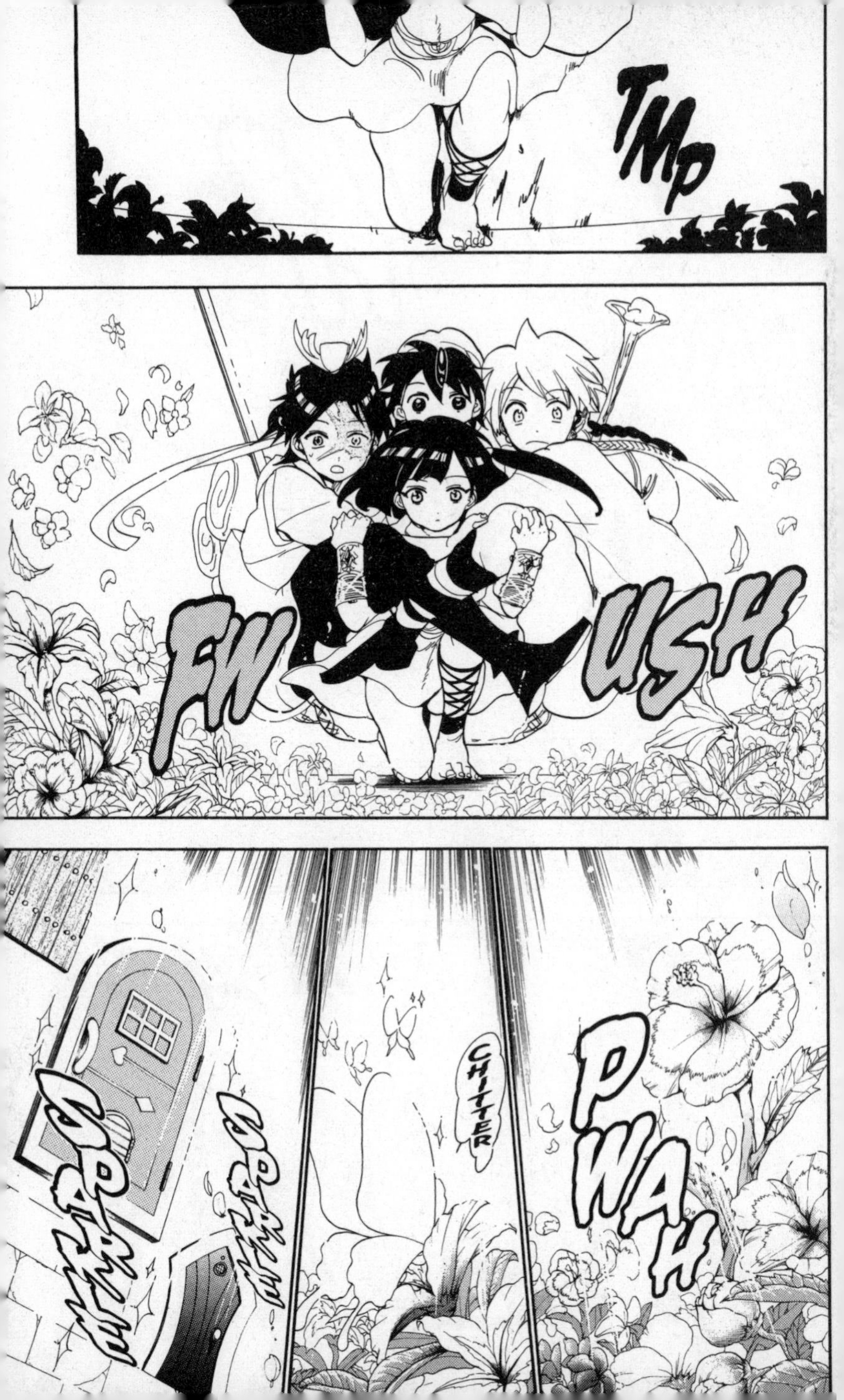
TMP
FWUSH
PWAH
CHITTER

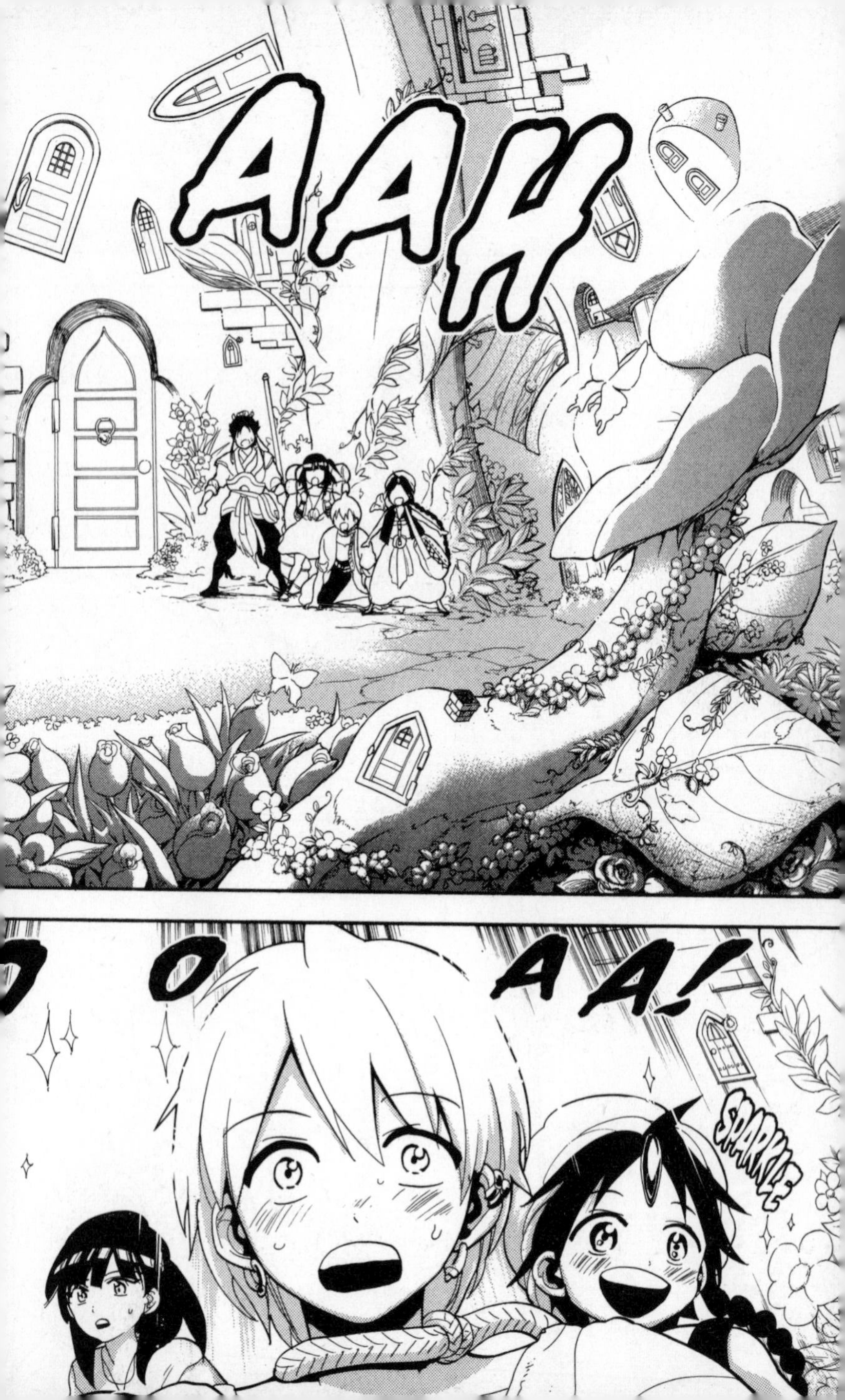
AAH
O AA!
SPARKLE

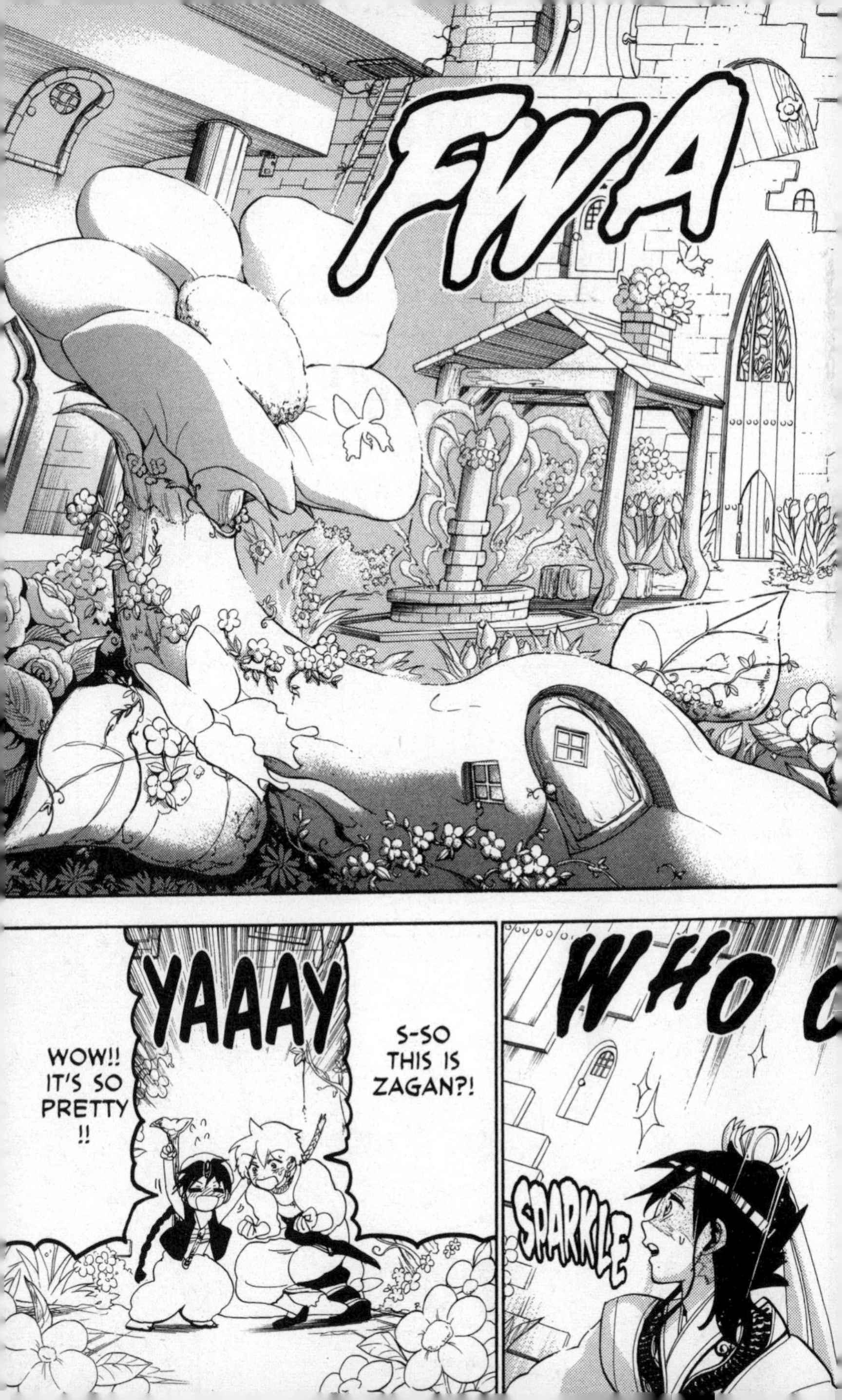
FWA
WHO O
SPARKLE
YAAAY
S-SO THIS IS ZAGAN?!
WOW!! IT'S SO PRETTY !!

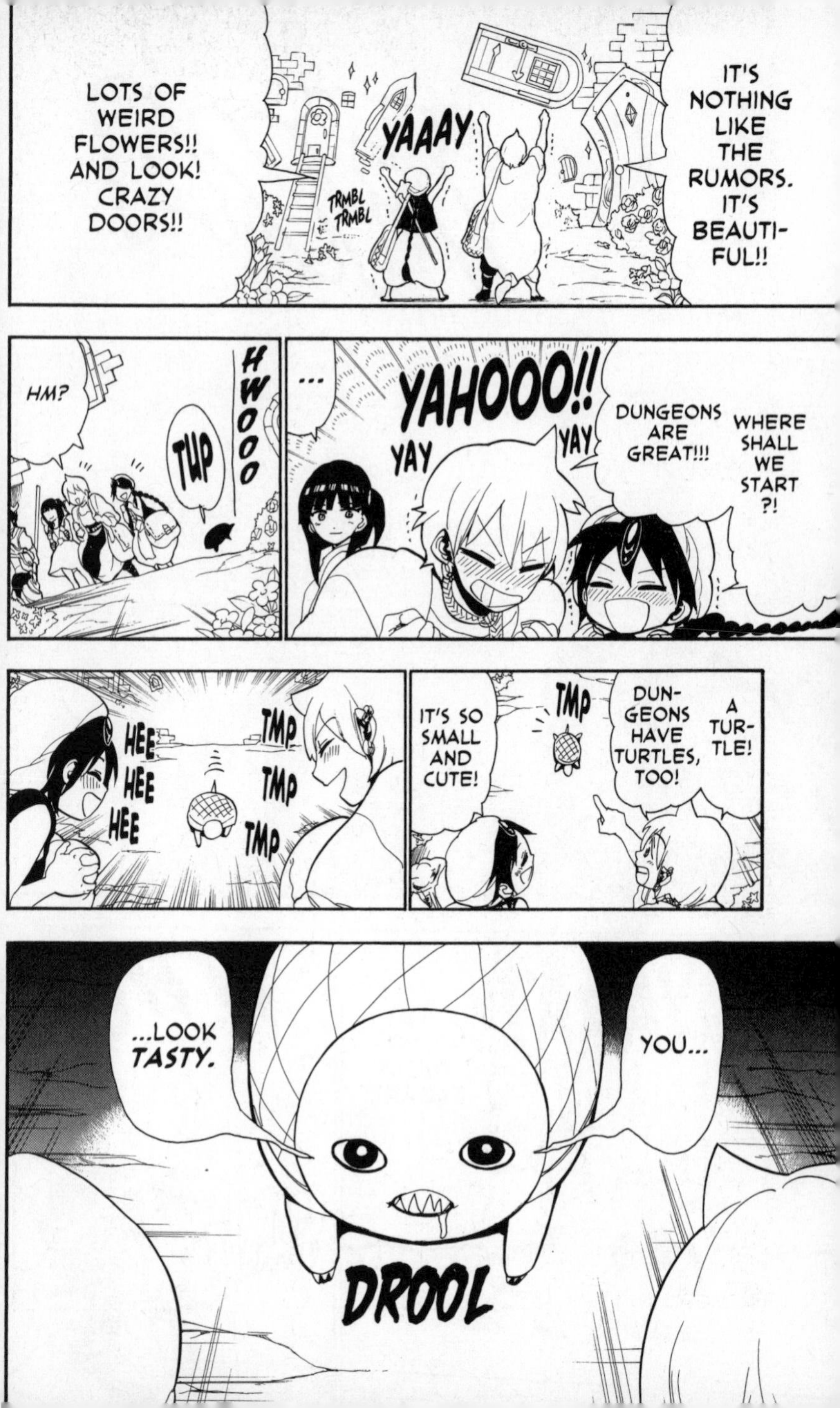
IT'S NOTHING LIKE THE RUMORS. IT'S BEAUTIFUL!!
YAAAY
TRMBL TRMBL
LOTS OF WEIRD FLOWERS!! AND LOOK! CRAZY DOORS!!
WHERE SHALL WE START?!
DUNGEONS ARE GREAT!!!
YAHOOO!!
YAY
YAY
...
HWOOO
TUP
HM?
A TURTLE!
DUNGEONS HAVE TURTLES, TOO!
TMP
IT'S SO SMALL AND CUTE!
TMP
TMP
TMP
HEE HEE HEE
YOU...
...LOOK *TASTY.*
DROOL

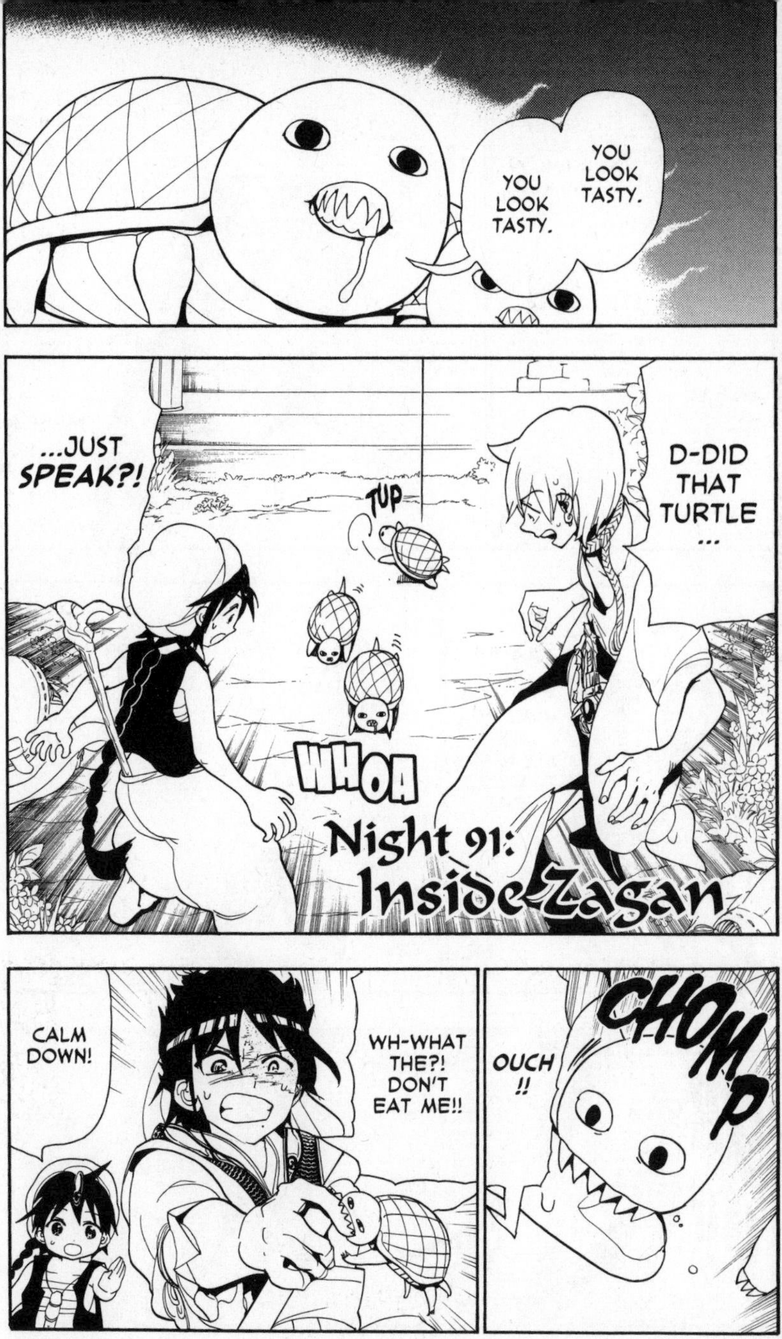
YOU LOOK TASTY.
YOU LOOK TASTY.
D-DID THAT TURTLE ...
TUP
...JUST SPEAK?!
WHOA
Night 91: Inside Zagan
CHOMP
OUCH !!
WH-WHAT THE?! DON'T EAT ME!!
CALM DOWN!

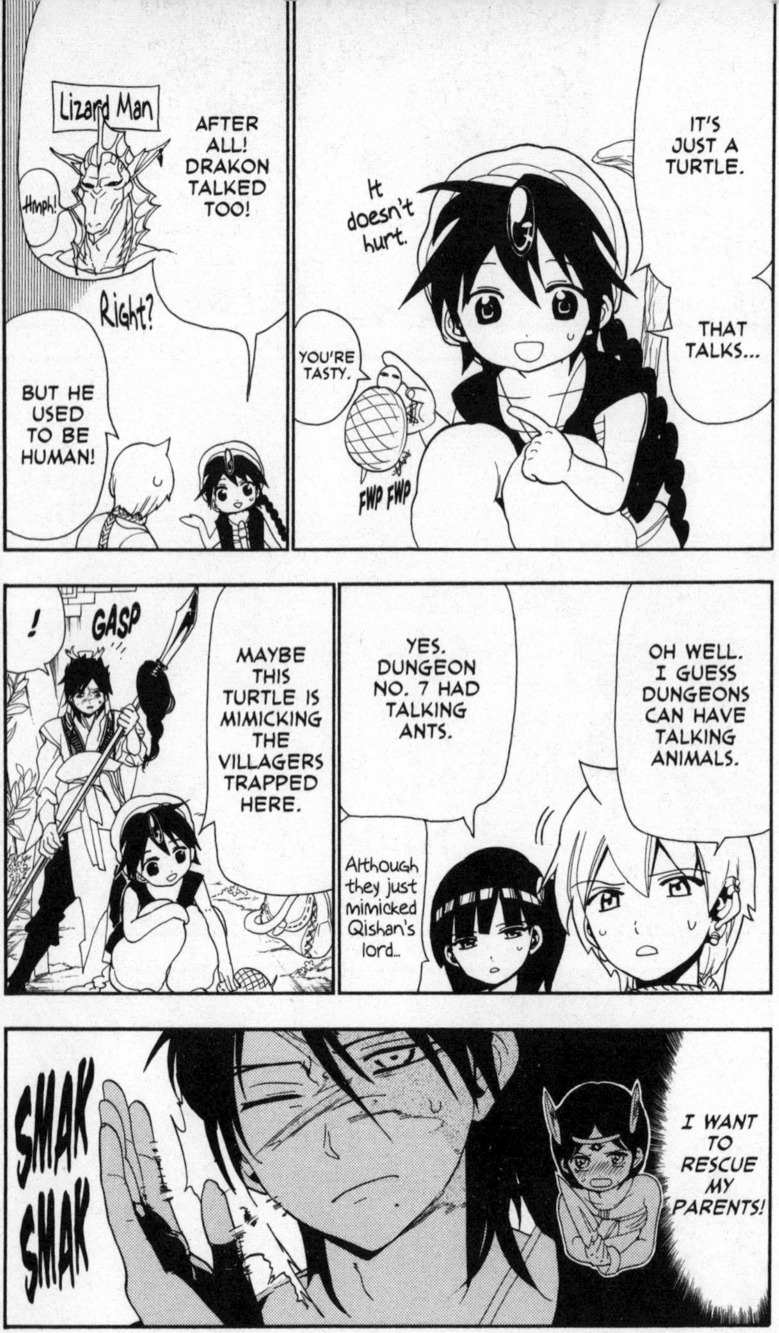
IT'S JUST A TURTLE.
THAT TALKS...
It doesn't hurt.
YOU'RE TASTY.
FWP FWP
AFTER ALL! DRAKON TALKED TOO!
Lizard Man
Hmph!
Right?
BUT HE USED TO BE HUMAN!
OH WELL. I GUESS DUNGEONS CAN HAVE TALKING ANIMALS.
YES. DUNGEON NO. 7 HAD TALKING ANTS.
Although they just mimicked Qishan's lord...
MAYBE THIS TURTLE IS MIMICKING THE VILLAGERS TRAPPED HERE.
GASP
!
I WANT TO RESCUE MY PARENTS!
SMAK SMAK

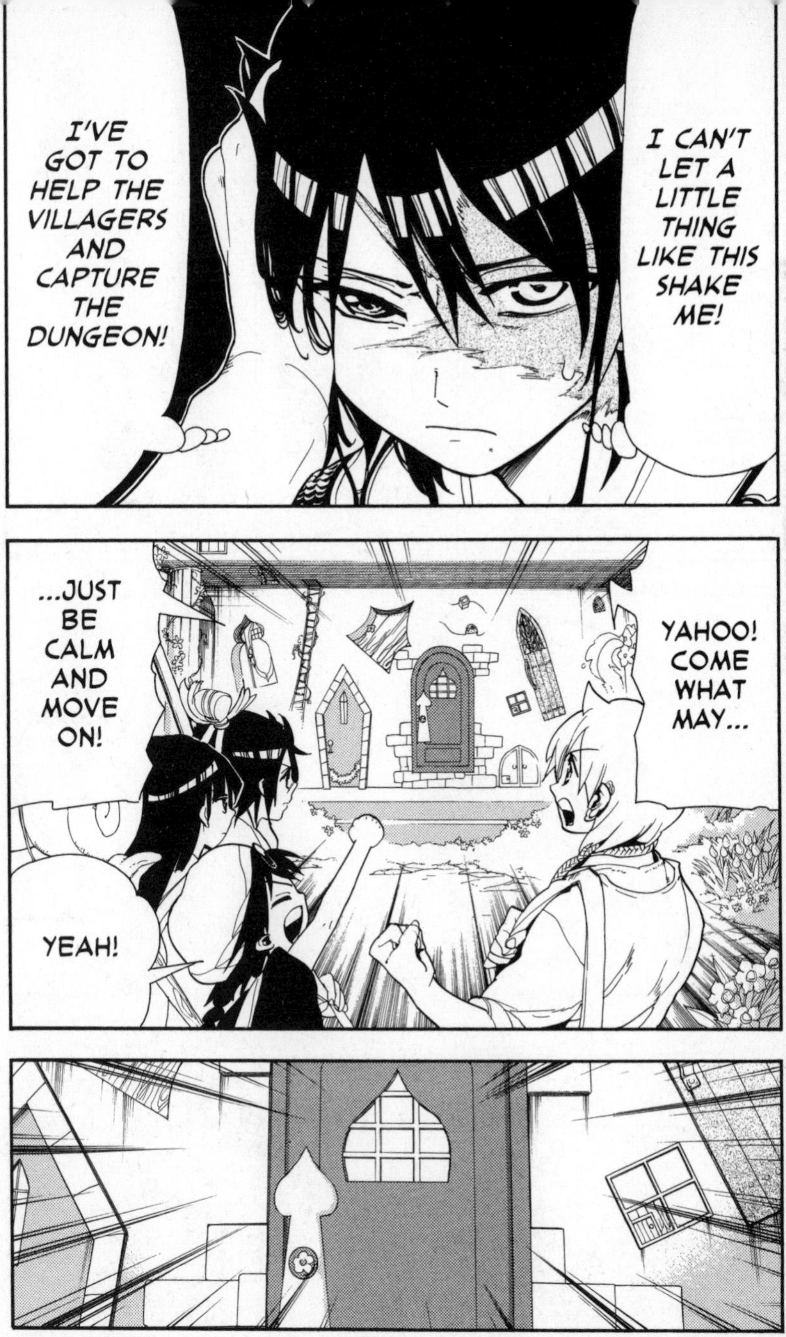
I CAN'T LET A LITTLE THING LIKE THIS SHAKE ME!
I'VE GOT TO HELP THE VILLAGERS AND CAPTURE THE DUNGEON!
YAHOO! COME WHAT MAY...
...JUST BE CALM AND MOVE ON!
YEAH!

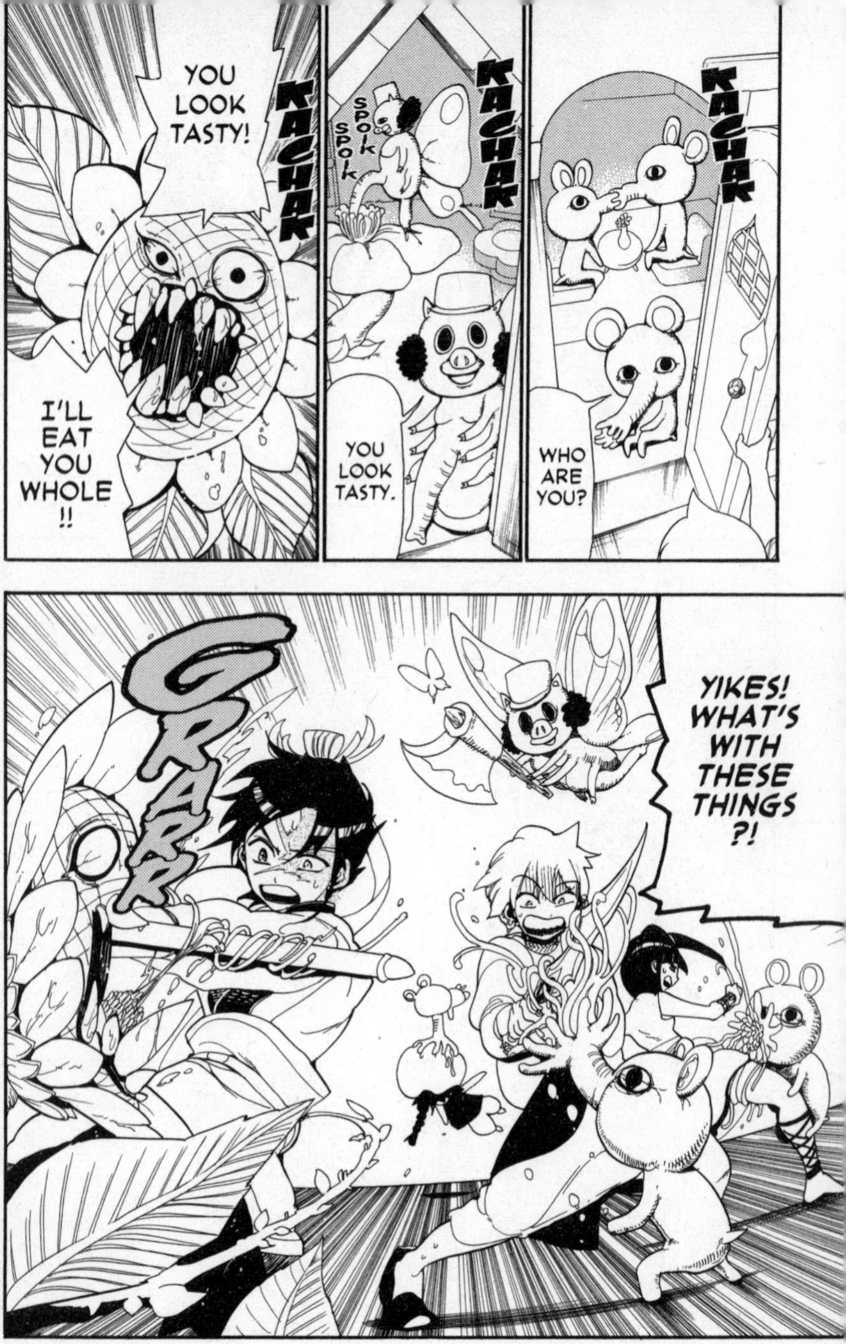
KACHAK
WHO ARE YOU?
KACHAK
SPOK SPOK
YOU LOOK TASTY.
KACHAK
YOU LOOK TASTY!
I'LL EAT YOU WHOLE!!
YIKES! WHAT'S WITH THESE THINGS?!
GRARR

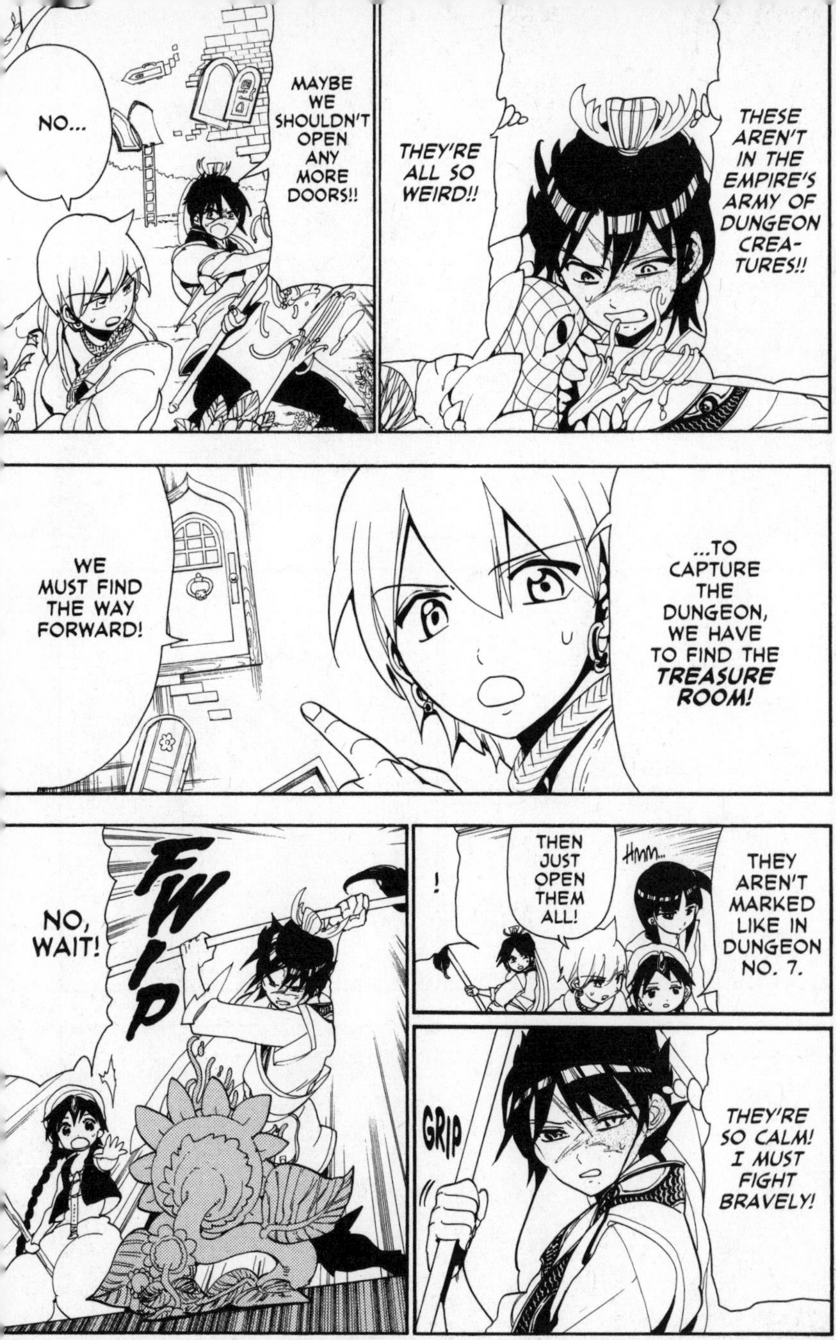
THESE AREN'T IN THE EMPIRE'S ARMY OF DUNGEON CREATURES!!
THEY'RE ALL SO WEIRD!!
MAYBE WE SHOULDN'T OPEN ANY MORE DOORS!!
NO...
...TO CAPTURE THE DUNGEON, WE HAVE TO FIND THE TREASURE ROOM!
WE MUST FIND THE WAY FORWARD!
THEY AREN'T MARKED LIKE IN DUNGEON NO. 7.
HMM...
THEN JUST OPEN THEM ALL!
!
THEY'RE SO CALM! I MUST FIGHT BRAVELY!
GRIP
FWIP
NO, WAIT!

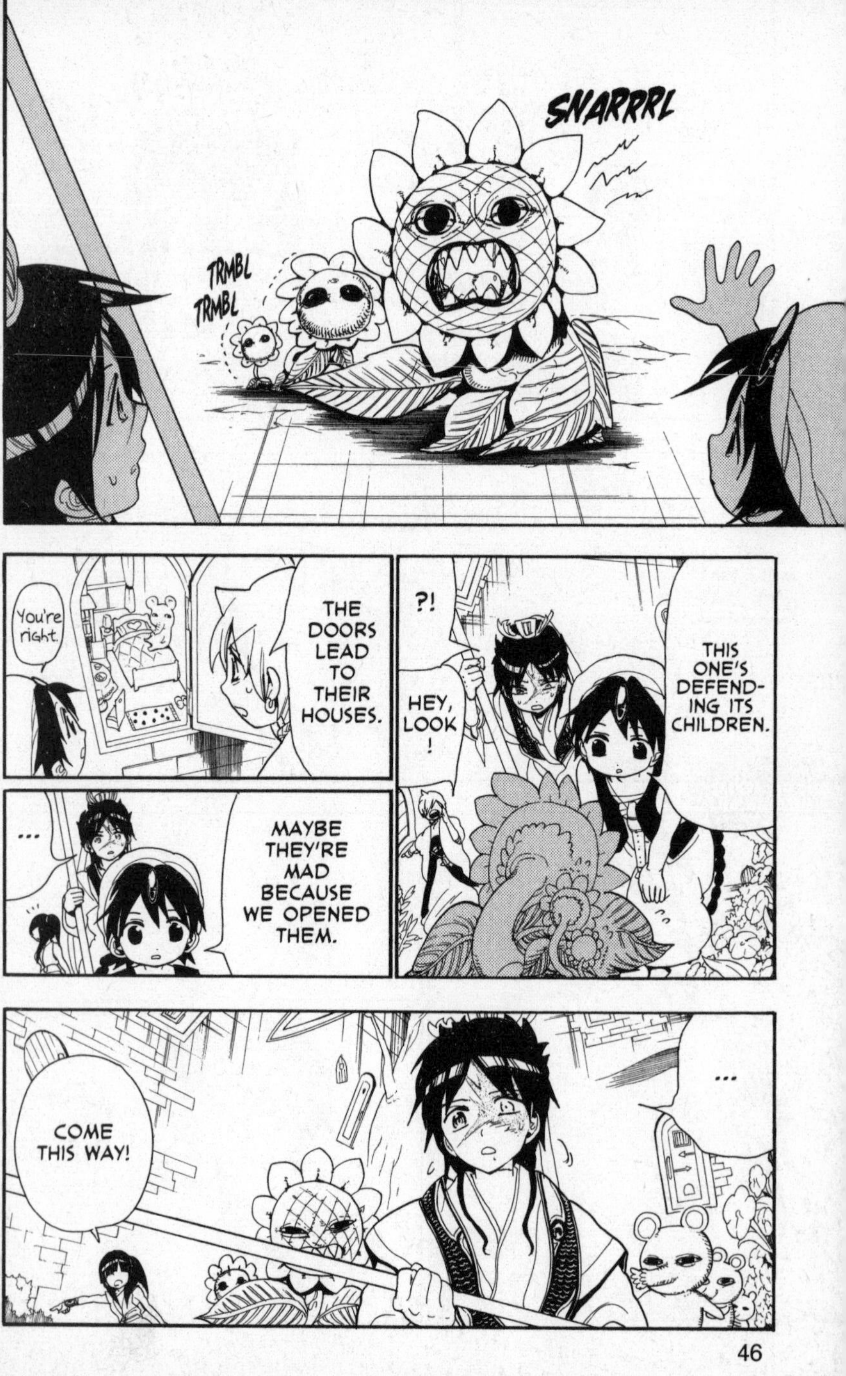
SNARRRL
TRMBL TRMBL
THIS ONE'S DEFENDING ITS CHILDREN.
?!
HEY, LOOK!
THE DOORS LEAD TO THEIR HOUSES.
You're right.
MAYBE THEY'RE MAD BECAUSE WE OPENED THEM.
...
...
COME THIS WAY!

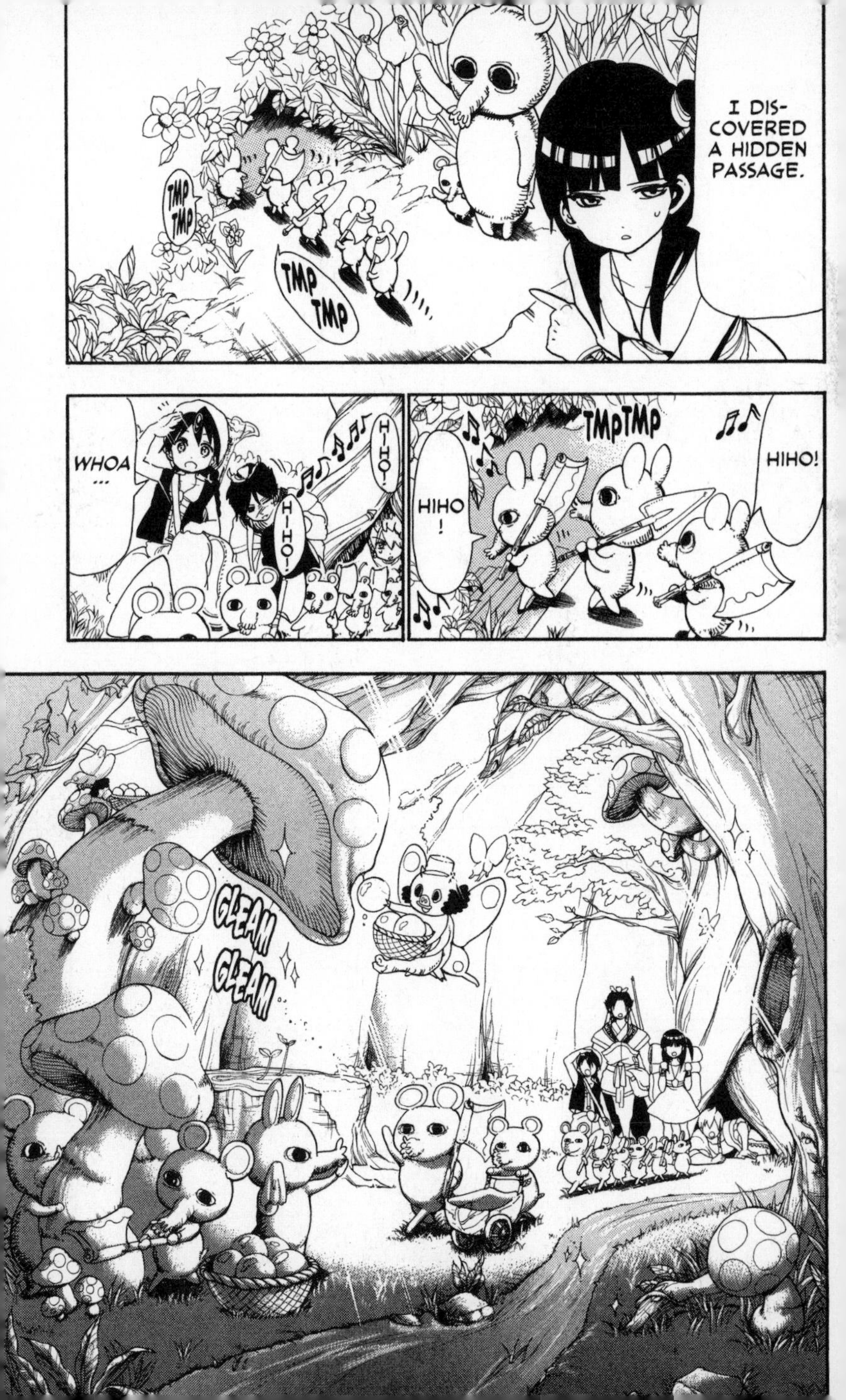
I DIS-
COVERED
A HIDDEN
PASSAGE.
TMP TMP
TMP TMP
HIHO!
TMPTMP
HIHO
!
HI HO!
HI HO!
WHOA
...
GLEAM
GLEAM

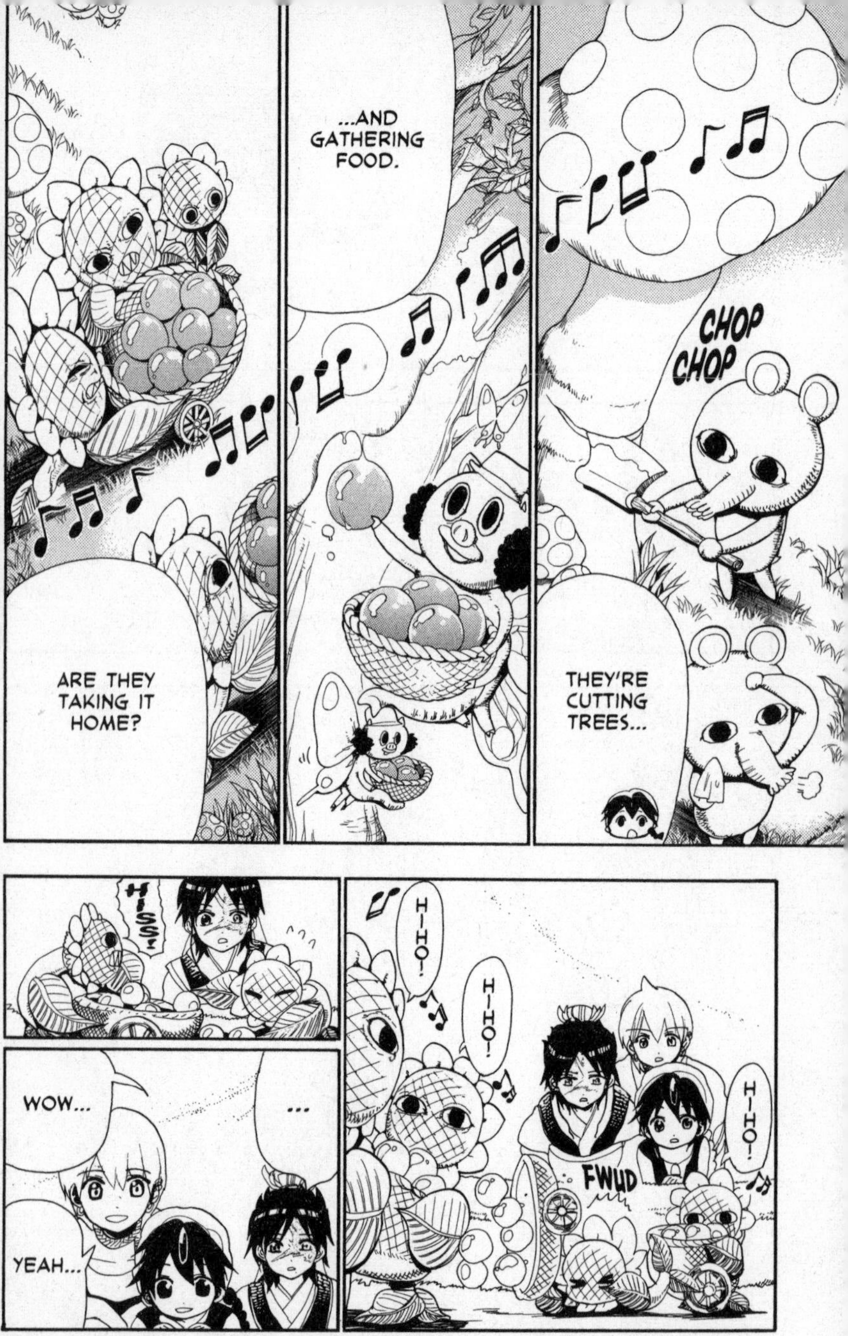

CHOP CHOP
THEY'RE CUTTING TREES...
...AND GATHERING FOOD.
ARE THEY TAKING IT HOME?
HI HO!
HI HO!
HI HO!
FWUD
HISS!
...
WOW...
YEAH...

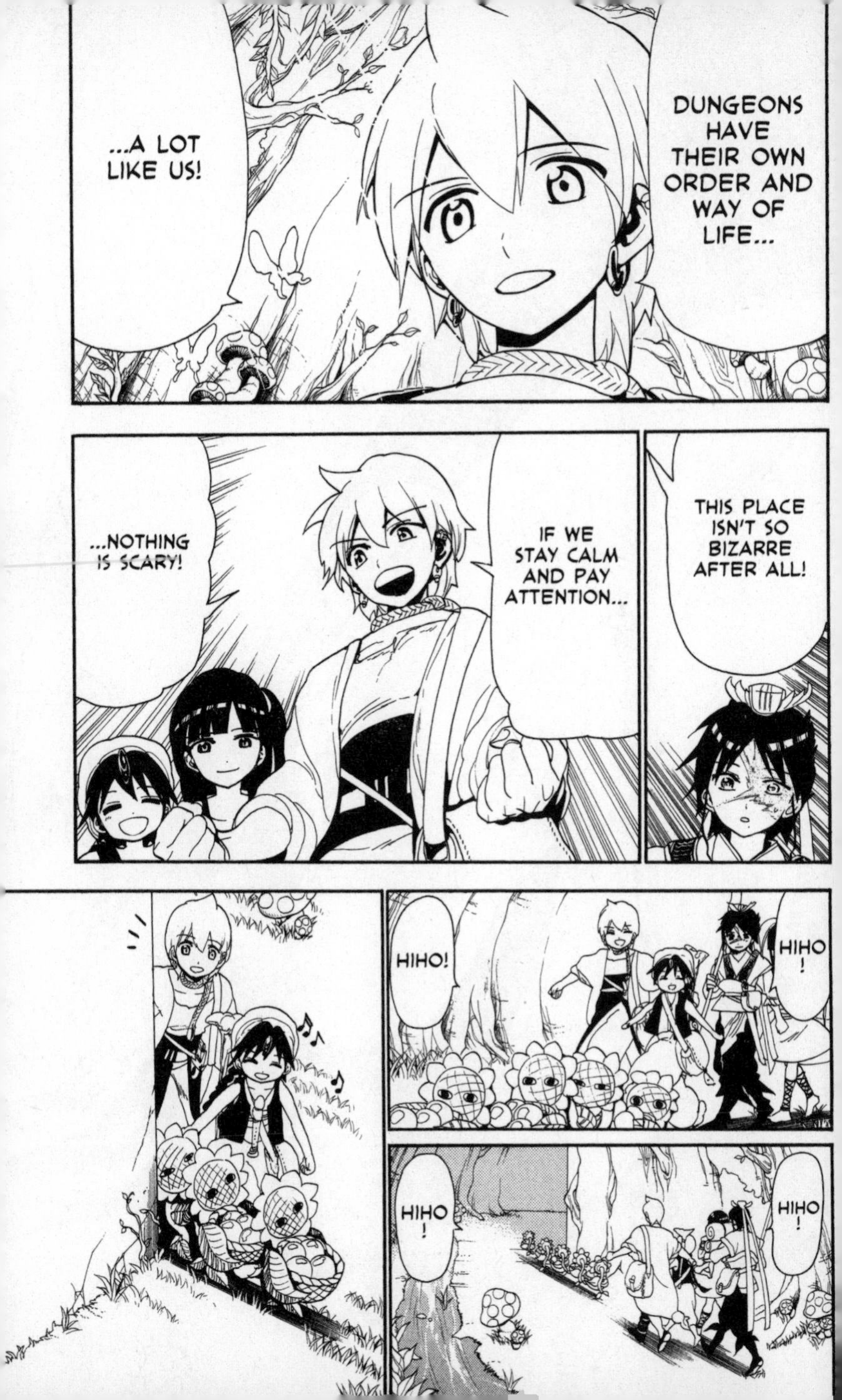
DUNGEONS HAVE THEIR OWN ORDER AND WAY OF LIFE...
...A LOT LIKE US!
THIS PLACE ISN'T SO BIZARRE AFTER ALL!
IF WE STAY CALM AND PAY ATTENTION...
...NOTHING IS SCARY!
HIHO!
HIHO!
HIHO!
HIHO!

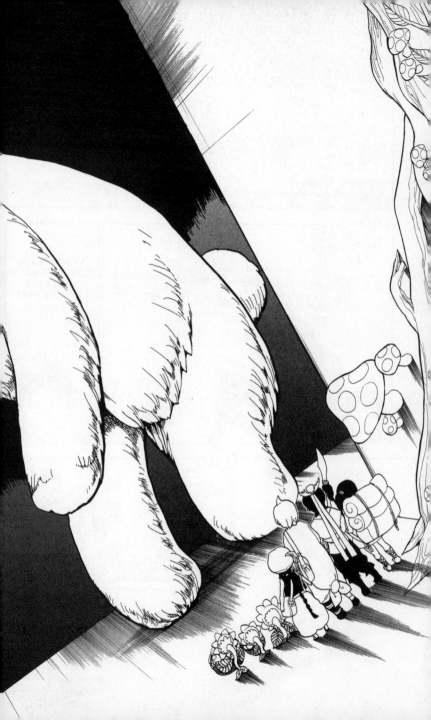

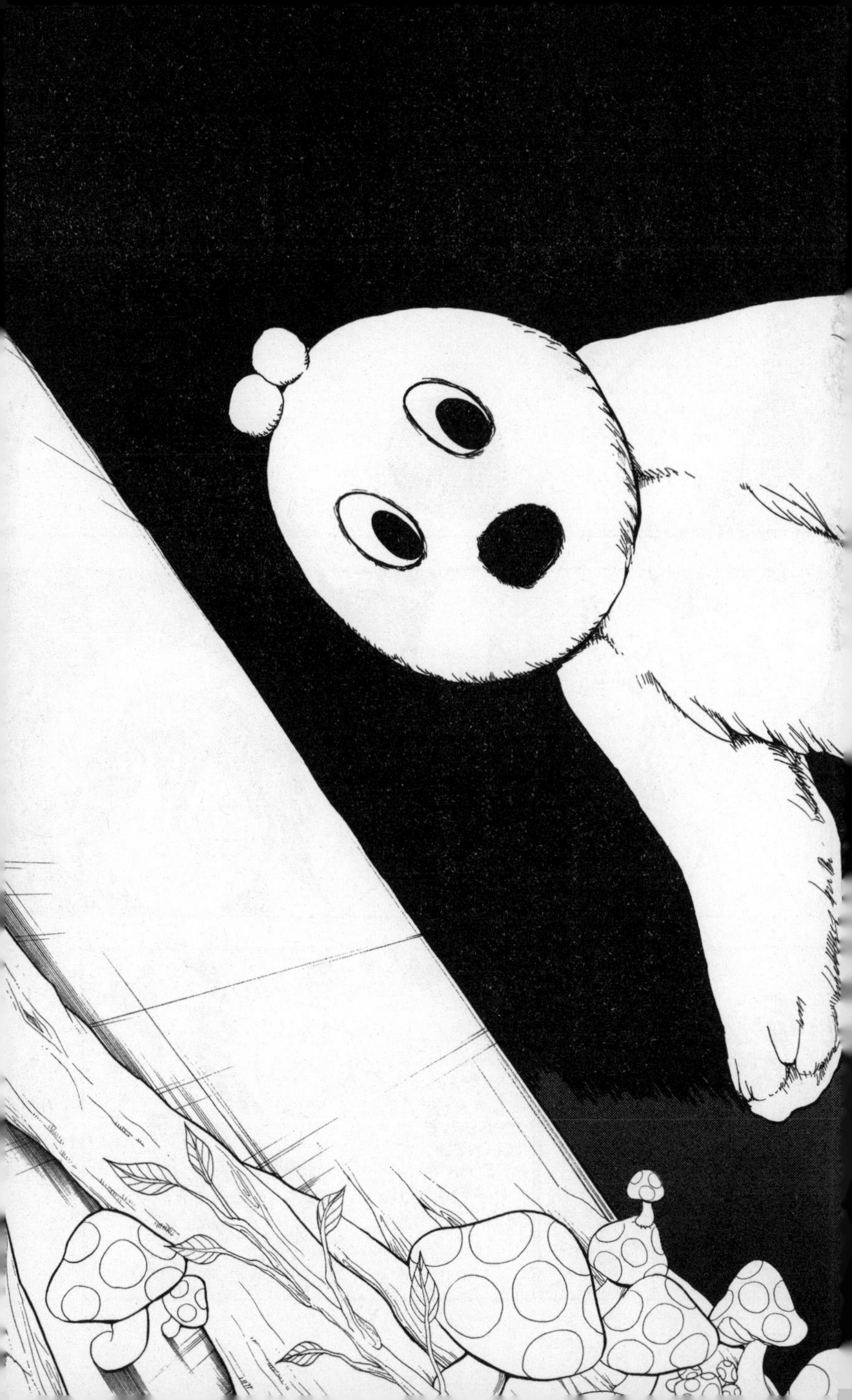

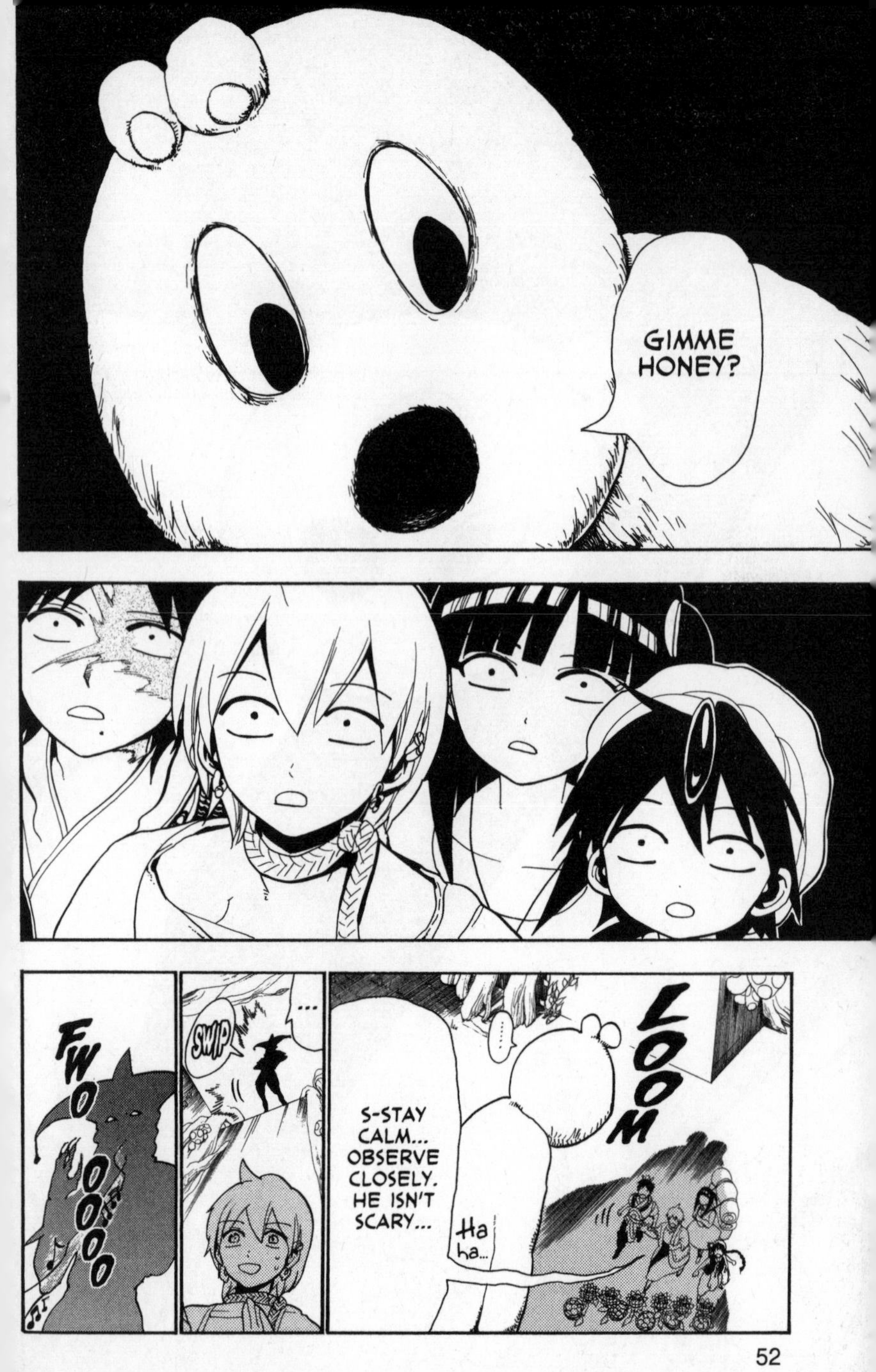
GIMME HONEY?
LOOOM
......
S-STAY CALM... OBSERVE CLOSELY. HE ISN'T SCARY...
Ha ha...
...
SWIP
FWOOOOOO

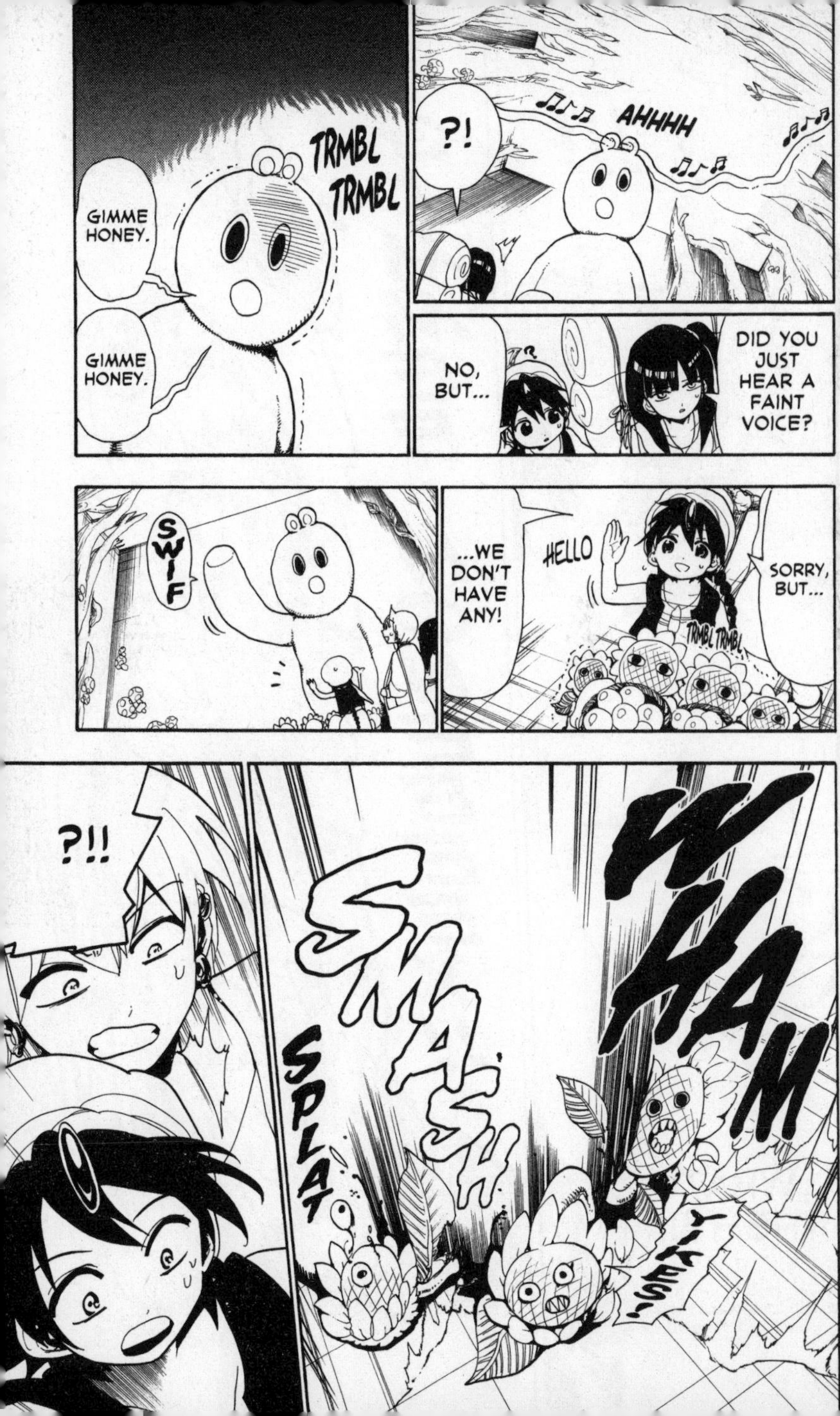
AHHHH
?!
DID YOU JUST HEAR A FAINT VOICE?
NO, BUT...
TRMBL TRMBL
GIMME HONEY.
GIMME HONEY.
SORRY, BUT...
HELLO
TRMBL TRMBL
...WE DON'T HAVE ANY!
SWIF
WHAM
YIKES!
SMASH
SPLAT
?!!

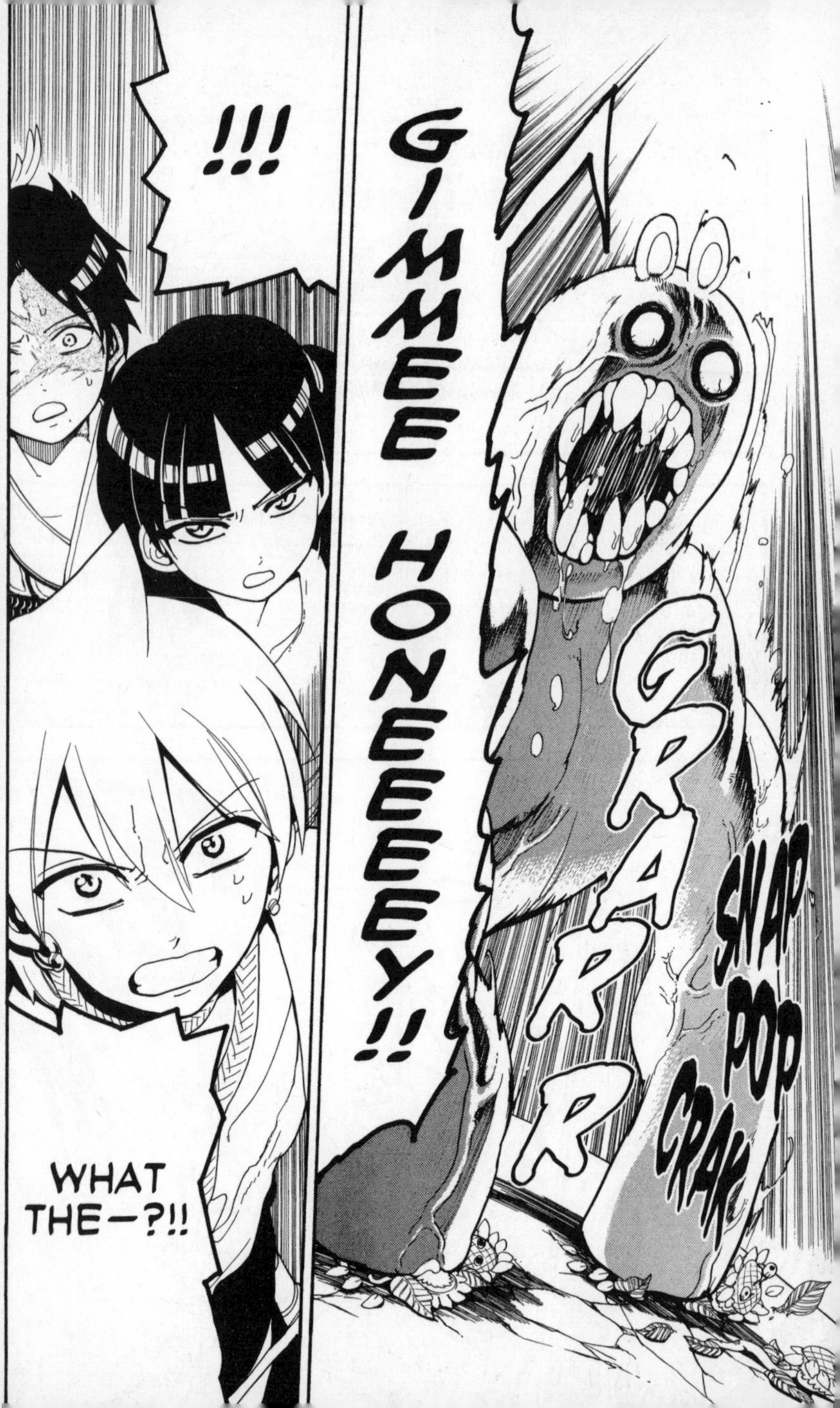
GIMME HONEEEEEY!!
GRARR
SNAP
POP
CRAK
!!!
WHAT THE—?!!

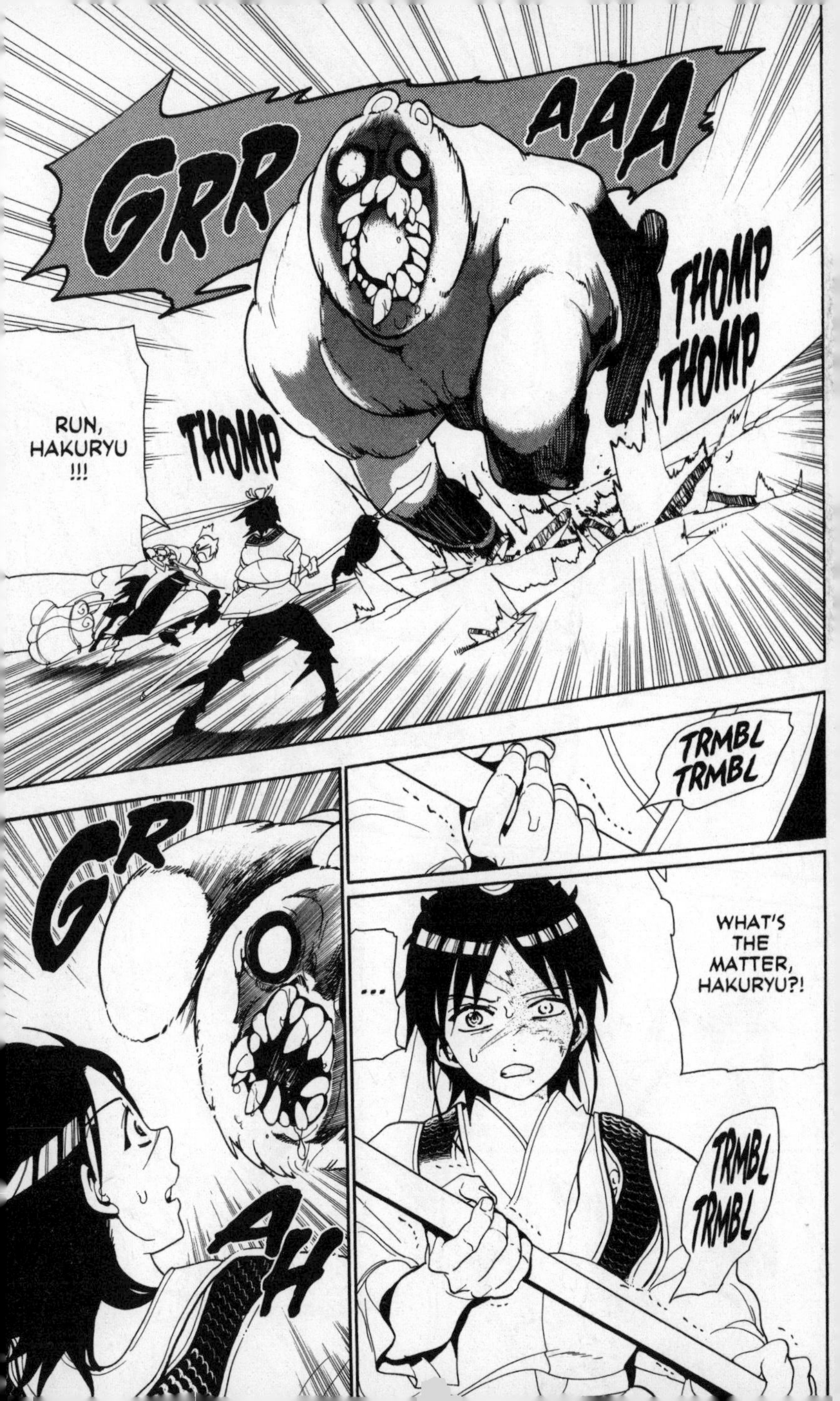
GRR AAA
THOMP THOMP
RUN, HAKURYU !!!
THOMP
TRMBL TRMBL
WHAT'S THE MATTER, HAKURYU?!
...
TRMBL TRMBL
GR
AH

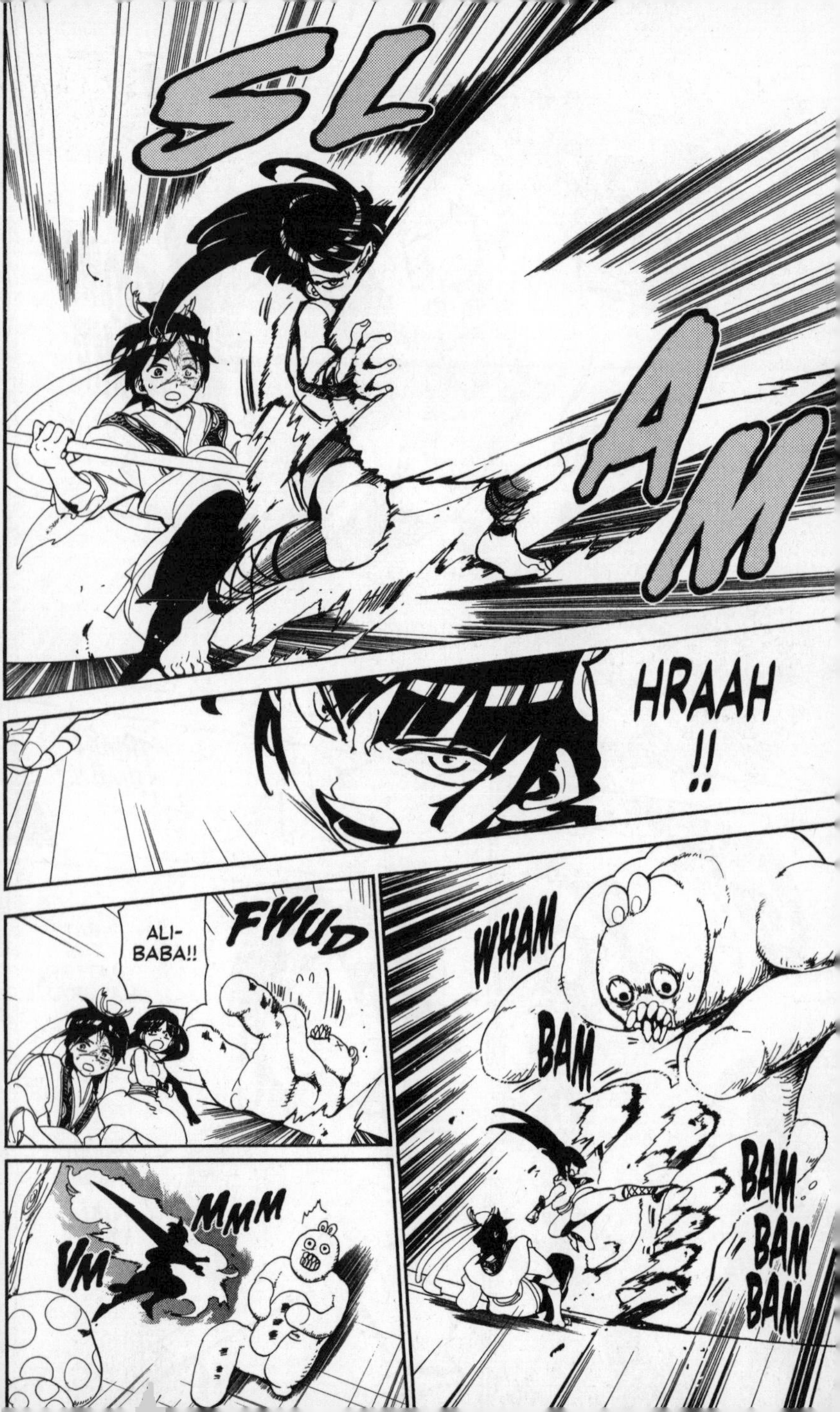
SL
AM
HRAAH!!
WHAM
BAM
BAM BAM BAM
ALI-BABA!!
FWUD
MMM
VM

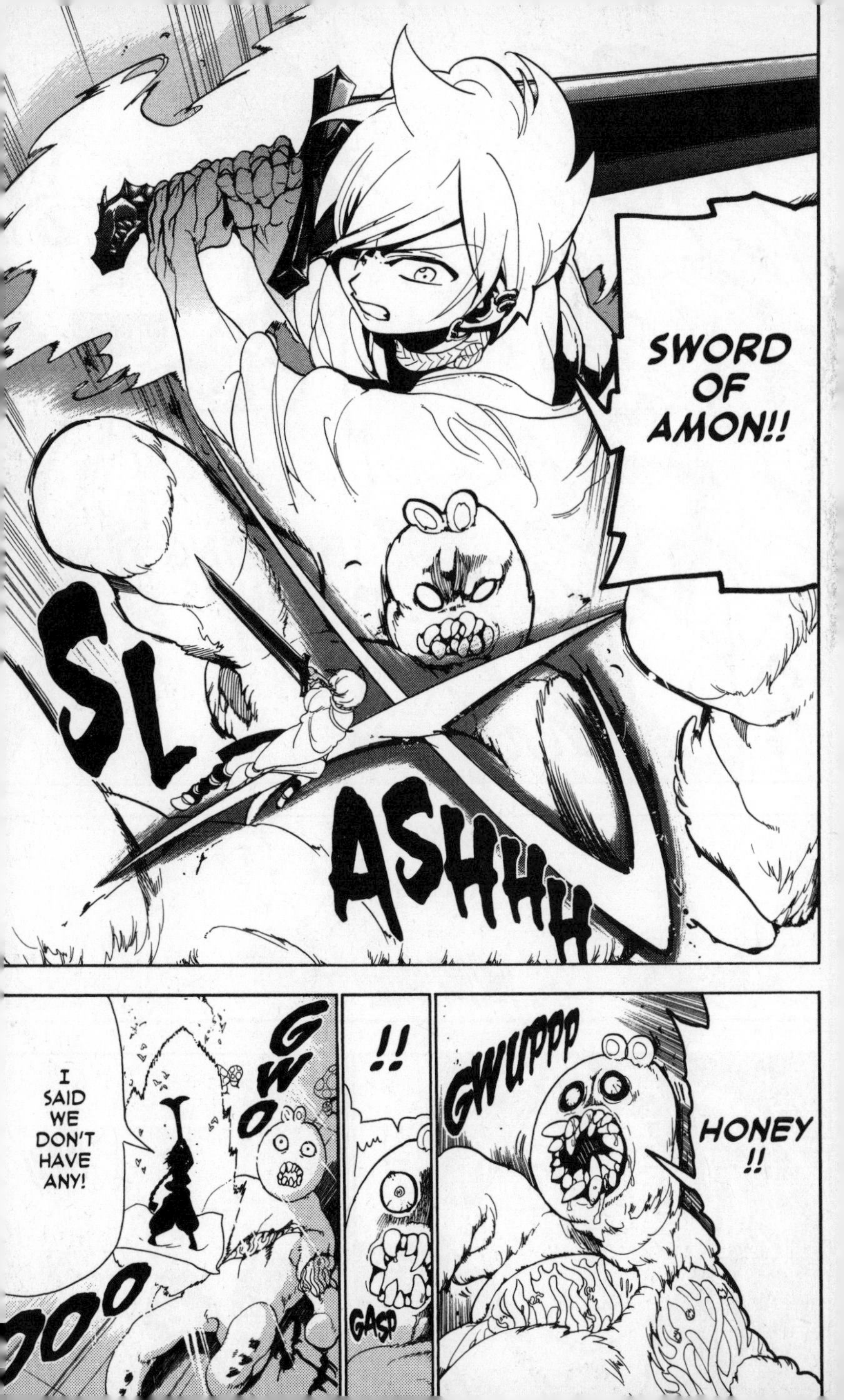
SWORD OF AMON!!
SL
ASHHH
GWUPPP
HONEY!!
!!
GASP
GWOO
I SAID WE DON'T HAVE ANY!
OOO

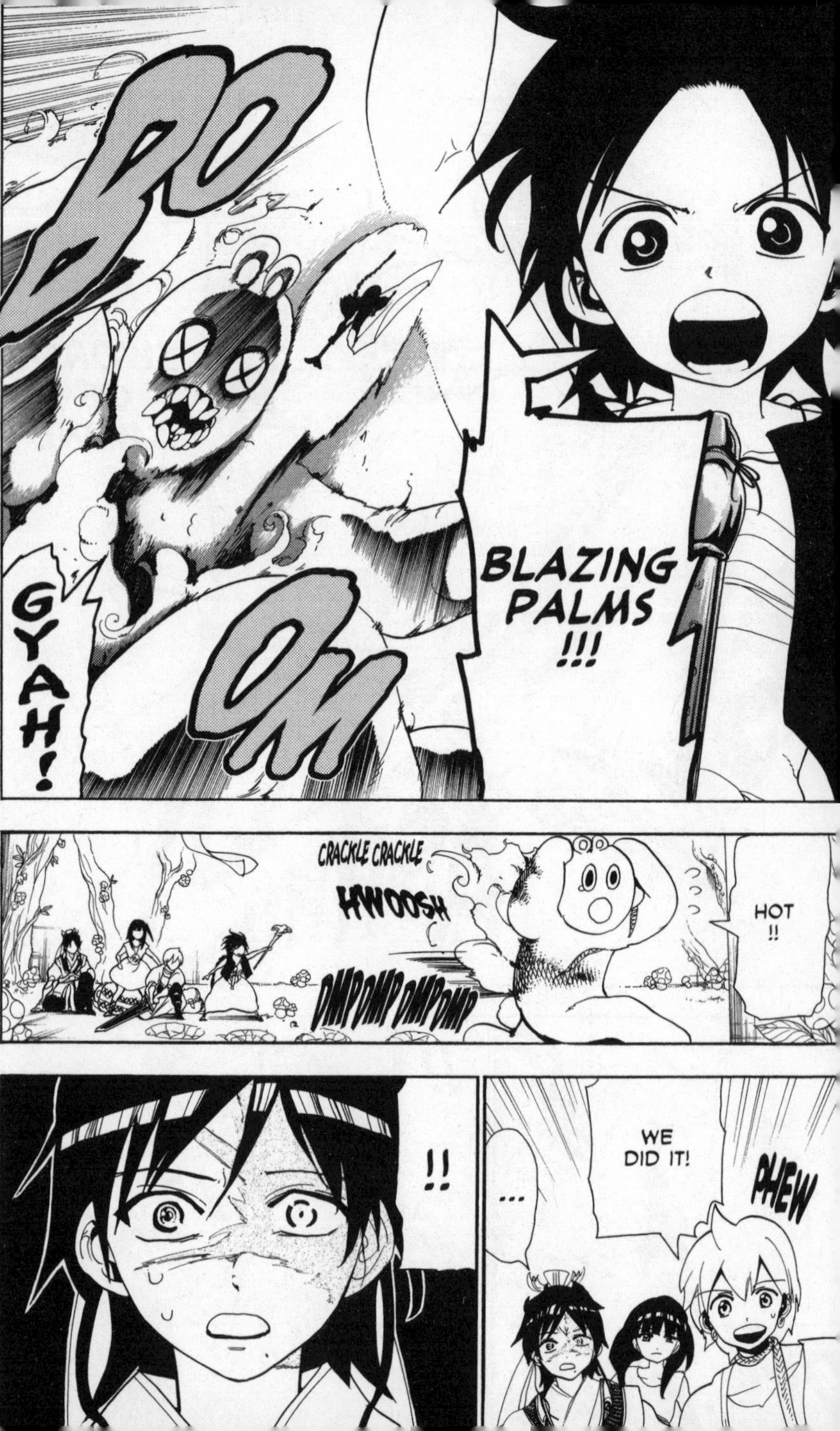
BLAZING PALMS !!!
BOOM
GYAH!
HOT !!
CRACKLE CRACKLE
HWOOSH
DMP DMP DMP DMP
WE DID IT!
PHEW
...
!!

# Night 92: Zagan Appears

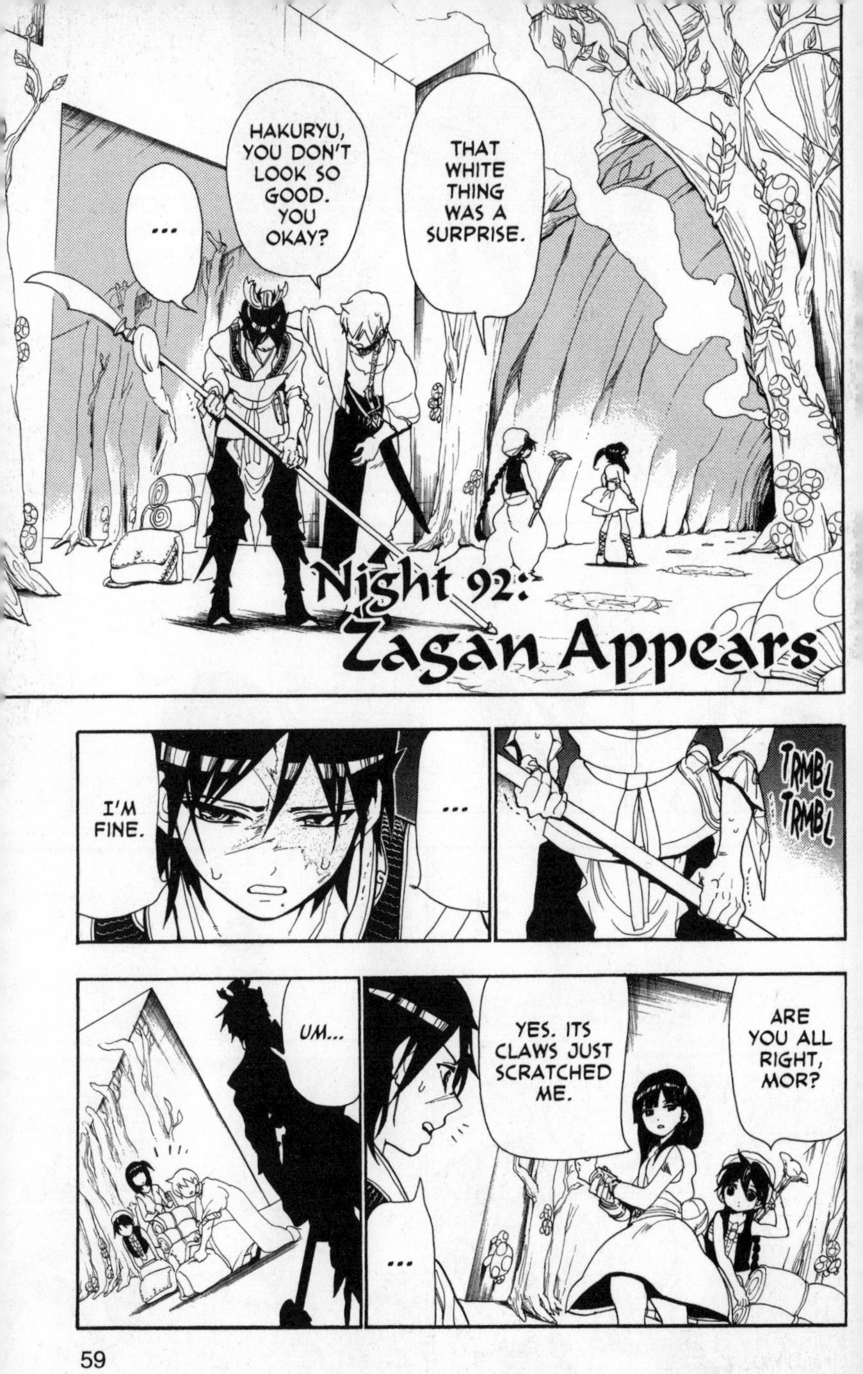
THAT WHITE THING WAS A SURPRISE.
HAKURYU, YOU DON'T LOOK SO GOOD. YOU OKAY?
...
TRMBL TRMBL
...
I'M FINE.
ARE YOU ALL RIGHT, MOR?
YES. ITS CLAWS JUST SCRATCHED ME.
...
UM...

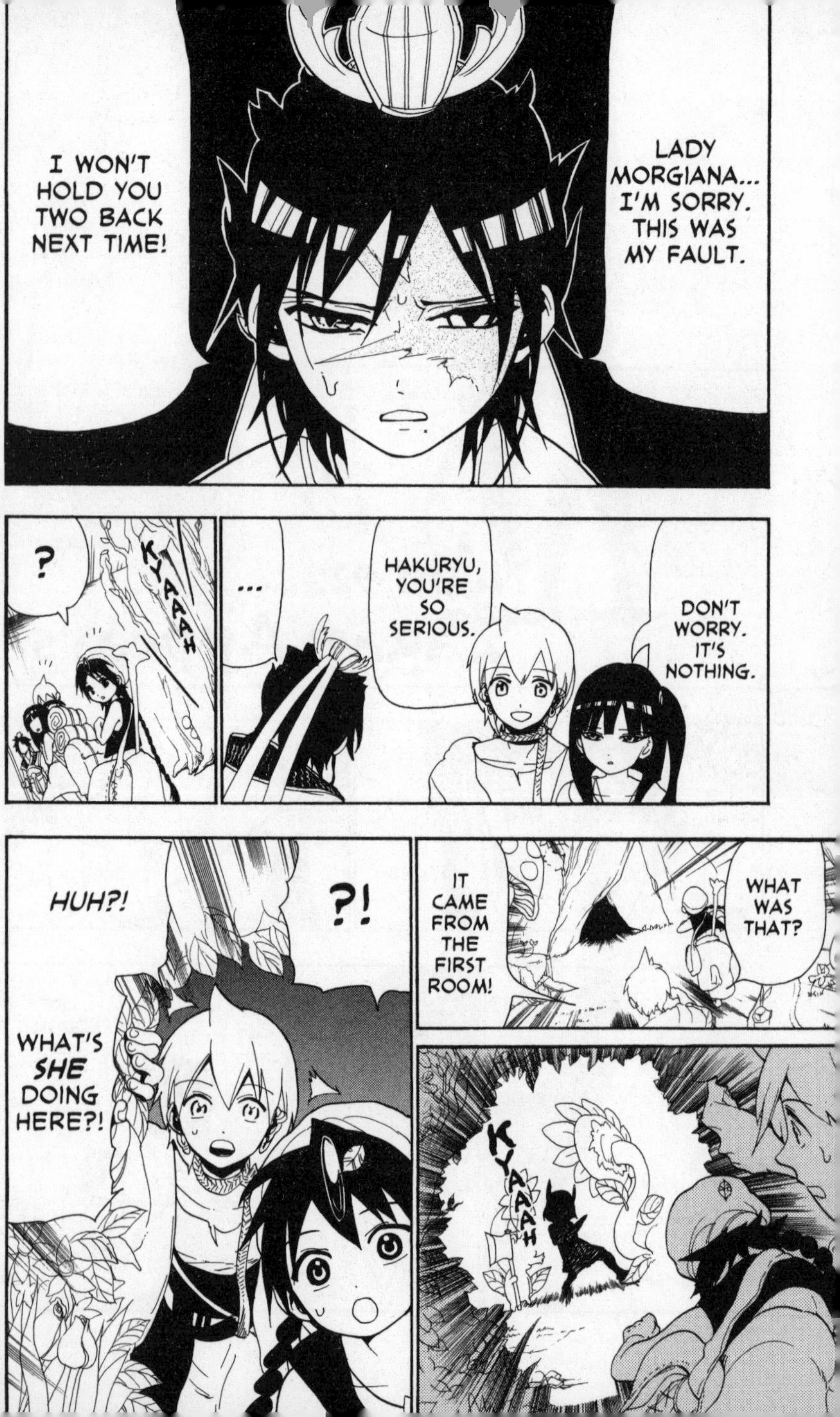
LADY MORGIANA... I'M SORRY. THIS WAS MY FAULT.
I WON'T HOLD YOU TWO BACK NEXT TIME!
DON'T WORRY. IT'S NOTHING.
HAKURYU, YOU'RE SO SERIOUS.
...
KYAAAH
?
WHAT WAS THAT?
IT CAME FROM THE FIRST ROOM!
KYAAAH
HUH?!
?!
WHAT'S *SHE* DOING HERE?!

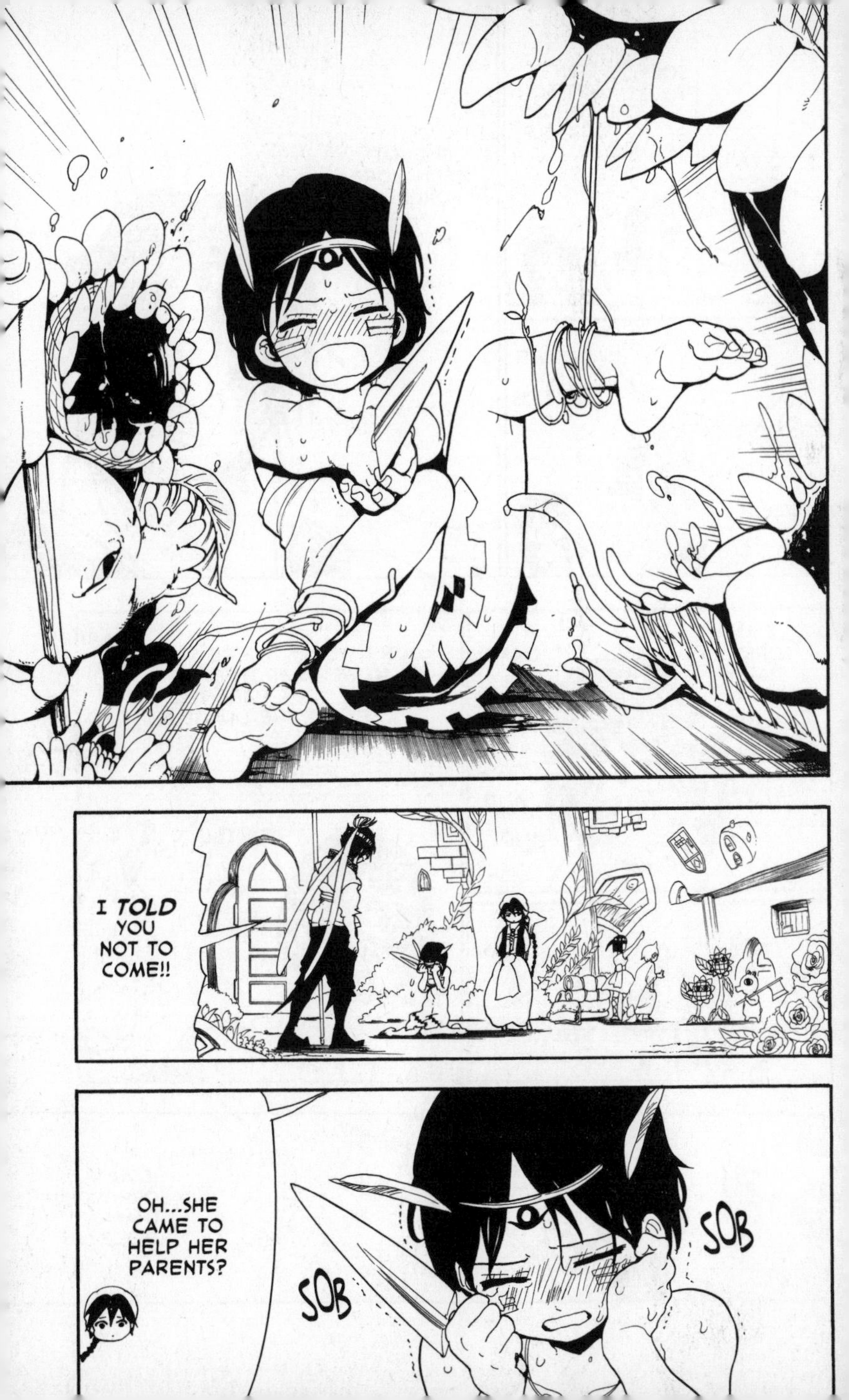
I TOLD YOU NOT TO COME!!
SOB
SOB
OH...SHE CAME TO HELP HER PARENTS?

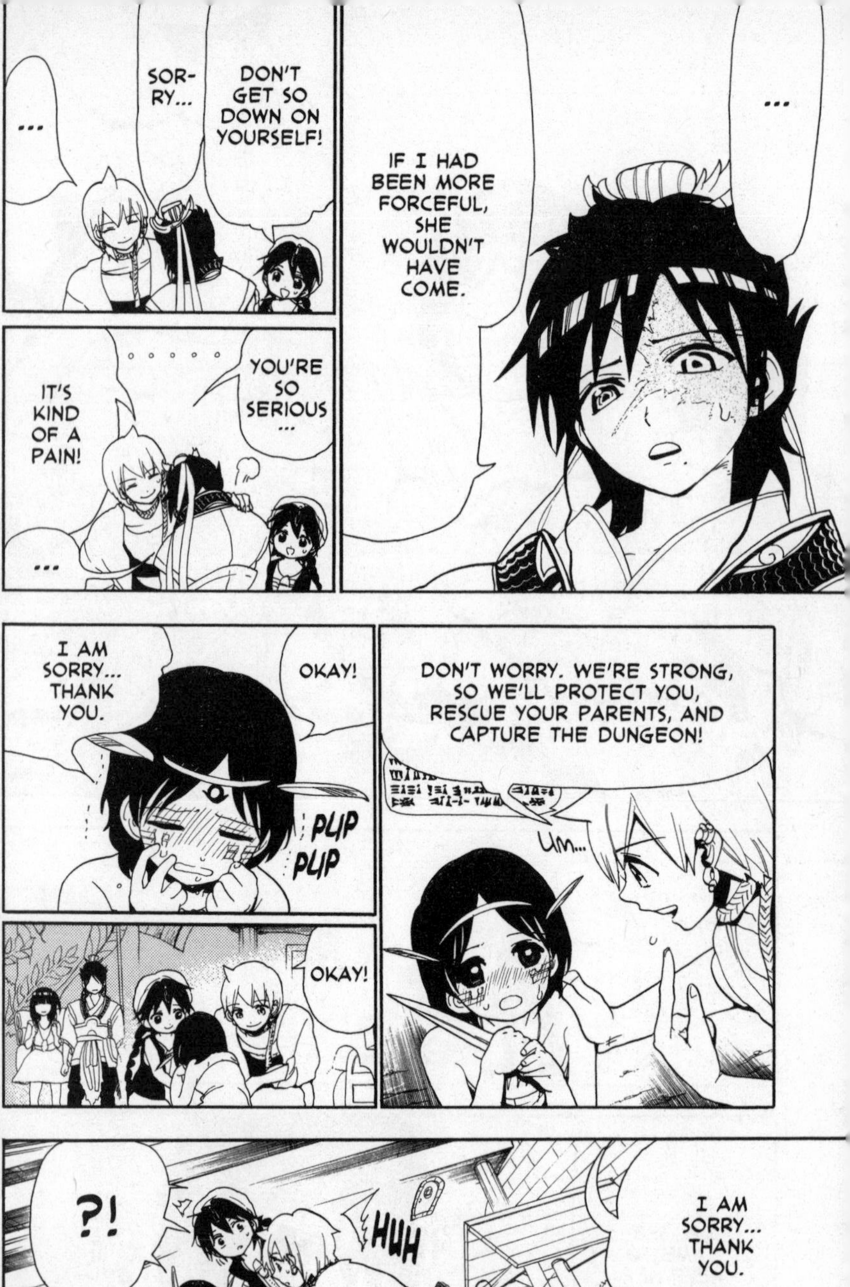
...
IF I HAD BEEN MORE FORCEFUL, SHE WOULDN'T HAVE COME.
DON'T GET SO DOWN ON YOURSELF!
SOR-RY...
...
YOU'RE SO SERIOUS...
。。。。。
IT'S KIND OF A PAIN!
...
DON'T WORRY. WE'RE STRONG, SO WE'LL PROTECT YOU, RESCUE YOUR PARENTS, AND CAPTURE THE DUNGEON!
Um...
OKAY!
I AM SORRY... THANK YOU.
PLIP PLIP
OKAY!
I AM SORRY... THANK YOU.
HUH
?!

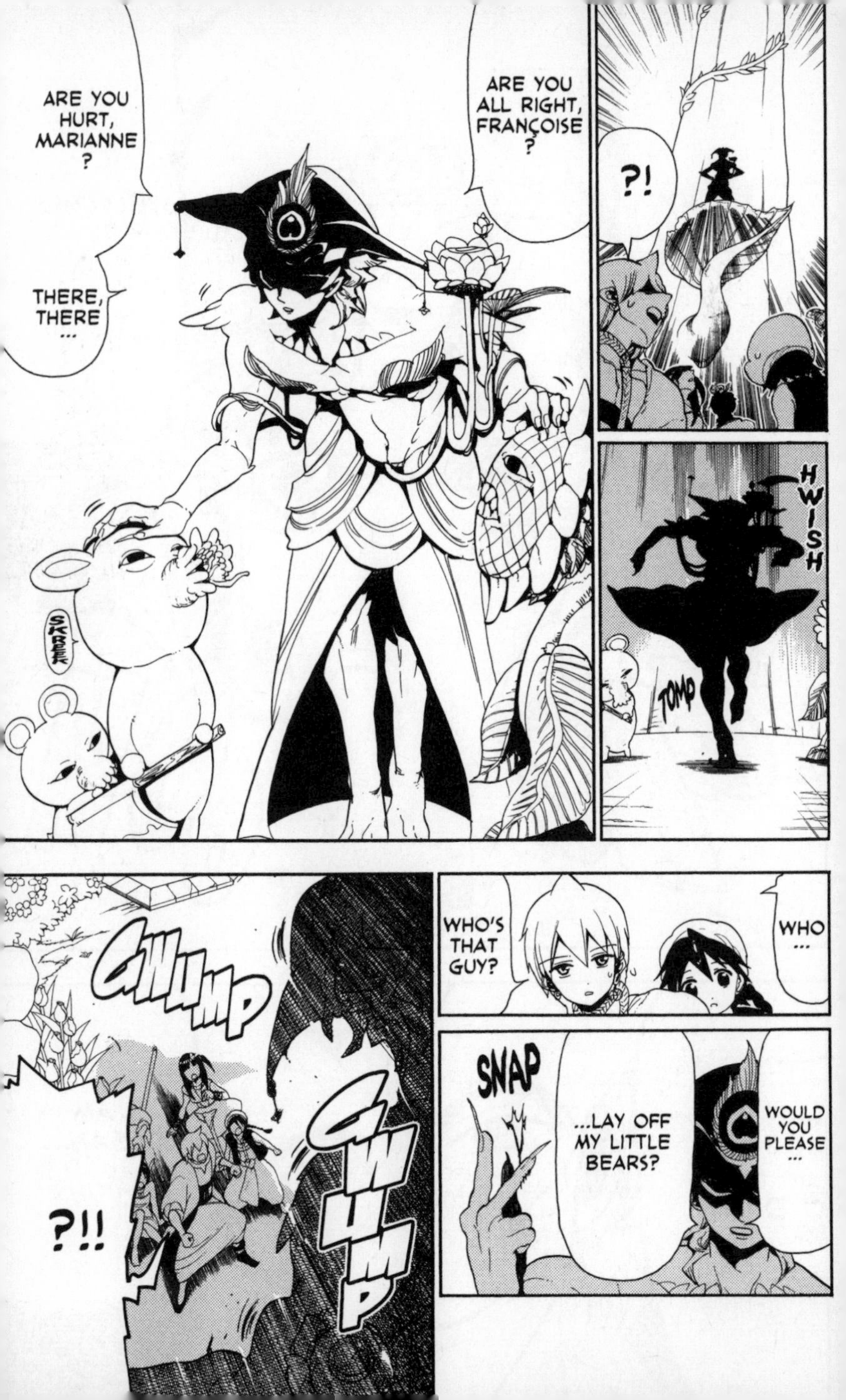
?!
HWISH
TOMP
ARE YOU ALL RIGHT, FRANÇOISE?
ARE YOU HURT, MARIANNE?
THERE, THERE...
SKREEK
WHO...
WHO'S THAT GUY?
WOULD YOU PLEASE...
SNAP
...LAY OFF MY LITTLE BEARS?
GWUMP
GWUMP
?!!

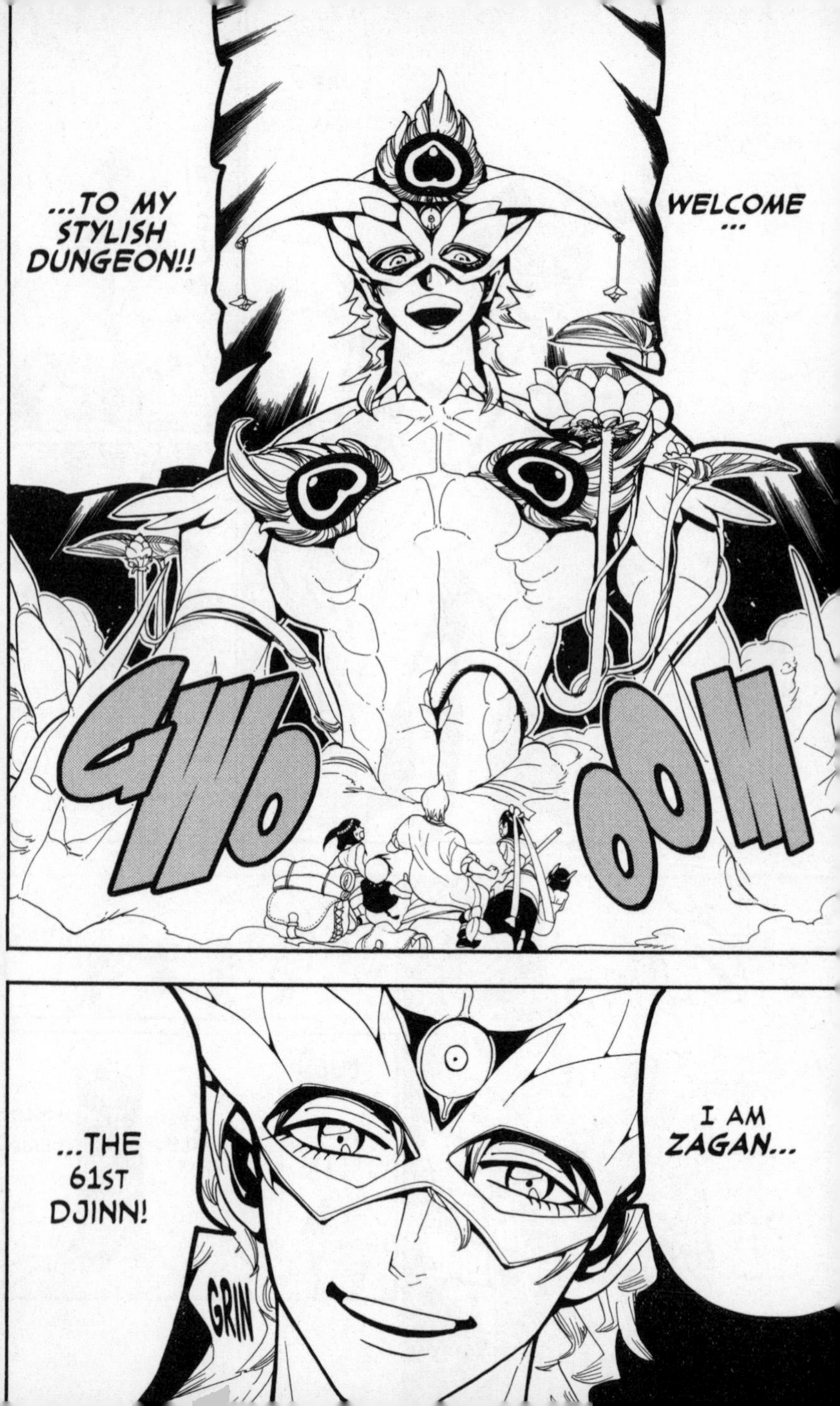
WELCOME ...
...TO MY STYLISH DUNGEON!!
GWOOOM
I AM ZAGAN...
...THE 61ST DJINN!
GRIN

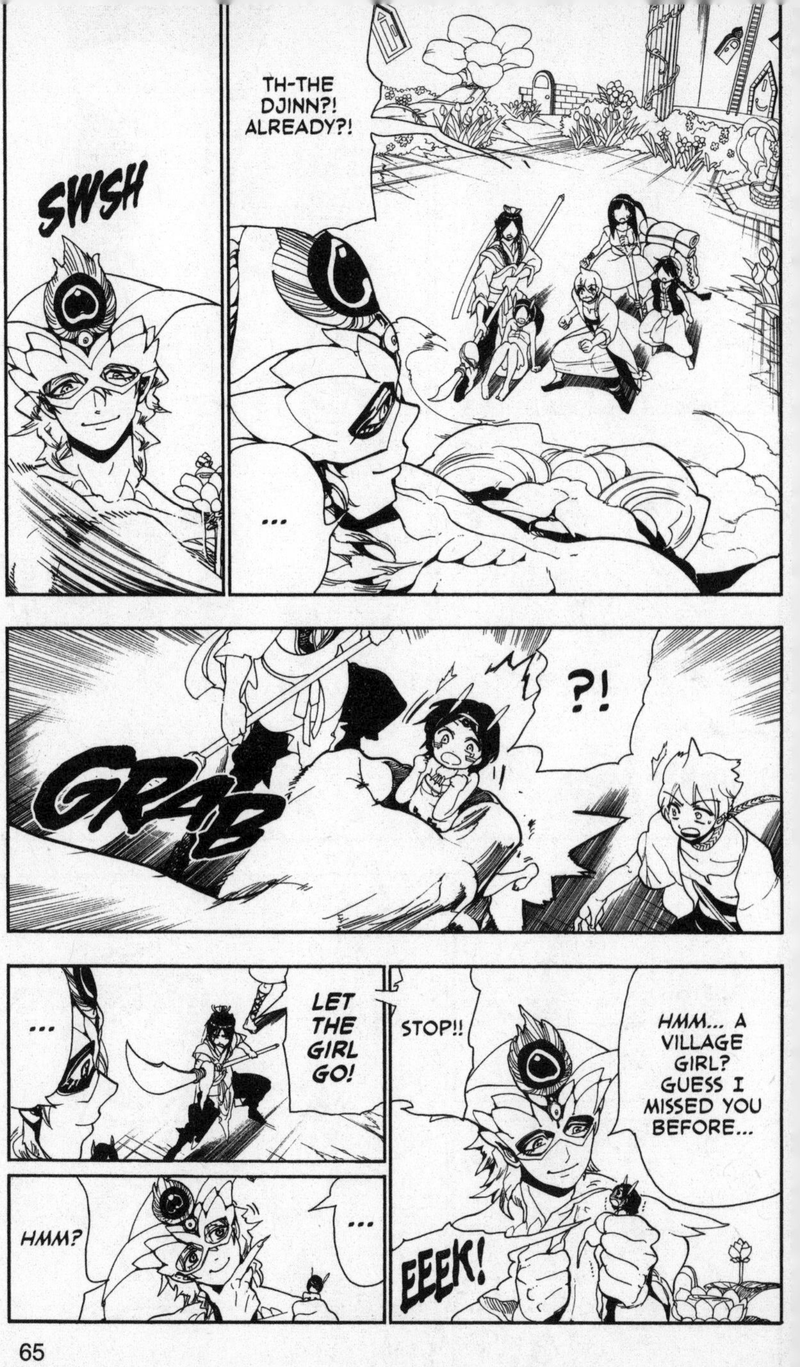
TH-THE DJINN?! ALREADY?!
...
SWSH
?!
GRAB
HMM... A VILLAGE GIRL? GUESS I MISSED YOU BEFORE...
STOP!!
EEEK!
LET THE GIRL GO!
...
...
HMM?

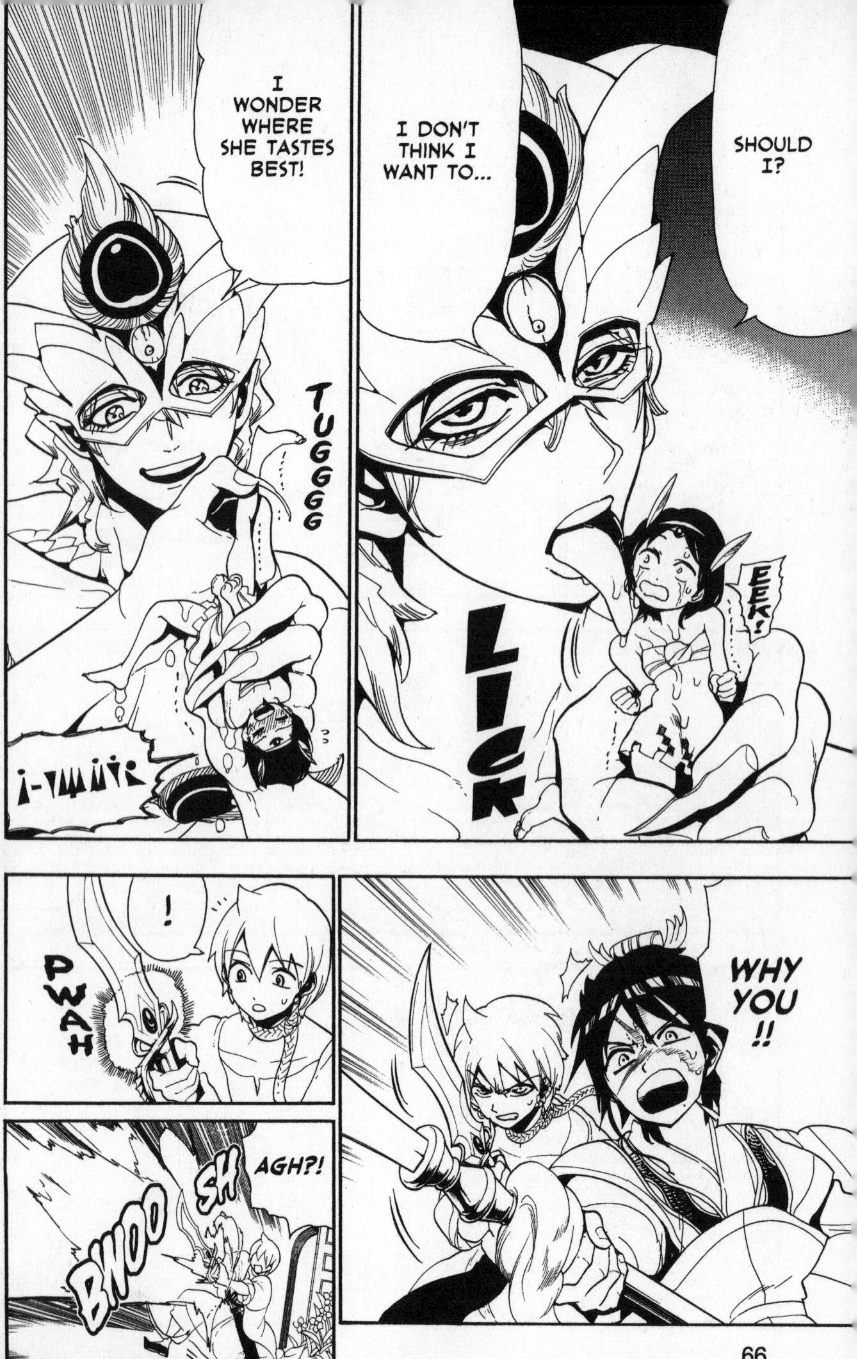

SHOULD I?
I DON'T THINK I WANT TO...
EEK!
LICK
I WONDER WHERE SHE TASTES BEST!
TUGGGG
WHY YOU!!
!
PWAH
AGH?!
BWOOSH

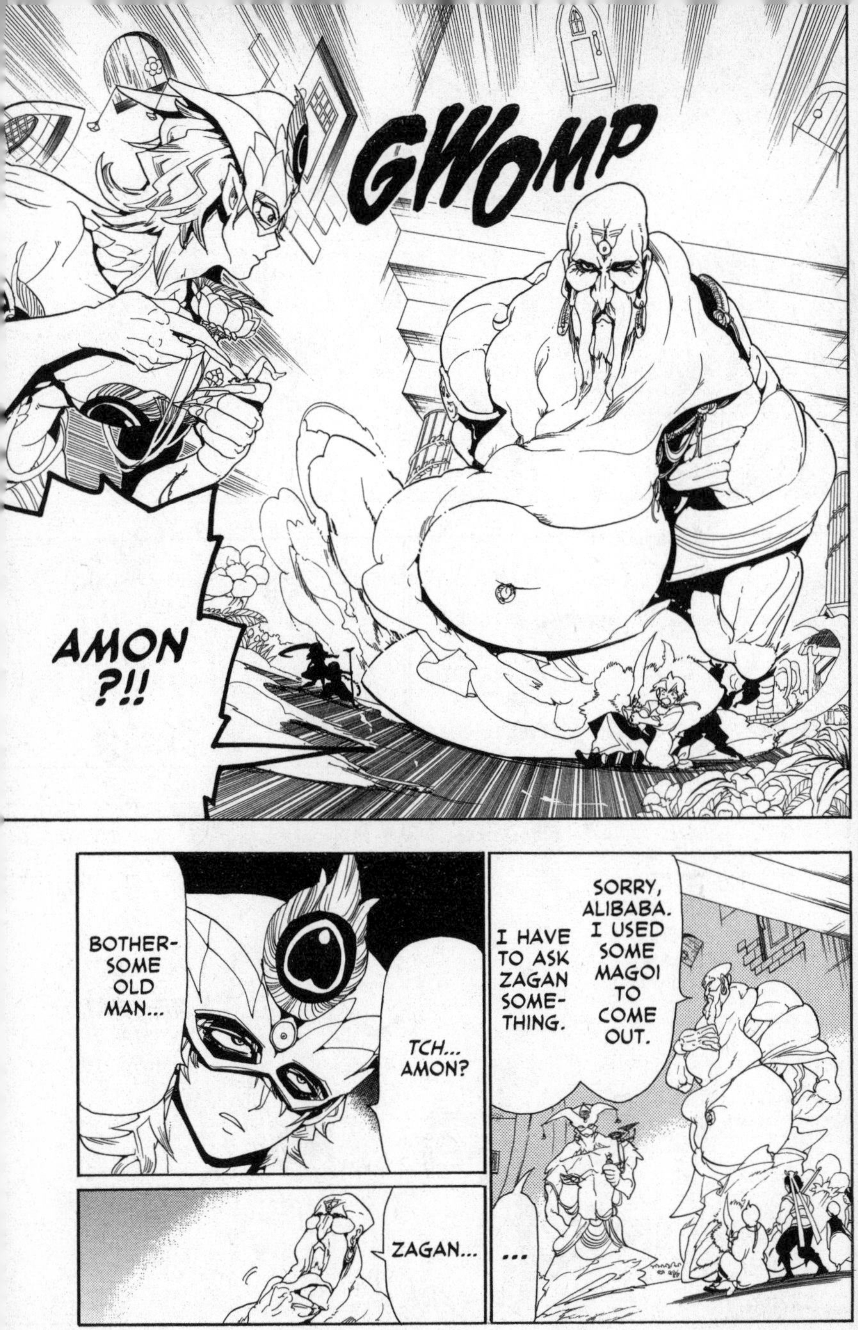
GWOMP
AMON ?!!
SORRY, ALIBABA. I USED SOME MAGOI TO COME OUT.
I HAVE TO ASK ZAGAN SOME-THING.
...
TCH... AMON?
BOTHER-SOME OLD MAN...
ZAGAN...

...DO YOU NOT INTEND TO CHOOSE A KING?

OF COURSE NOT!

HEH...

?!!

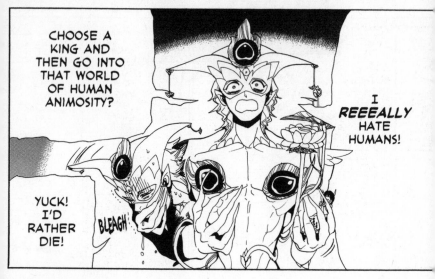

CHOOSE A KING AND THEN GO INTO THAT WORLD OF HUMAN ANIMOSITY?

I *REEEALLY* HATE HUMANS!

YUCK! I'D RATHER DIE!

BLEAGH

68

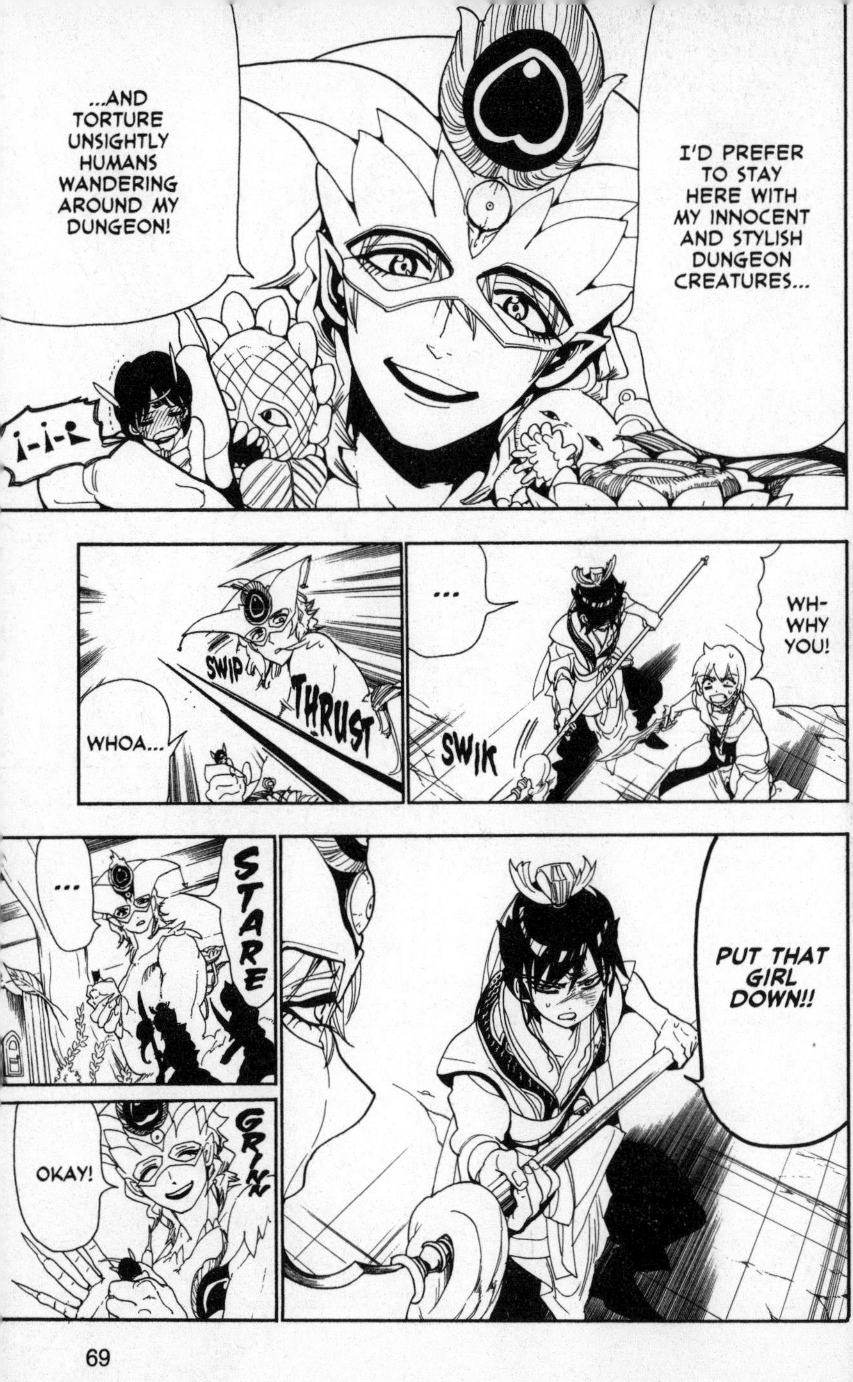
I'D PREFER TO STAY HERE WITH MY INNOCENT AND STYLISH DUNGEON CREATURES...
...AND TORTURE UNSIGHTLY HUMANS WANDERING AROUND MY DUNGEON!
WH- WHY YOU!
...
SWIK
SWIP
THRUST
WHOA...
PUT THAT GIRL DOWN!!
...
STARE
GRIN
OKAY!

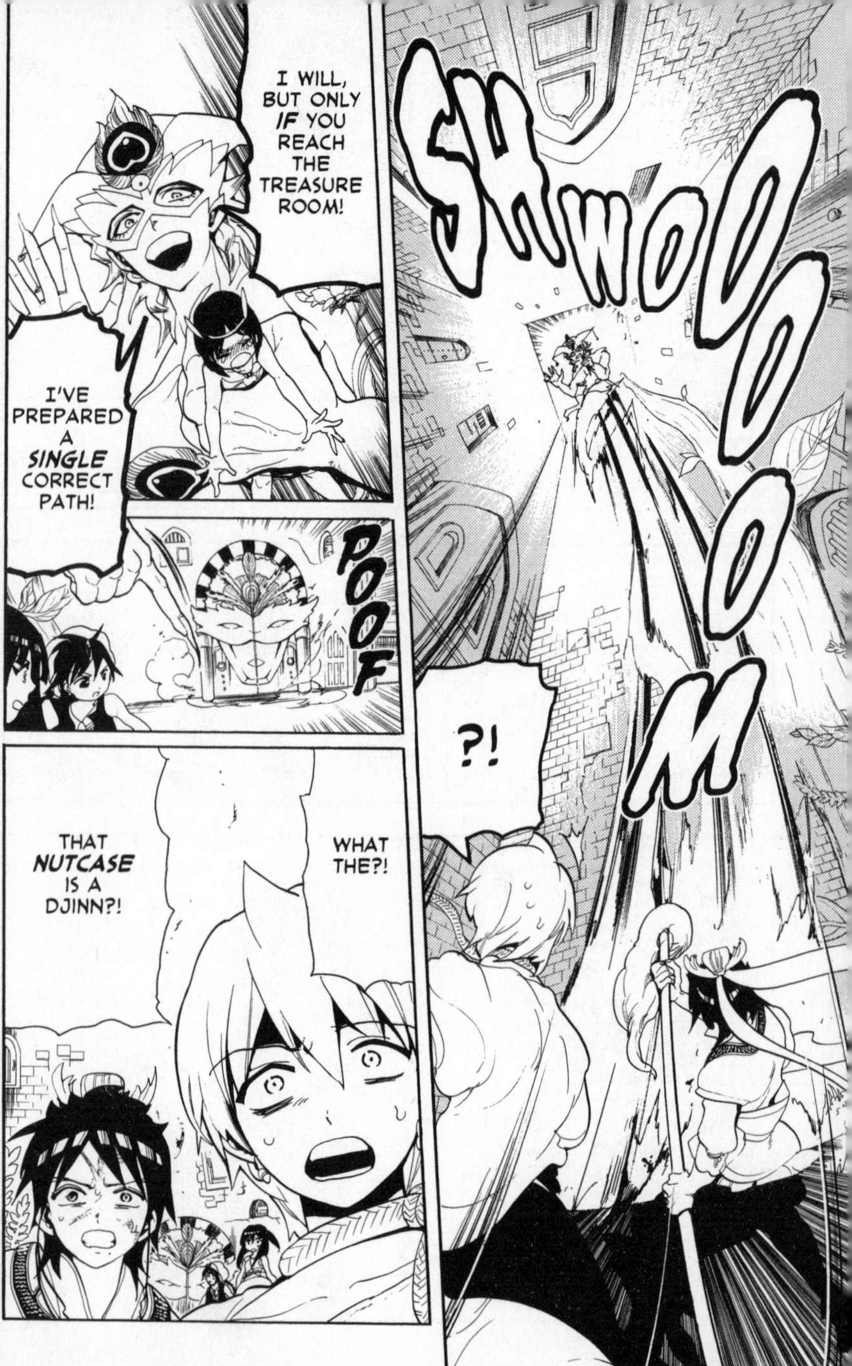
SHWOOOOM
?!
I WILL, BUT ONLY *IF* YOU REACH THE TREASURE ROOM!
I'VE PREPARED A *SINGLE* CORRECT PATH!
POOOF
WHAT THE?!
THAT *NUTCASE* IS A DJINN?!

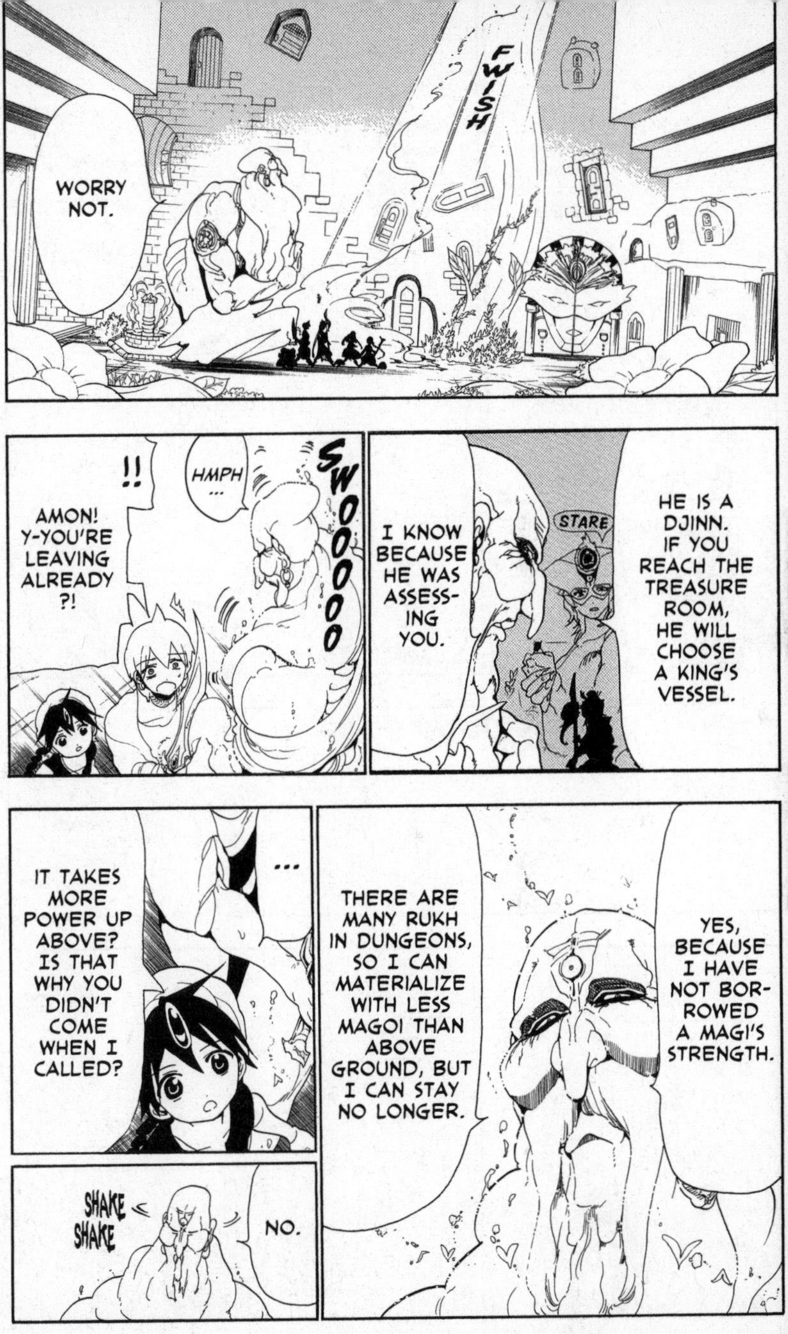
FWISH
WORRY NOT.
HE IS A DJINN. IF YOU REACH THE TREASURE ROOM, HE WILL CHOOSE A KING'S VESSEL.
STARE
I KNOW BECAUSE HE WAS ASSESS-ING YOU.
SWOOOOOO
HMPH ...
!!
AMON! Y-YOU'RE LEAVING ALREADY ?!
YES, BECAUSE I HAVE NOT BOR-ROWED A MAGI'S STRENGTH.
THERE ARE MANY RUKH IN DUNGEONS, SO I CAN MATERIALIZE WITH LESS MAGOI THAN ABOVE GROUND, BUT I CAN STAY NO LONGER.
...
IT TAKES MORE POWER UP ABOVE? IS THAT WHY YOU DIDN'T COME WHEN I CALLED?
NO.
SHAKE SHAKE

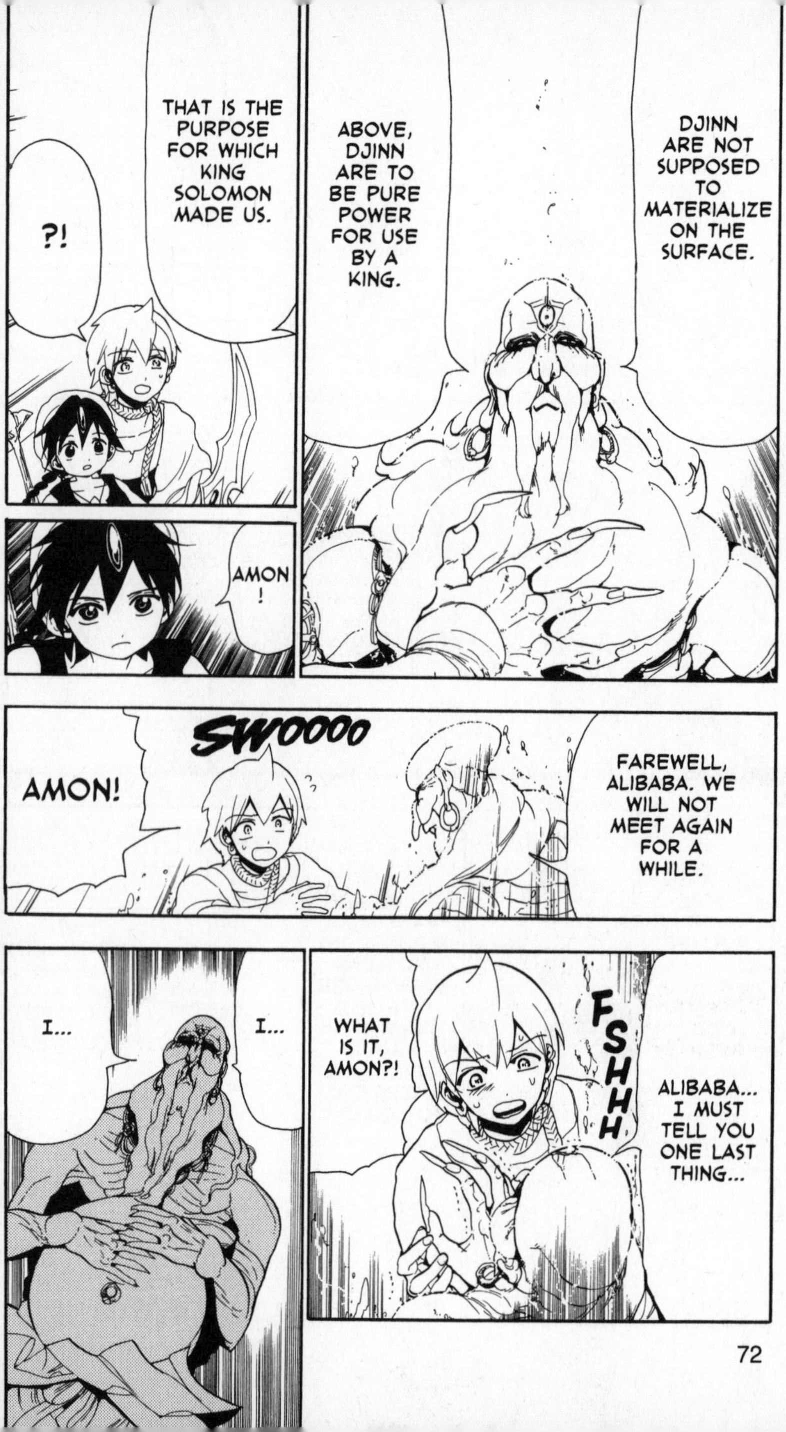
DJINN ARE NOT SUPPOSED TO MATERIALIZE ON THE SURFACE.
ABOVE, DJINN ARE TO BE PURE POWER FOR USE BY A KING.
THAT IS THE PURPOSE FOR WHICH KING SOLOMON MADE US.
?!
AMON!
FAREWELL, ALIBABA. WE WILL NOT MEET AGAIN FOR A WHILE.
SWOOOO
AMON!
ALIBABA... I MUST TELL YOU ONE LAST THING...
FSHHH
WHAT IS IT, AMON?!
I...
I...

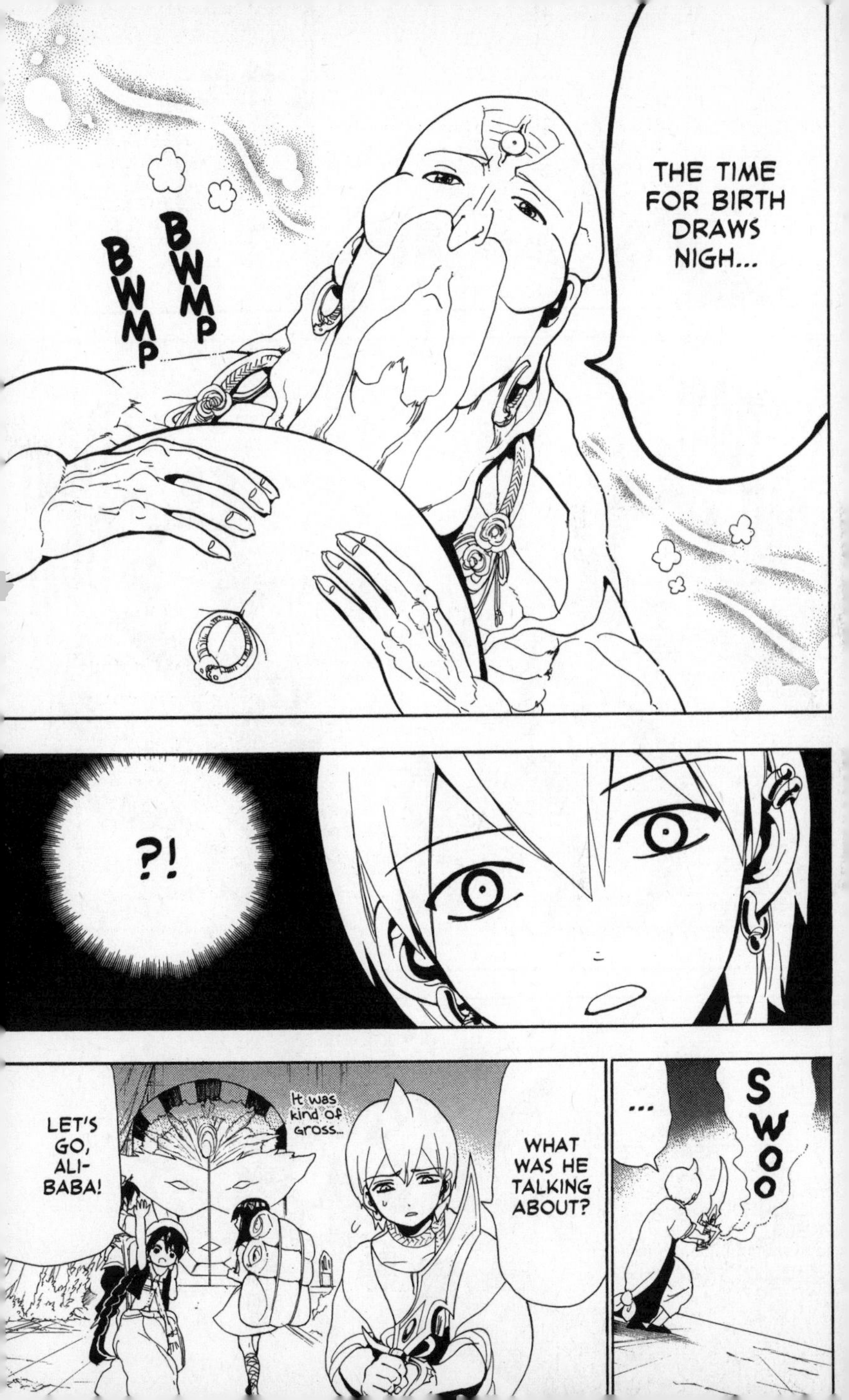
THE TIME FOR BIRTH DRAWS NIGH...
BWMP BWMP
?!
SWOO
...
WHAT WAS HE TALKING ABOUT?
It was kind of gross...
LET'S GO, ALI-BABA!

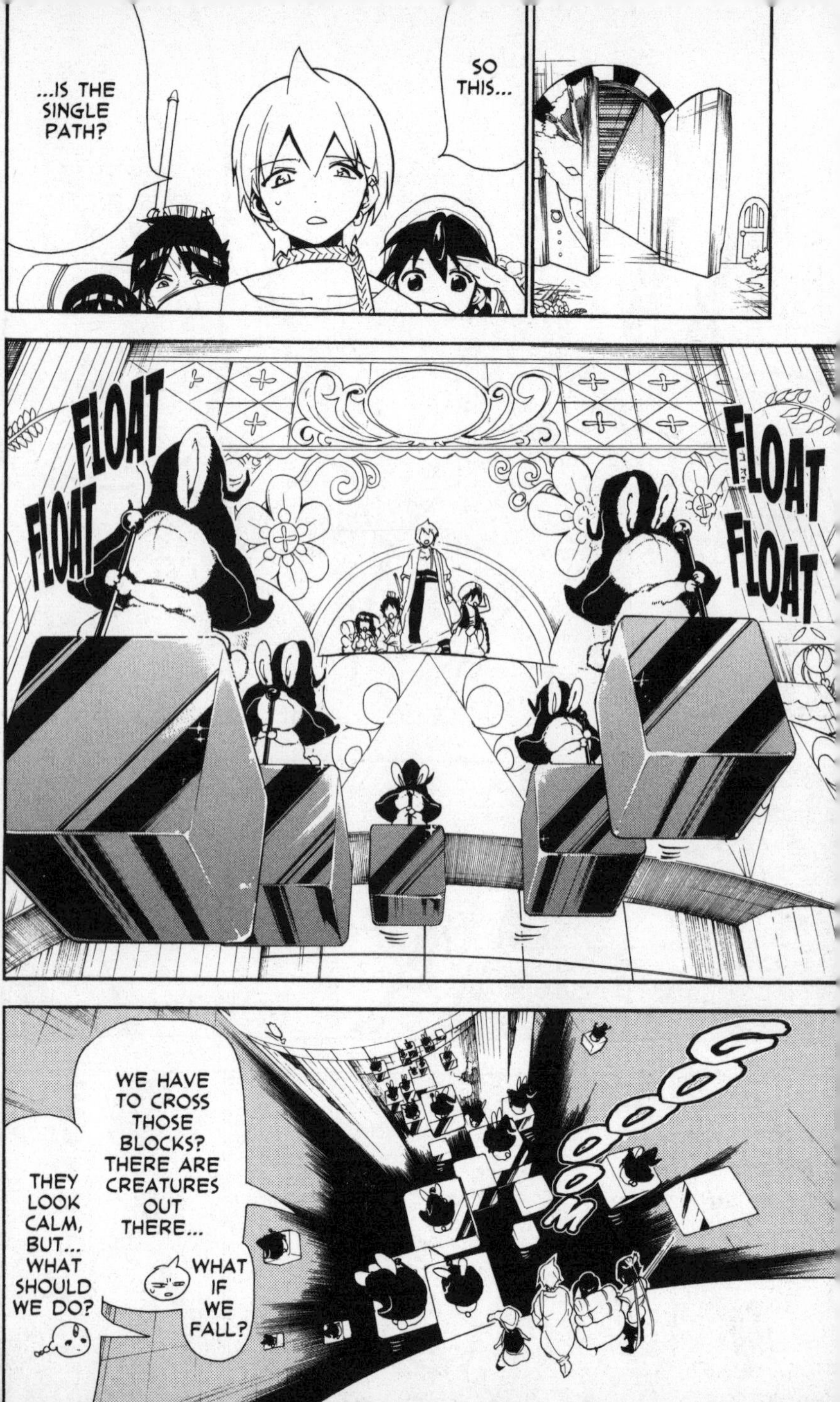
SO THIS...
...IS THE SINGLE PATH?
FLOAT FLOAT
FLOAT FLOAT
GOOOOOM
WE HAVE TO CROSS THOSE BLOCKS? THERE ARE CREATURES OUT THERE...
WHAT IF WE FALL?
THEY LOOK CALM, BUT... WHAT SHOULD WE DO?

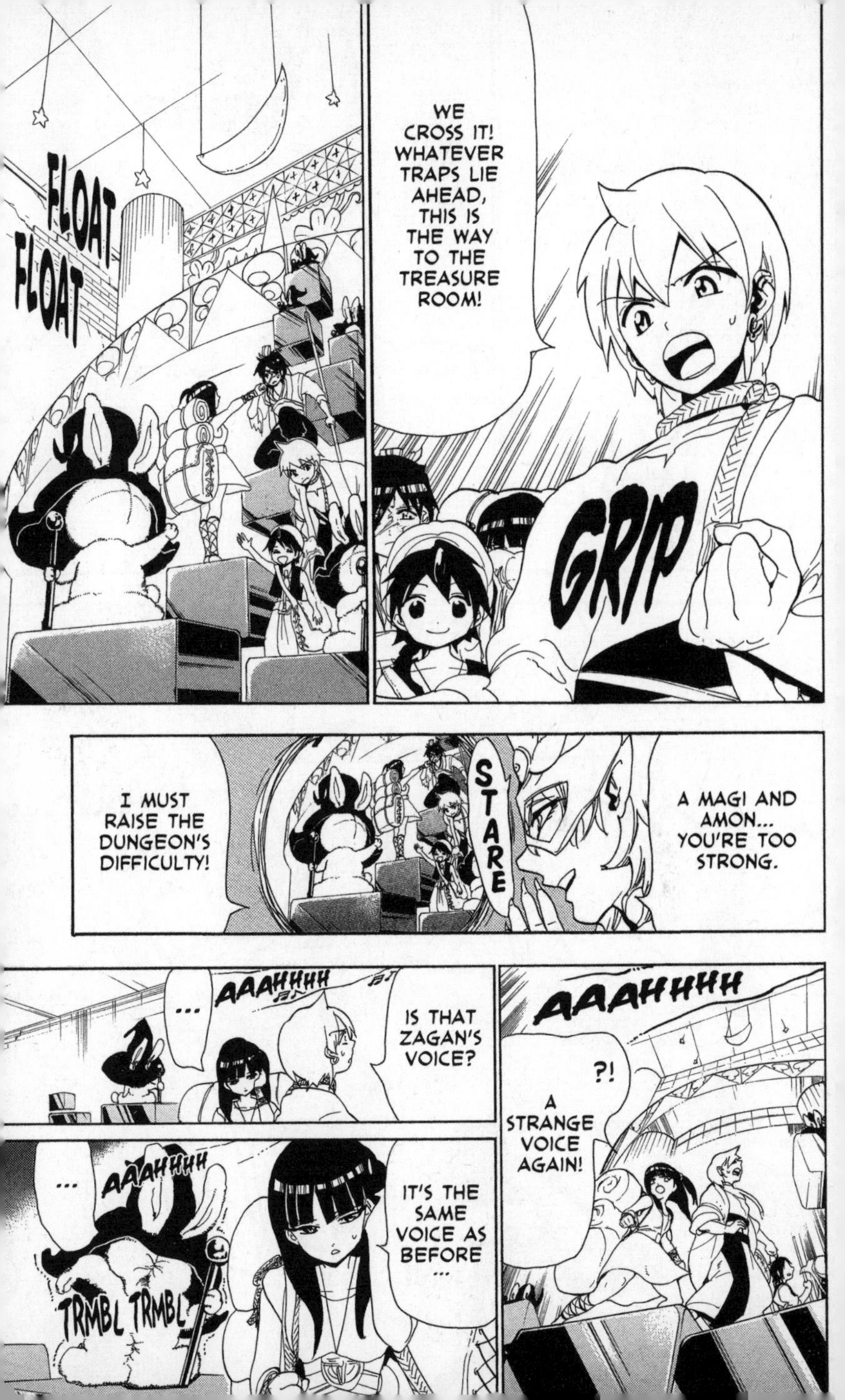
WE CROSS IT! WHATEVER TRAPS LIE AHEAD, THIS IS THE WAY TO THE TREASURE ROOM!
GRIP
FLOAT FLOAT
A MAGI AND AMON... YOU'RE TOO STRONG.
STARE
I MUST RAISE THE DUNGEON'S DIFFICULTY!
AAAHHHH
?!
A STRANGE VOICE AGAIN!
IS THAT ZAGAN'S VOICE?
AAAHHHH
...
IT'S THE SAME VOICE AS BEFORE ...
AAAHHHH
...
TRMBL TRMBL

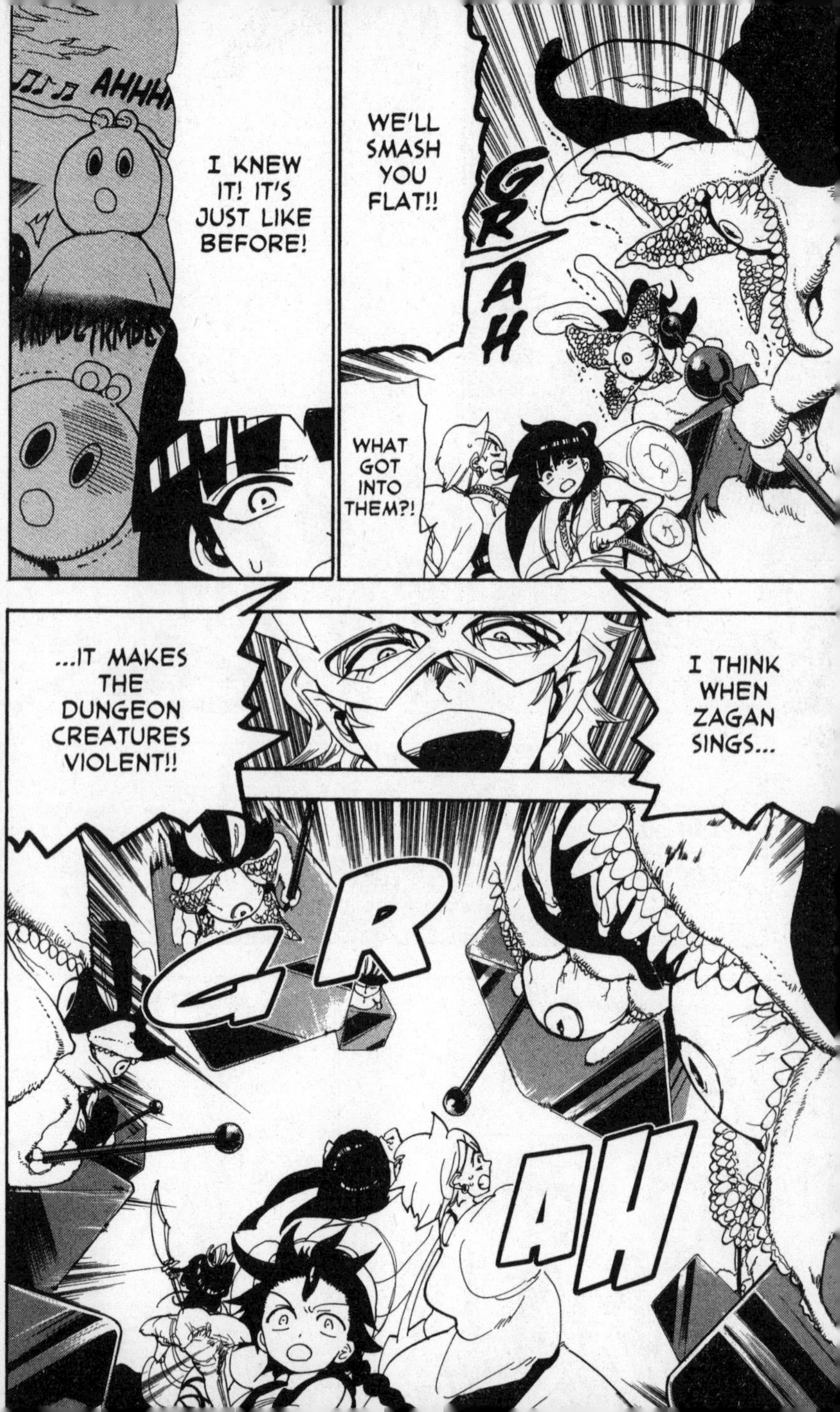
WE'LL SMASH YOU FLAT!!
GRAH
WHAT GOT INTO THEM?!
AHHH
I KNEW IT! IT'S JUST LIKE BEFORE!
I THINK WHEN ZAGAN SINGS...
...IT MAKES THE DUNGEON CREATURES VIOLENT!!
GRAH

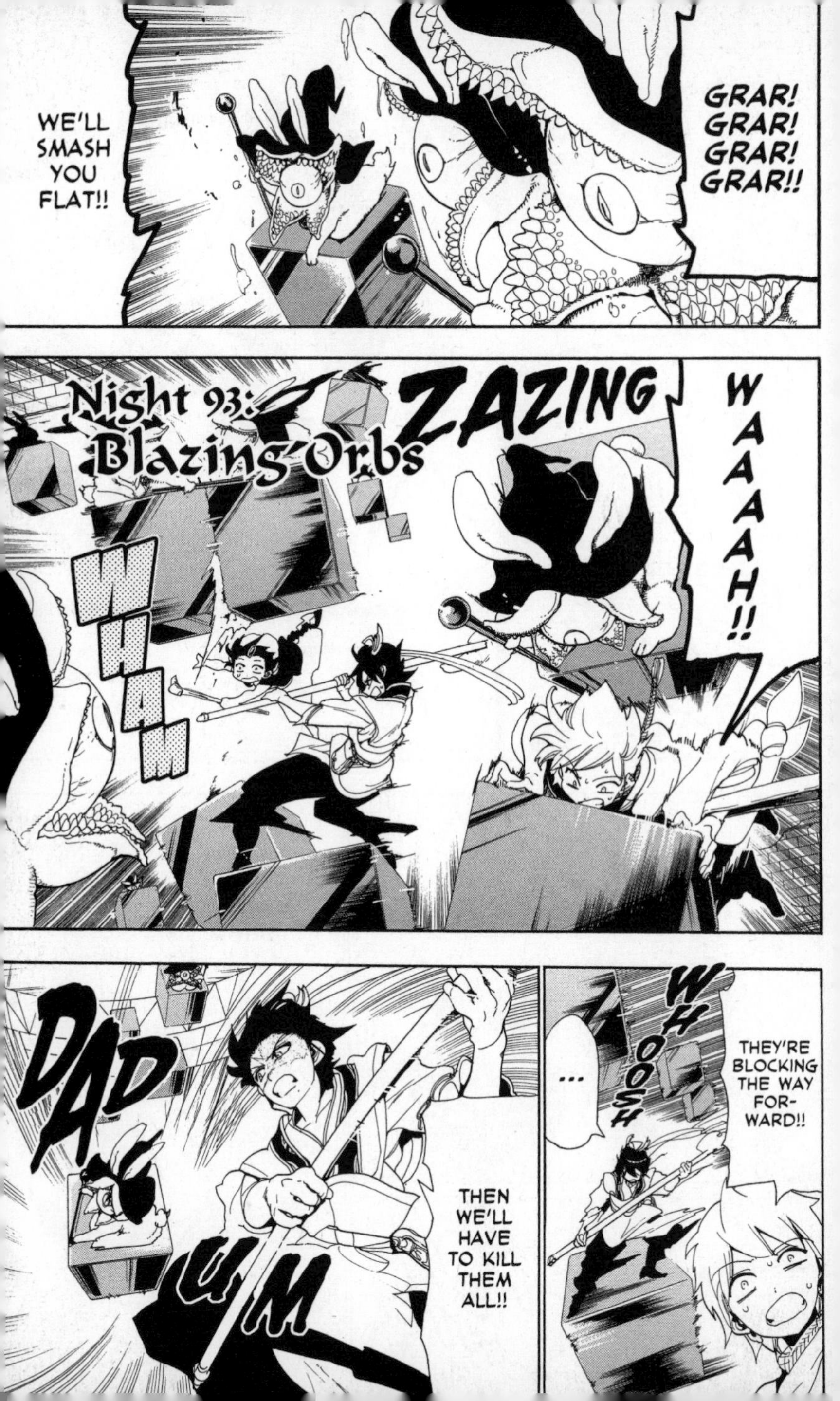
GRAR! GRAR! GRAR! GRAR!!
WE'LL SMASH YOU FLAT!!
WAAAAAH!!
ZAZING
Night 93: Blazing Orbs
WHAM
THEY'RE BLOCKING THE WAY FOR-WARD!!
WHOOSH
...
THEN WE'LL HAVE TO KILL THEM ALL!!
DADUM

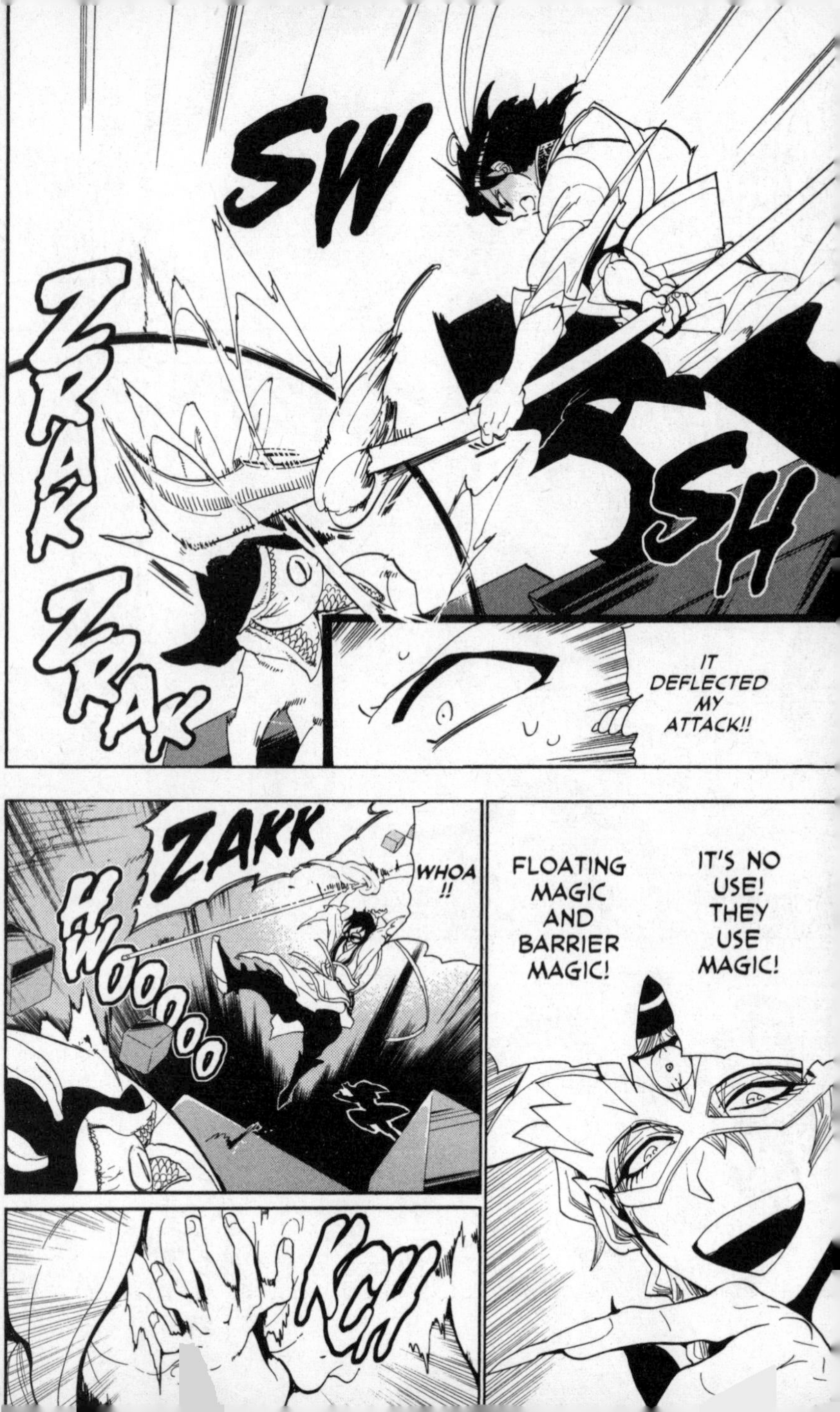
SW
SH
ZRAK
ZRAK
IT DEFLECTED MY ATTACK!!
IT'S NO USE! THEY USE MAGIC!
FLOATING MAGIC AND BARRIER MAGIC!
WHOA !!
ZAKK
HWOOOOO
KCH

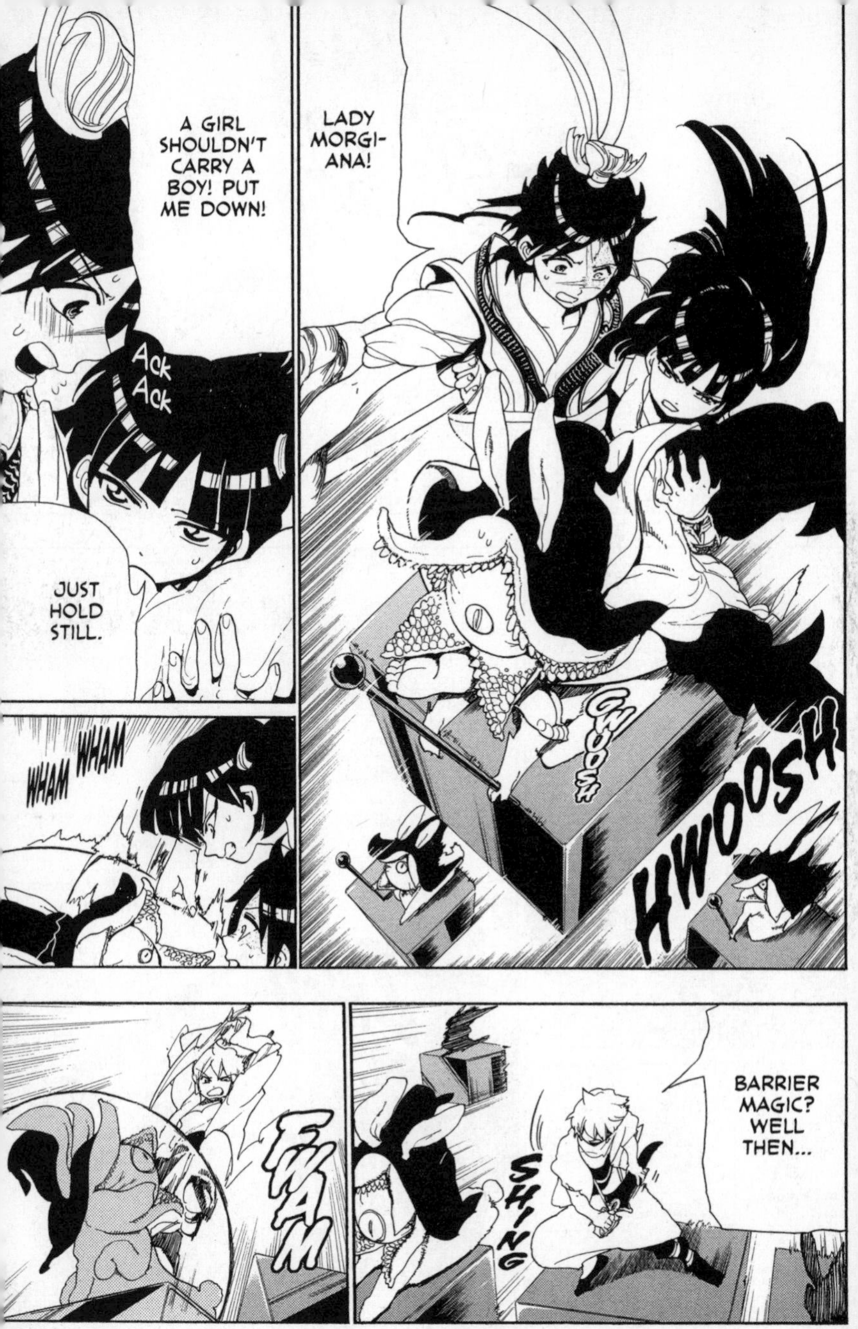
LADY MORGIANA!
GWOOSH
HWOOSH
A GIRL SHOULDN'T CARRY A BOY! PUT ME DOWN!
Ack Ack
JUST HOLD STILL.
WHAM WHAM
BARRIER MAGIC? WELL THEN...
SHING
FWAM

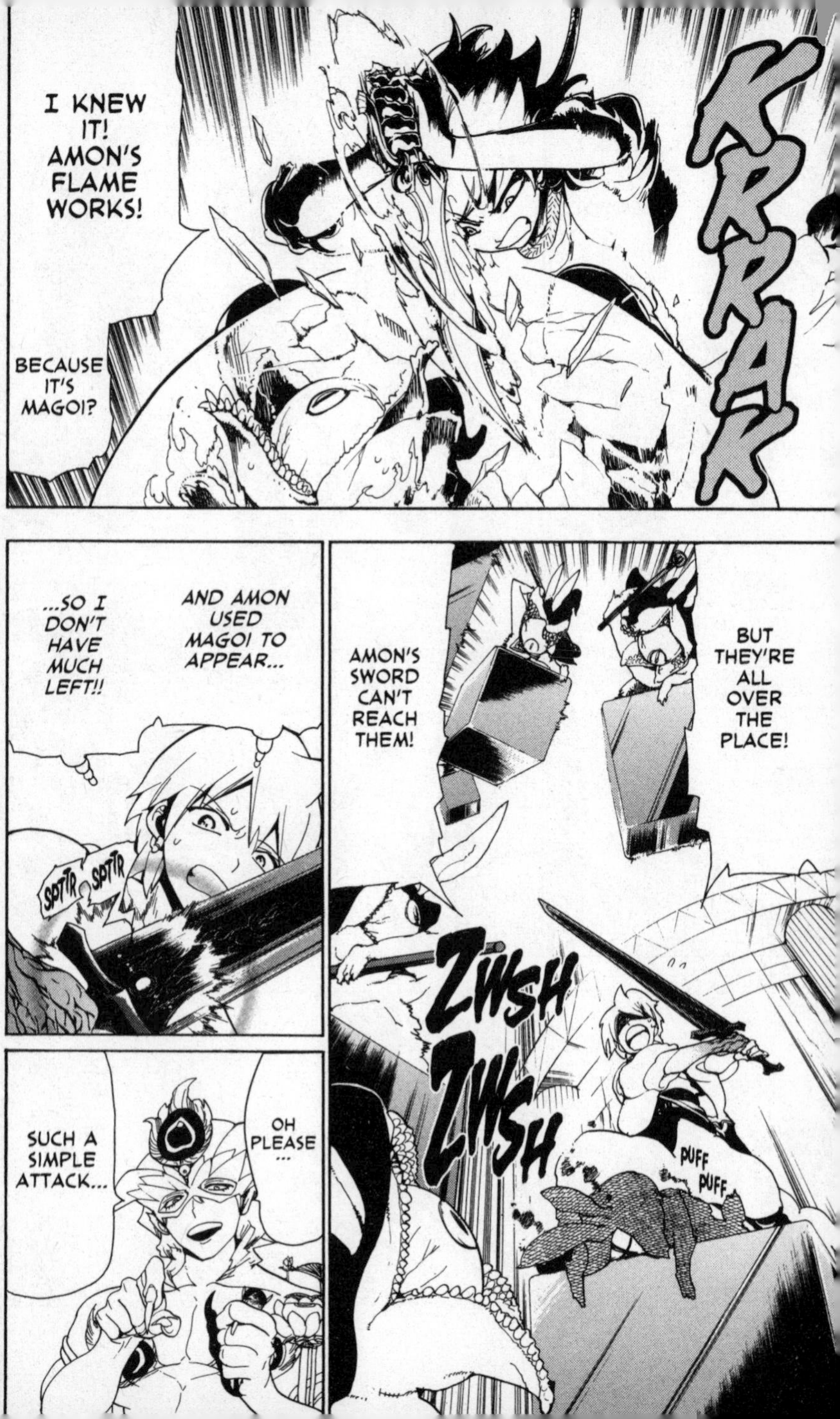
KRAK
I KNEW IT! AMON'S FLAME WORKS!
BECAUSE IT'S MAGOI?
BUT THEY'RE ALL OVER THE PLACE!
AMON'S SWORD CAN'T REACH THEM!
ZWSH ZWSH
PUFF PUFF
AND AMON USED MAGOI TO APPEAR...
...SO I DON'T HAVE MUCH LEFT!!
SPTTR SPTTR
OH PLEASE ...
SUCH A SIMPLE ATTACK...

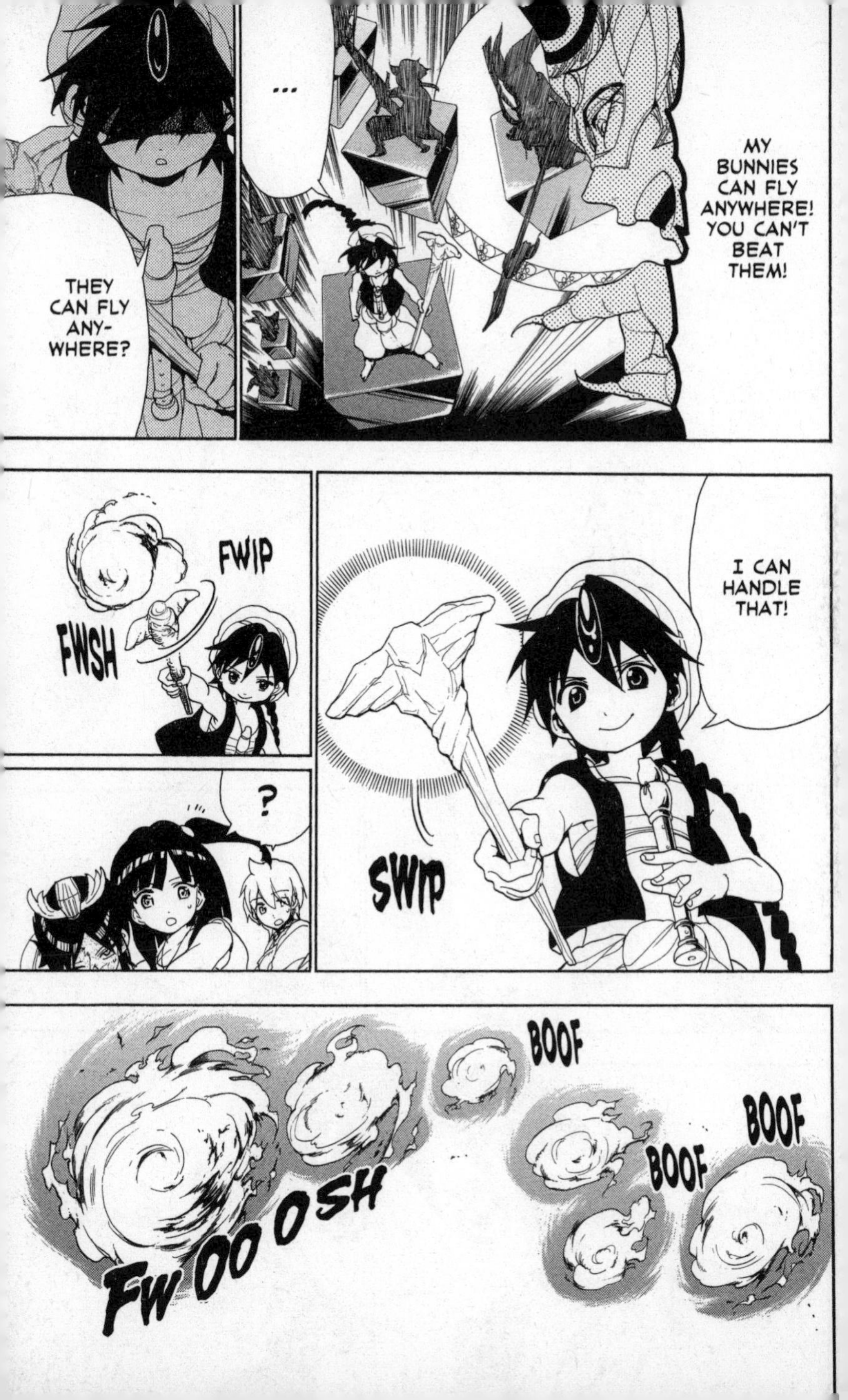
MY BUNNIES CAN FLY ANYWHERE! YOU CAN'T BEAT THEM!
...
THEY CAN FLY ANY-WHERE?
I CAN HANDLE THAT!
SWIP
FWIP
FWSH
?
BOOF
BOOF
BOOF
FWOOOSH

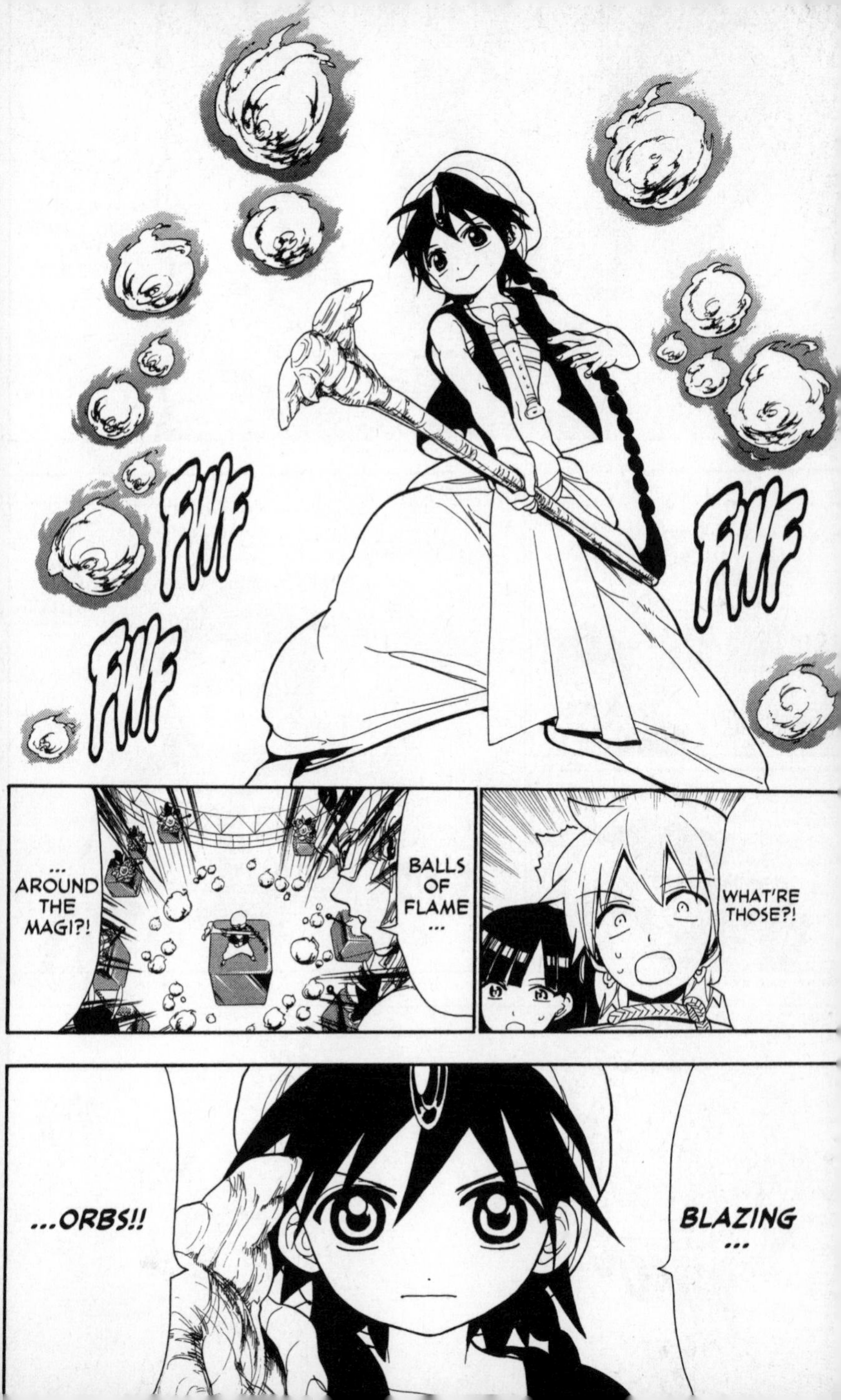
FWF
FWF
FWF
WHAT'RE THOSE?!
BALLS OF FLAME ...
... AROUND THE MAGI?!
BLAZING ...
...ORBS!!

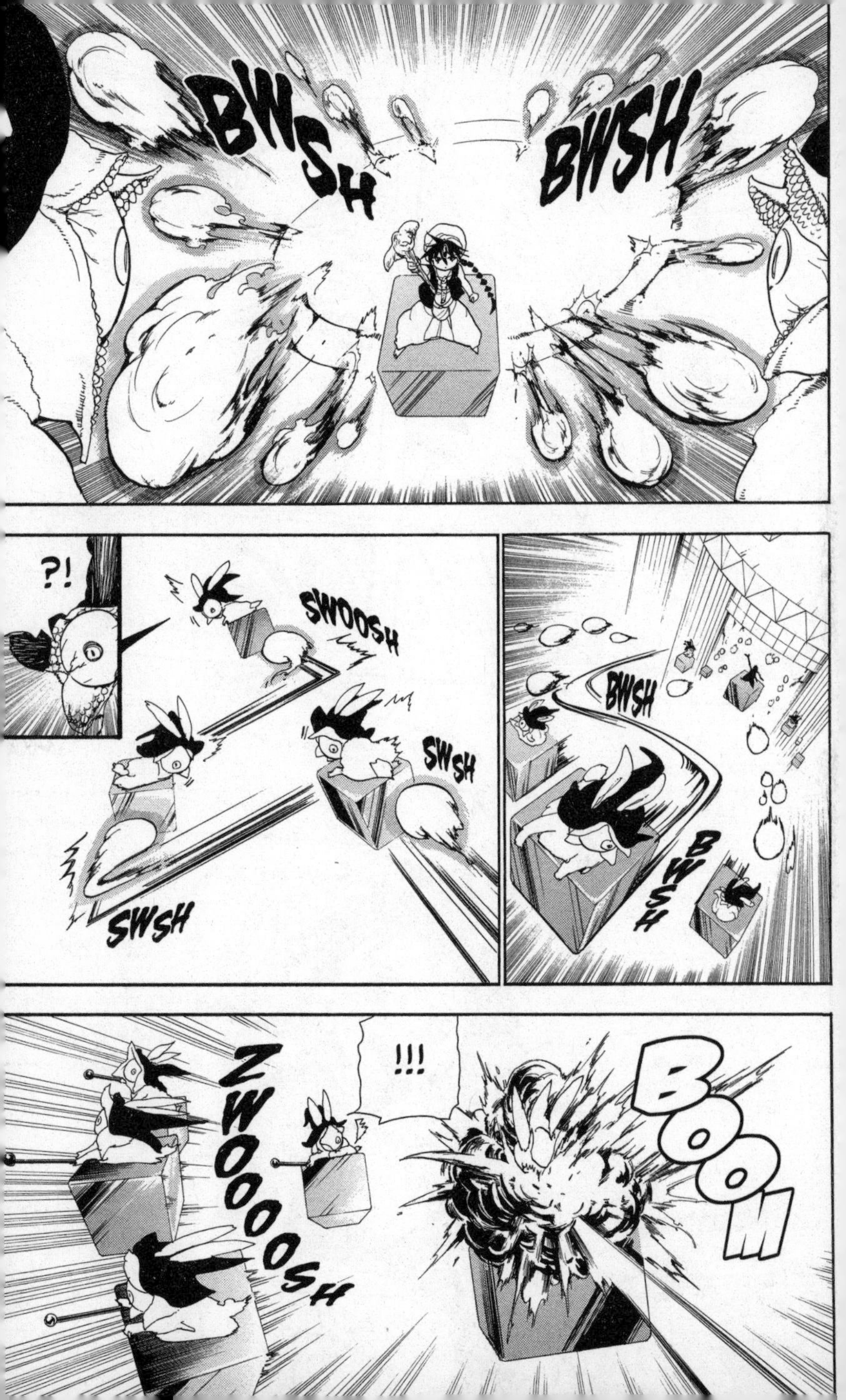
BWSH
BWSH
BWSH
BWSH
?!
SWOOSH
SWSH
SWSH
BOOM
!!!
ZWOOOOOSH

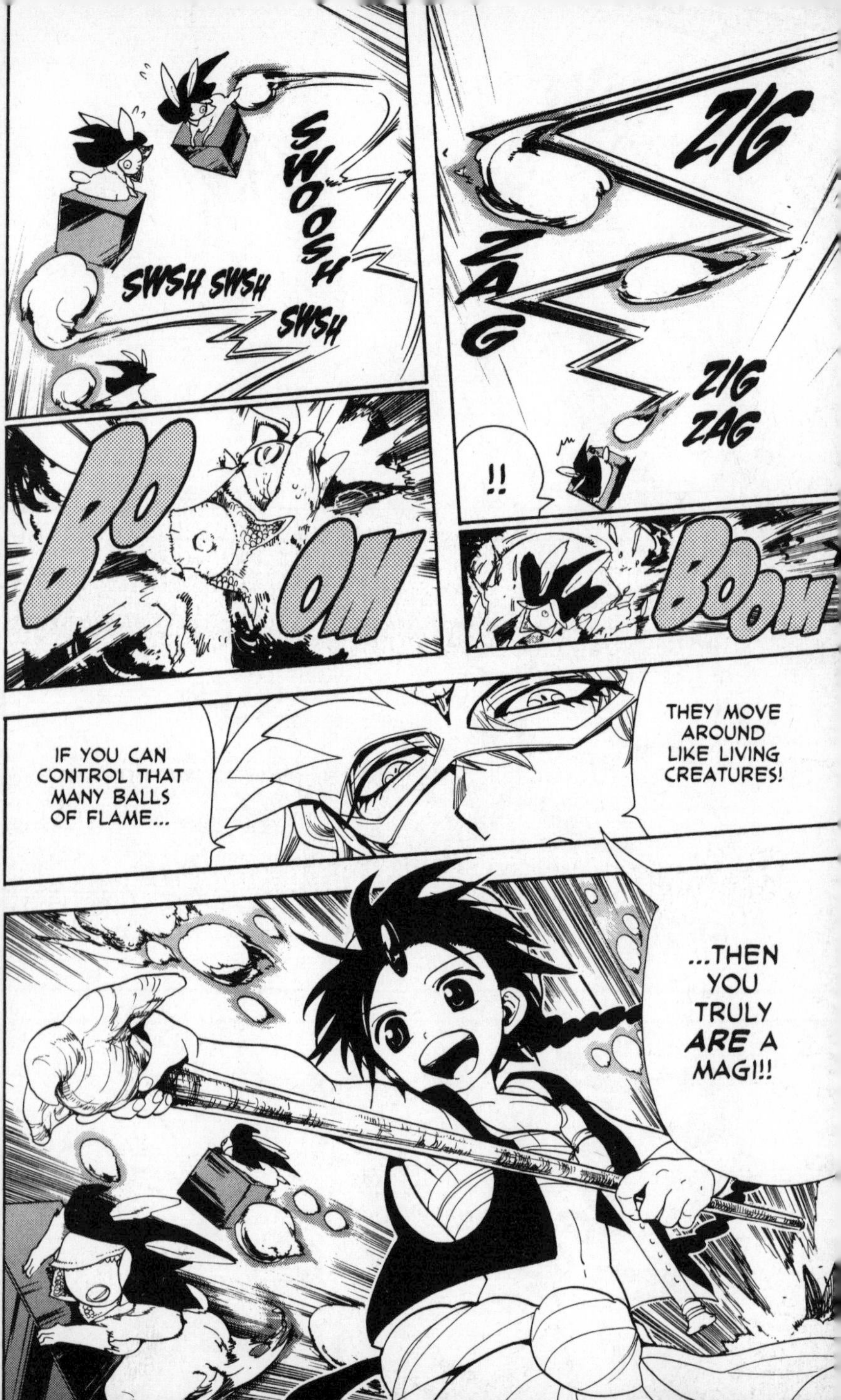
ZIG
ZAG
ZIG ZAG
!!
SWOOOSH
SWSH SWSH
SWSH
BOOM
BOOM
THEY MOVE AROUND LIKE LIVING CREATURES!
IF YOU CAN CONTROL THAT MANY BALLS OF FLAME...
...THEN YOU TRULY *ARE* A MAGI!!

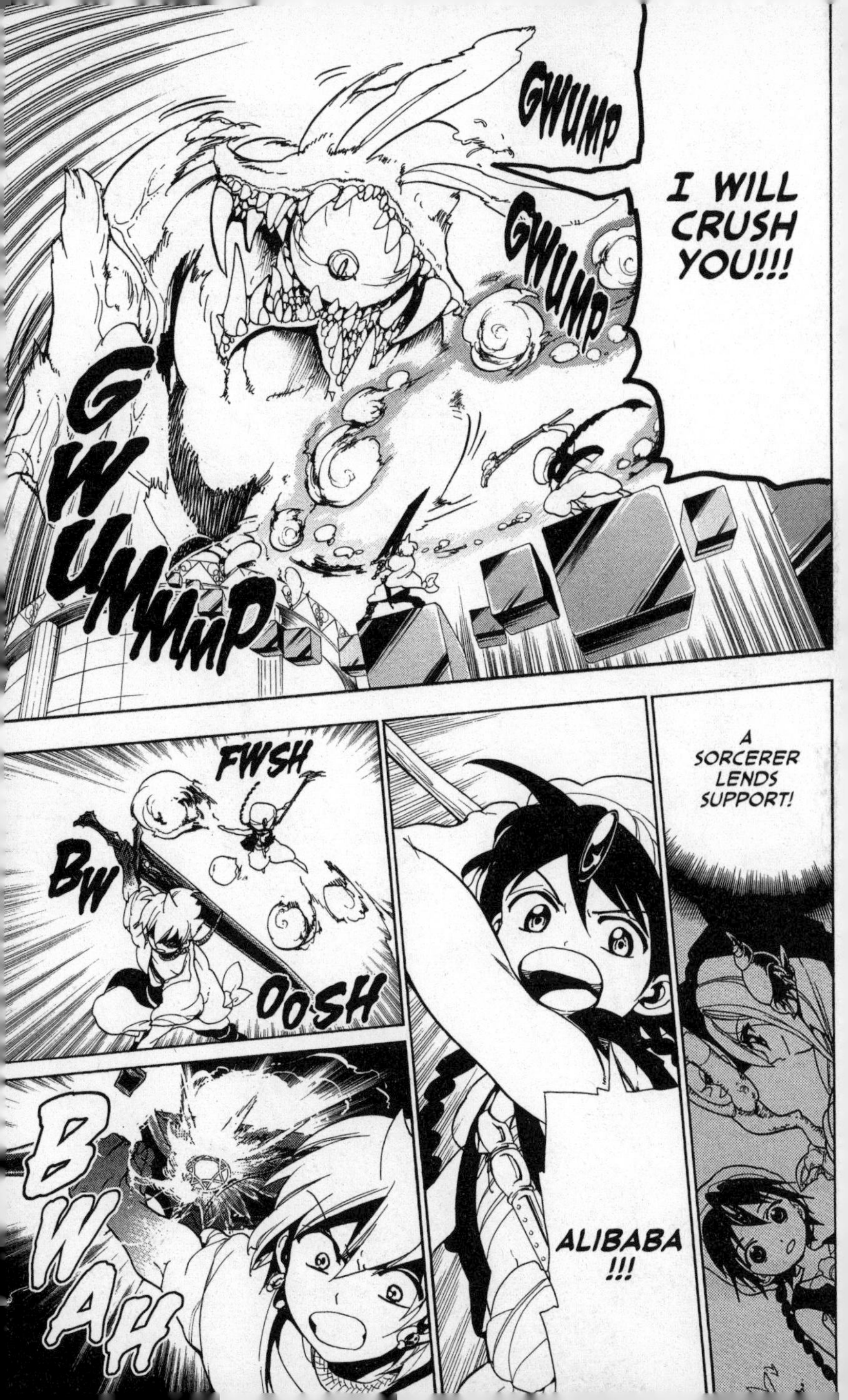

GWUMP
I WILL CRUSH YOU!!!
GWUMP
GWUMMMP
A SORCERER LENDS SUPPORT!
ALIBABA !!!
FWSH
BW
OOSH
BWAH

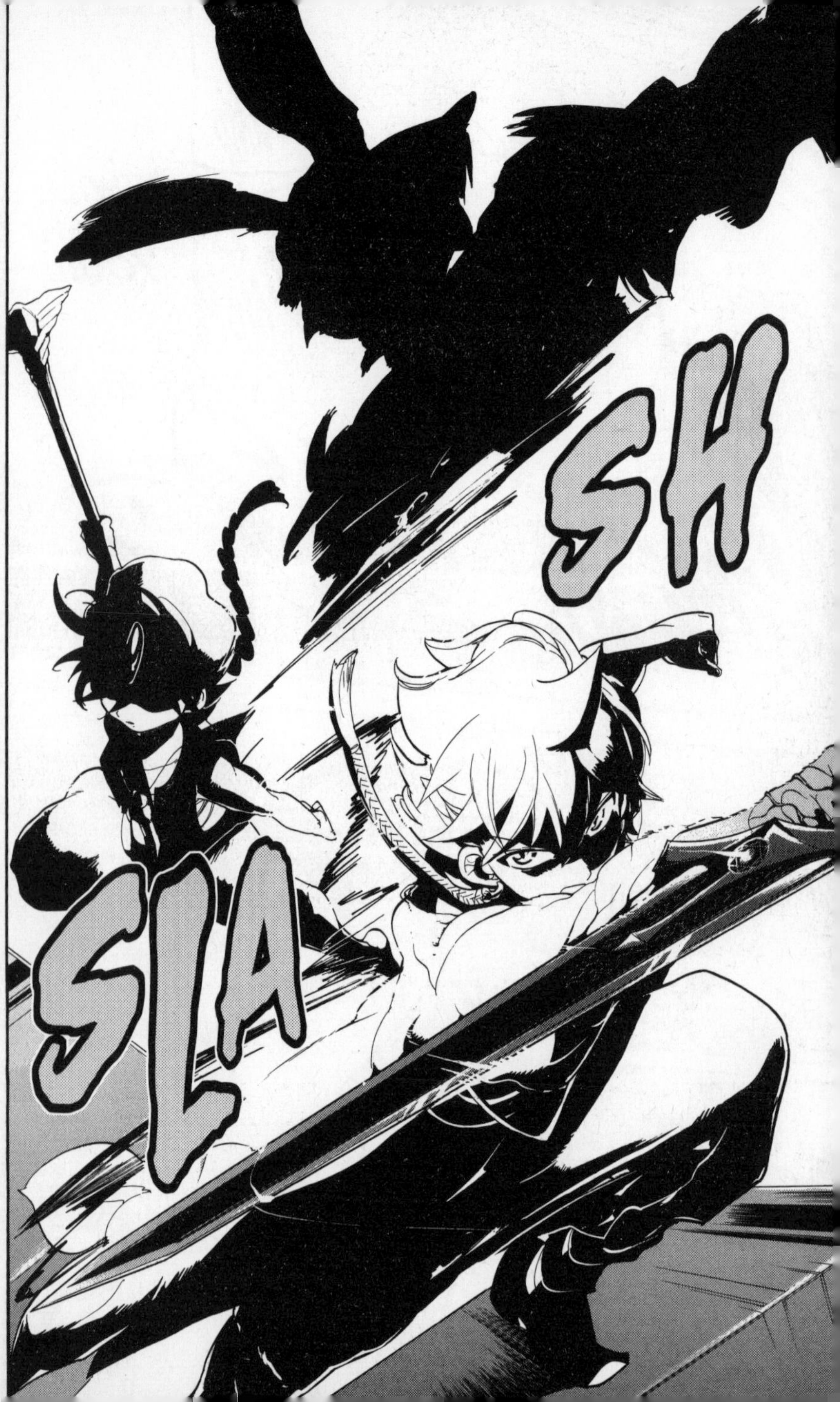
SLA
SH

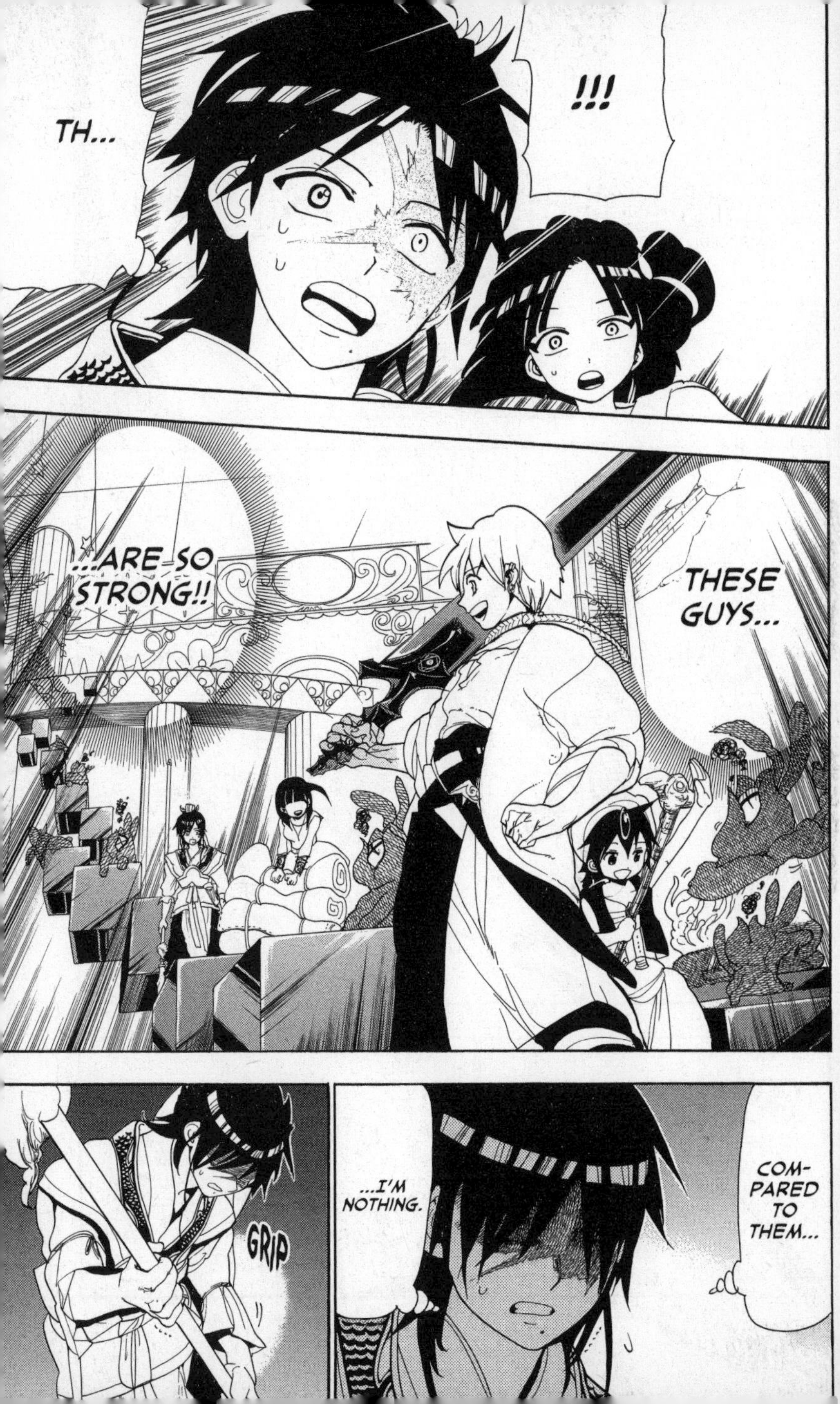
!!!
TH...
THESE GUYS...
...ARE SO STRONG!!
COM-PARED TO THEM...
...I'M NOTHING.
GRIP

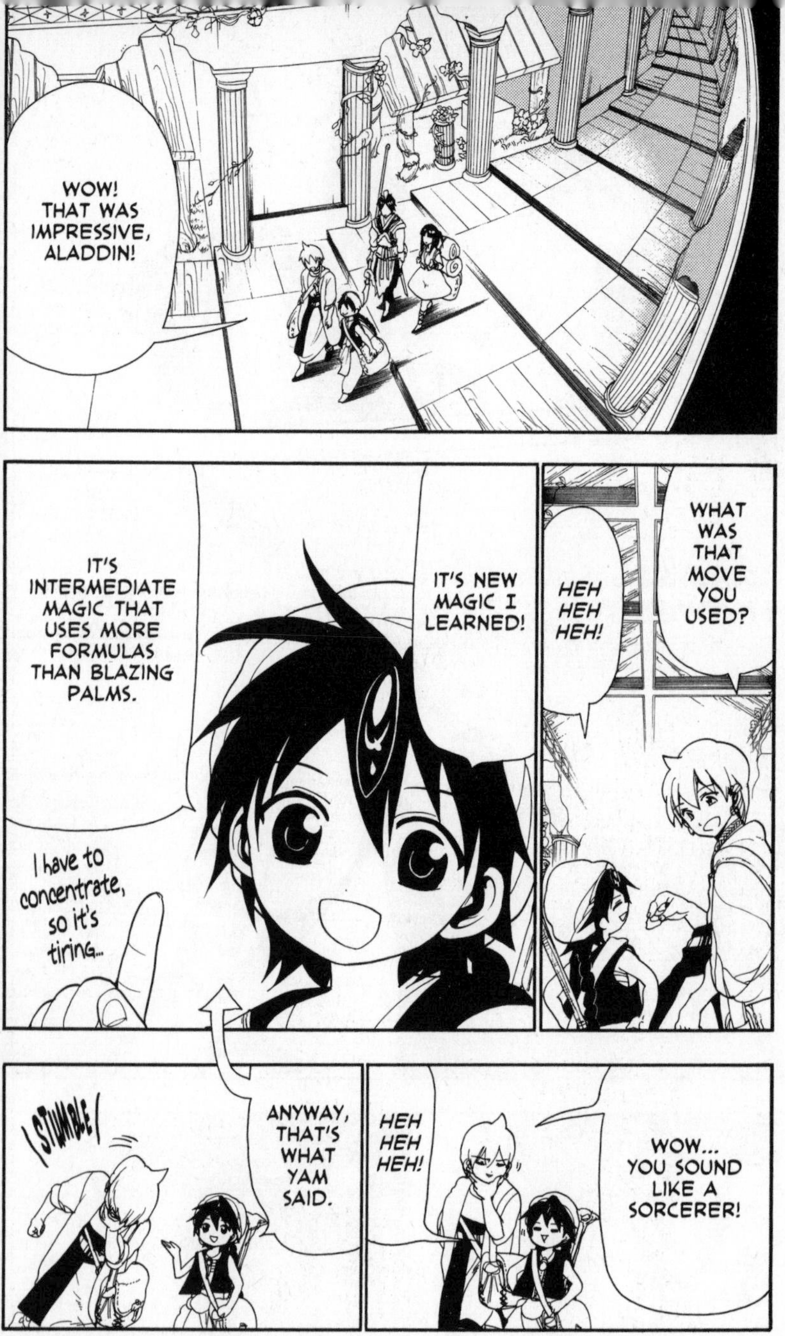
WOW! THAT WAS IMPRESSIVE, ALADDIN!
WHAT WAS THAT MOVE YOU USED?
HEH HEH HEH!
IT'S NEW MAGIC I LEARNED!
IT'S INTERMEDIATE MAGIC THAT USES MORE FORMULAS THAN BLAZING PALMS.
I have to concentrate, so it's tiring...
WOW... YOU SOUND LIKE A SORCERER!
HEH HEH HEH!
ANYWAY, THAT'S WHAT YAM SAID.
STUMBLE

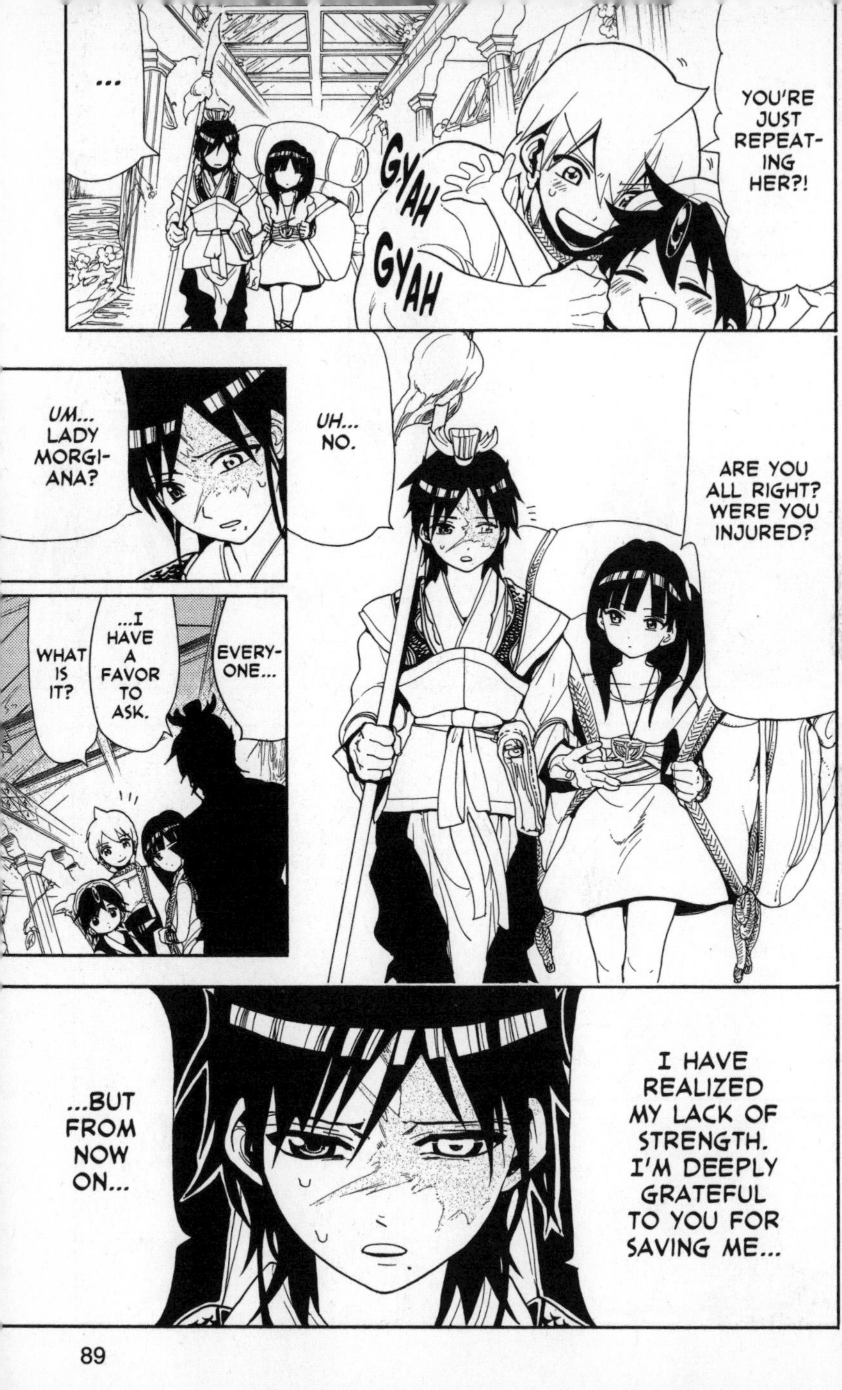
YOU'RE JUST REPEAT-ING HER?!
GYAH GYAH
...
ARE YOU ALL RIGHT? WERE YOU INJURED?
UH... NO.
UM... LADY MORGI-ANA?
EVERY-ONE...
...I HAVE A FAVOR TO ASK.
WHAT IS IT?
I HAVE REALIZED MY LACK OF STRENGTH. I'M DEEPLY GRATEFUL TO YOU FOR SAVING ME...
...BUT FROM NOW ON...

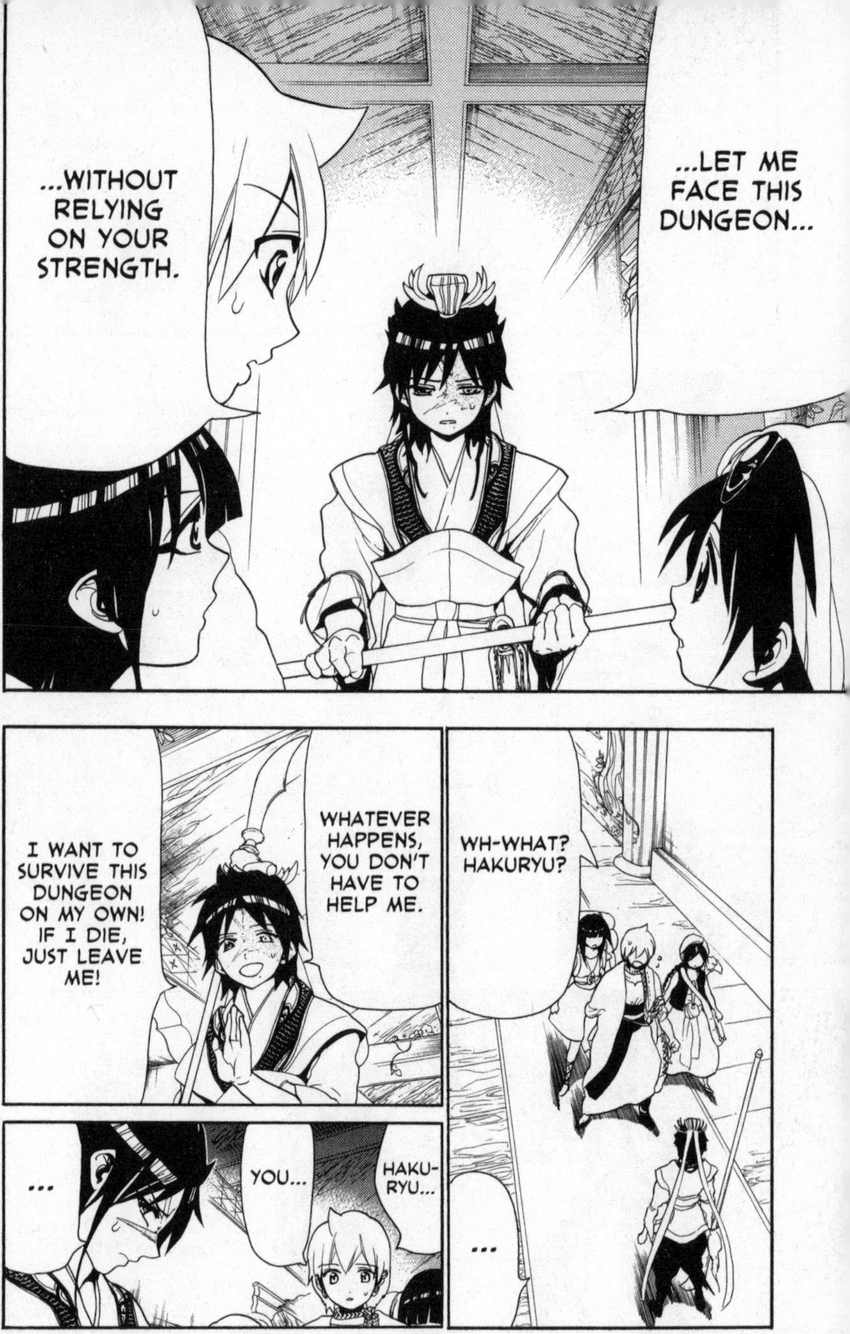
...LET ME FACE THIS DUNGEON...
...WITHOUT RELYING ON YOUR STRENGTH.
WH-WHAT? HAKURYU?
...
WHATEVER HAPPENS, YOU DON'T HAVE TO HELP ME.
I WANT TO SURVIVE THIS DUNGEON ON MY OWN! IF I DIE, JUST LEAVE ME!
HAKU-RYU...
YOU...
...

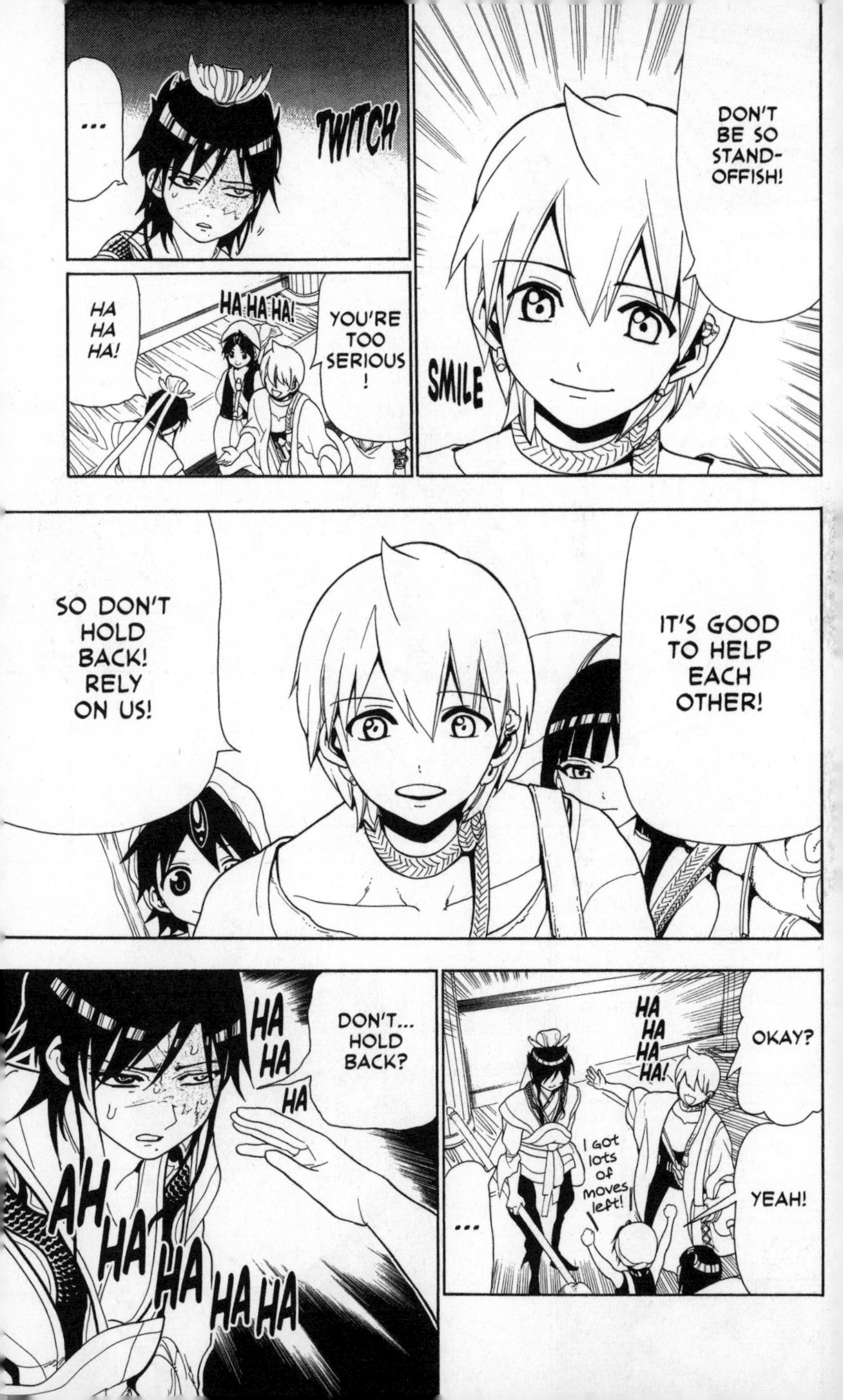
DON'T BE SO STAND-OFFISH!
SMILE
...
TWITCH
YOU'RE TOO SERIOUS!
HA HA HA!
HA HA HA!
IT'S GOOD TO HELP EACH OTHER!
SO DON'T HOLD BACK! RELY ON US!
OKAY?
HA HA HA HA!
YEAH!
I got lots of moves left!
...
DON'T... HOLD BACK?
HA HA HA
AH HA HA HA HA HA

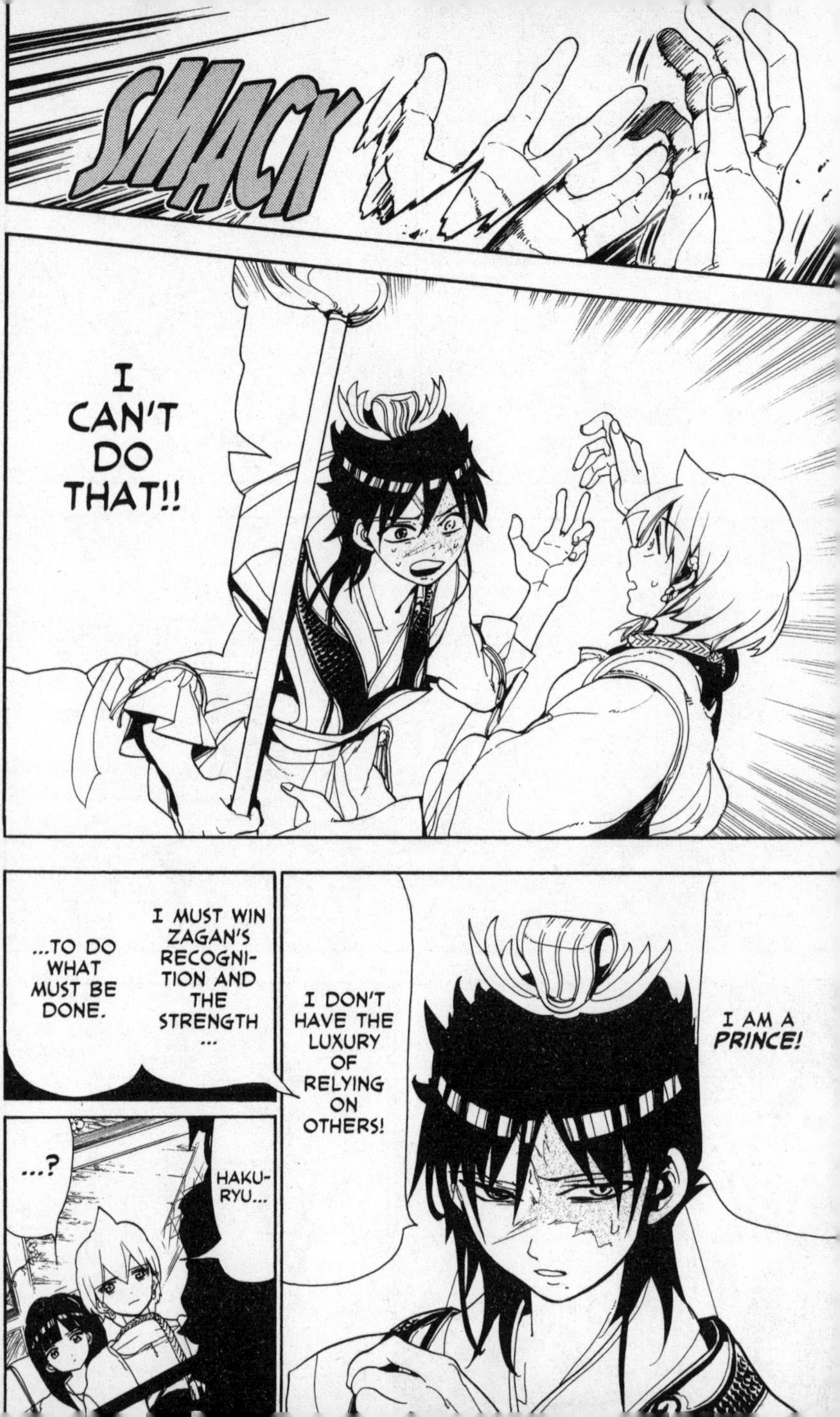
SMACK
I CAN'T DO THAT!!
I AM A PRINCE!
I DON'T HAVE THE LUXURY OF RELYING ON OTHERS!
I MUST WIN ZAGAN'S RECOGNITION AND THE STRENGTH ...
...TO DO WHAT MUST BE DONE.
HAKU-RYU...
...?

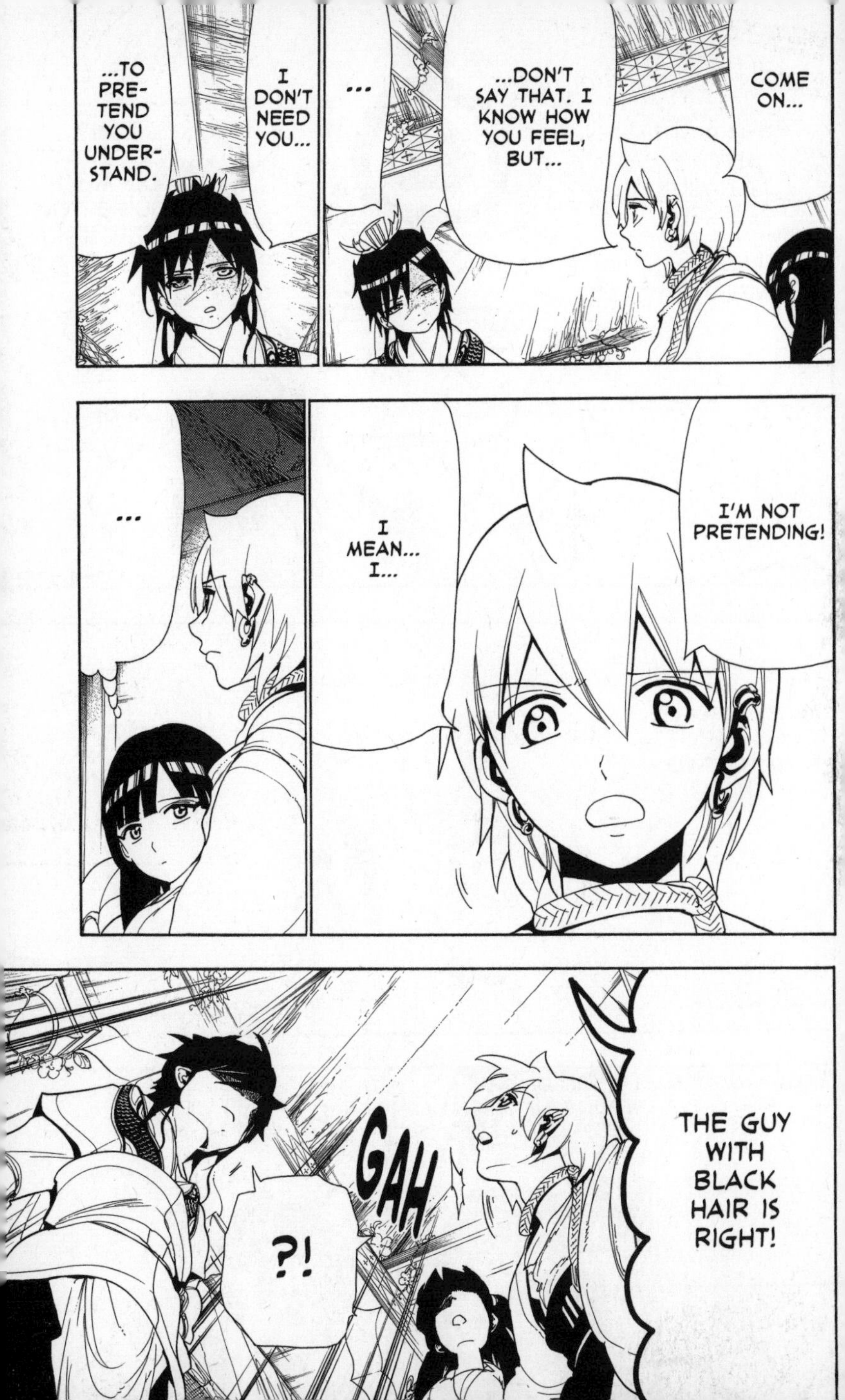
COME ON...
...DON'T SAY THAT. I KNOW HOW YOU FEEL, BUT...
...
I DON'T NEED YOU...
...TO PRETEND YOU UNDERSTAND.
I'M NOT PRETENDING!
I MEAN... I...
...
THE GUY WITH BLACK HAIR IS RIGHT!
GAH
?!

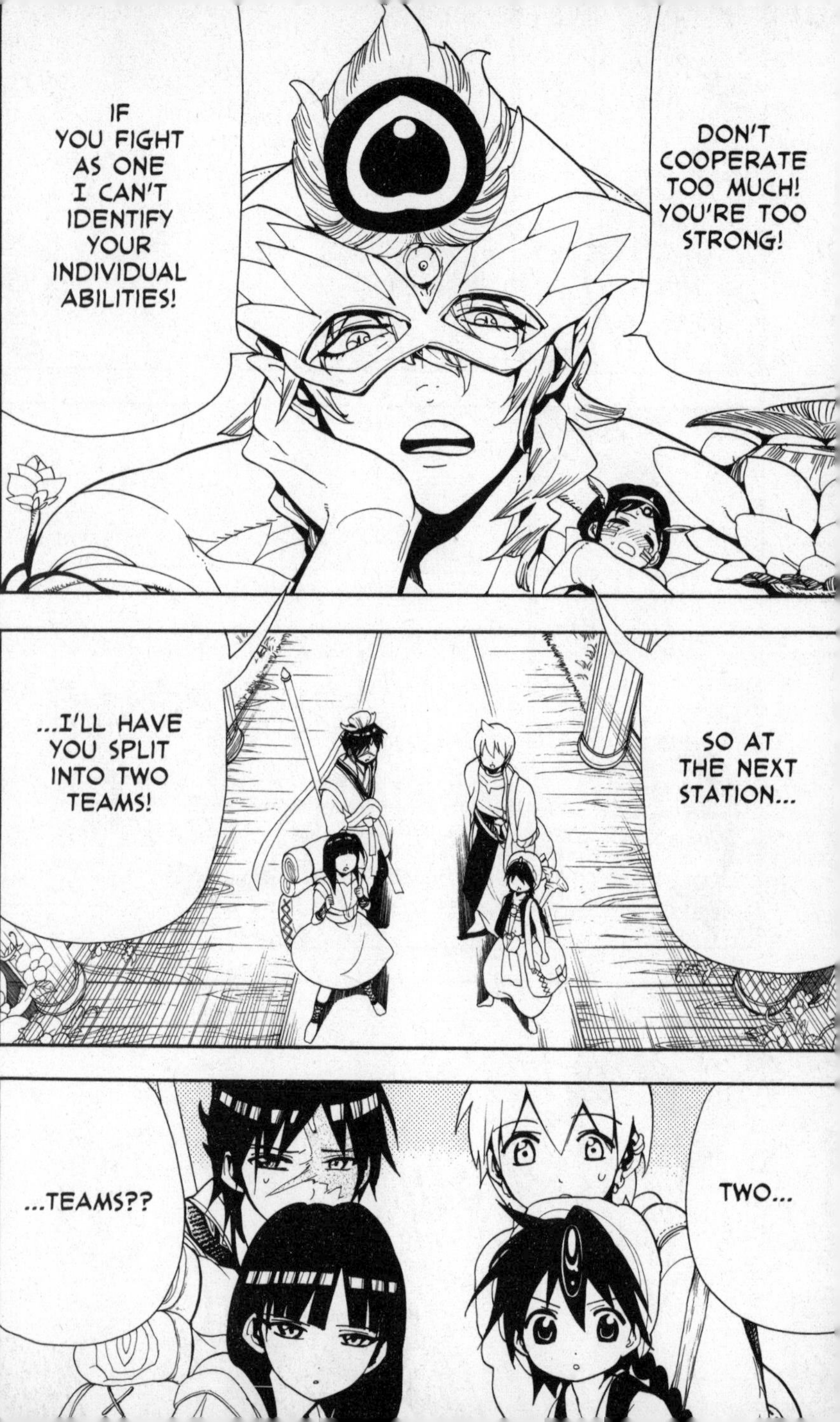
DON'T COOPERATE TOO MUCH! YOU'RE TOO STRONG!
IF YOU FIGHT AS ONE I CAN'T IDENTIFY YOUR INDIVIDUAL ABILITIES!
SO AT THE NEXT STATION...
...I'LL HAVE YOU SPLIT INTO TWO TEAMS!
TWO...
...TEAMS??

# Night 94: Your Strength

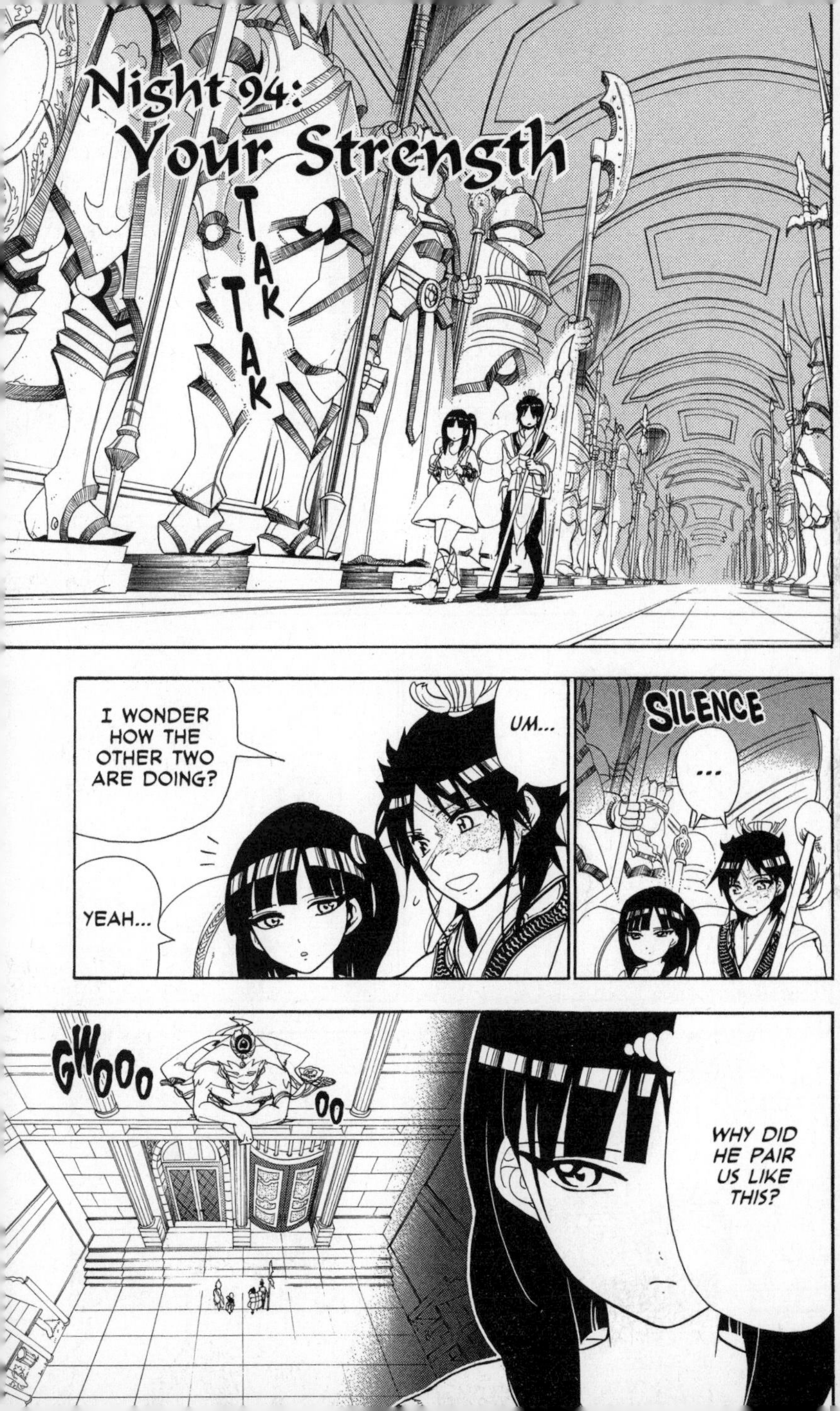
TAK TAK
SILENCE
...
UM...
I WONDER HOW THE OTHER TWO ARE DOING?
YEAH...
WHY DID HE PAIR US LIKE THIS?
GWOOOOO

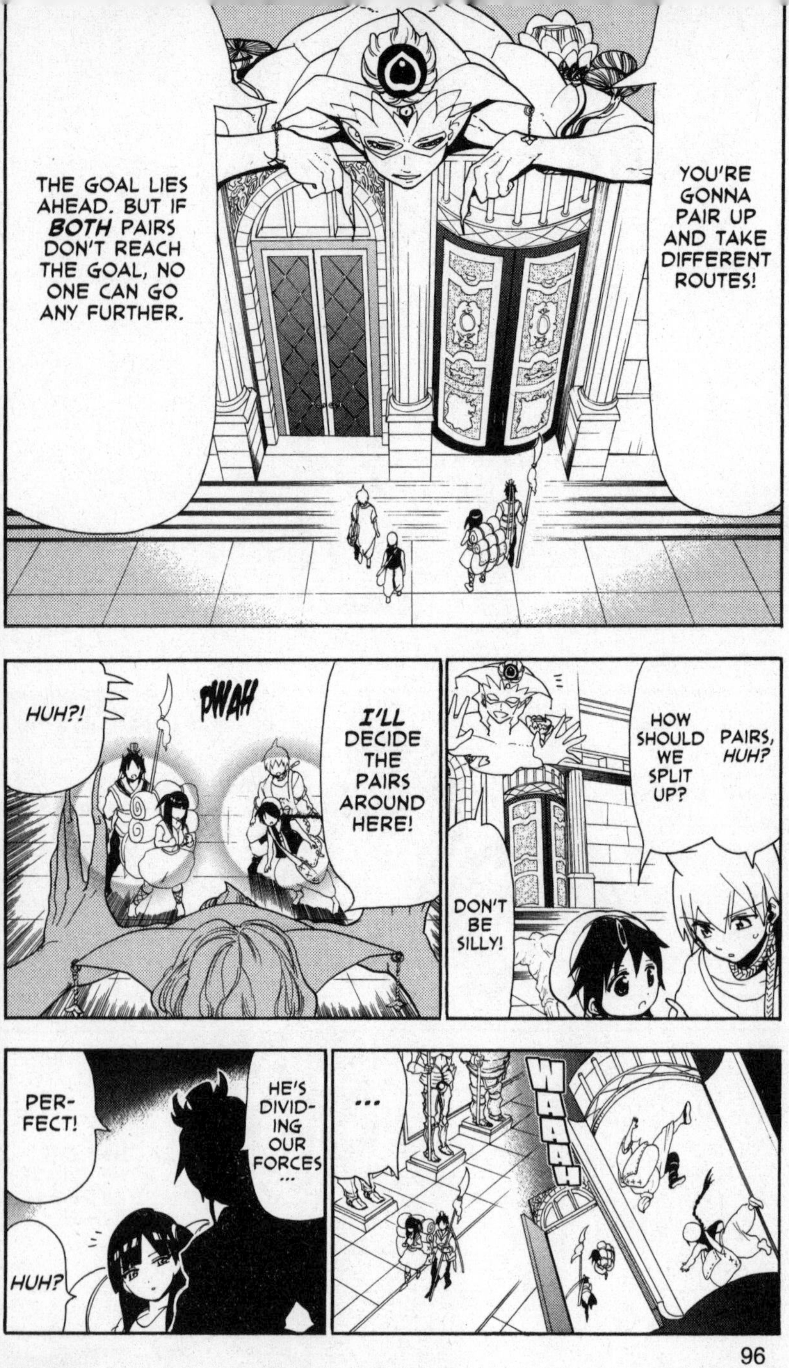
YOU'RE GONNA PAIR UP AND TAKE DIFFERENT ROUTES!
THE GOAL LIES AHEAD. BUT IF *BOTH* PAIRS DON'T REACH THE GOAL, NO ONE CAN GO ANY FURTHER.
PAIRS, *HUH?*
HOW SHOULD WE SPLIT UP?
DON'T BE SILLY!
*I'LL* DECIDE THE PAIRS AROUND HERE!
PWAH
*HUH?!*
WAAAH
...
HE'S DIVID-ING OUR FORCES ...
PER-FECT!
*HUH?*

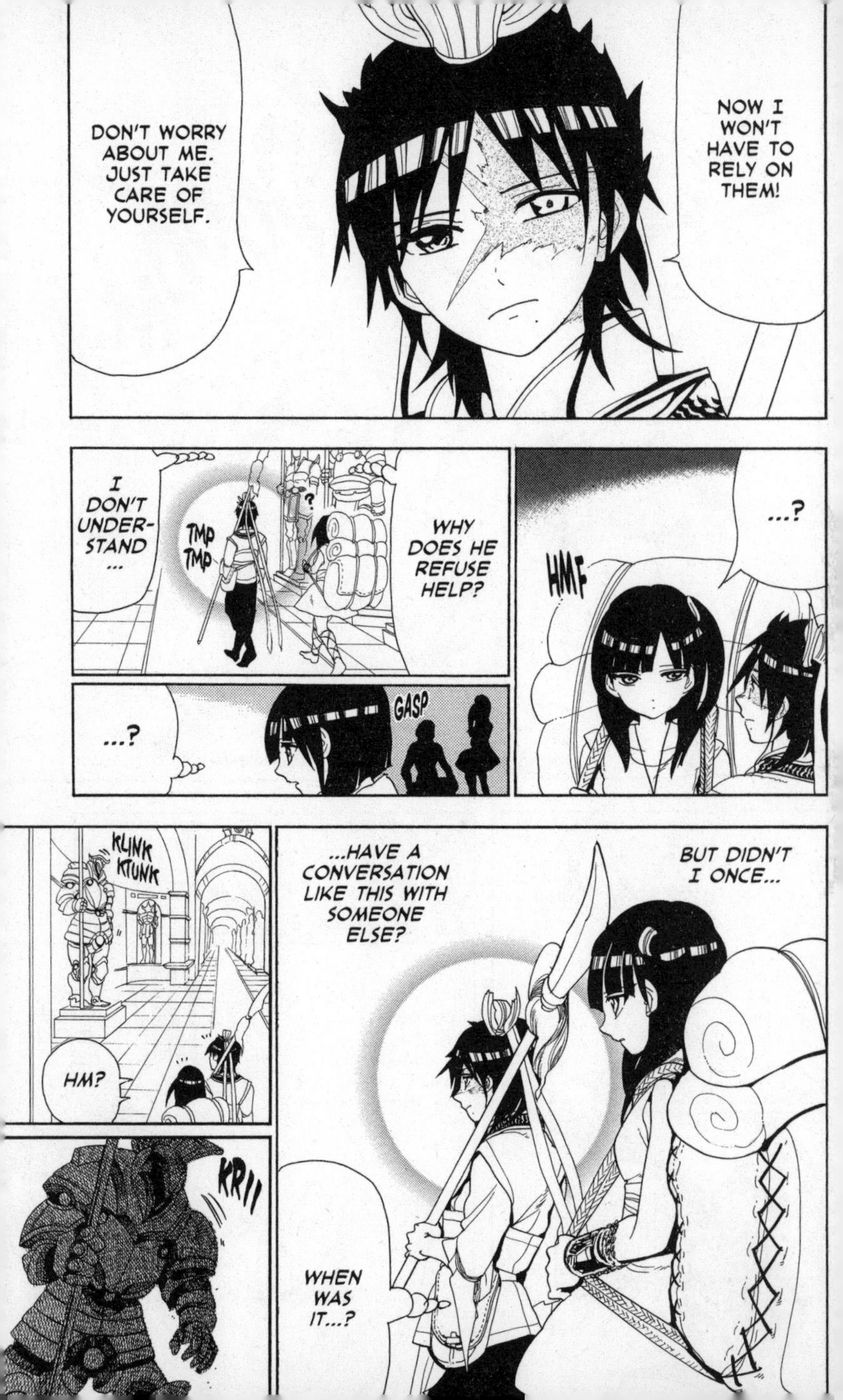
NOW I WON'T HAVE TO RELY ON THEM!
DON'T WORRY ABOUT ME. JUST TAKE CARE OF YOURSELF.
...?
HMF
WHY DOES HE REFUSE HELP?
?
TMP TMP
I DON'T UNDER-STAND ...
GASP
...?
BUT DIDN'T I ONCE...
...HAVE A CONVERSATION LIKE THIS WITH SOMEONE ELSE?
WHEN WAS IT...?
KLINK KLUNK
HM?
KRII

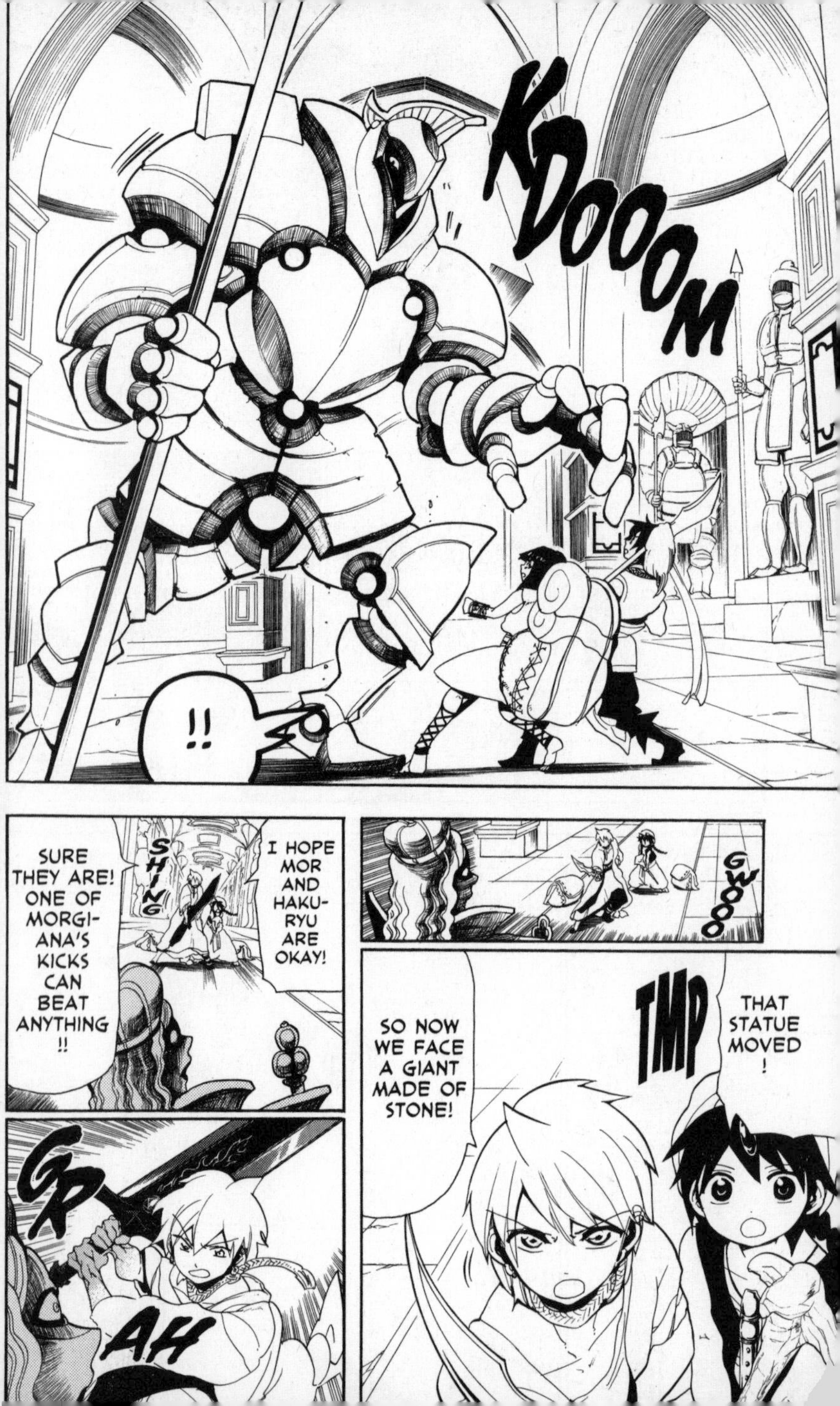
KDOOOM
!!
GWOOOO
SHING
I HOPE MOR AND HAKURYU ARE OKAY!
SURE THEY ARE! ONE OF MORGIANA'S KICKS CAN BEAT ANYTHING!!
TMP
THAT STATUE MOVED!
SO NOW WE FACE A GIANT MADE OF STONE!
GR
AH

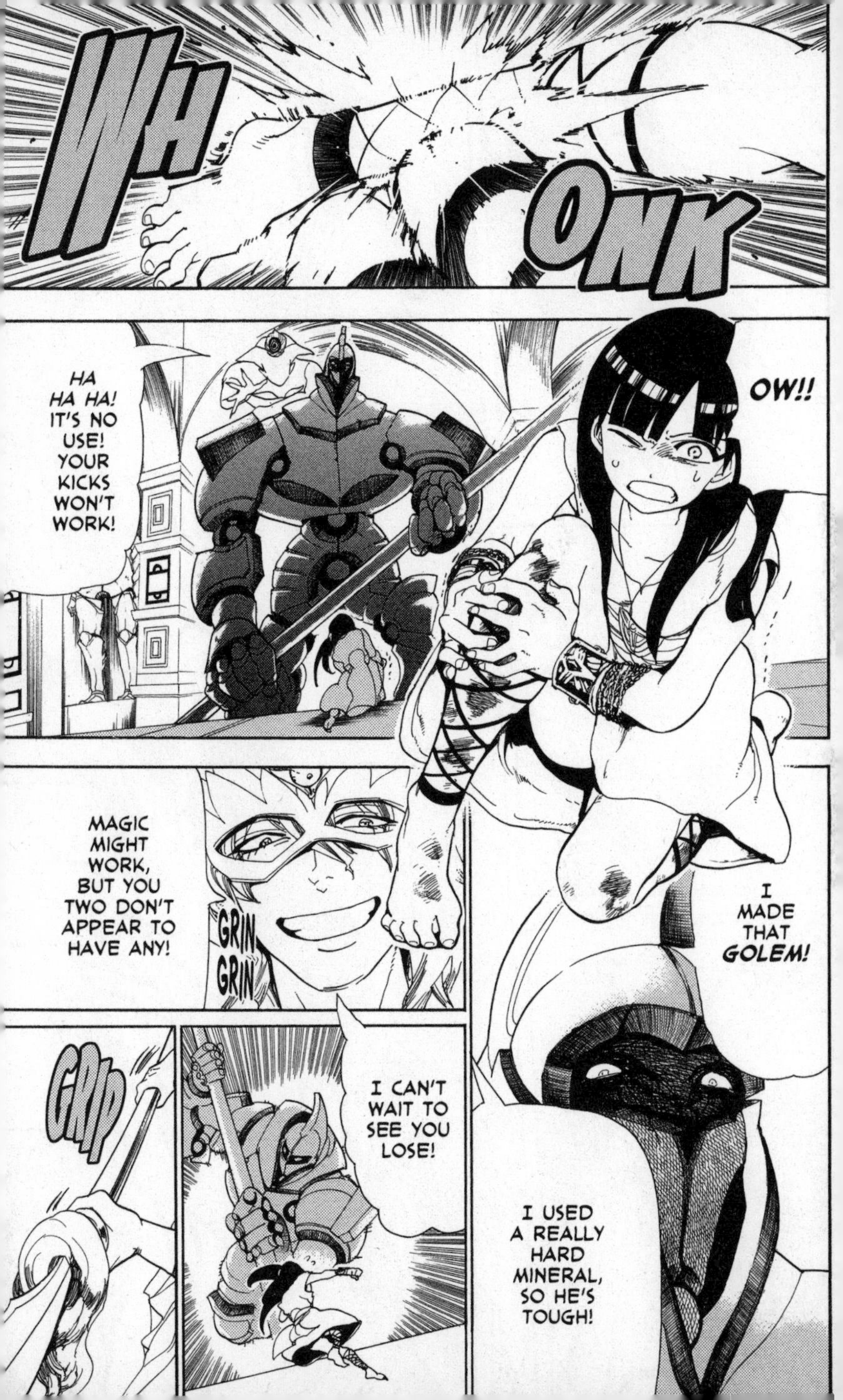
WHA
ONK
OW!!
HA HA HA! IT'S NO USE! YOUR KICKS WON'T WORK!
I MADE THAT GOLEM!
I USED A REALLY HARD MINERAL, SO HE'S TOUGH!
MAGIC MIGHT WORK, BUT YOU TWO DON'T APPEAR TO HAVE ANY!
GRIN GRIN
I CAN'T WAIT TO SEE YOU LOSE!
GRIP

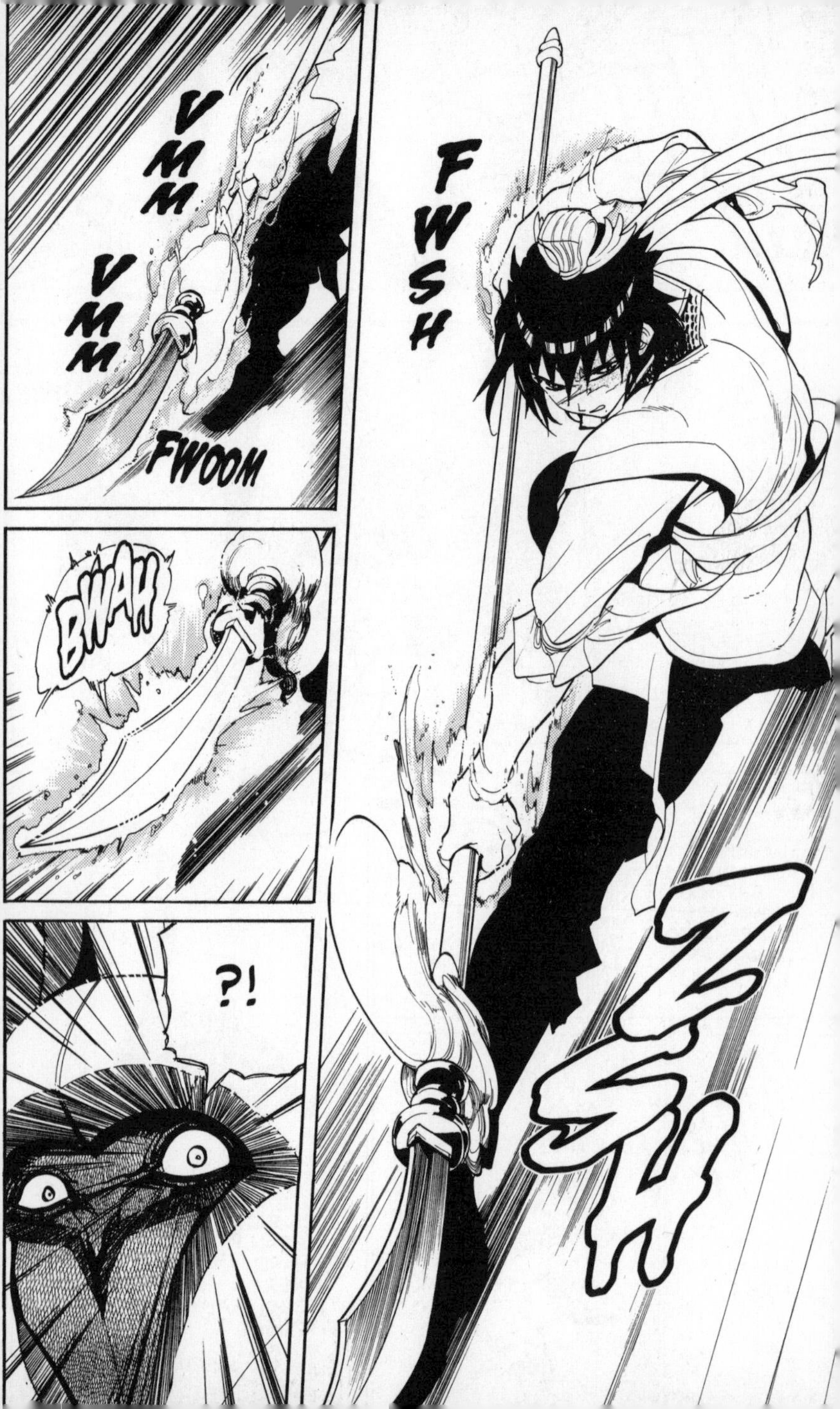
FWSH
ZSH
VMM
VMM
FWOOM
BWAH
?!

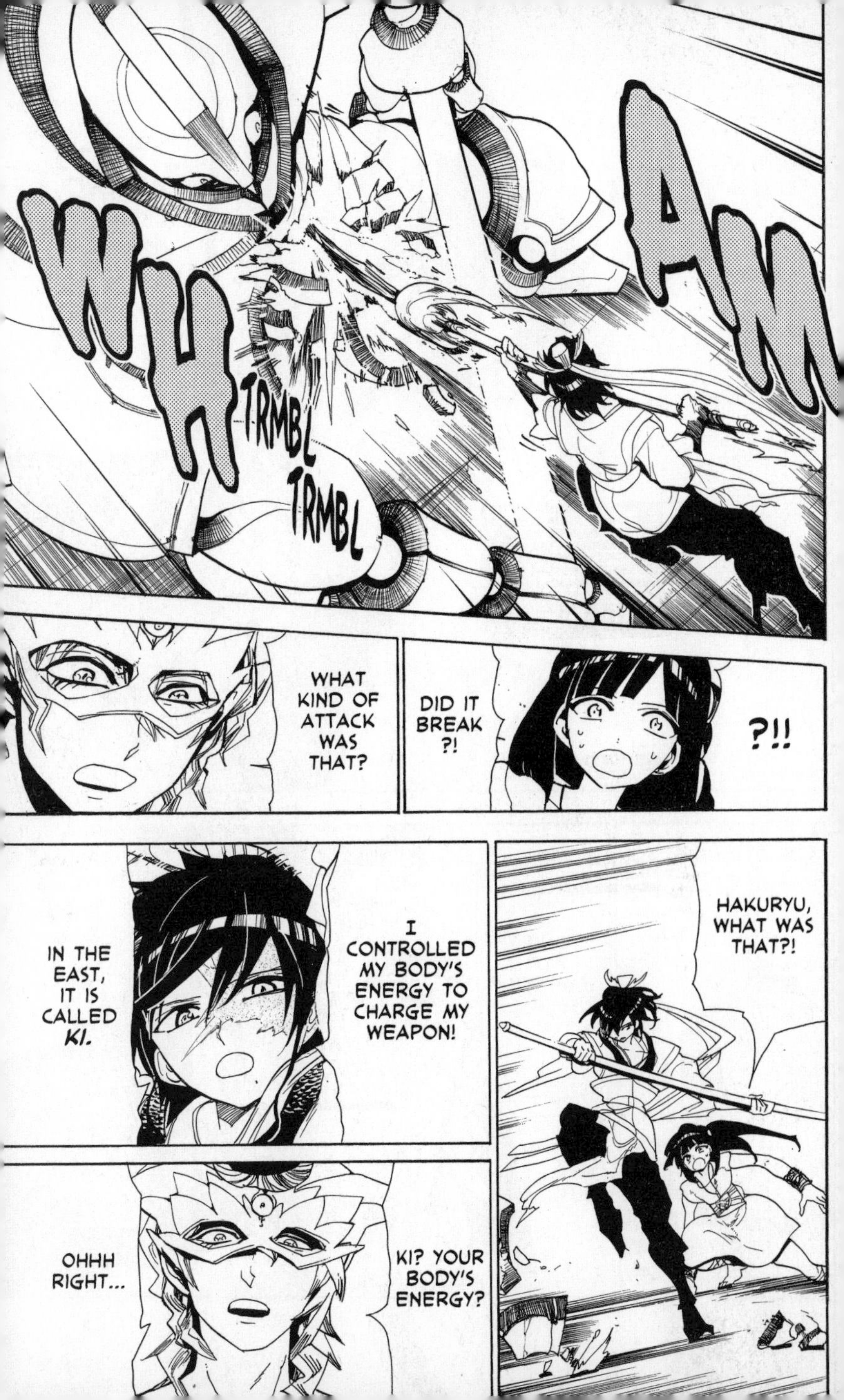
WHAM
TRMBL
TRMBL
?!!
DID IT BREAK ?!
WHAT KIND OF ATTACK WAS THAT?
HAKURYU, WHAT WAS THAT?!
I CONTROLLED MY BODY'S ENERGY TO CHARGE MY WEAPON!
IN THE EAST, IT IS CALLED *KI*.
KI? YOUR BODY'S ENERGY?
OHHH RIGHT...

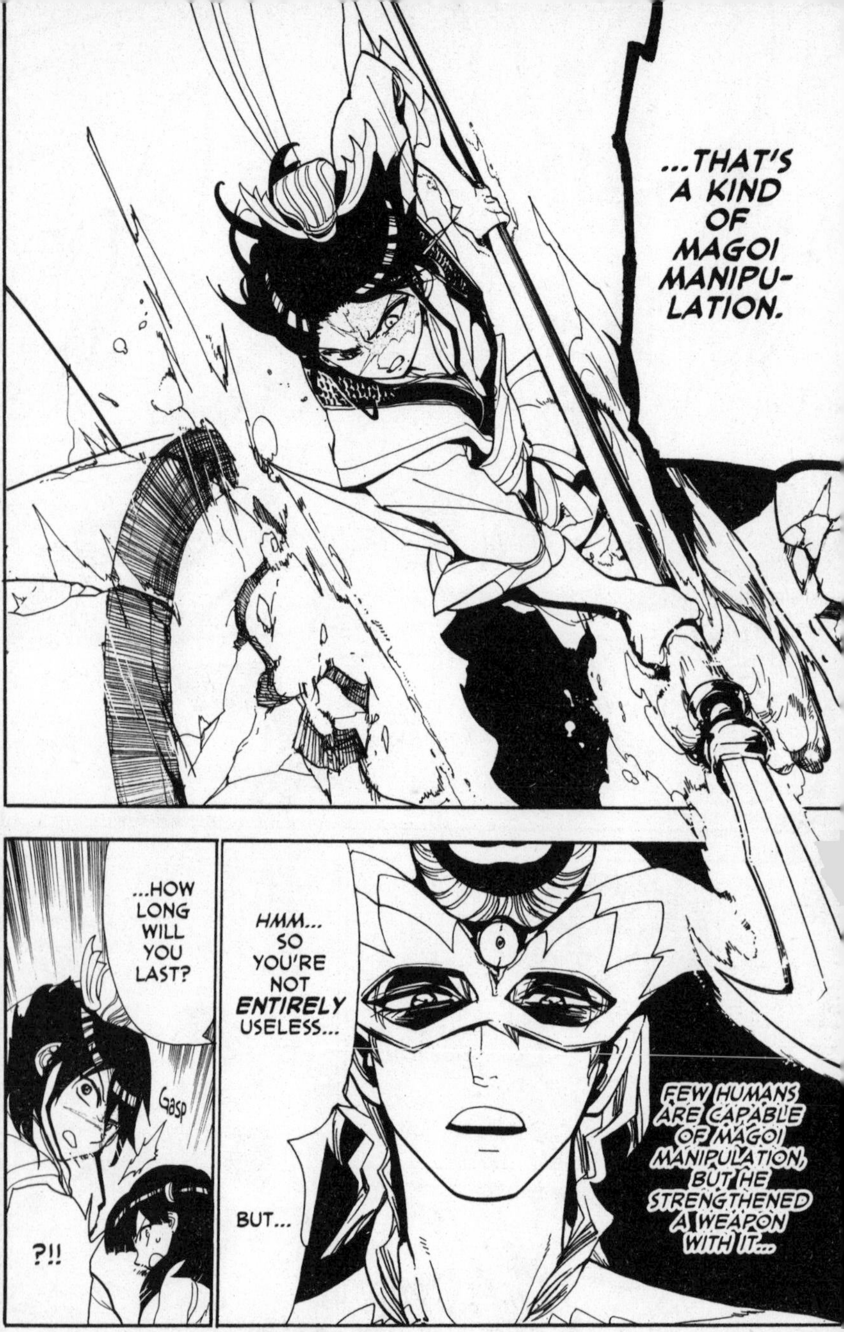
...THAT'S A KIND OF MAGOI MANIPULATION.
FEW HUMANS ARE CAPABLE OF MAGOI MANIPULATION, BUT HE STRENGTHENED A WEAPON WITH IT...
HMM... SO YOU'RE NOT ENTIRELY USELESS...
BUT...
...HOW LONG WILL YOU LAST?
Gasp
?!!

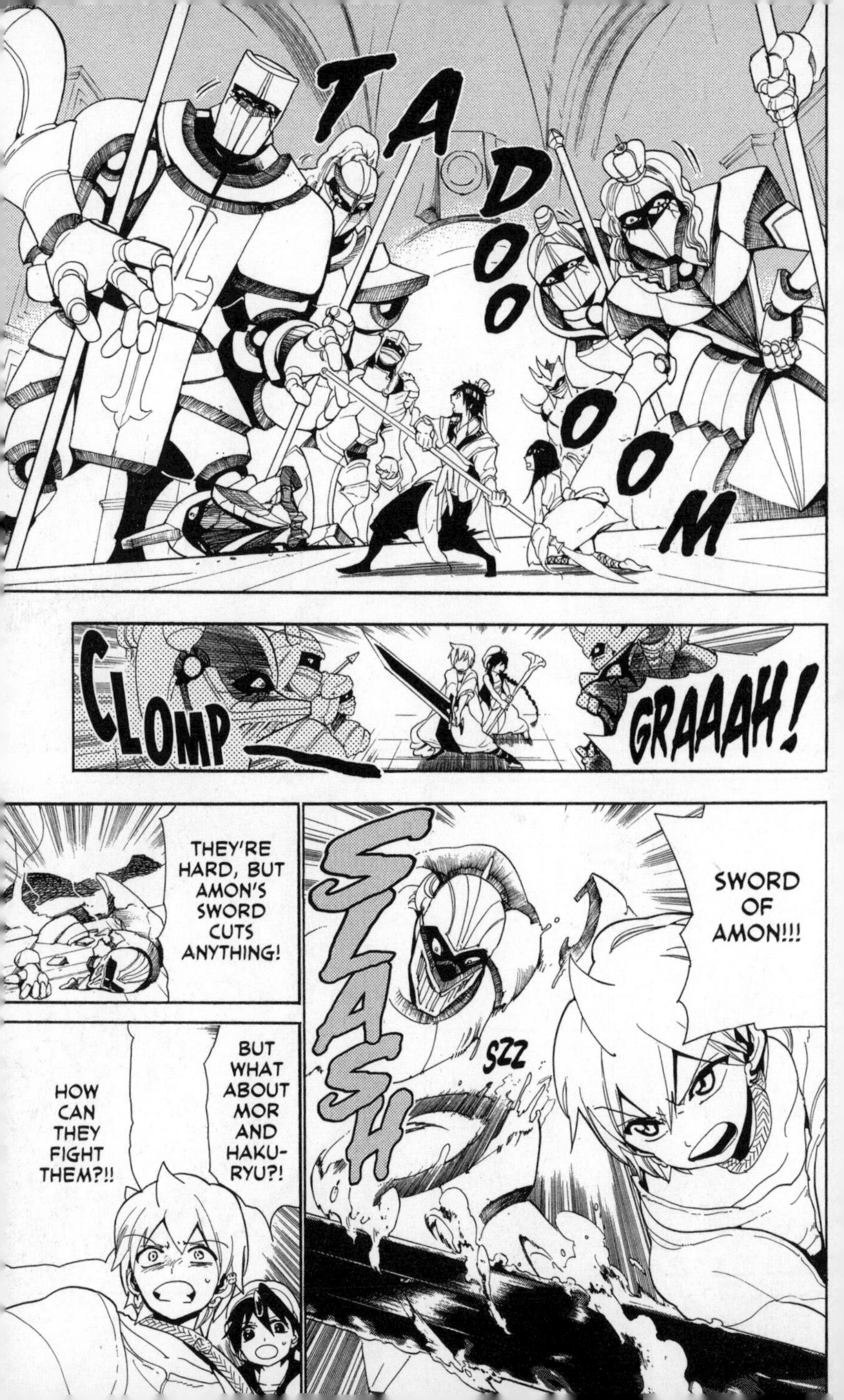
TA
DOOOOOM
GRAAAH!
CLOMP
SWORD OF AMON!!!
SZZ
SLASH
THEY'RE HARD, BUT AMON'S SWORD CUTS ANYTHING!
BUT WHAT ABOUT MOR AND HAKU-RYU?!
HOW CAN THEY FIGHT THEM?!!

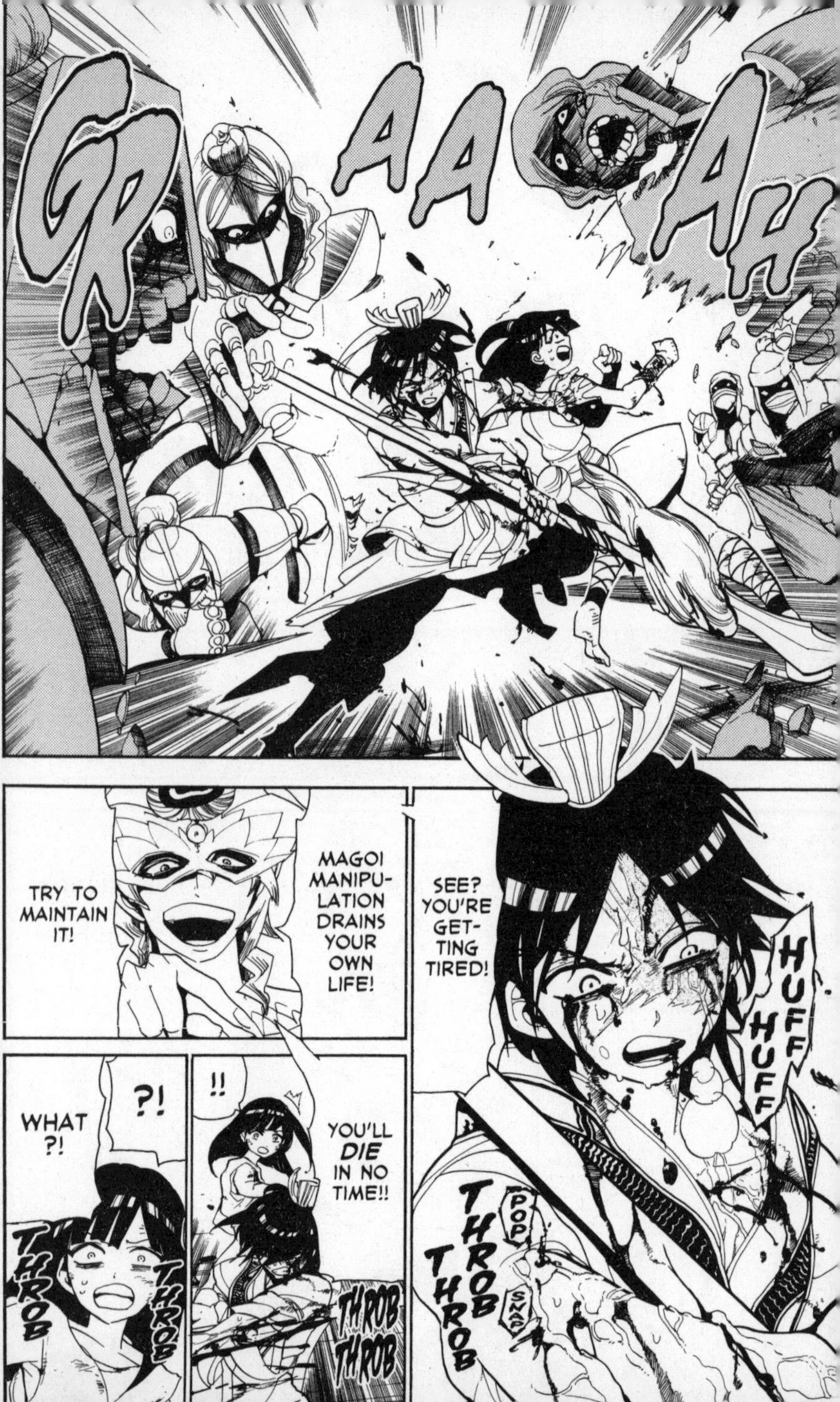
GRAAAAH
SEE? YOU'RE GETTING TIRED!
HUFF HUFF
HUFF HUFF
POP
SNAP
THROB THROB
THROB THROB
MAGOI MANIPULATION DRAINS YOUR OWN LIFE!
TRY TO MAINTAIN IT!
YOU'LL *DIE* IN NO TIME!!
!!
THROB THROB
?!
WHAT ?!
THROB THROB

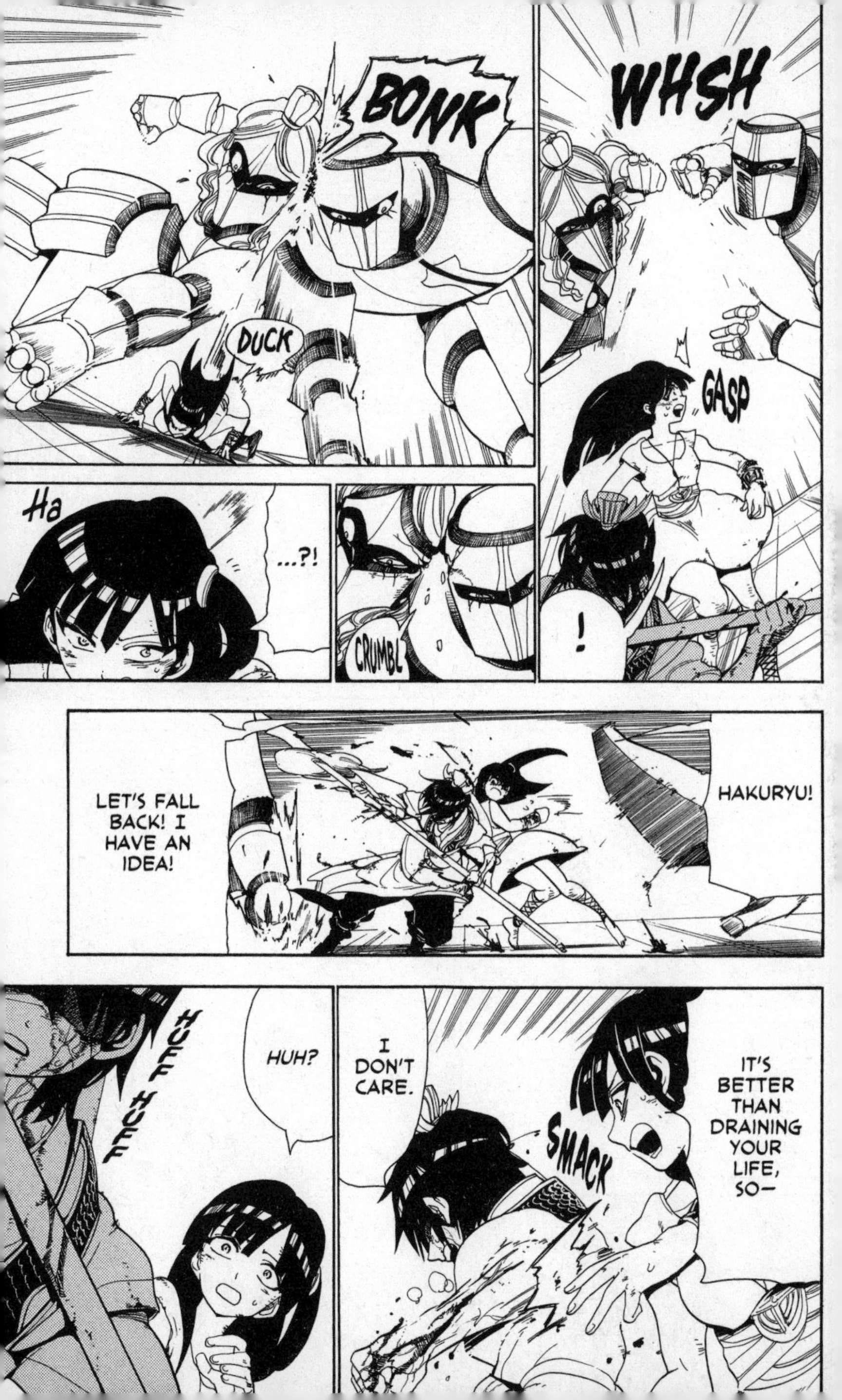
WHSH
GASP
!
BONK
DUCK
CRUMBL
Ha
...?!
HAKURYU!
LET'S FALL BACK! I HAVE AN IDEA!
IT'S BETTER THAN DRAINING YOUR LIFE, SO—
SMACK
I DON'T CARE.
HUH?
HUFF HUFF

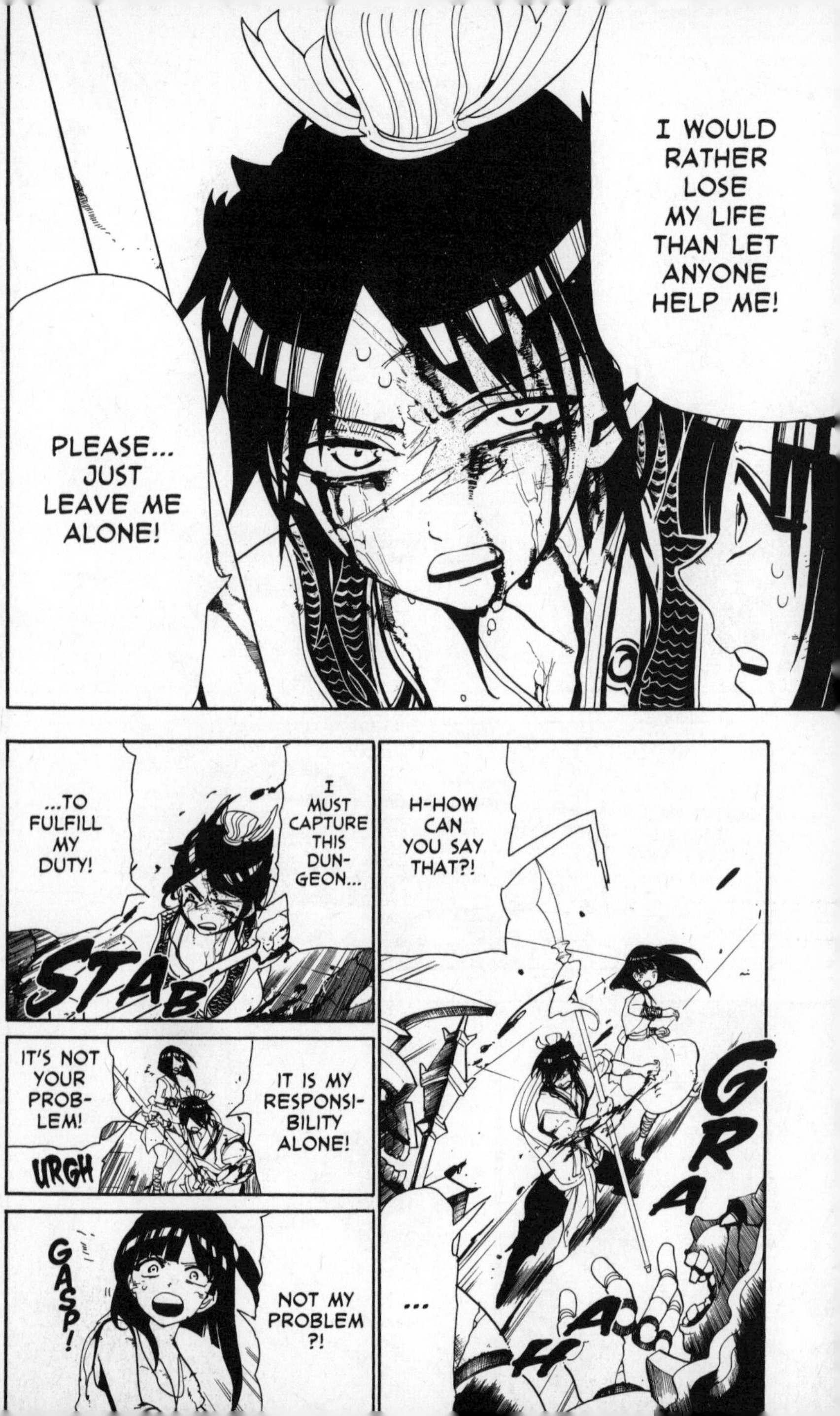
I WOULD RATHER LOSE MY LIFE THAN LET ANYONE HELP ME!
PLEASE... JUST LEAVE ME ALONE!
H-HOW CAN YOU SAY THAT?!
GRA
HA...
...
I MUST CAPTURE THIS DUN-GEON...
...TO FULFILL MY DUTY!
STAB
IT IS MY RESPONSI-BILITY ALONE!
IT'S NOT YOUR PROB-LEM!
URGH
NOT MY PROBLEM ?!
GASP!

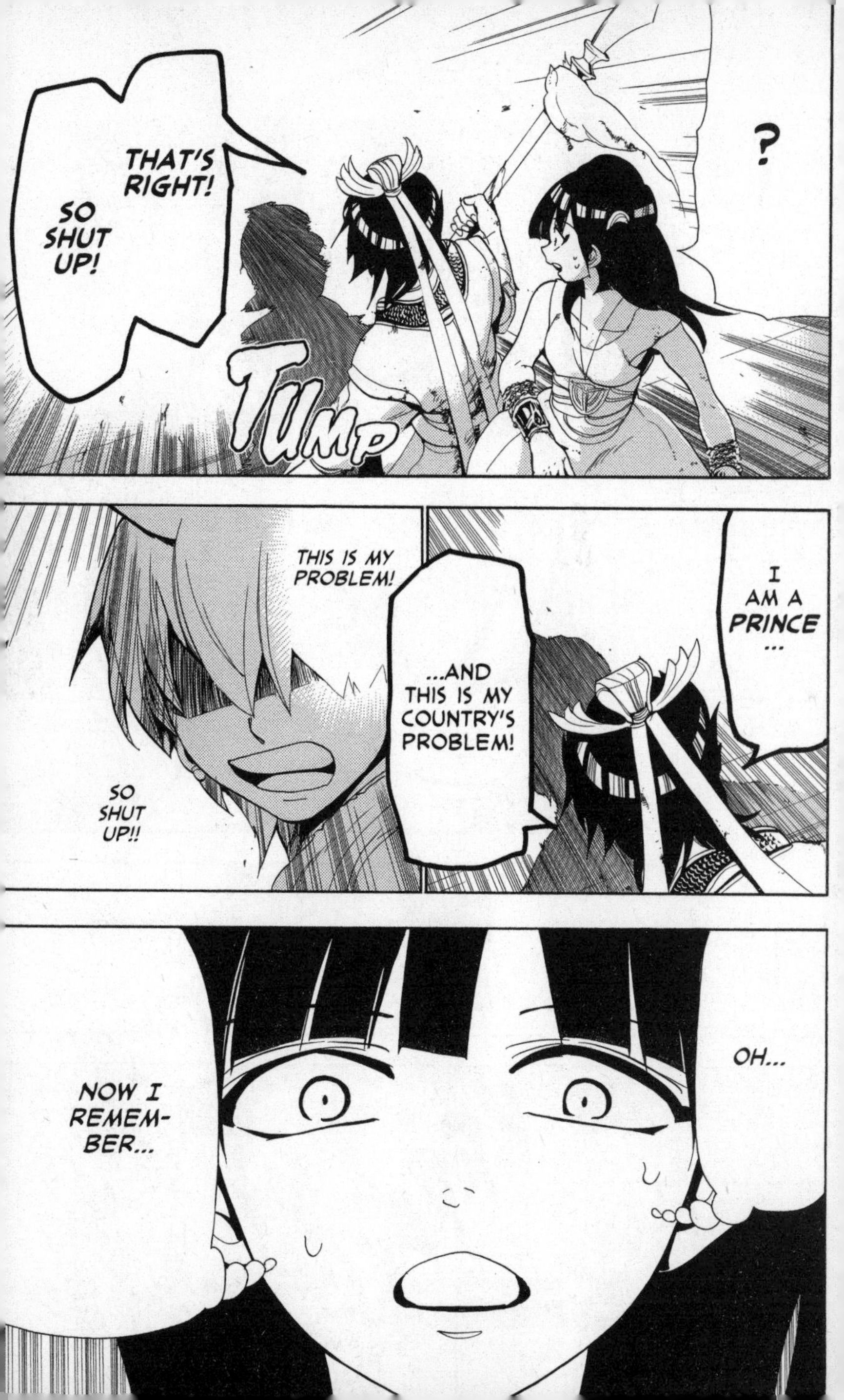
?
THAT'S RIGHT!
SO SHUT UP!
TUMP
I AM A PRINCE...
THIS IS MY PROBLEM!
...AND THIS IS MY COUNTRY'S PROBLEM!
SO SHUT UP!!
OH...
NOW I REMEMBER...

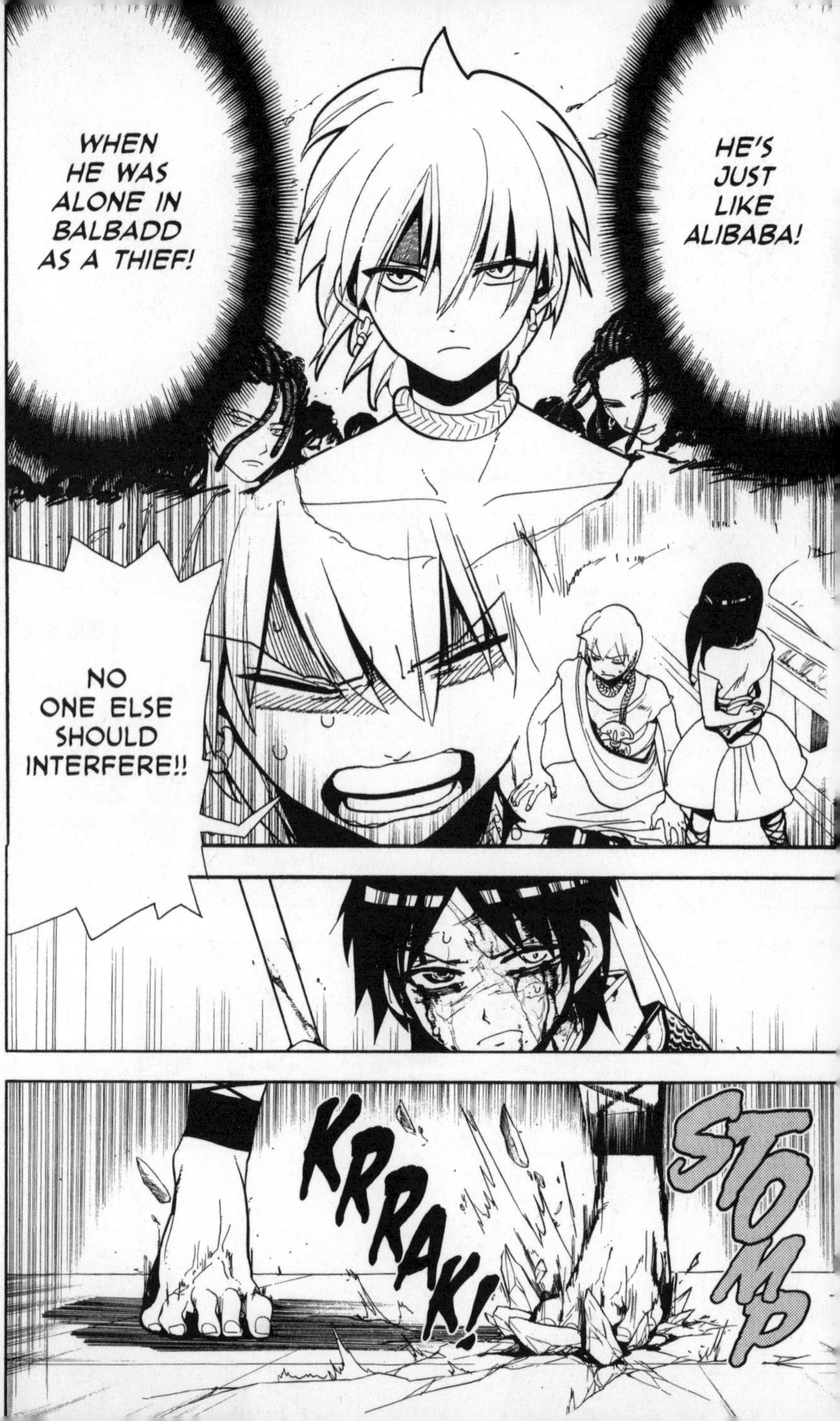
HE'S JUST LIKE ALIBABA!
WHEN HE WAS ALONE IN BALBADD AS A THIEF!
NO ONE ELSE SHOULD INTERFERE!!
STOMP
KRRAK!

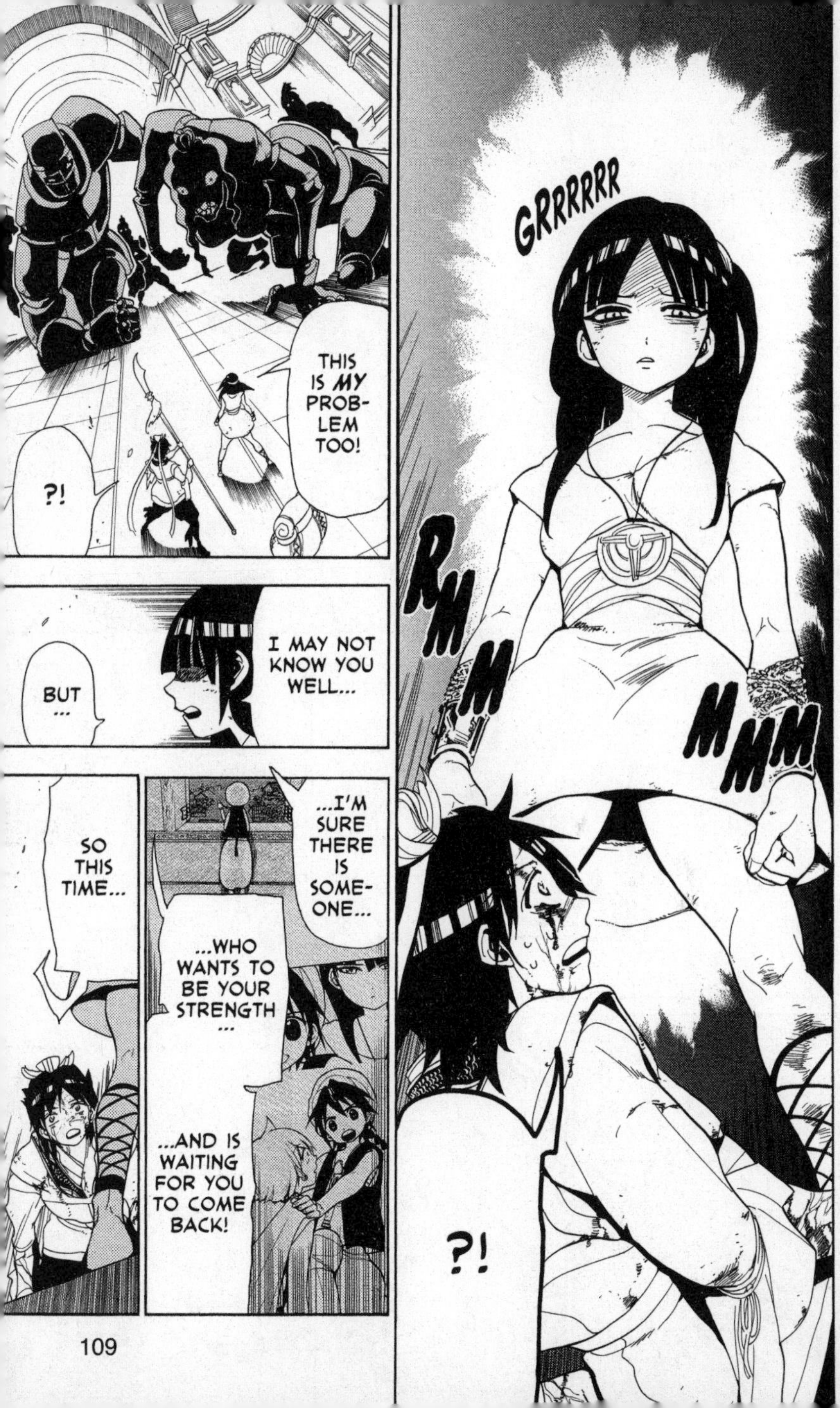
GRRRRRR
RMM
MMM
?!
THIS IS *MY* PROB-LEM TOO!
?!
I MAY NOT KNOW YOU WELL...
BUT ...
...I'M SURE THERE IS SOME-ONE...
...WHO WANTS TO BE YOUR STRENGTH ...
...AND IS WAITING FOR YOU TO COME BACK!
SO THIS TIME...

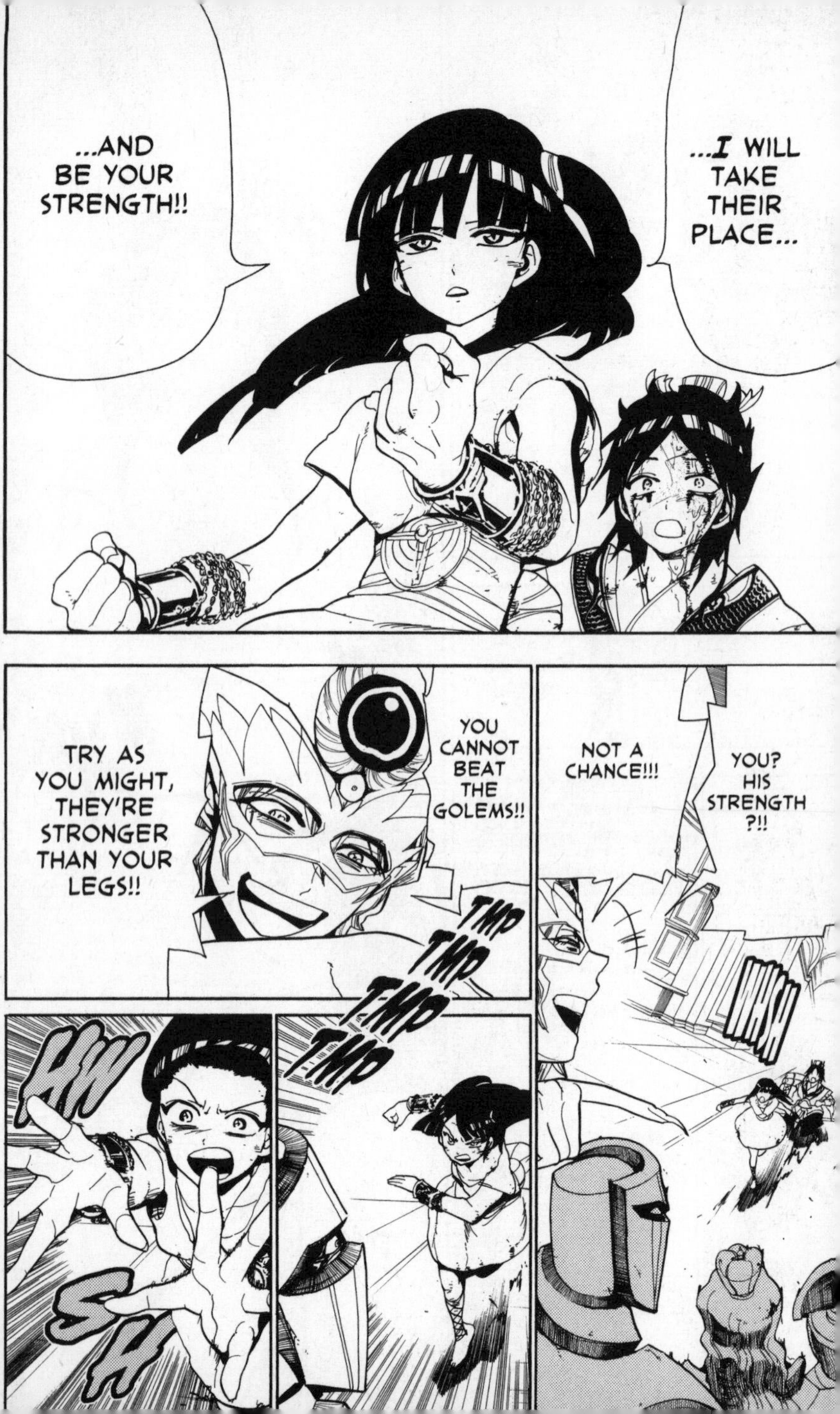
...I WILL TAKE THEIR PLACE...
...AND BE YOUR STRENGTH!!
YOU? HIS STRENGTH ?!!
NOT A CHANCE!!!
WHSH
YOU CANNOT BEAT THE GOLEMS!!
TRY AS YOU MIGHT, THEY'RE STRONGER THAN YOUR LEGS!!
TMP TMP T-MP TMP
HN
SH

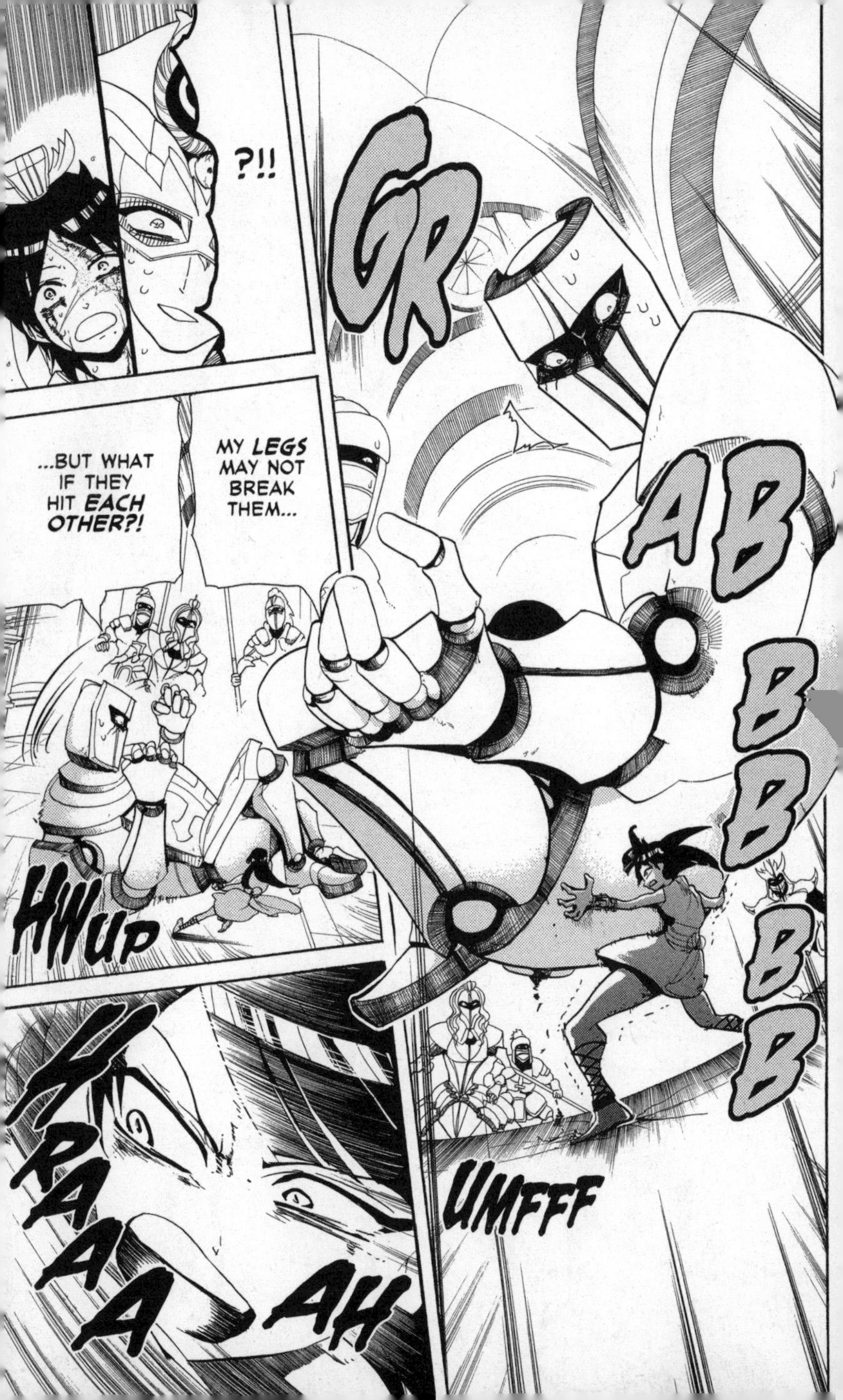
GR
AB
BBBB
UMFFF
?!!
MY LEGS MAY NOT BREAK THEM...
...BUT WHAT IF THEY HIT EACH OTHER?!
HWUP
HRAAAAAH

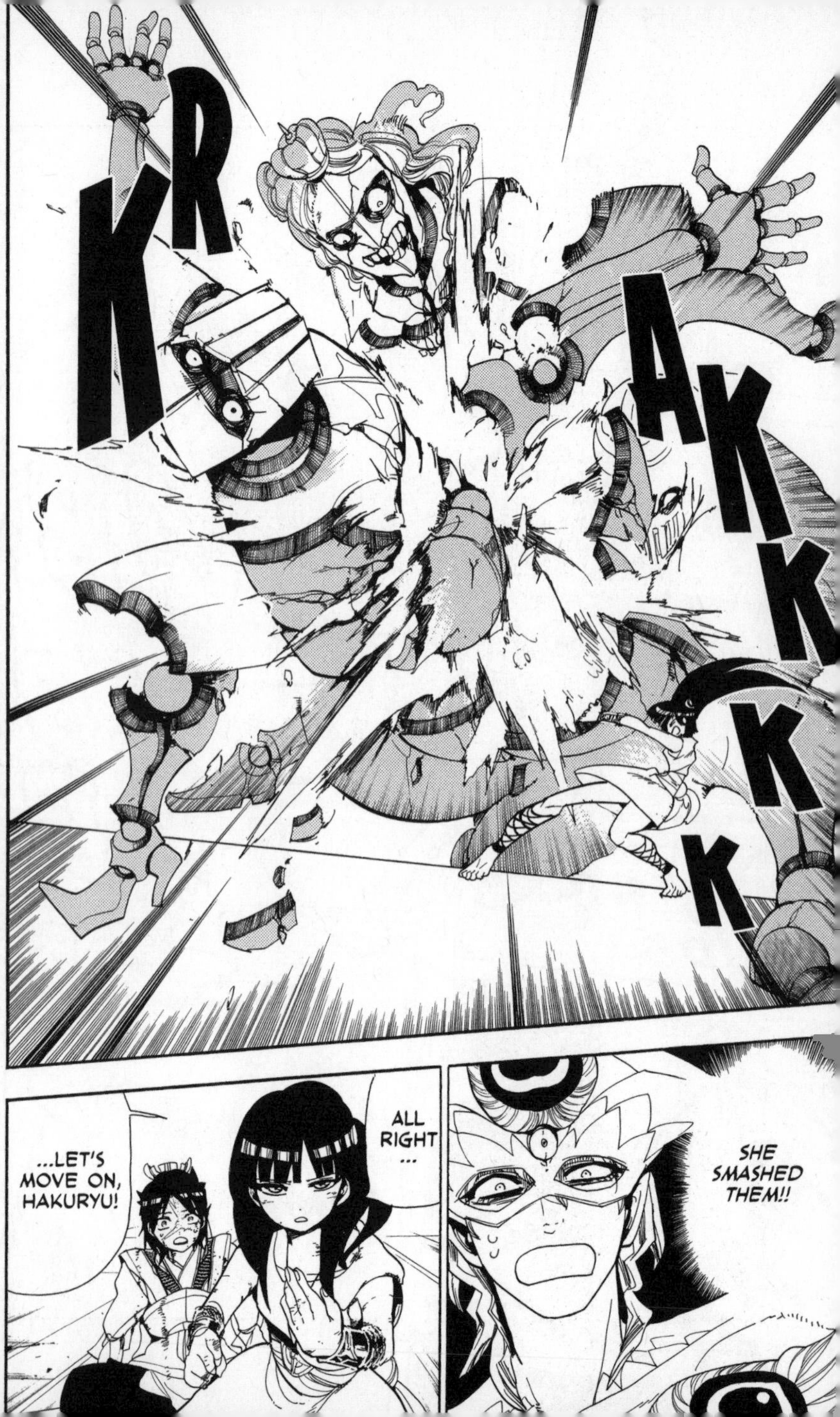
KRAKKKK
SHE SMASHED THEM!!
ALL RIGHT ...
...LET'S MOVE ON, HAKURYU!

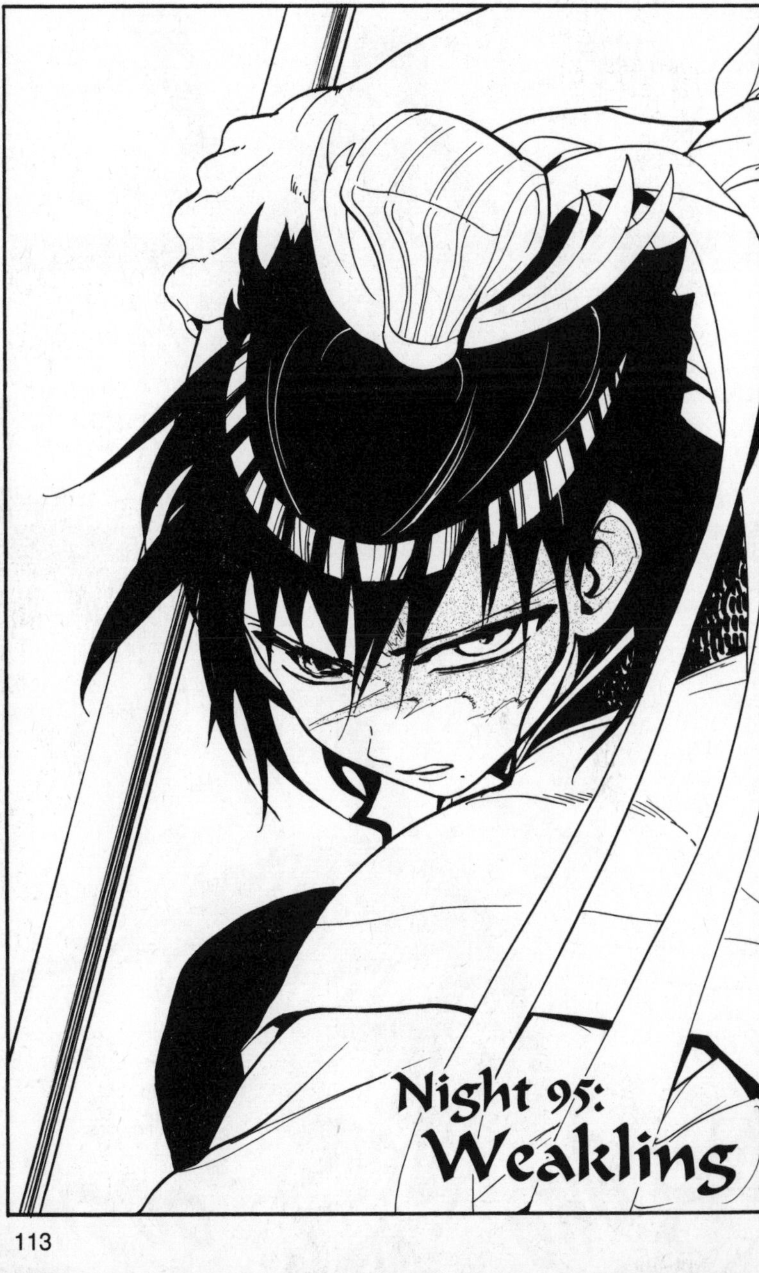
Night 95:
Weakling

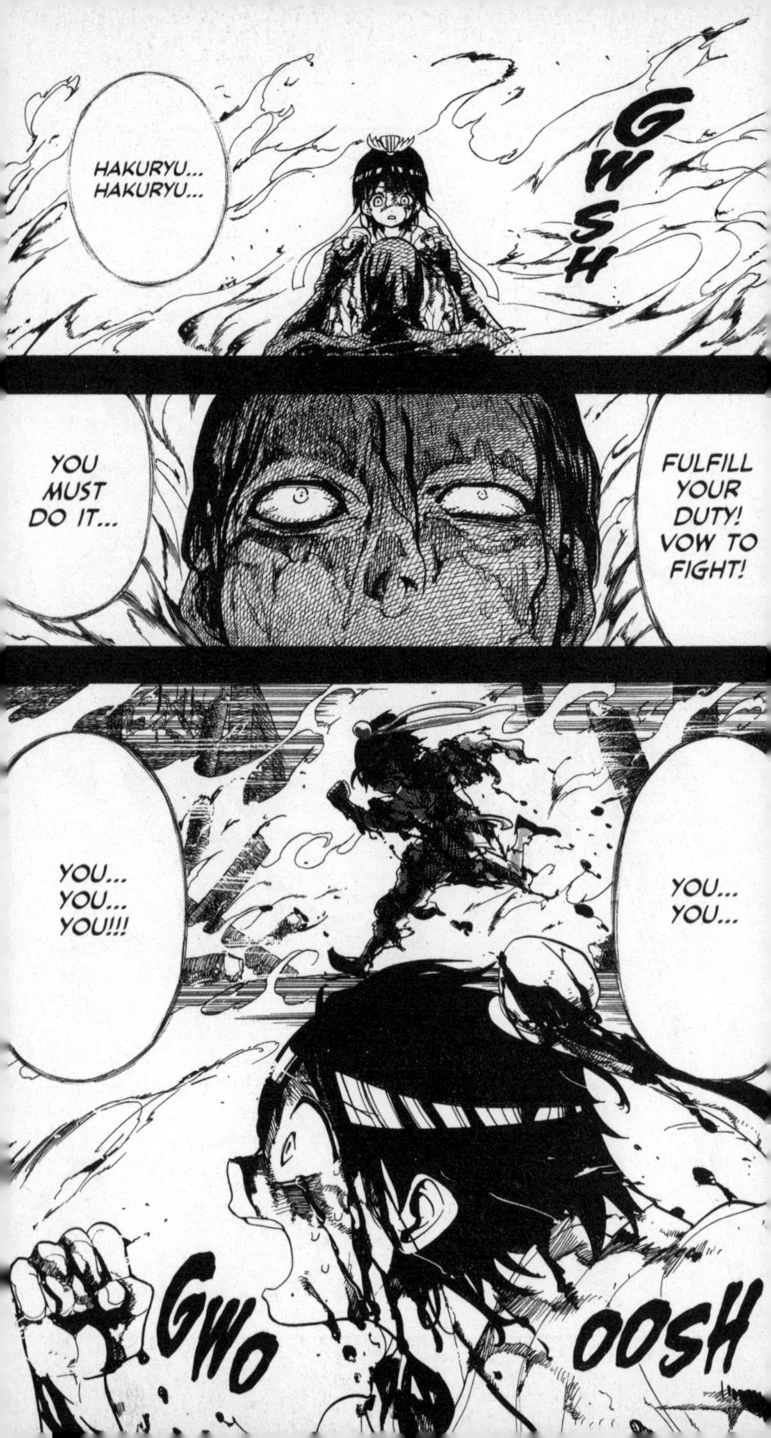
GWSH
HAKURYU... HAKURYU...
FULFILL YOUR DUTY! VOW TO FIGHT!
YOU MUST DO IT...
YOU... YOU...
YOU... YOU... YOU!!!
GWO OOSH

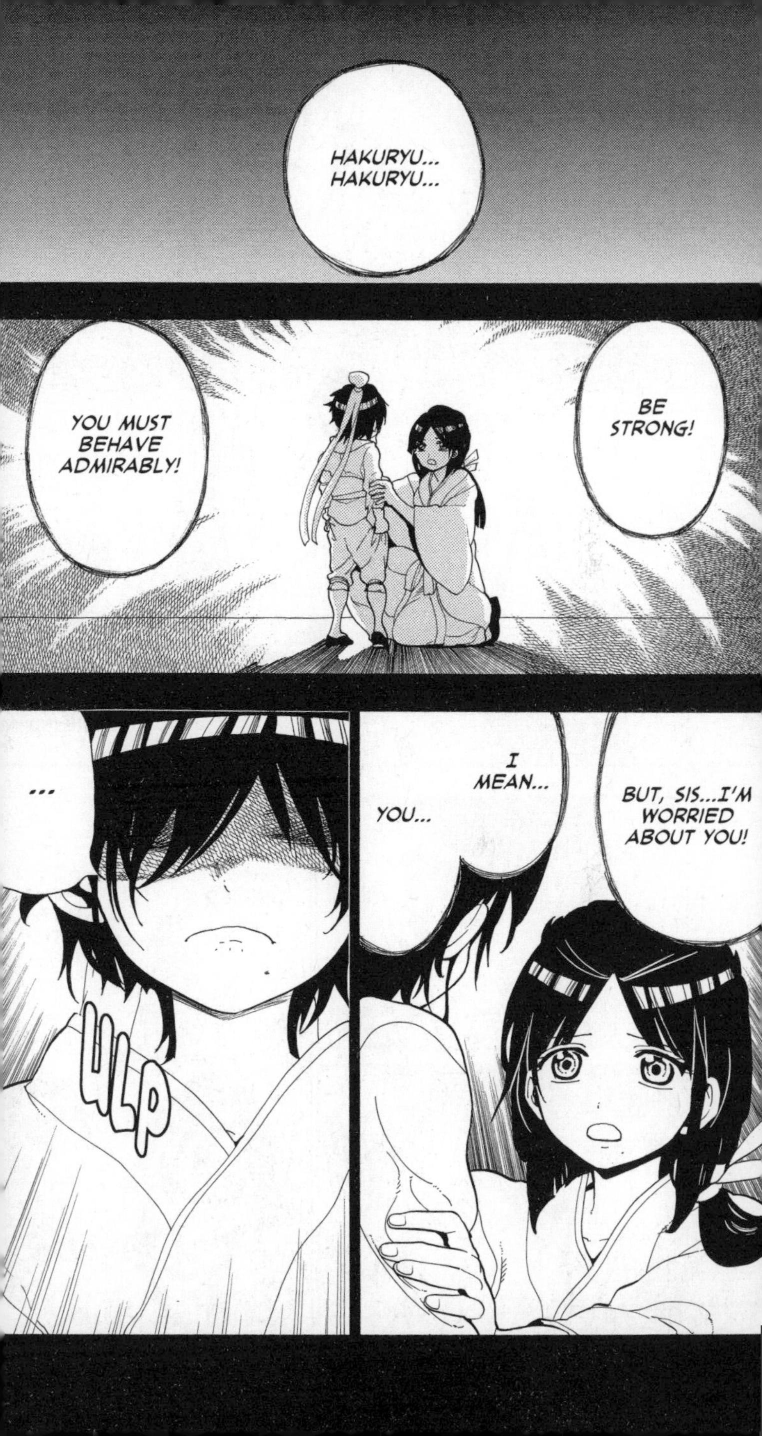
HAKURYU... HAKURYU...
BE STRONG!
YOU MUST BEHAVE ADMIRABLY!
BUT, SIS...I'M WORRIED ABOUT YOU!
I MEAN...
YOU...
...
ULP

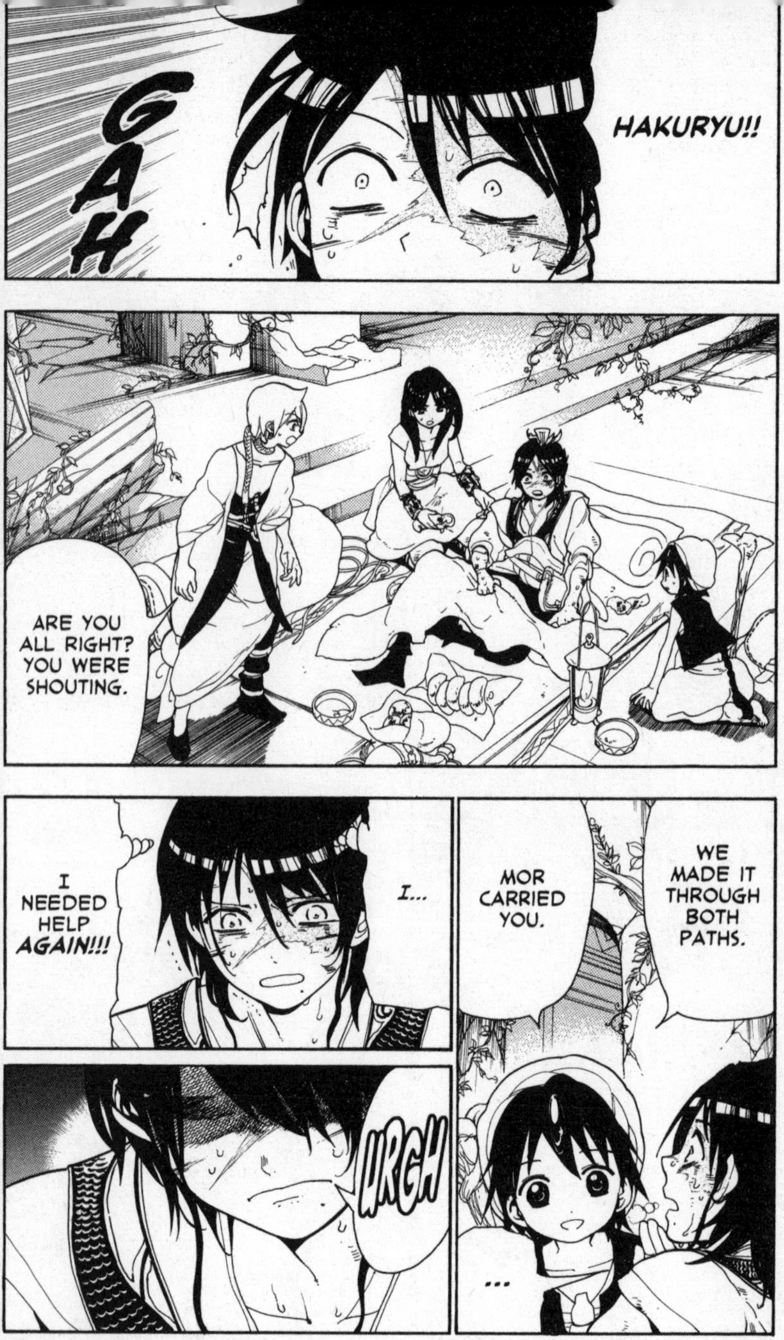
HAKURYU!!
GAH
ARE YOU ALL RIGHT? YOU WERE SHOUTING.
WE MADE IT THROUGH BOTH PATHS.
MOR CARRIED YOU.
I...
I NEEDED HELP AGAIN!!!
...
URGH

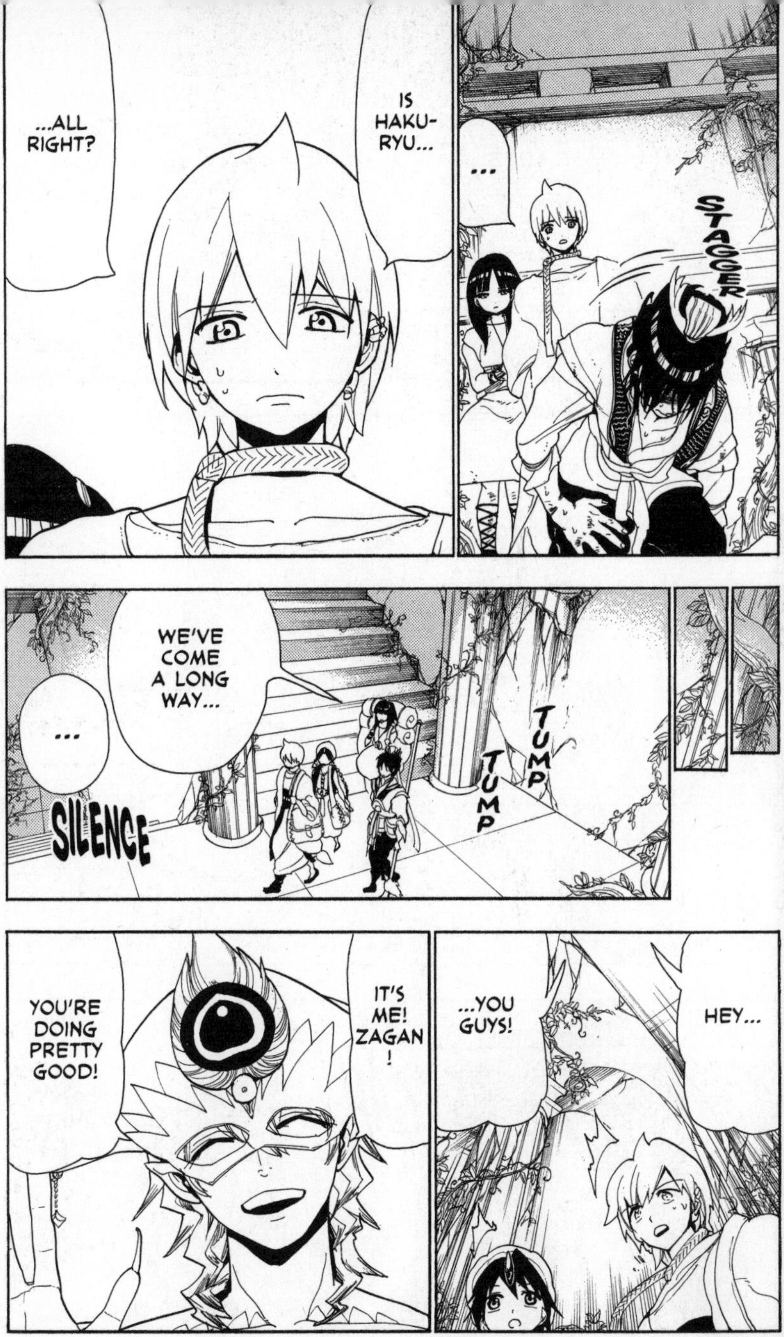
...
STAGGER
IS HAKU-RYU...
...ALL RIGHT?
WE'VE COME A LONG WAY...
TUMP
TUMP
...
SILENCE
HEY...
...YOU GUYS!
IT'S ME! ZAGAN!
YOU'RE DOING PRETTY GOOD!

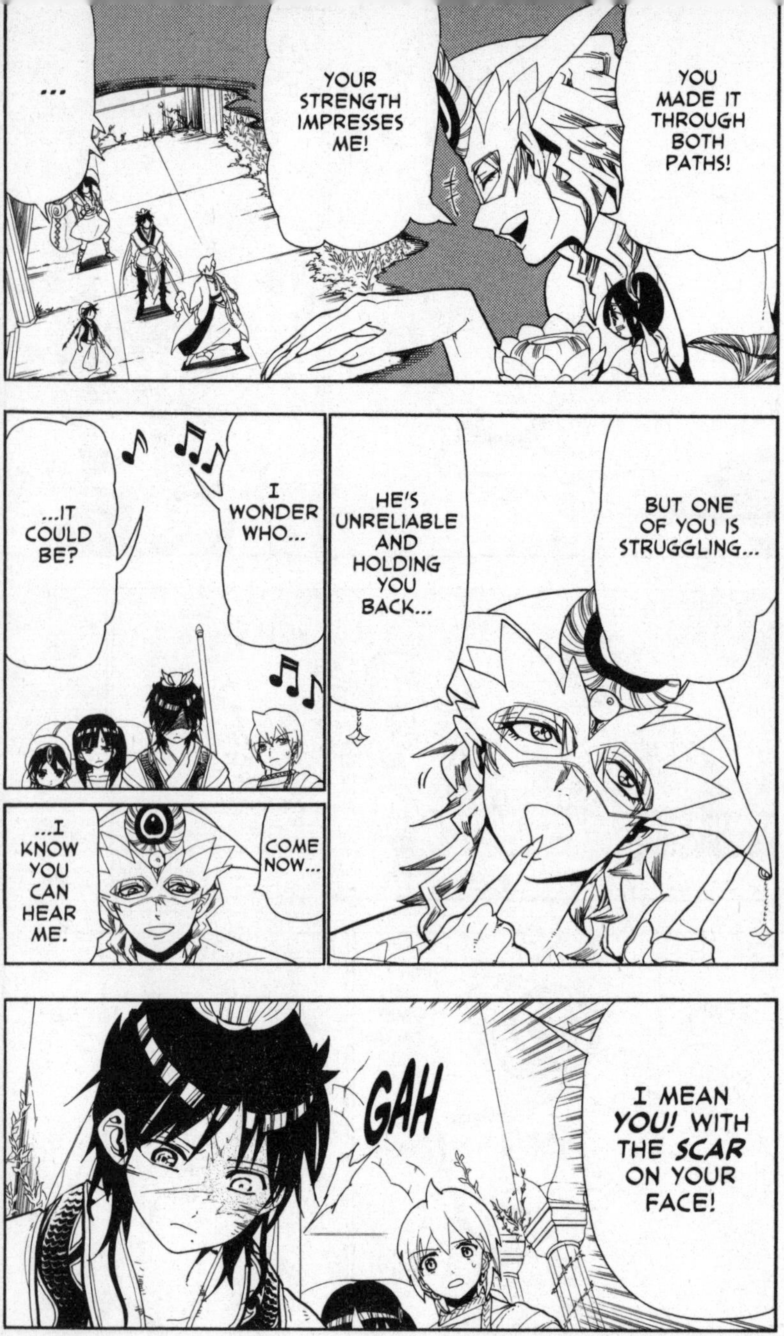
YOU MADE IT THROUGH BOTH PATHS!
YOUR STRENGTH IMPRESSES ME!
...
BUT ONE OF YOU IS STRUGGLING...
HE'S UNRELIABLE AND HOLDING YOU BACK...
I WONDER WHO...
...IT COULD BE?
COME NOW...
...I KNOW YOU CAN HEAR ME.
I MEAN YOU! WITH THE SCAR ON YOUR FACE!
GAH

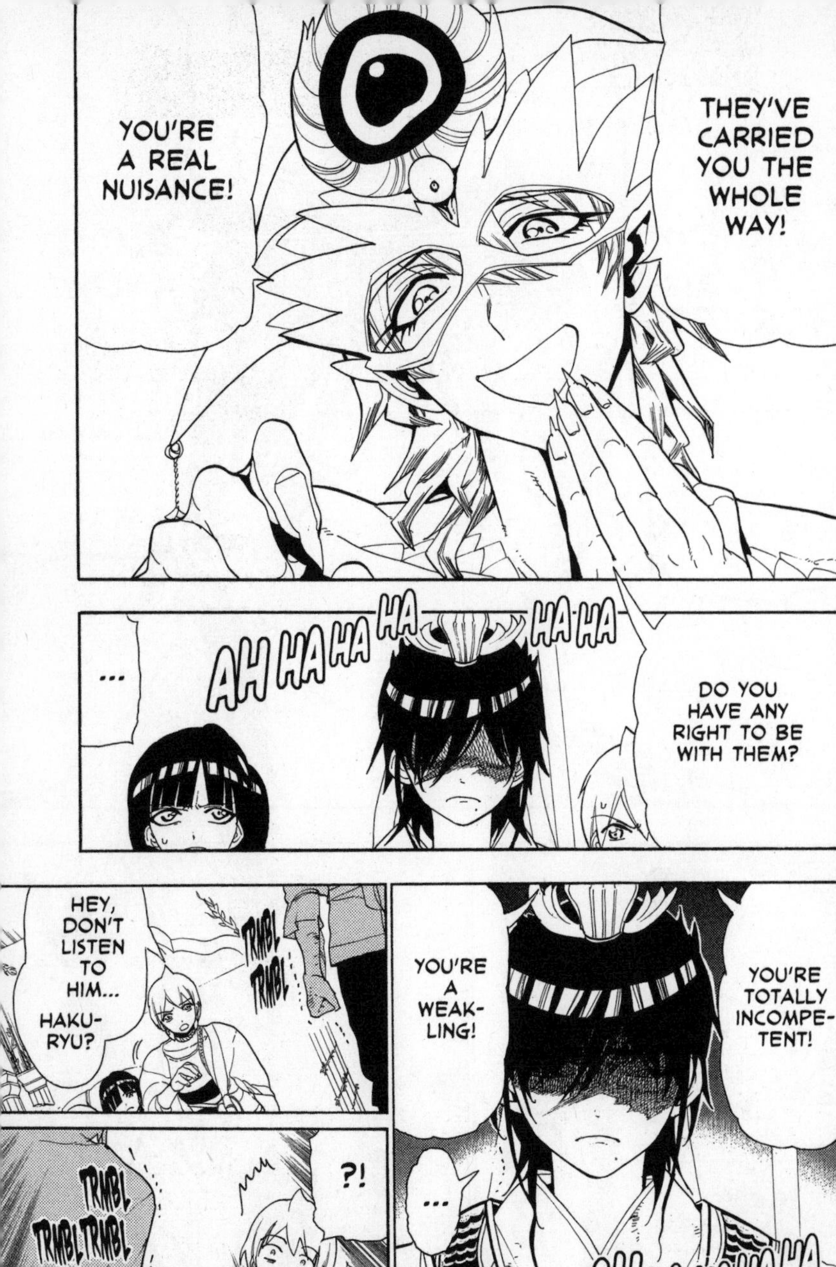
THEY'VE CARRIED YOU THE WHOLE WAY!
YOU'RE A REAL NUISANCE!
DO YOU HAVE ANY RIGHT TO BE WITH THEM?
AH HA HA HA HA HA
...
YOU'RE TOTALLY INCOMPETENT!
YOU'RE A WEAKLING!
...
AH HA HA HA HA HA
HEY, DON'T LISTEN TO HIM...
HAKURYU?
TRMBL TRMBL
?!
TRMBL TRMBL TRMBL

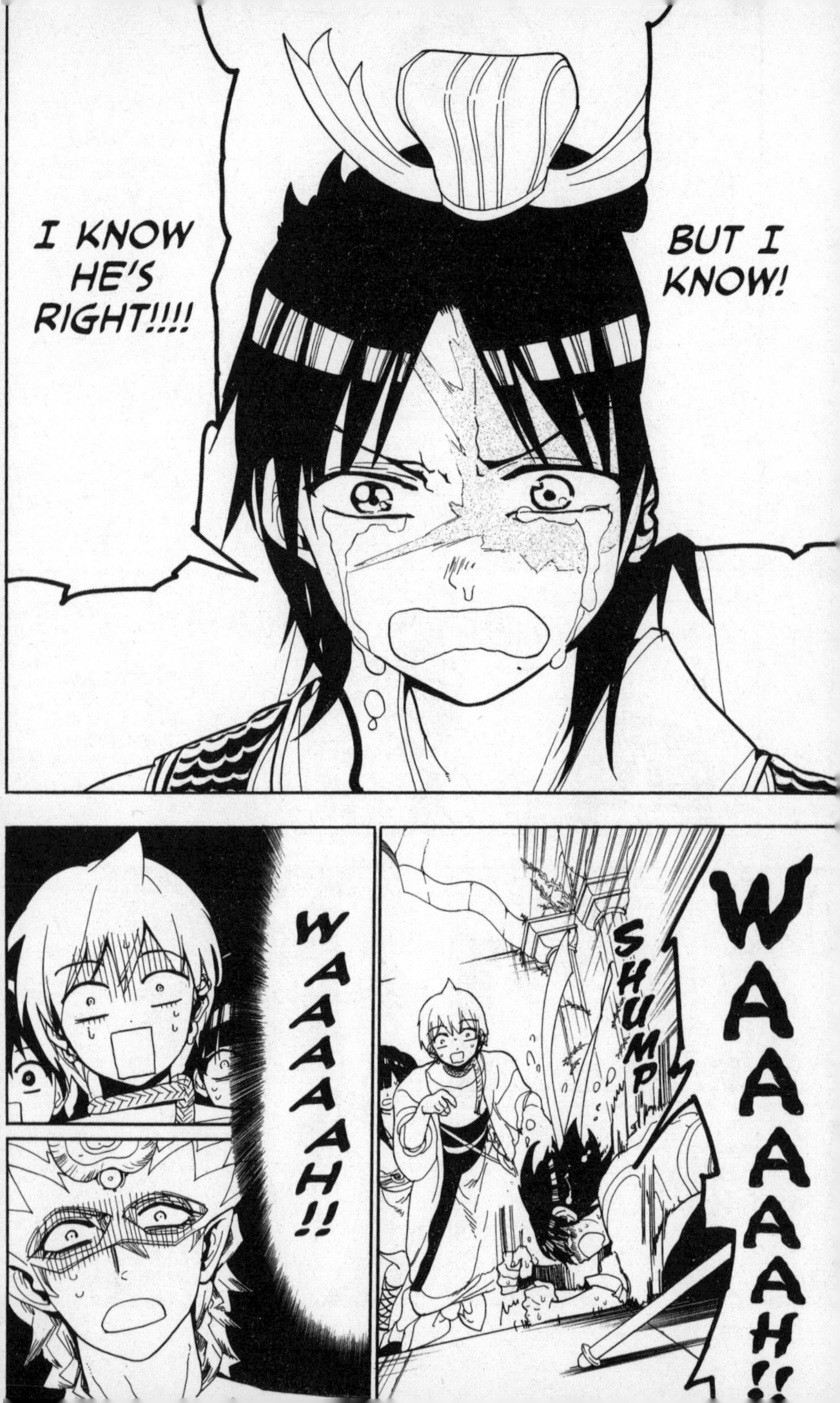
BUT I KNOW!
I KNOW HE'S RIGHT!!!!
WAAAAAH!!
SHUMP
WAAAAAH!!

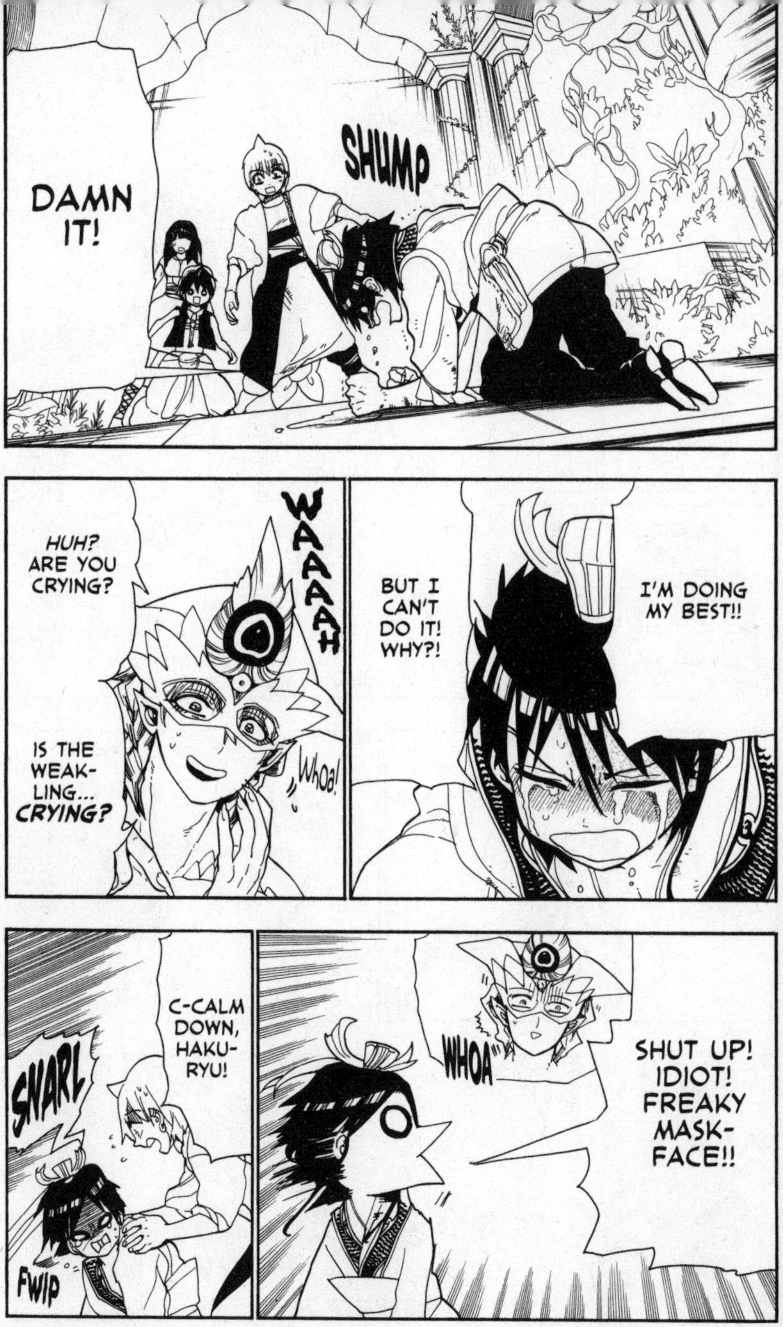
SHUMP
DAMN IT!
I'M DOING MY BEST!!
BUT I CAN'T DO IT! WHY?!
WAAAAAH
HUH? ARE YOU CRYING?
Whoa!
IS THE WEAKLING... *CRYING?*
SHUT UP! IDIOT! FREAKY MASK-FACE!!
WHOA
C-CALM DOWN, HAKURYU!
SNARL
FWIP

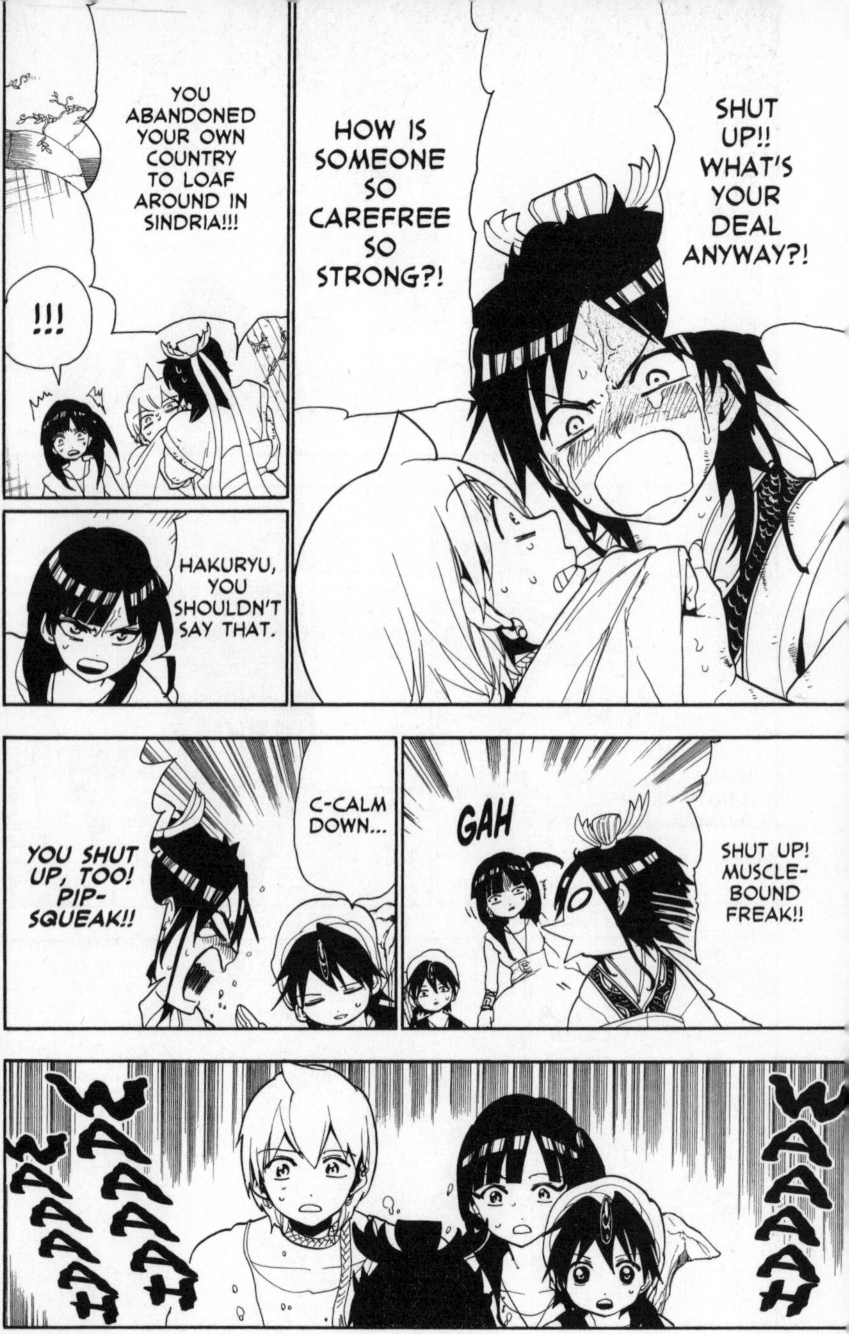
SHUT UP!! WHAT'S YOUR DEAL ANYWAY?!
HOW IS SOMEONE SO CAREFREE SO STRONG?!
YOU ABANDONED YOUR OWN COUNTRY TO LOAF AROUND IN SINDRIA!!!
!!!
HAKURYU, YOU SHOULDN'T SAY THAT.
GAH
SHUT UP! MUSCLE-BOUND FREAK!!
C-CALM DOWN...
YOU SHUT UP, TOO! PIP-SQUEAK!!
WAAAAH
WAAAAAH
WAAAAAH

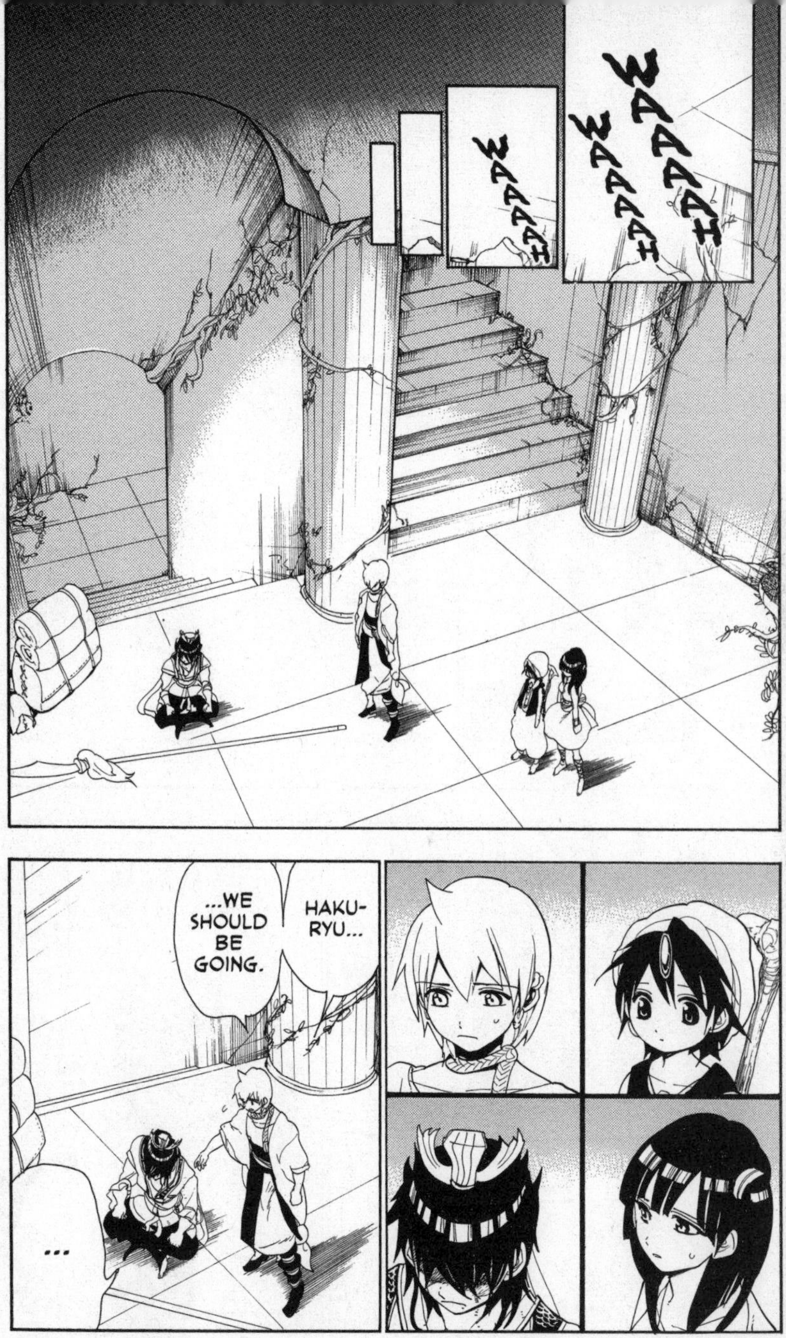
WAAAAH
WAAAAH
WAAAAH
HAKU-RYU...
...WE SHOULD BE GOING.
...

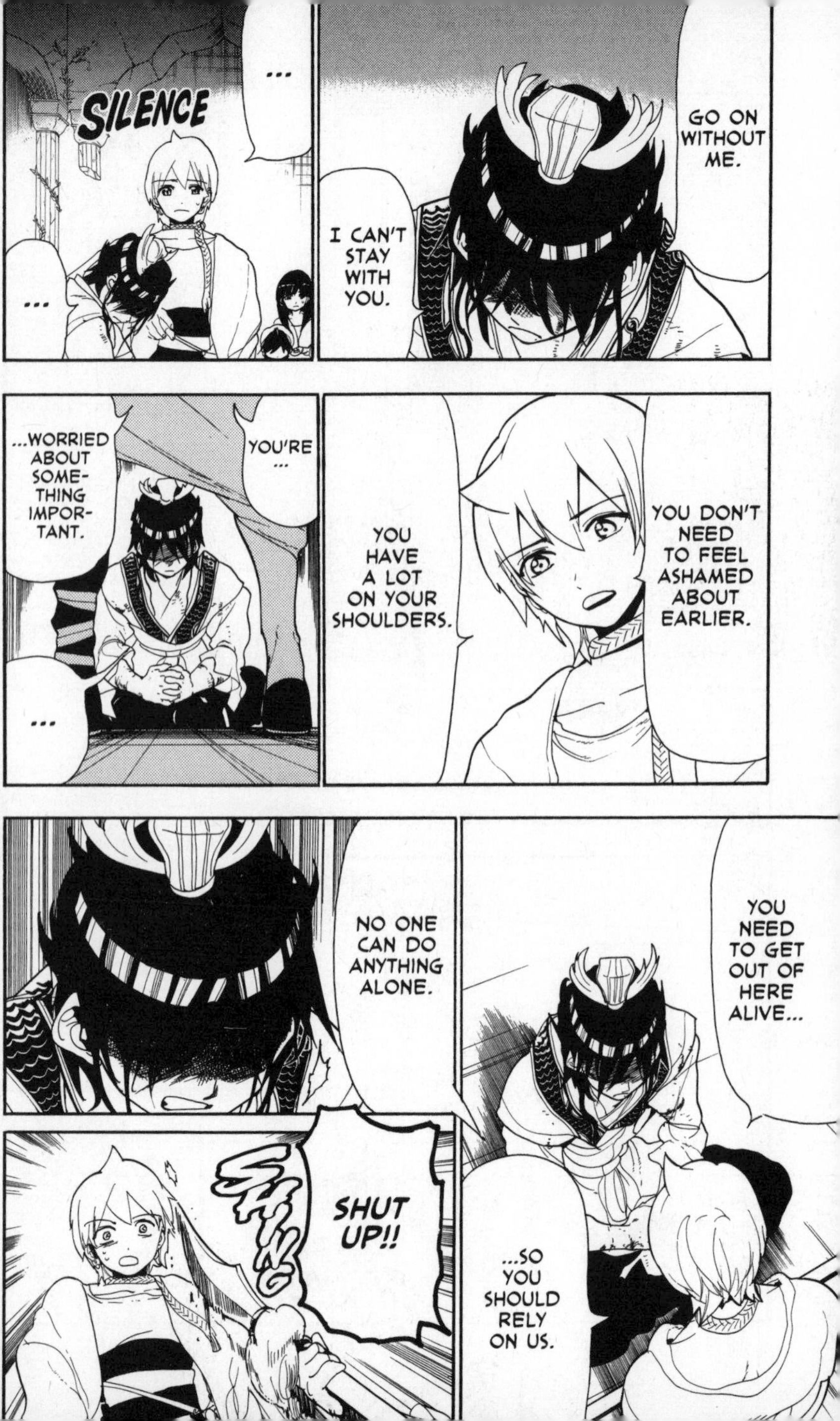
GO ON WITHOUT ME.
I CAN'T STAY WITH YOU.
...
SILENCE
...
YOU DON'T NEED TO FEEL ASHAMED ABOUT EARLIER.
YOU HAVE A LOT ON YOUR SHOULDERS.
YOU'RE ...
...WORRIED ABOUT SOME-THING IMPOR-TANT.
...
YOU NEED TO GET OUT OF HERE ALIVE...
...SO YOU SHOULD RELY ON US.
NO ONE CAN DO ANYTHING ALONE.
SHUT UP!!
SHING

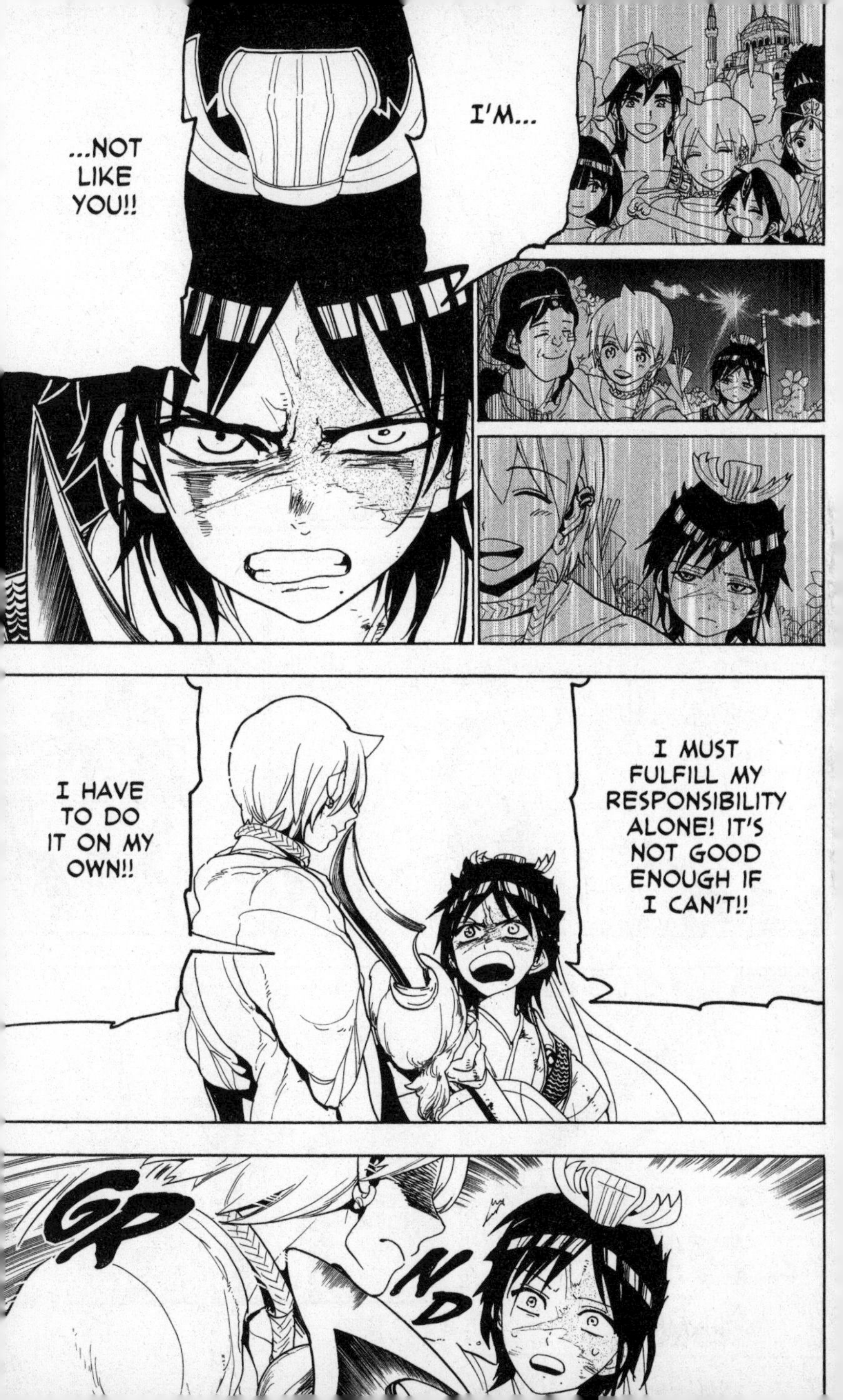
I'M...
...NOT LIKE YOU!!
I MUST FULFILL MY RESPONSIBILITY ALONE! IT'S NOT GOOD ENOUGH IF I CAN'T!!
I HAVE TO DO IT ON MY OWN!!
GRND

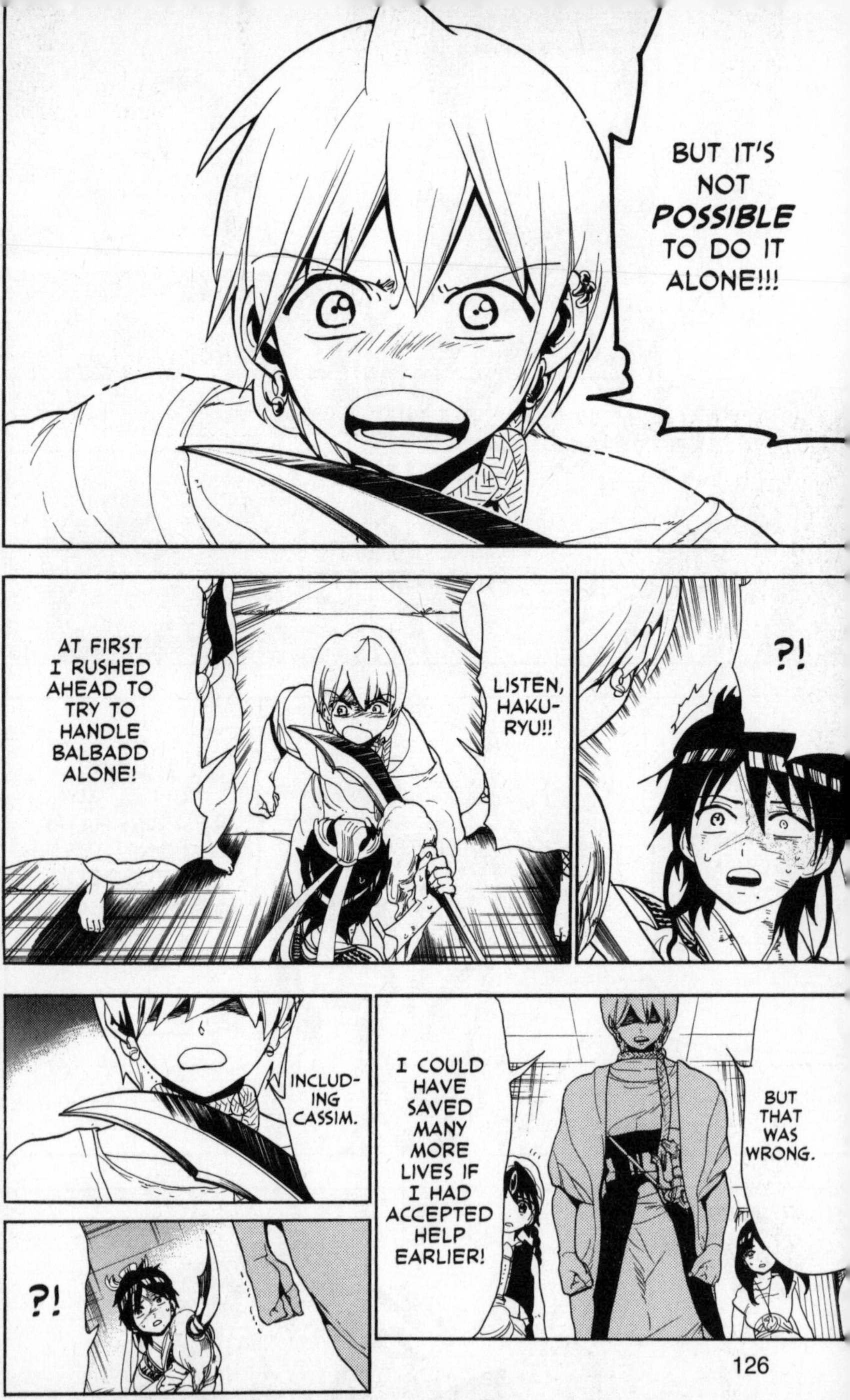
BUT IT'S NOT *POSSIBLE* TO DO IT ALONE!!!
?!
LISTEN, HAKU-RYU!!
AT FIRST I RUSHED AHEAD TO TRY TO HANDLE BALBADD ALONE!
BUT THAT WAS WRONG.
I COULD HAVE SAVED MANY MORE LIVES IF I HAD ACCEPTED HELP EARLIER!
INCLUD-ING CASSIM.
?!

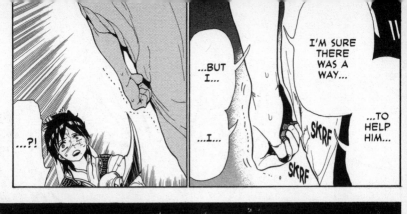

...?!

...BUT I...

...I...

SKRF

SKRF

I'M SURE THERE WAS A WAY...

...TO HELP HIM...

IT'S LIKE *I* KILLED HIM!

WHAT IS HE TALKING ABOUT...?

?!

ALIBABA!!

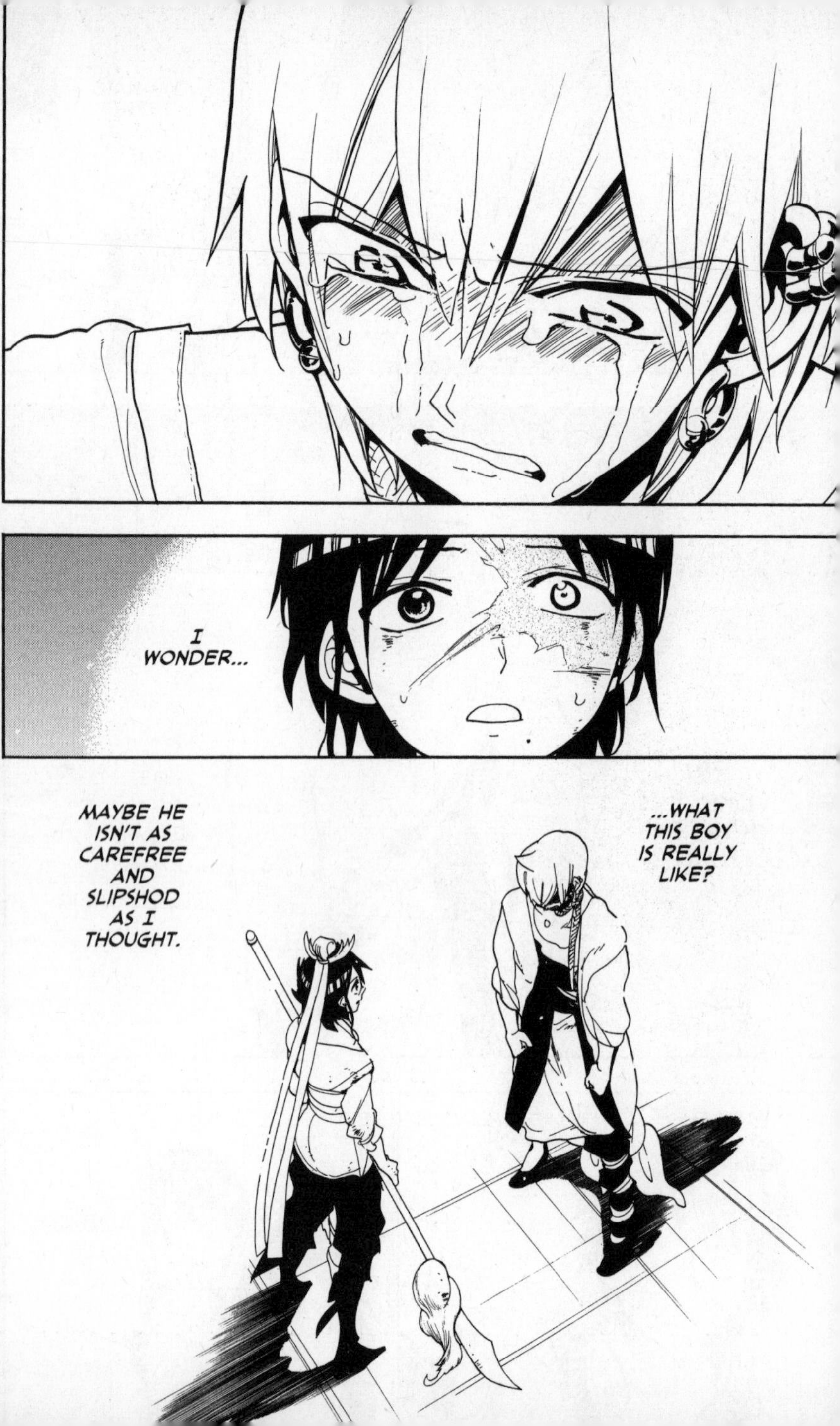
I WONDER...
...WHAT THIS BOY IS REALLY LIKE?
MAYBE HE ISN'T AS CAREFREE AND SLIPSHOD AS I THOUGHT.

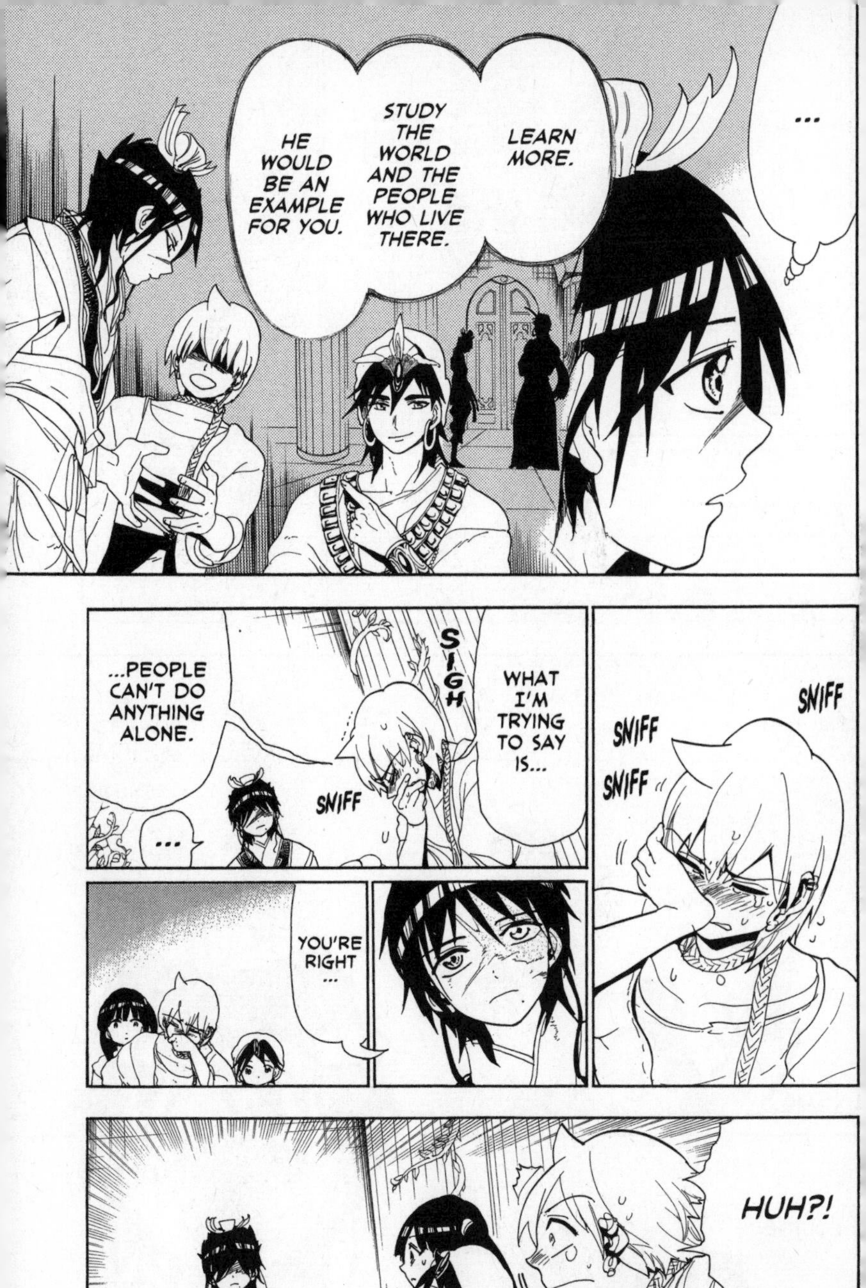
...
LEARN MORE.
STUDY THE WORLD AND THE PEOPLE WHO LIVE THERE.
HE WOULD BE AN EXAMPLE FOR YOU.
SNIFF
SNIFF
SNIFF
SIGH
WHAT I'M TRYING TO SAY IS...
SNIFF
...PEOPLE CAN'T DO ANYTHING ALONE.
...
YOU'RE RIGHT...
HUH?!

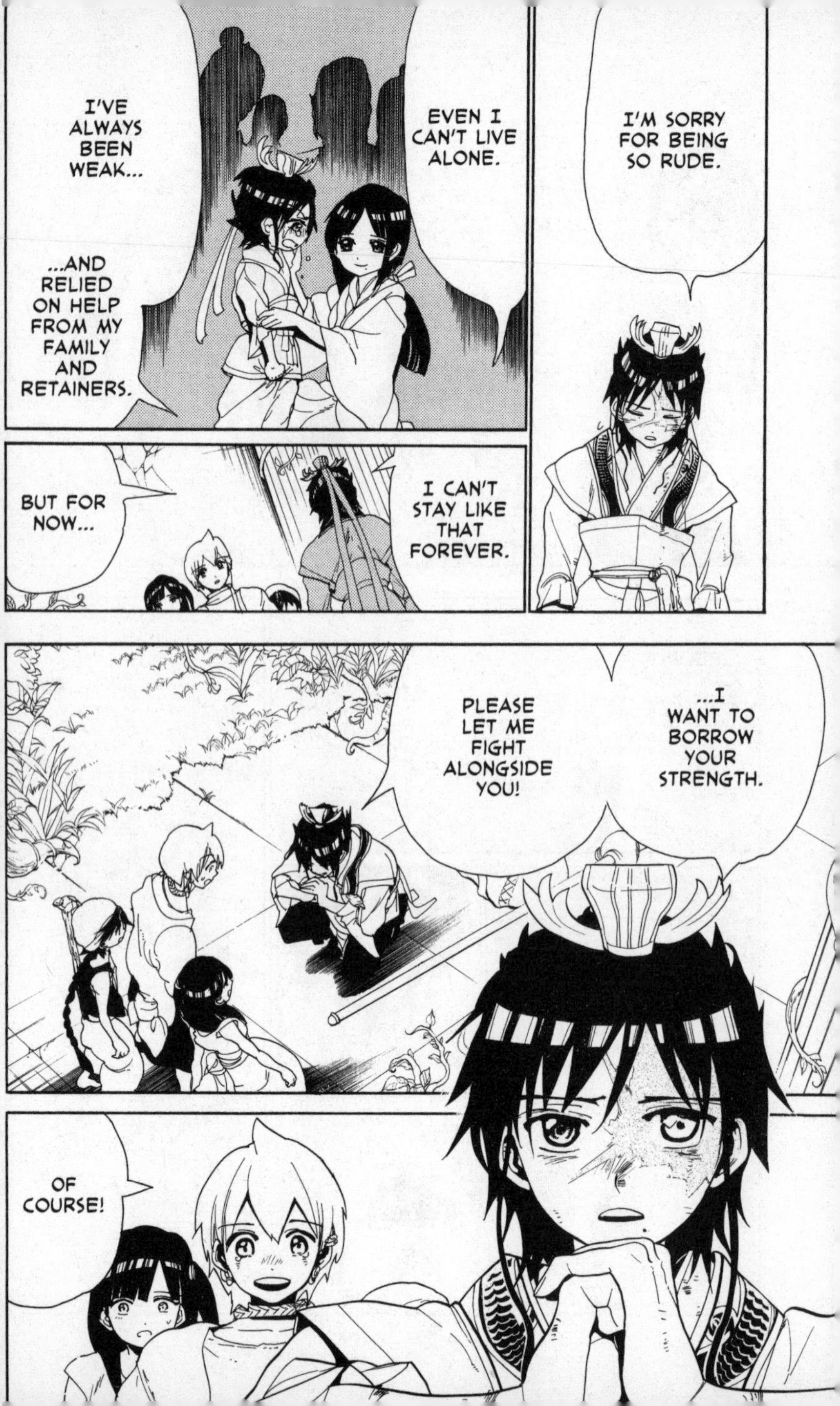
I'M SORRY FOR BEING SO RUDE.
EVEN I CAN'T LIVE ALONE.
I'VE ALWAYS BEEN WEAK...
...AND RELIED ON HELP FROM MY FAMILY AND RETAINERS.
I CAN'T STAY LIKE THAT FOREVER.
BUT FOR NOW...
...I WANT TO BORROW YOUR STRENGTH.
PLEASE LET ME FIGHT ALONGSIDE YOU!
OF COURSE!

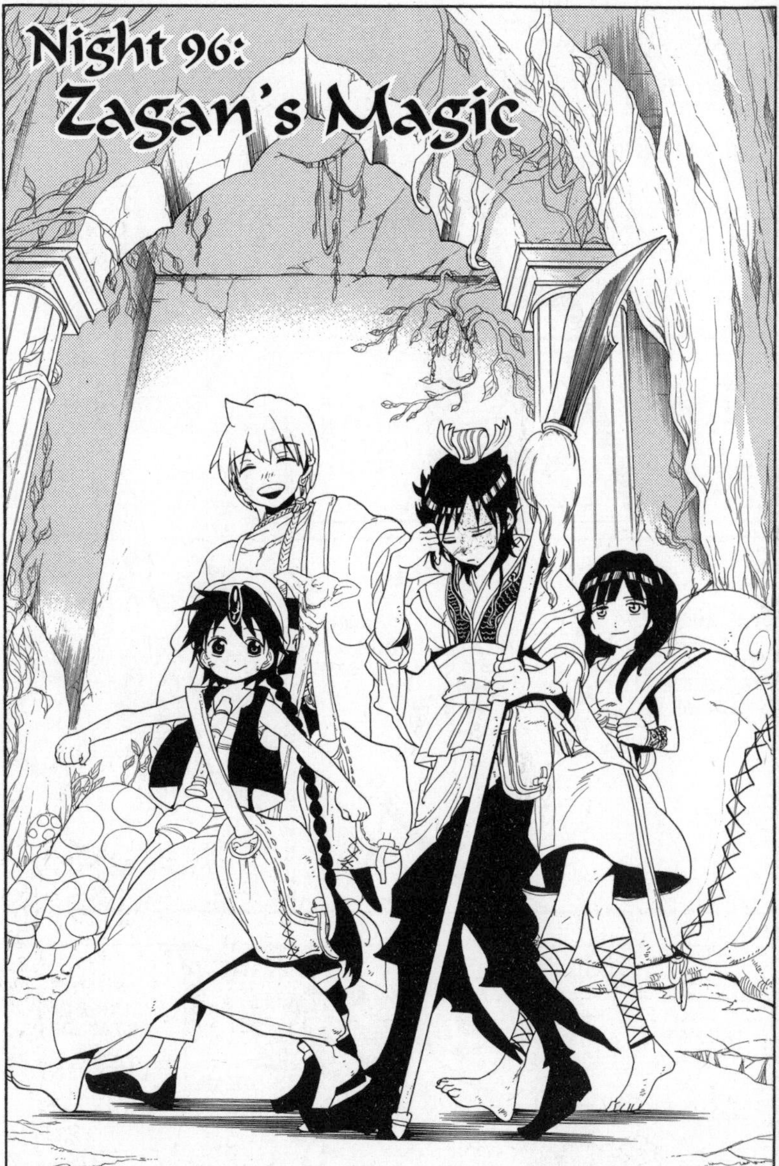
Night 96:
Zagan's Magic

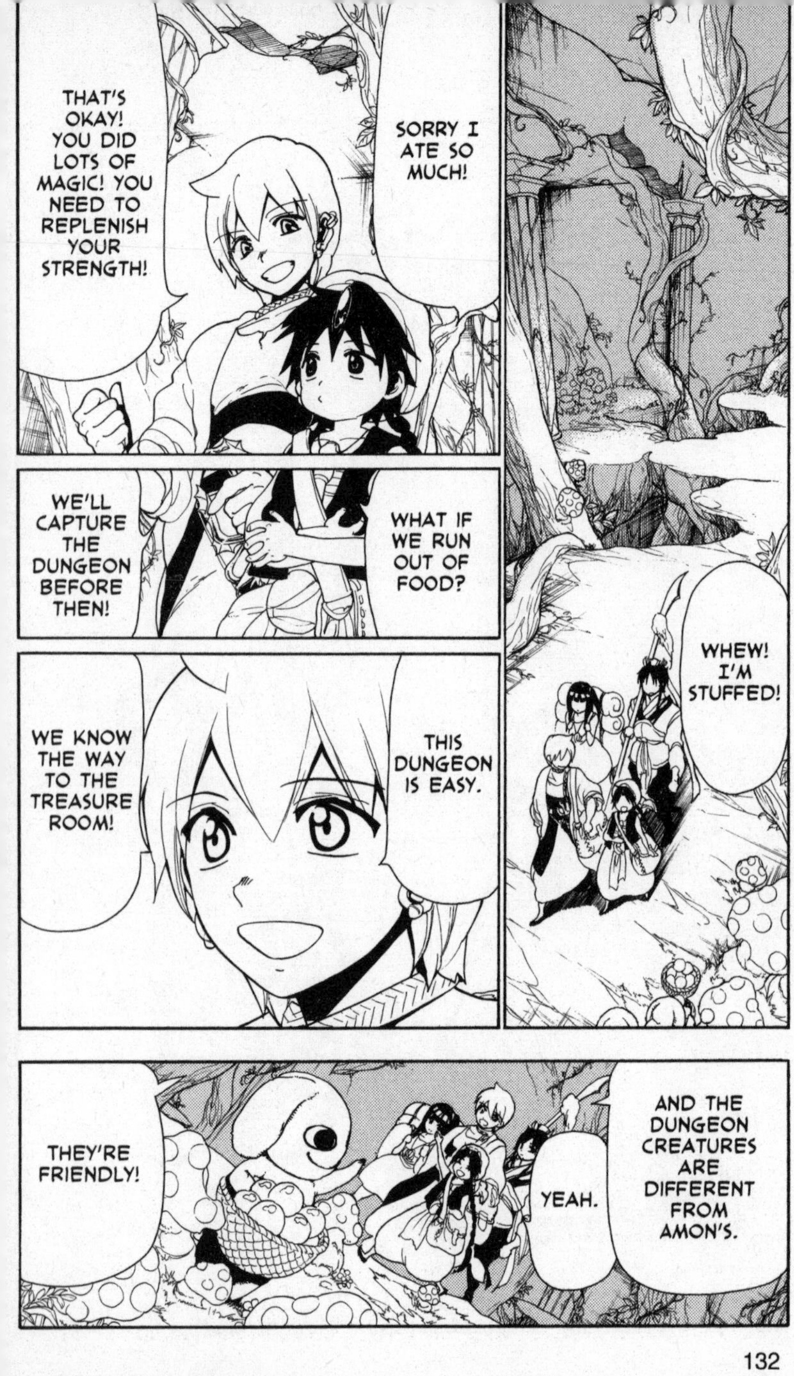
WHEW! I'M STUFFED!
SORRY I ATE SO MUCH!
THAT'S OKAY! YOU DID LOTS OF MAGIC! YOU NEED TO REPLENISH YOUR STRENGTH!
WHAT IF WE RUN OUT OF FOOD?
WE'LL CAPTURE THE DUNGEON BEFORE THEN!
THIS DUNGEON IS EASY.
WE KNOW THE WAY TO THE TREASURE ROOM!
AND THE DUNGEON CREATURES ARE DIFFERENT FROM AMON'S.
YEAH.
THEY'RE FRIENDLY!

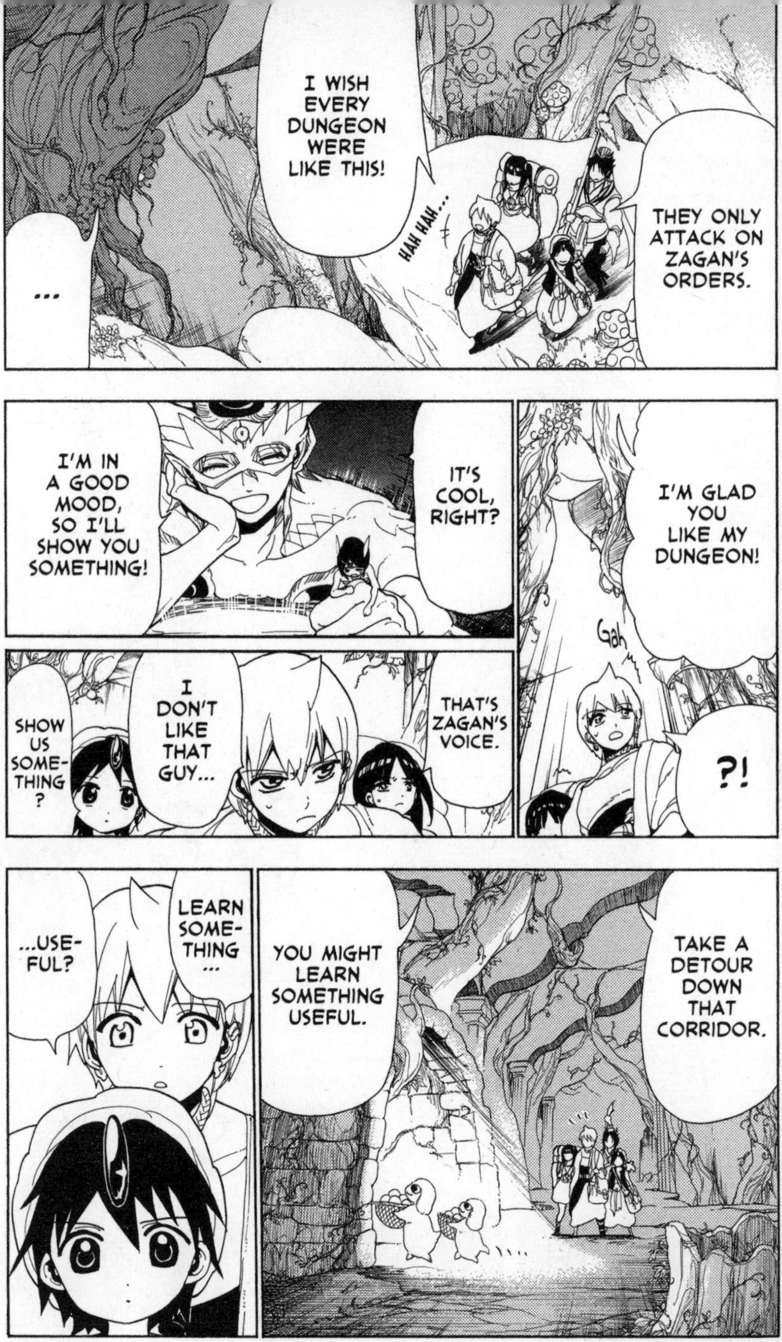
I WISH EVERY DUNGEON WERE LIKE THIS!
THEY ONLY ATTACK ON ZAGAN'S ORDERS.
HAH HAH...
...
I'M GLAD YOU LIKE MY DUNGEON!
Gah
?!
IT'S COOL, RIGHT?
I'M IN A GOOD MOOD, SO I'LL SHOW YOU SOMETHING!
THAT'S ZAGAN'S VOICE.
I DON'T LIKE THAT GUY...
SHOW US SOMETHING?
TAKE A DETOUR DOWN THAT CORRIDOR.
YOU MIGHT LEARN SOMETHING USEFUL.
LEARN SOMETHING...
...USEFUL?

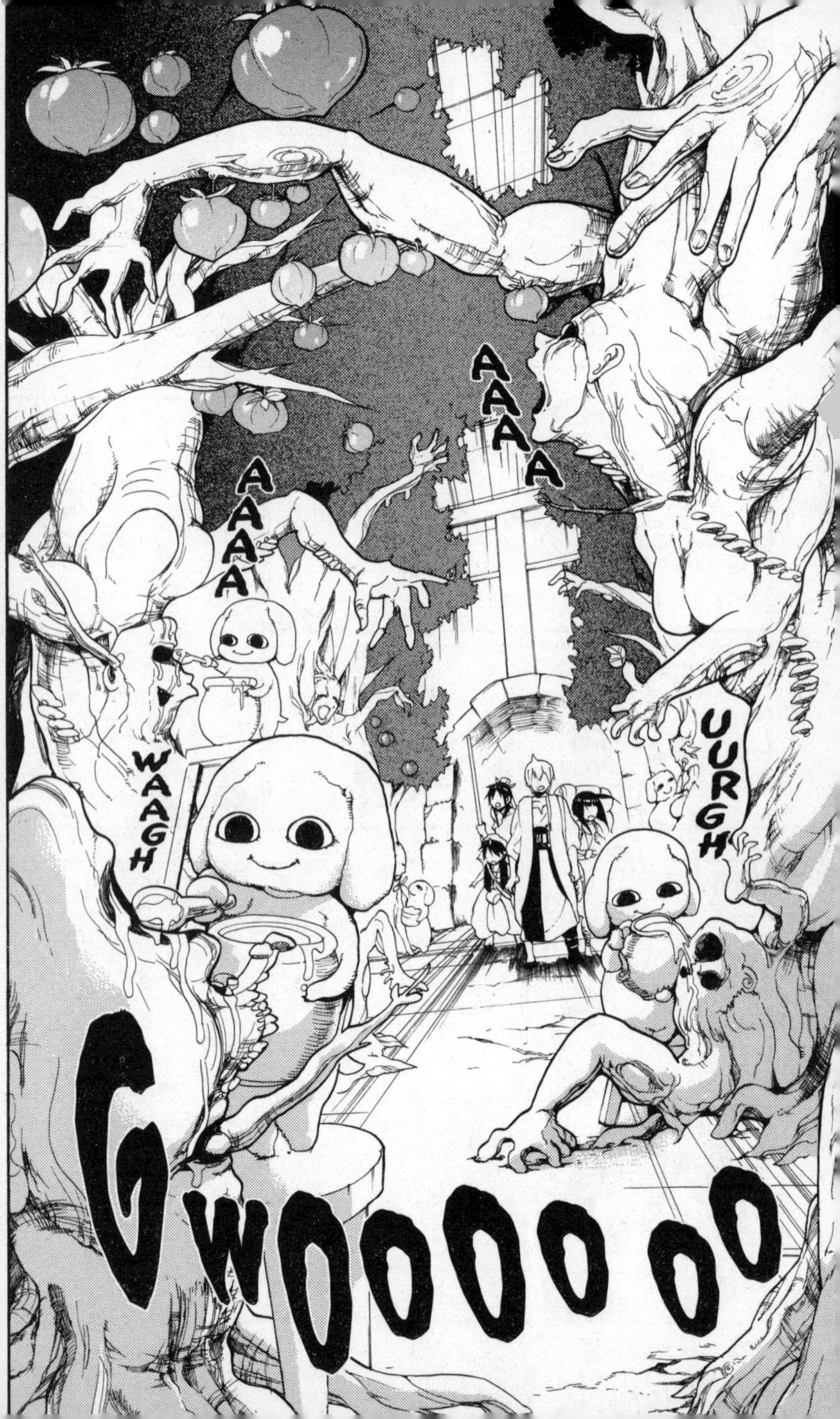
AAAA
AAAA
UURGH
WAAGH
GWOOOOOO

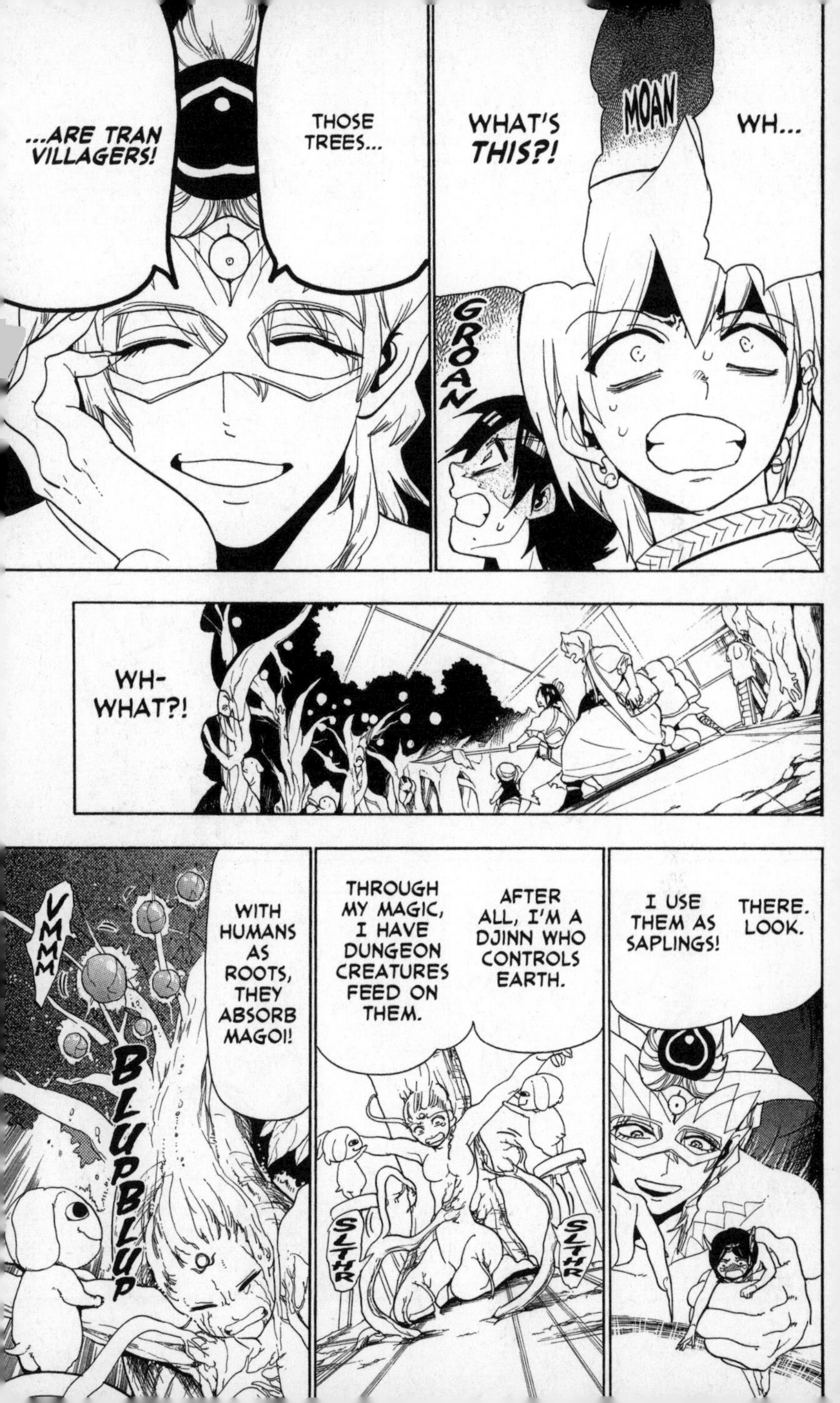
WH...
MOAN
WHAT'S THIS?!
GROAN
THOSE TREES...
...ARE TRAN VILLAGERS!
WH- WHAT?!
THERE. LOOK.
I USE THEM AS SAPLINGS!
AFTER ALL, I'M A DJINN WHO CONTROLS EARTH.
THROUGH MY MAGIC, I HAVE DUNGEON CREATURES FEED ON THEM.
SLTHR
SLTHR
WITH HUMANS AS ROOTS, THEY ABSORB MAGOI!
VMMM
BLUPBLUP

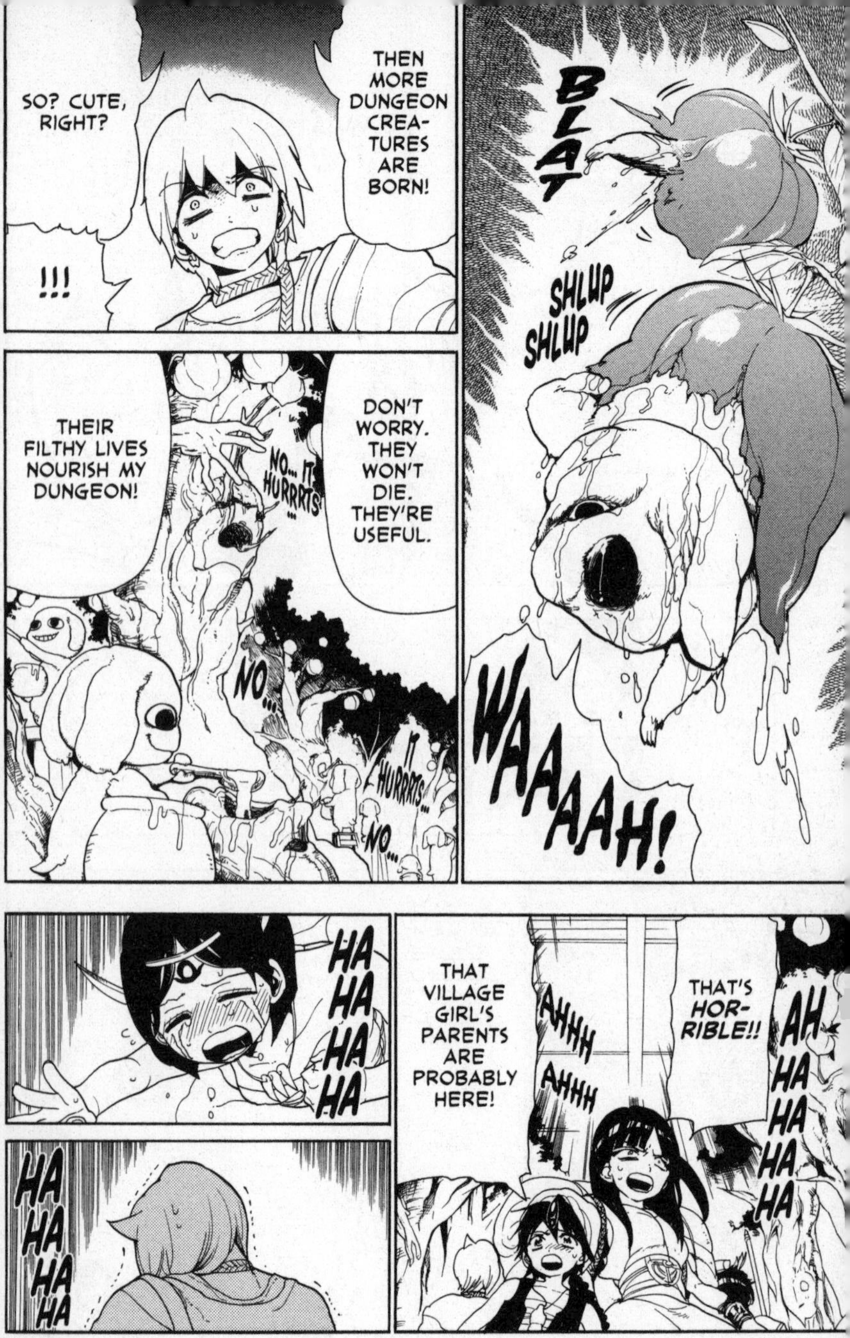
BLAT
SHLUP SHLUP
WAAAAAH!
THEN MORE DUNGEON CREA-TURES ARE BORN!
SO? CUTE, RIGHT?
!!!
DON'T WORRY. THEY WON'T DIE. THEY'RE USEFUL.
NO... IT HURRRTS...
THEIR FILTHY LIVES NOURISH MY DUNGEON!
NO...
IT HURRRTS... NO...
AH HA HA HA HA HA
THAT'S HOR-RIBLE!!
AHHH AHHH
THAT VILLAGE GIRL'S PARENTS ARE PROBABLY HERE!
HA HA HA HA HA
HA HA HA HA HA HA

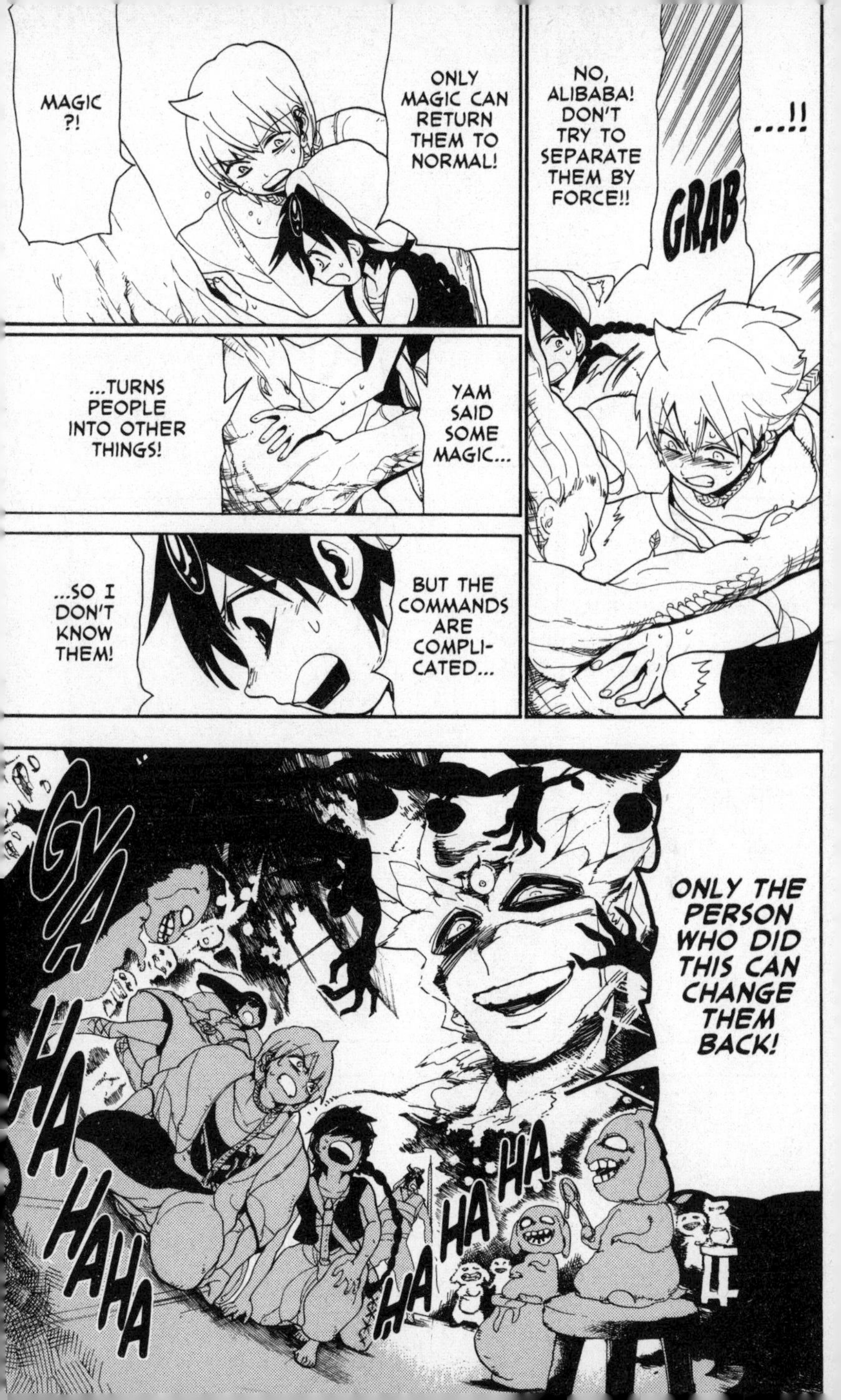
NO, ALIBABA! DON'T TRY TO SEPARATE THEM BY FORCE!!
GRAB
...!!
ONLY MAGIC CAN RETURN THEM TO NORMAL!
MAGIC ?!
YAM SAID SOME MAGIC...
...TURNS PEOPLE INTO OTHER THINGS!
BUT THE COMMANDS ARE COMPLICATED...
...SO I DON'T KNOW THEM!
ONLY THE PERSON WHO DID THIS CAN CHANGE THEM BACK!
HA HA HA
GYAHAHAHAHA

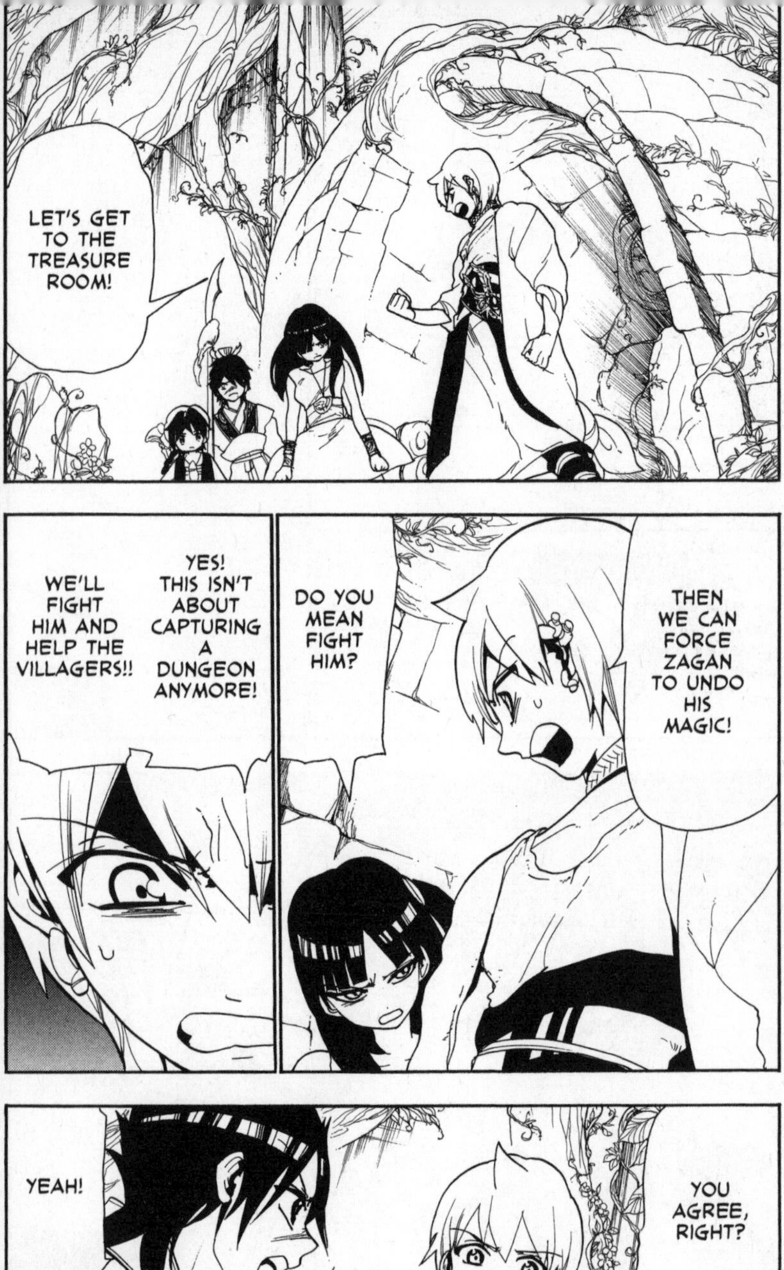
LET'S GET TO THE TREASURE ROOM!
THEN WE CAN FORCE ZAGAN TO UNDO HIS MAGIC!
DO YOU MEAN FIGHT HIM?
YES! THIS ISN'T ABOUT CAPTURING A DUNGEON ANYMORE!
WE'LL FIGHT HIM AND HELP THE VILLAGERS!!
YOU AGREE, RIGHT?
YEAH!

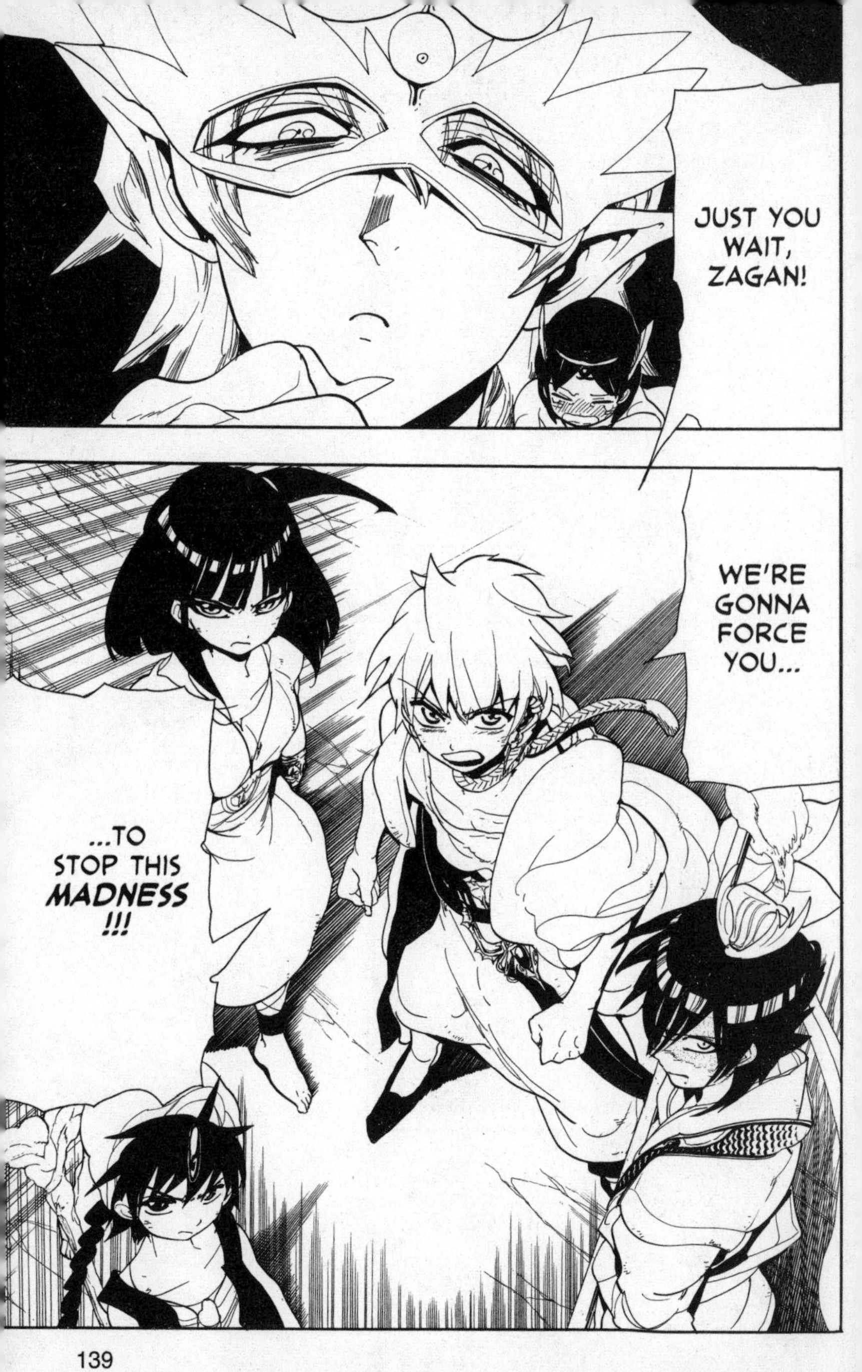
JUST YOU WAIT, ZAGAN!
WE'RE GONNA FORCE YOU...
...TO STOP THIS MADNESS!!!

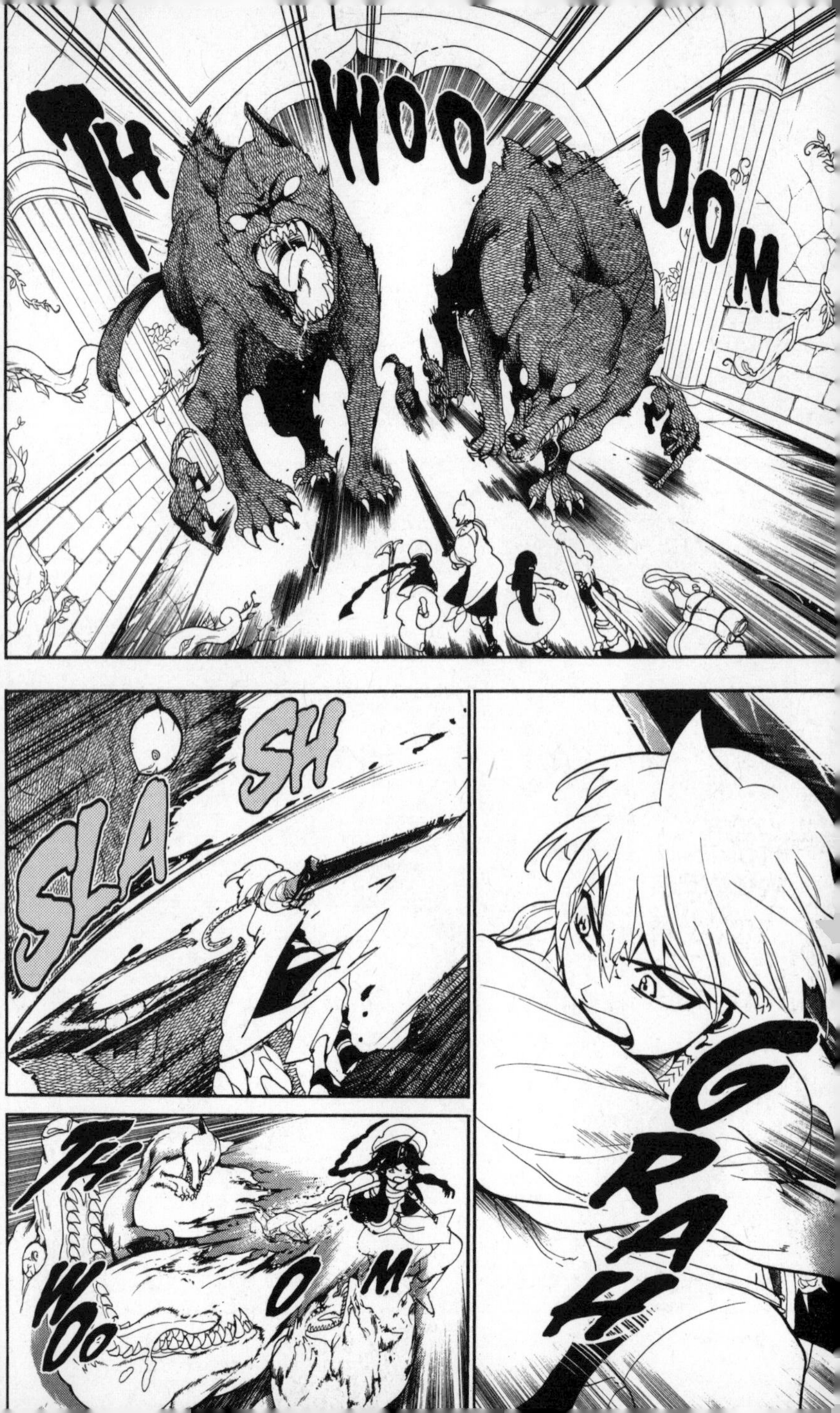
THWOOOOM
GRAAH
SLASH
THWOOOM

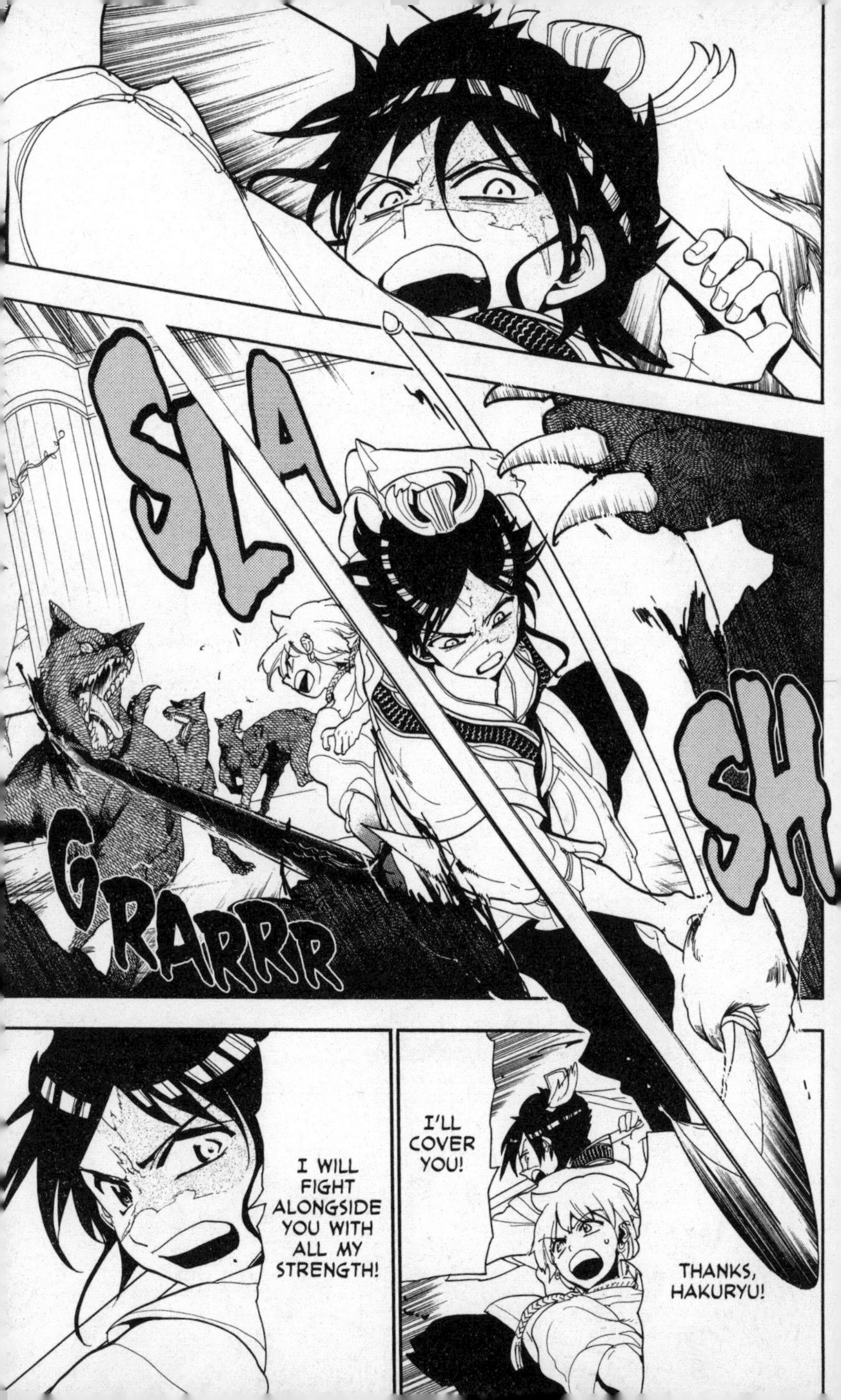
SLA
SH
GRARRR
I'LL COVER YOU!
THANKS, HAKURYU!
I WILL FIGHT ALONGSIDE YOU WITH ALL MY STRENGTH!

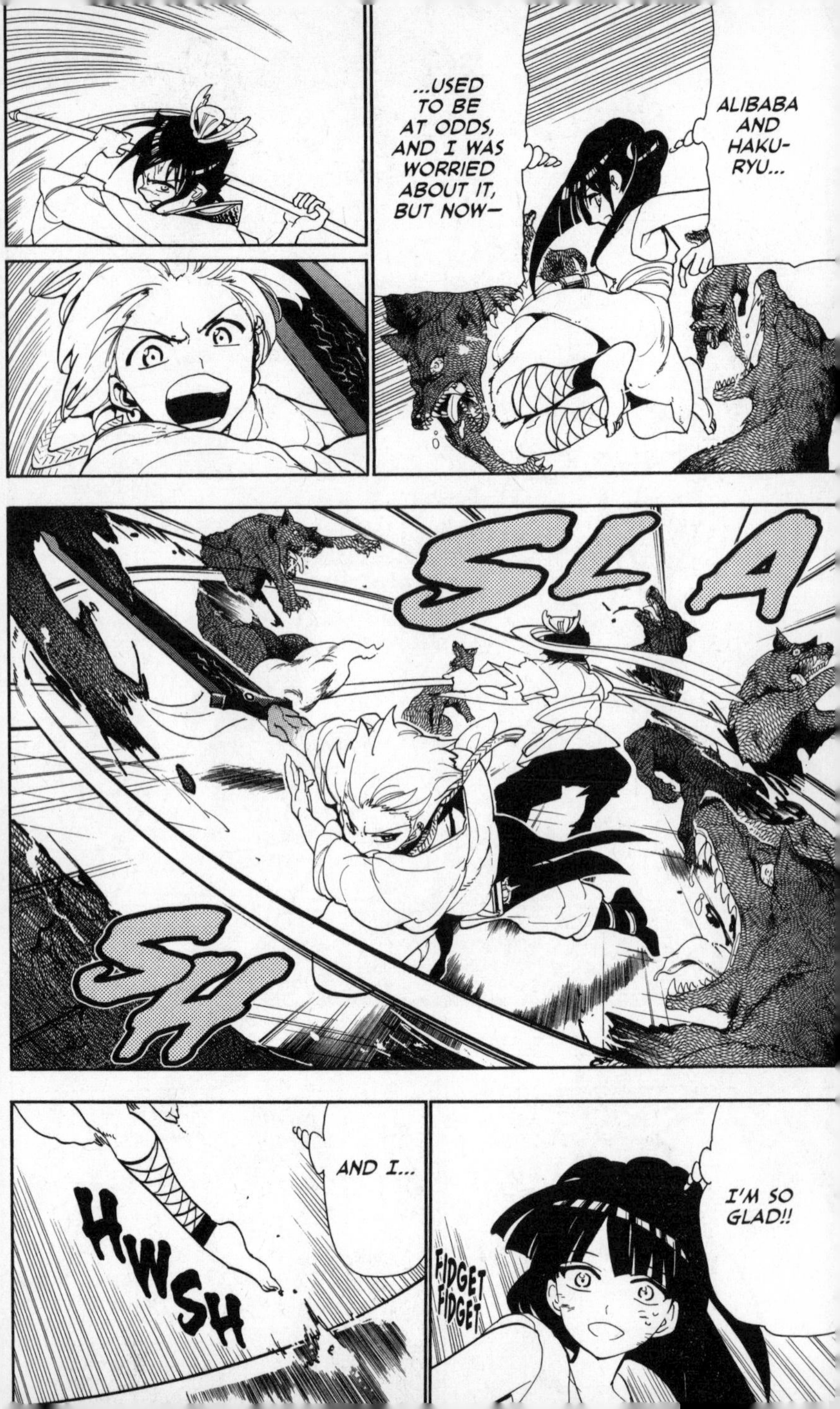
ALIBABA AND HAKU-RYU...
...USED TO BE AT ODDS, AND I WAS WORRIED ABOUT IT, BUT NOW—
SLA
SH
I'M SO GLAD!!
FIDGET FIDGET
AND I...
HWSH

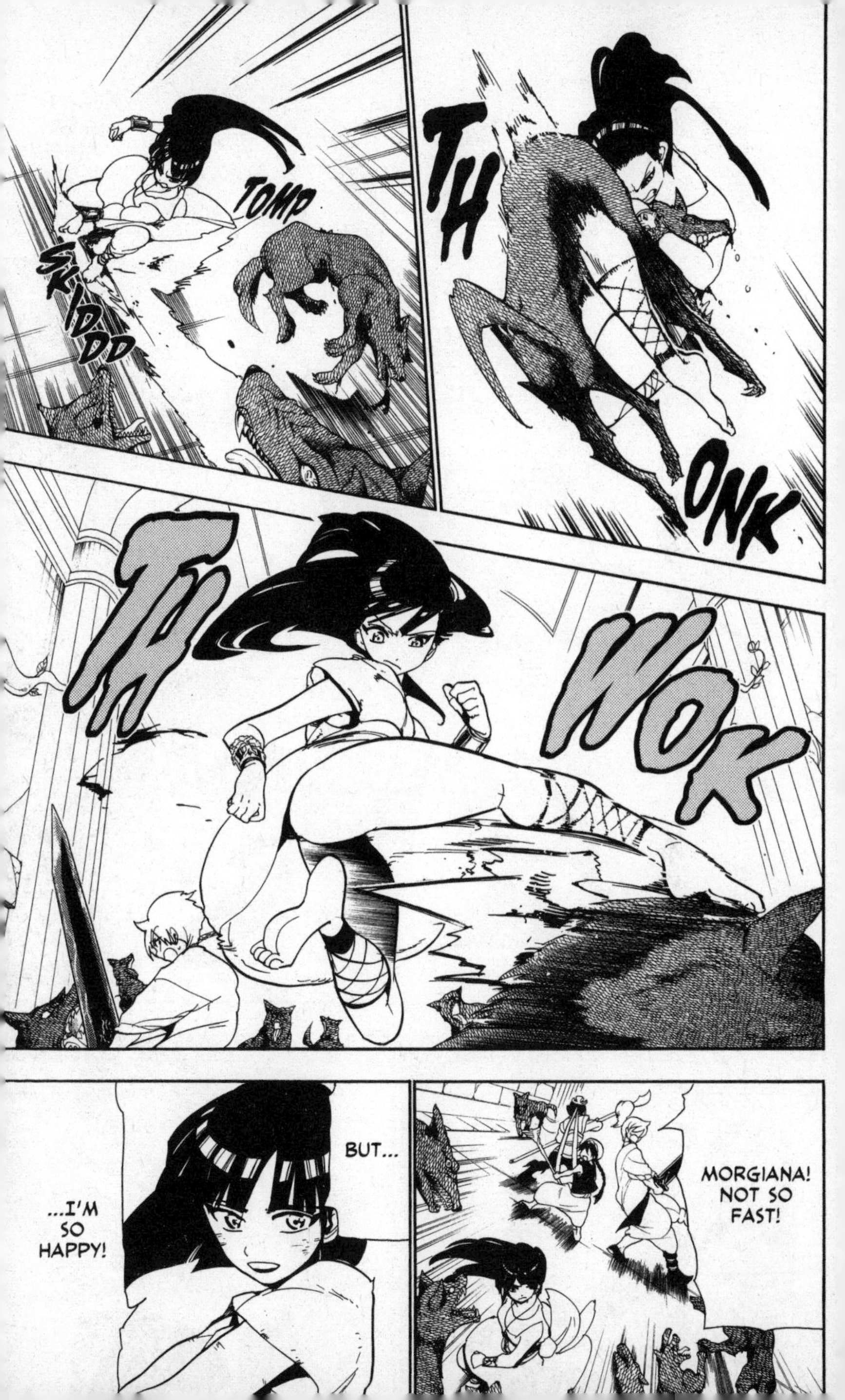
TH
ONK
TOMP
SKIDDD
TH
WOK
MORGIANA! NOT SO FAST!
BUT...
...I'M SO HAPPY!

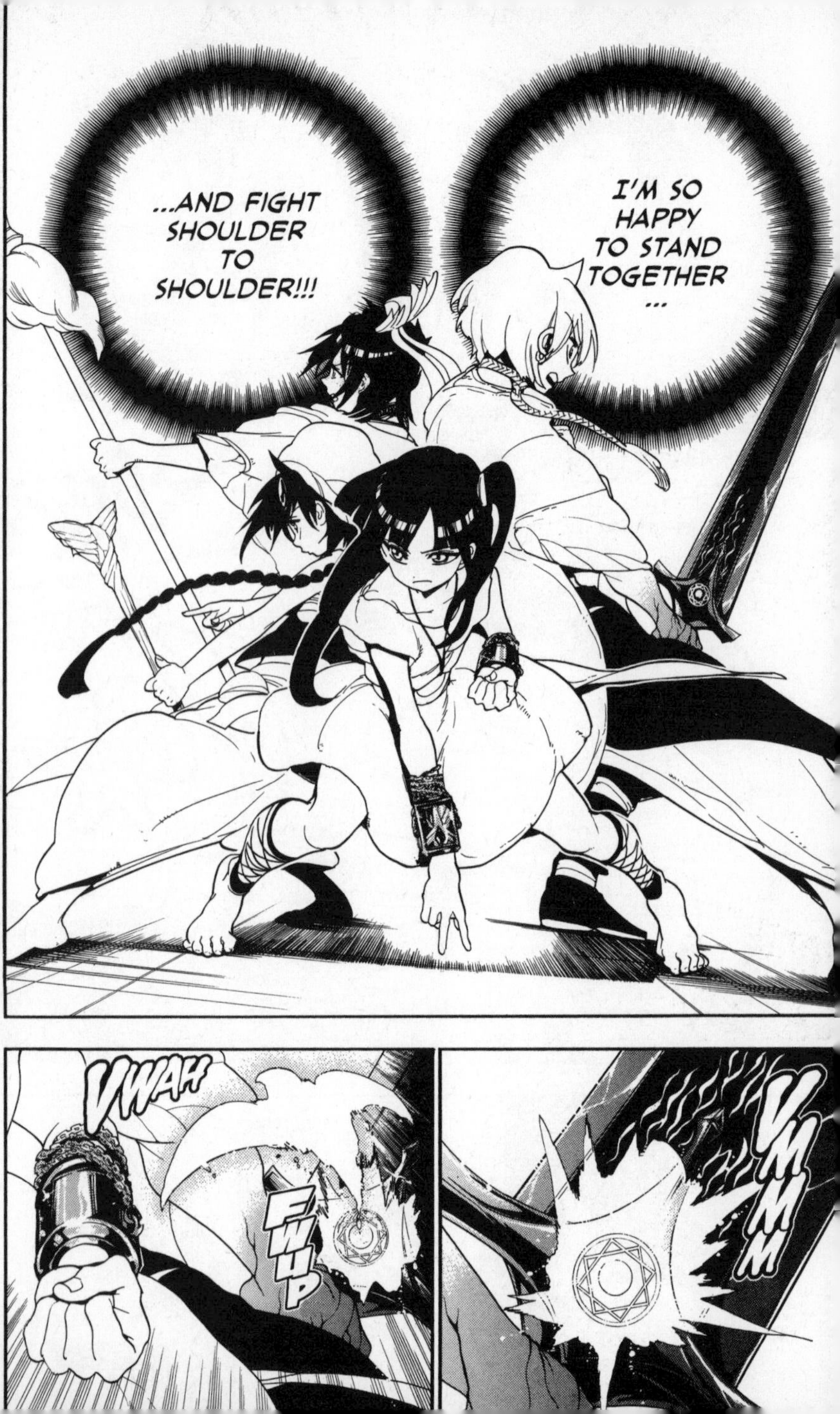
I'M SO HAPPY TO STAND TOGETHER ...
...AND FIGHT SHOULDER TO SHOULDER!!!
VMMM
VWAH
FWUP

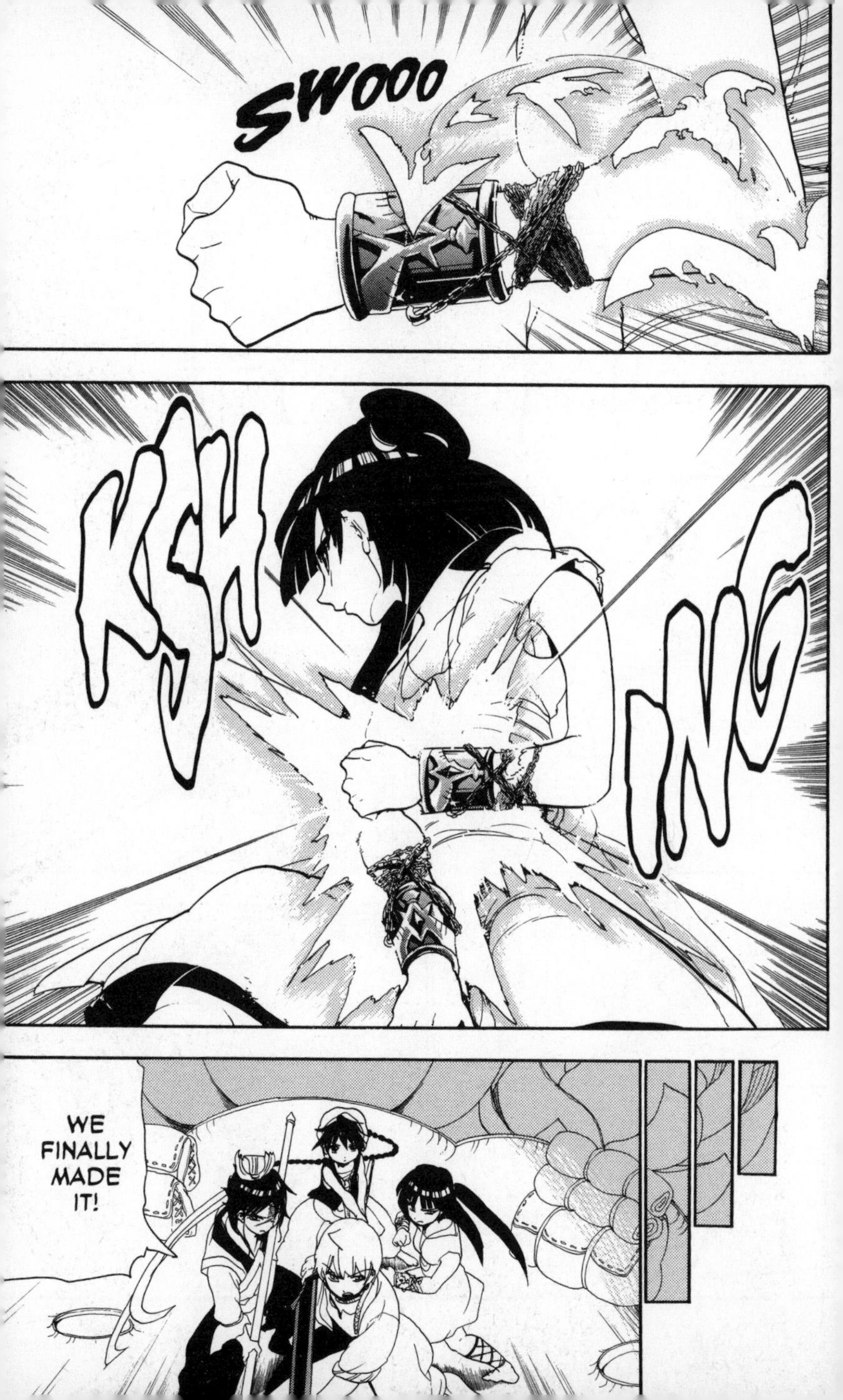
SWOOO
KSH
ING
WE FINALLY MADE IT!

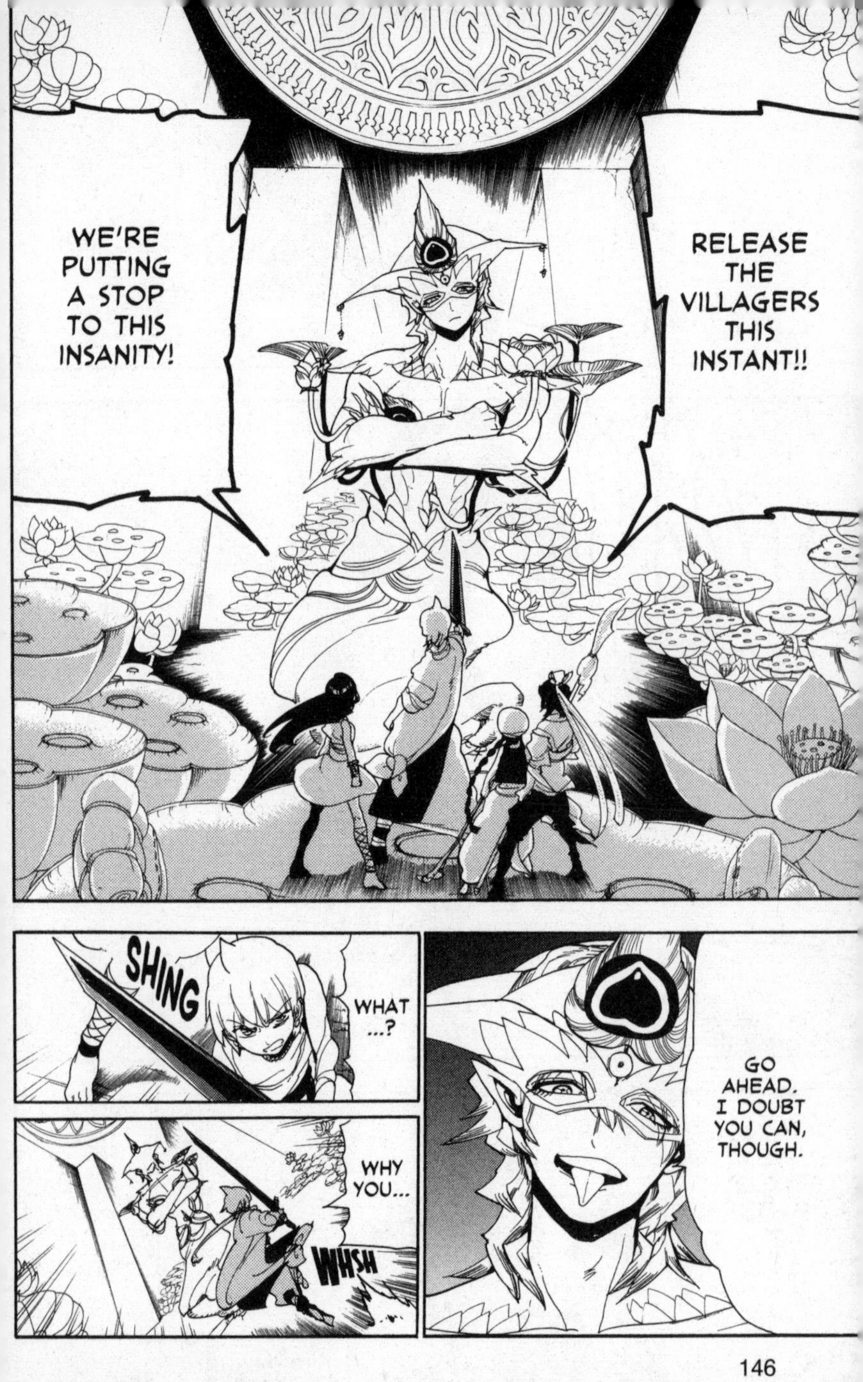
RELEASE THE VILLAGERS THIS INSTANT!!
WE'RE PUTTING A STOP TO THIS INSANITY!
GO AHEAD. I DOUBT YOU CAN, THOUGH.
SHING
WHAT ...?
WHY YOU...
WHSH

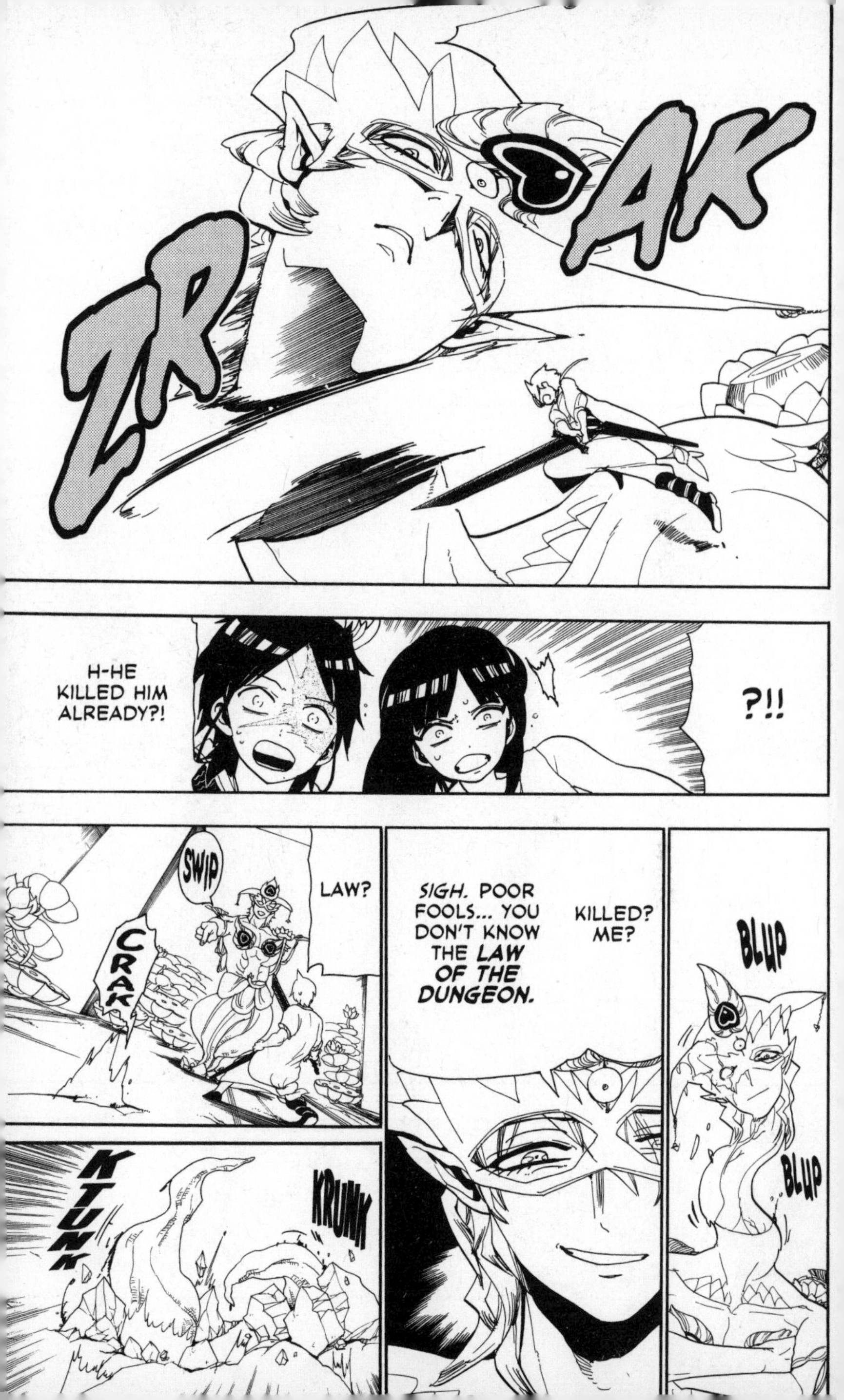
ZR
AK
?!!
H-HE KILLED HIM ALREADY?!
BLUP
BLUP
KILLED? ME?
SIGH. POOR FOOLS... YOU DON'T KNOW THE *LAW OF THE DUNGEON.*
LAW?
SWIP
CRAK
KRUNK
KTUNK

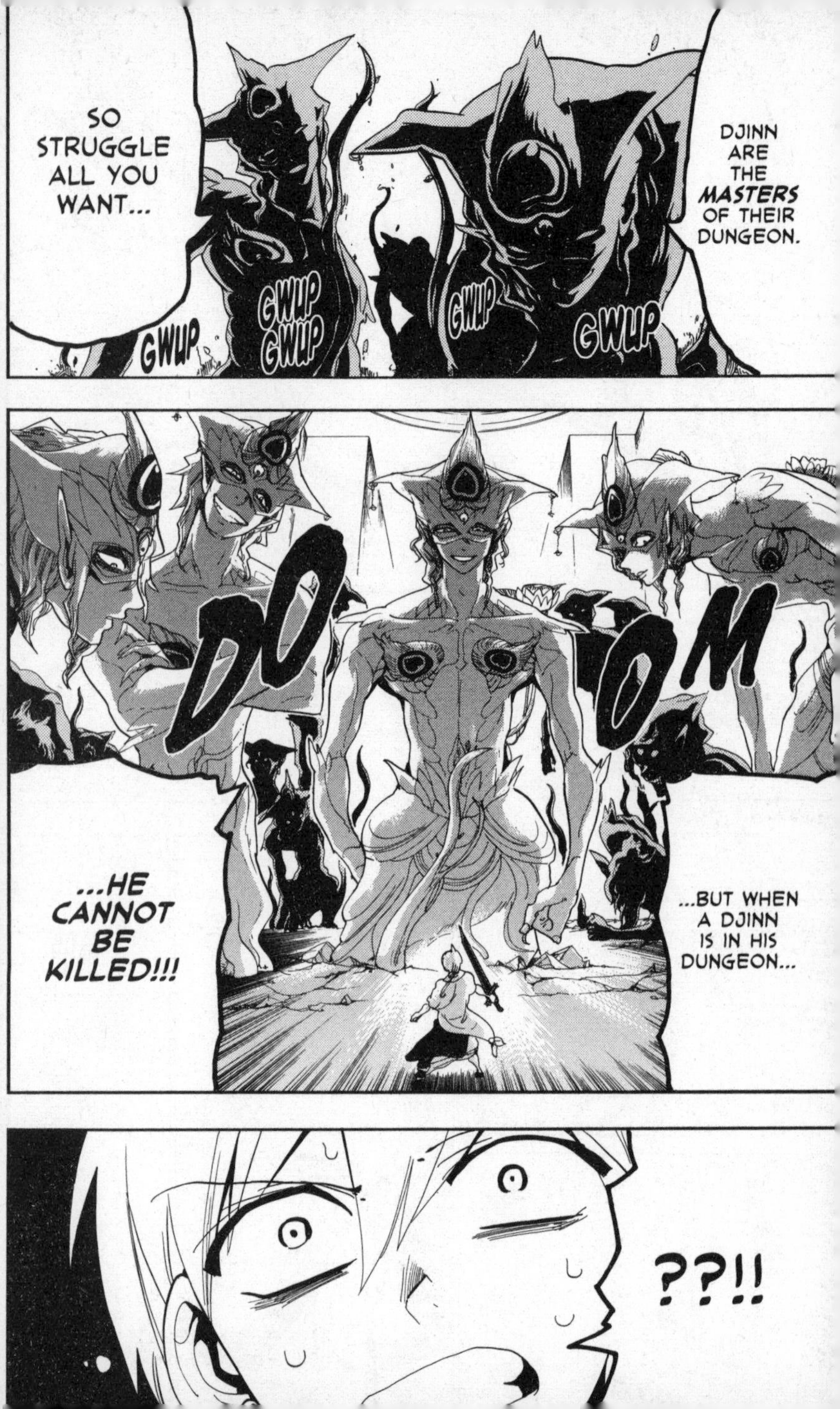

DJINN ARE THE *MASTERS* OF THEIR DUNGEON.
SO STRUGGLE ALL YOU WANT...
GWUP
GWUP
GWUP GWUP
GWUP
...BUT WHEN A DJINN IS IN HIS DUNGEON...
...HE CANNOT BE KILLED!!!
DOOM
??!!

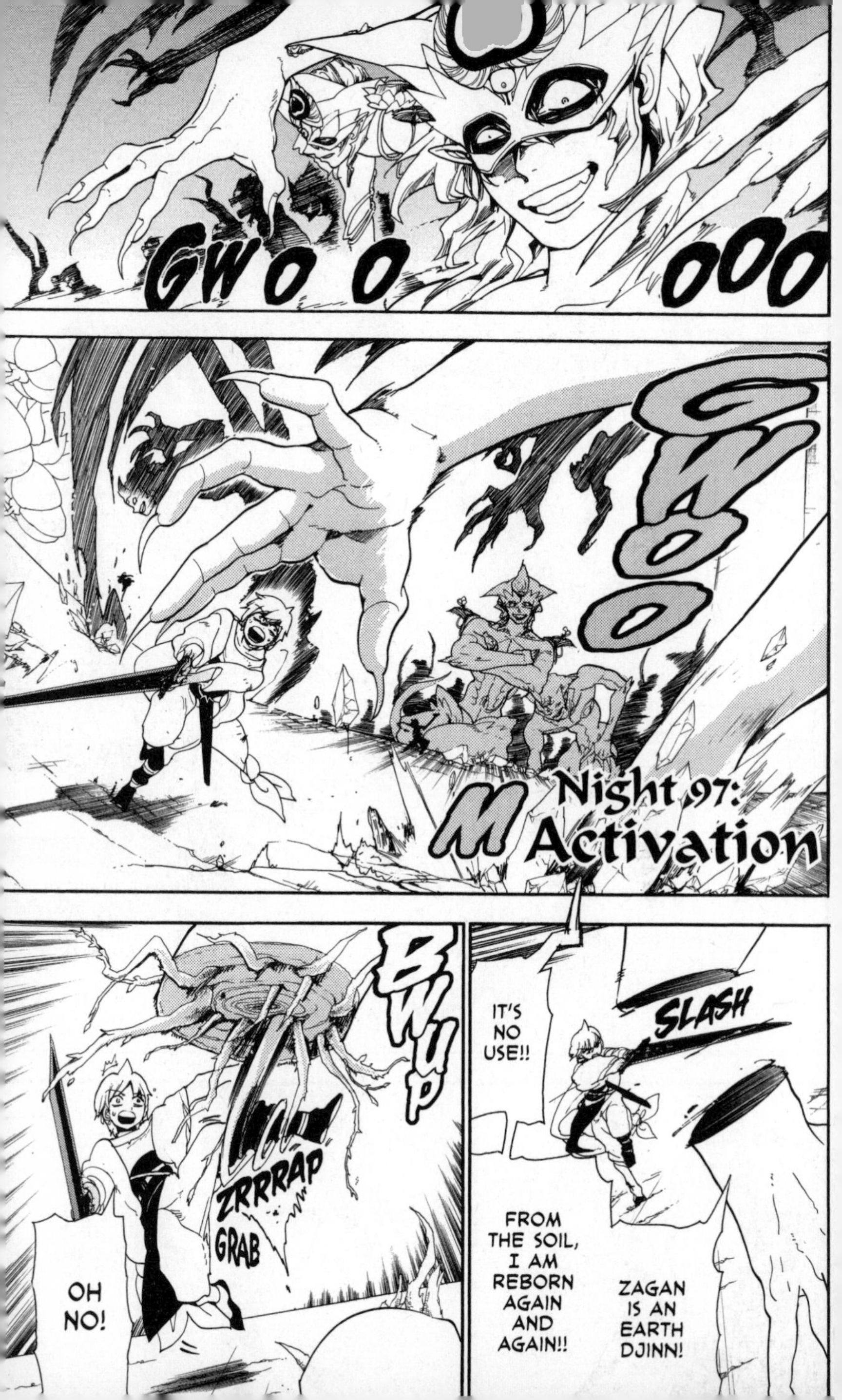
GWO O OOO
GWOOO
Night 97:
Activation
M
SLASH
IT'S NO USE!!
FROM THE SOIL, I AM REBORN AGAIN AND AGAIN!!
ZAGAN IS AN EARTH DJINN!
BWUP
ZRRRAP
GRAB
OH NO!

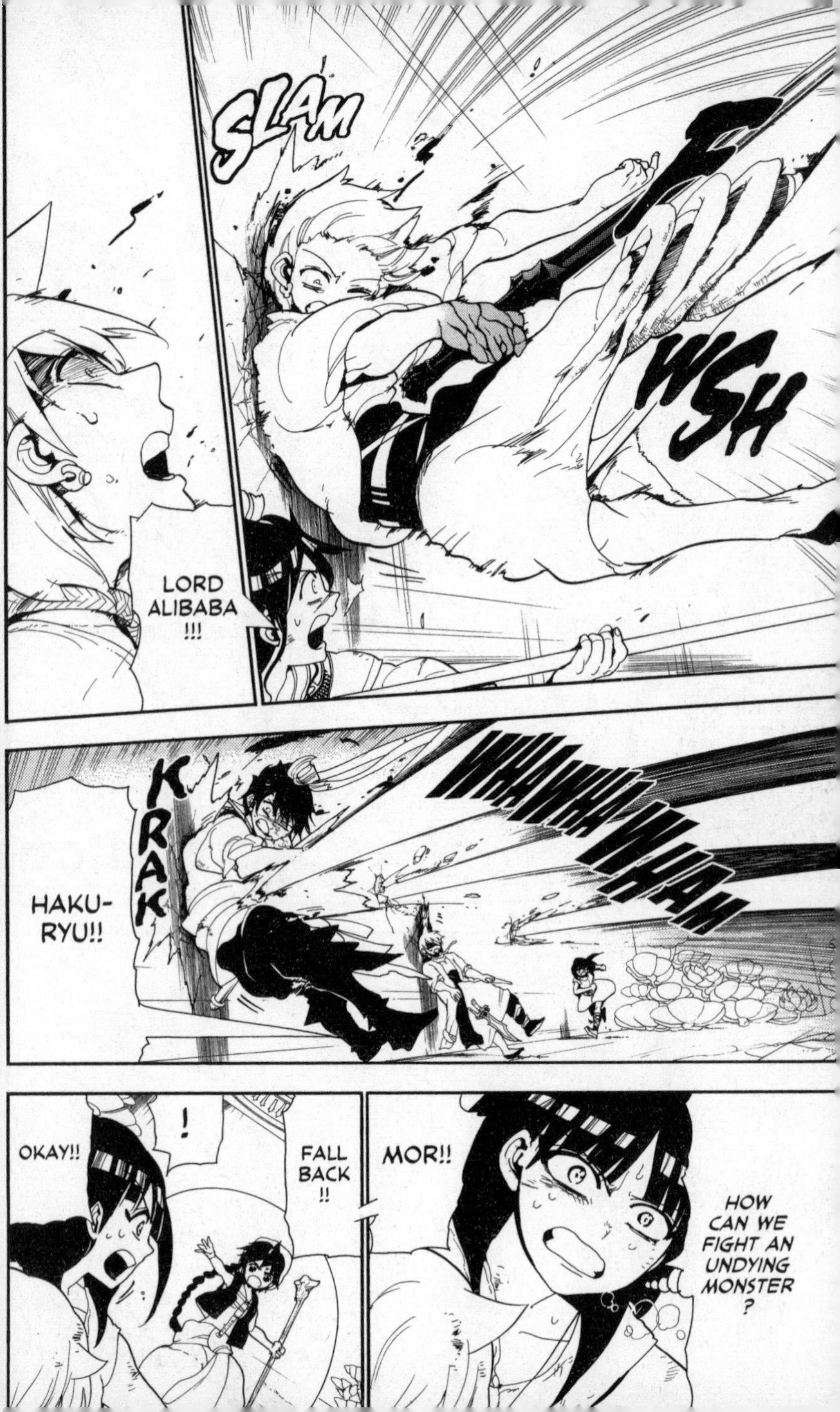
SLAM
WSH
LORD ALIBABA!!!
WHAWHAWHAM
KRAK
HAKU-RYU!!
HOW CAN WE FIGHT AN UNDYING MONSTER?
MOR!!
FALL BACK!!
!
OKAY!!

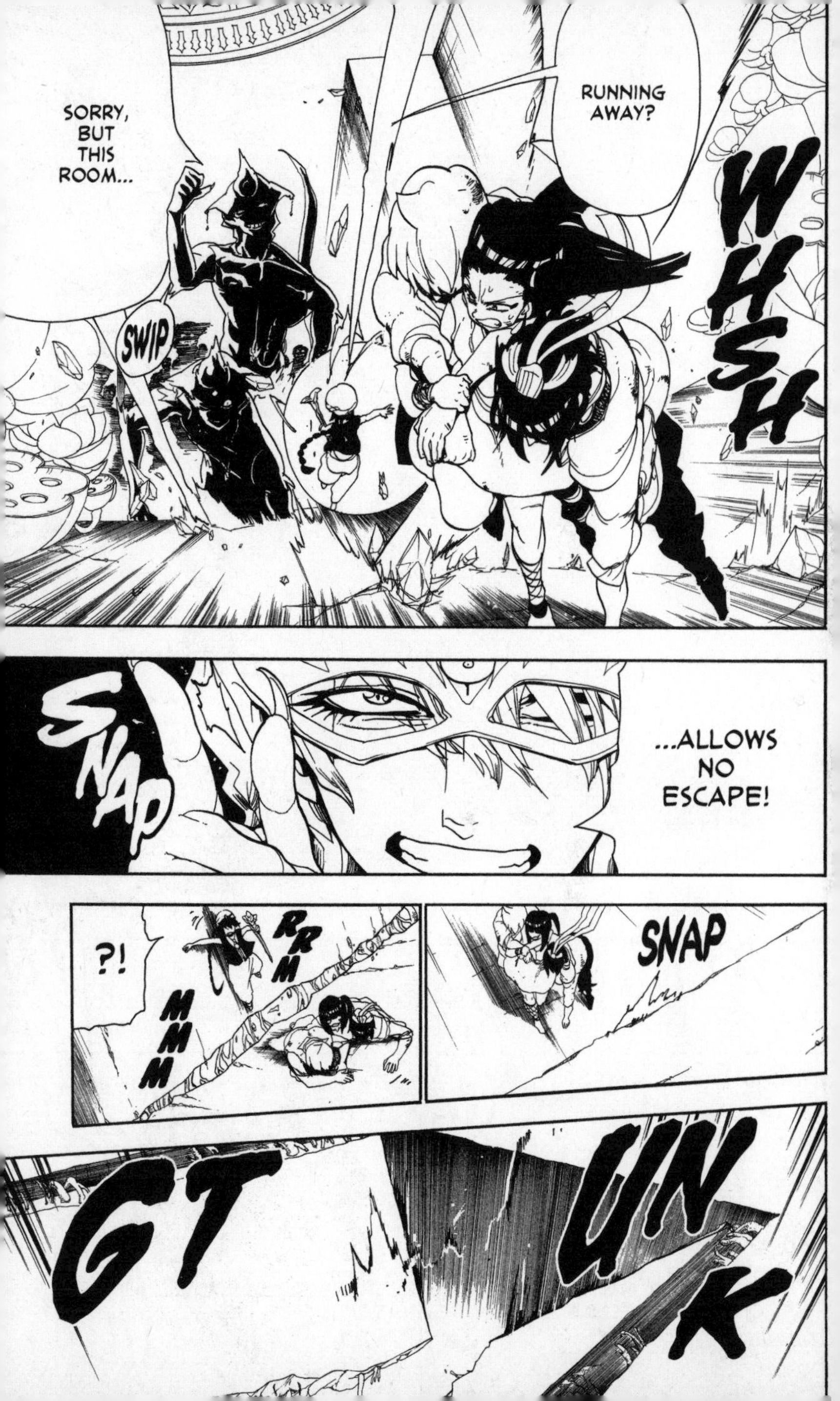
RUNNING AWAY?
WHSH
SORRY, BUT THIS ROOM...
SWIP
...ALLOWS NO ESCAPE!
SNAP
SNAP
RRMMMM
?!
GTUNK

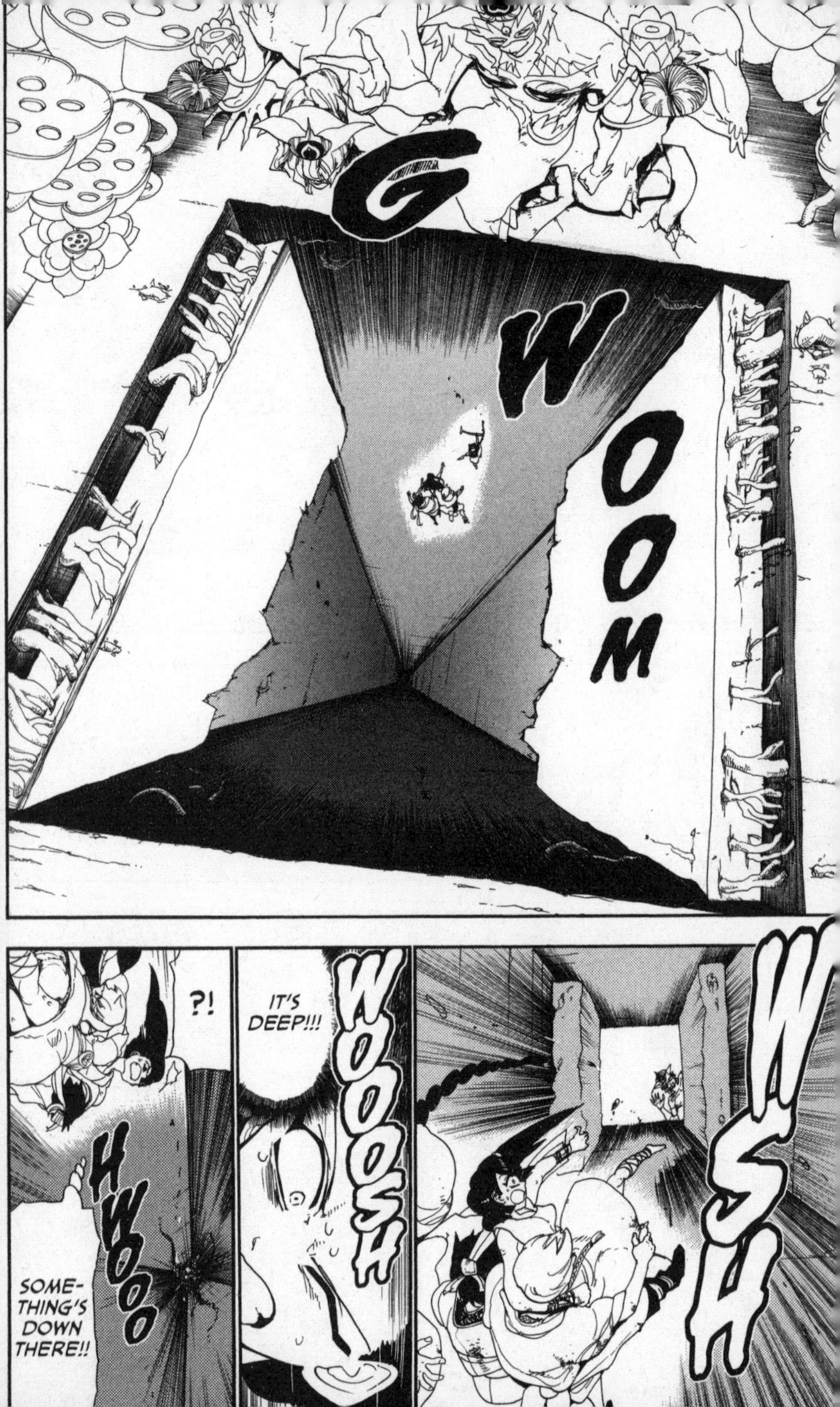
G
WOOM
WSH
WOOOSH
IT'S DEEP!!!
?!
HWOOO
SOME-THING'S DOWN THERE!!

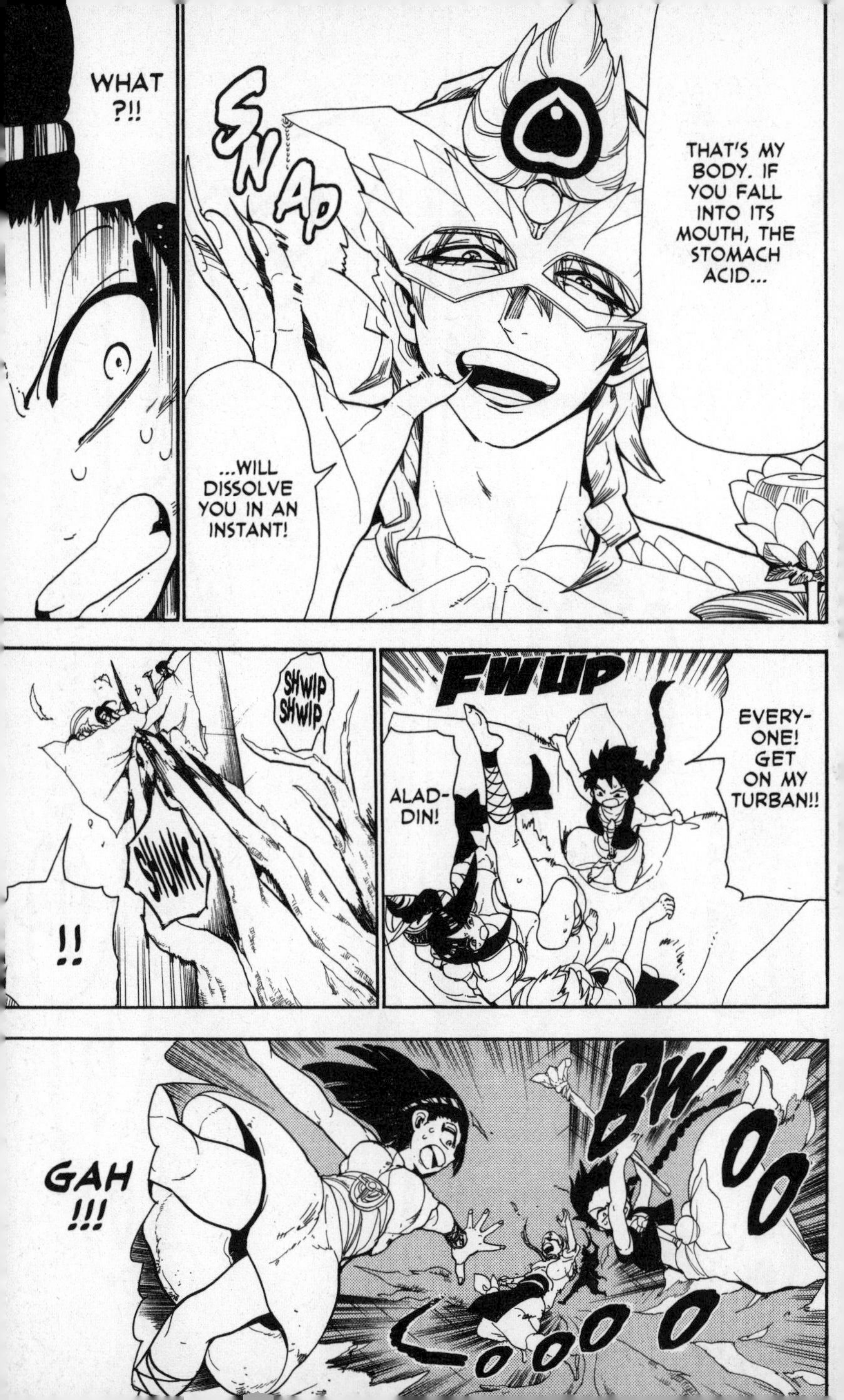
SNAP
THAT'S MY BODY. IF YOU FALL INTO ITS MOUTH, THE STOMACH ACID...
...WILL DISSOLVE YOU IN AN INSTANT!
WHAT ?!!
FWUP
EVERY-ONE! GET ON MY TURBAN!!
ALAD-DIN!
SHWIP SHWIP
SHUNK
!!
BWOO
GAH !!!
OOOOO

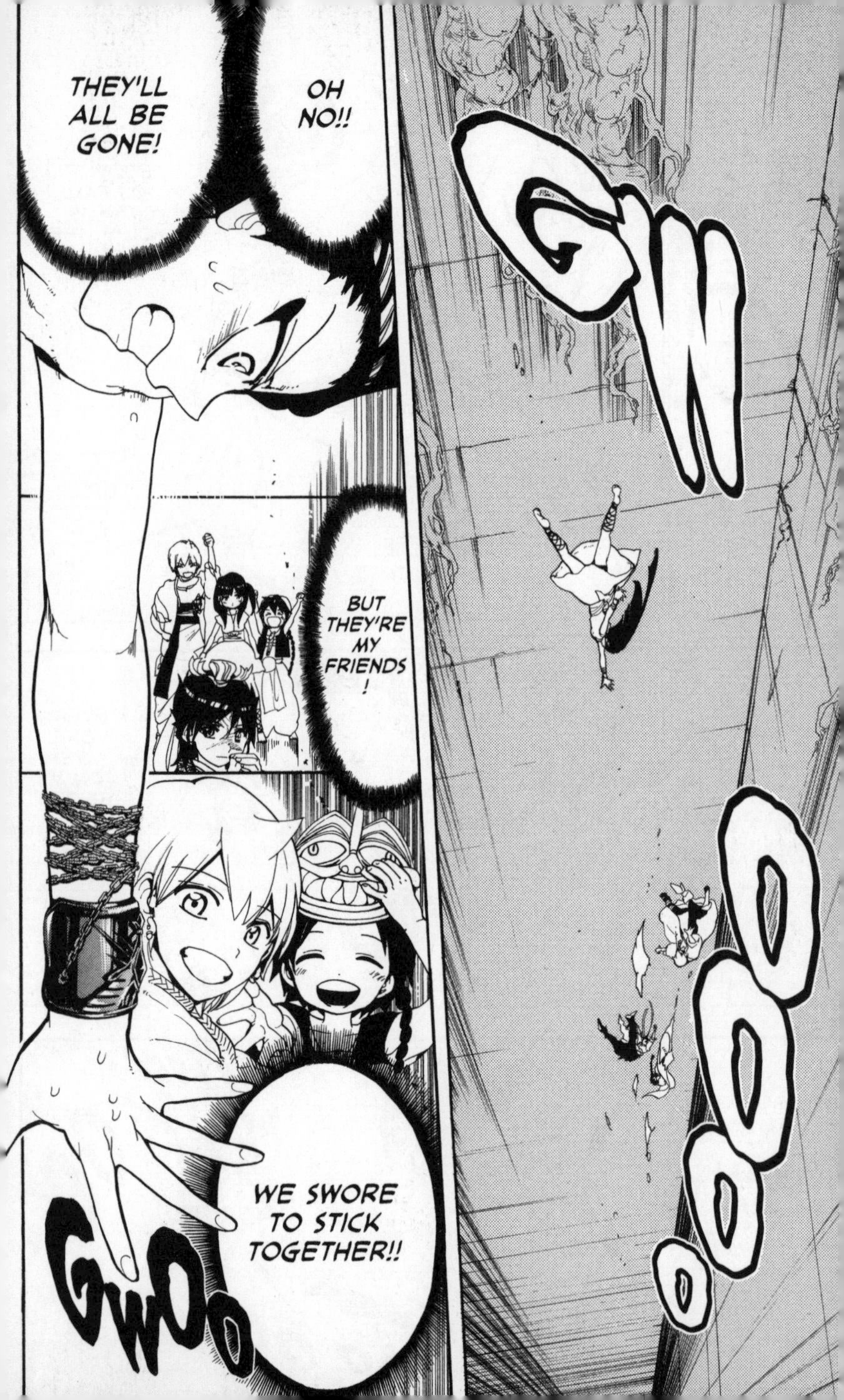
GW
OOOOOO
OH NO!!
THEY'LL ALL BE GONE!
BUT THEY'RE MY FRIENDS!
WE SWORE TO STICK TOGETHER!!
GWOO

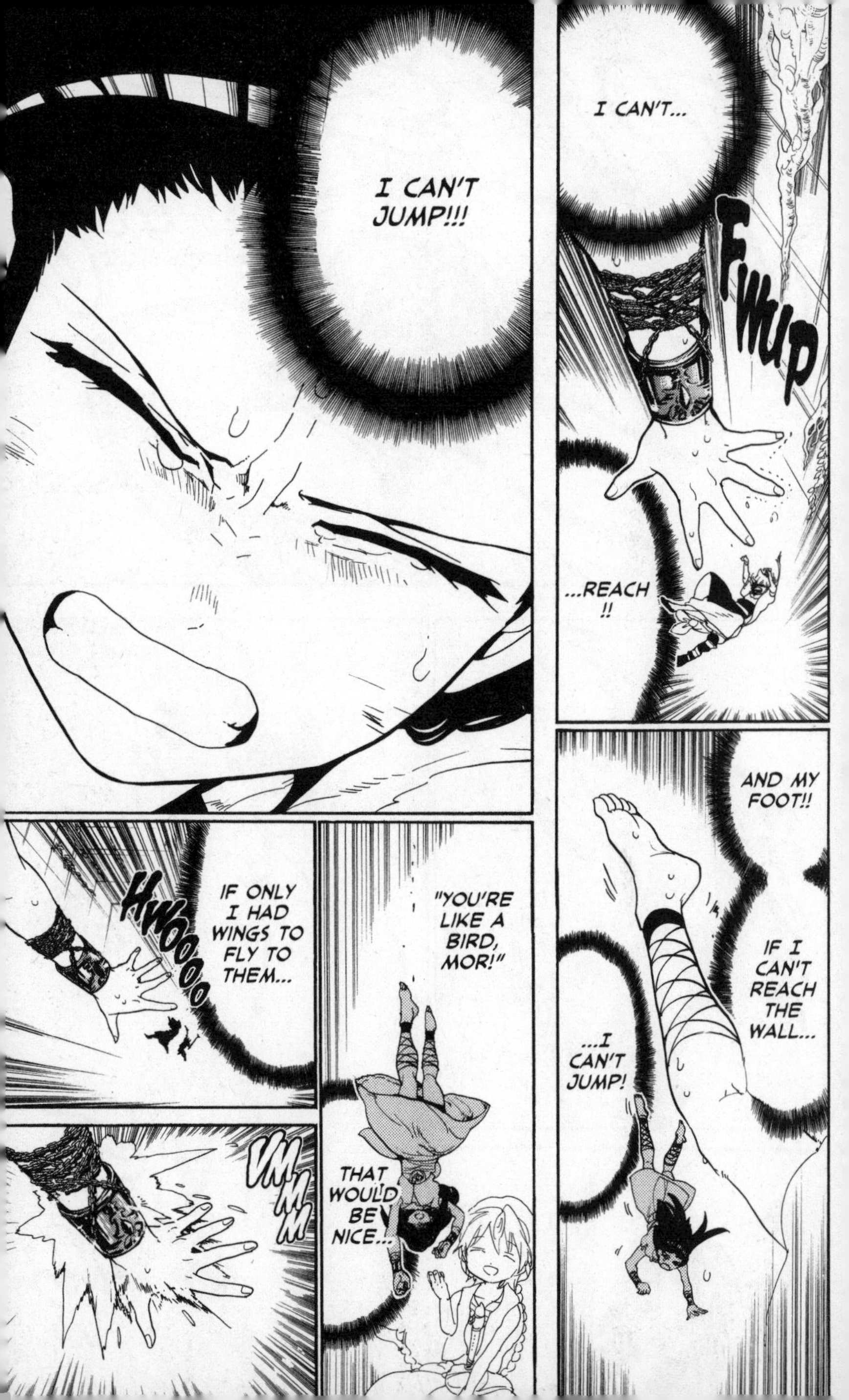
I CAN'T...
FWUP
...REACH!!
AND MY FOOT!!
IF I CAN'T REACH THE WALL...
...I CAN'T JUMP!
I CAN'T JUMP!!!
"YOU'RE LIKE A BIRD, MOR!"
THAT WOULD BE NICE...
IF ONLY I HAD WINGS TO FLY TO THEM...
HWOOOOO
VMMM

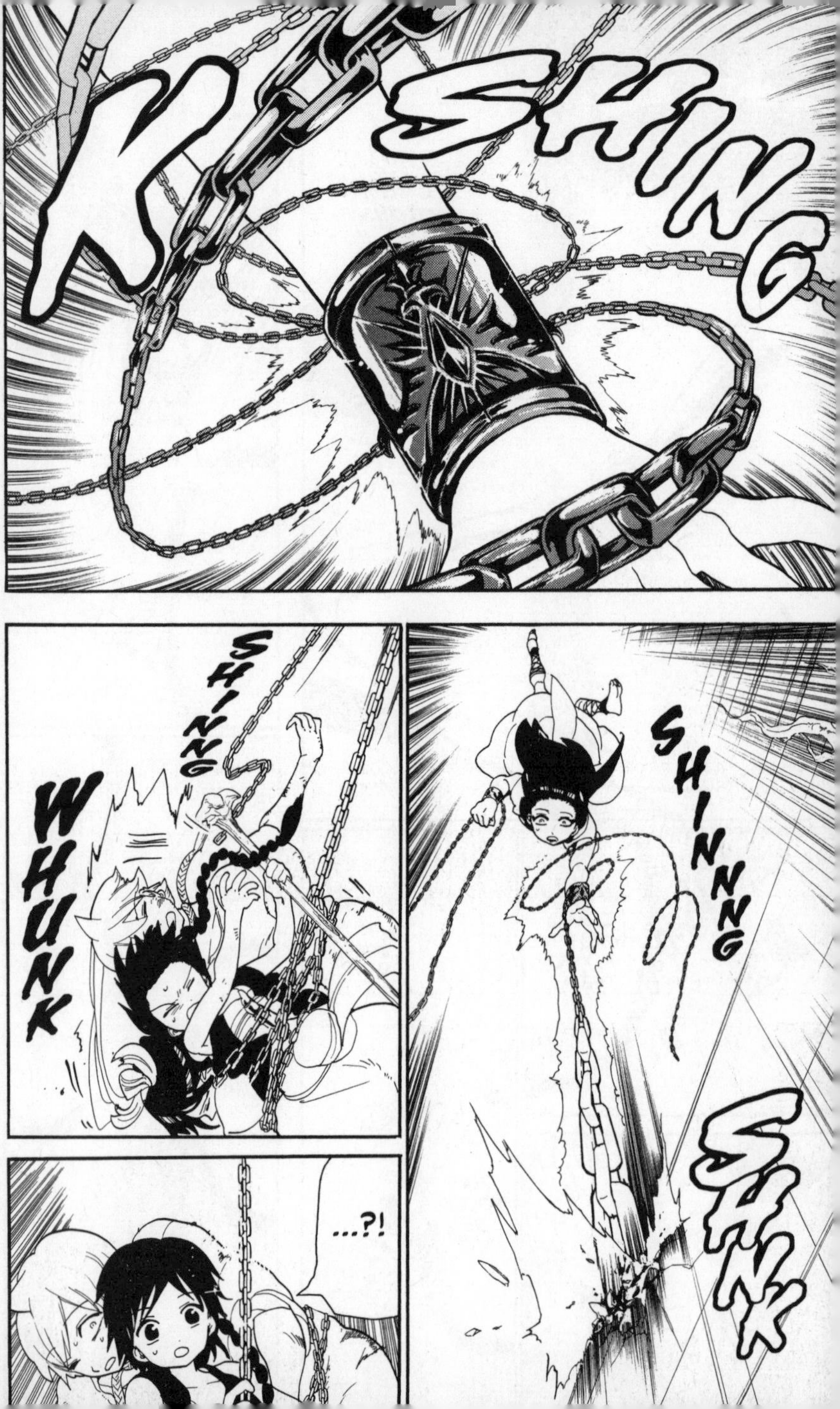
KSHING
SHINNNG
SHANK
SHINNG
WHUNK
...?!

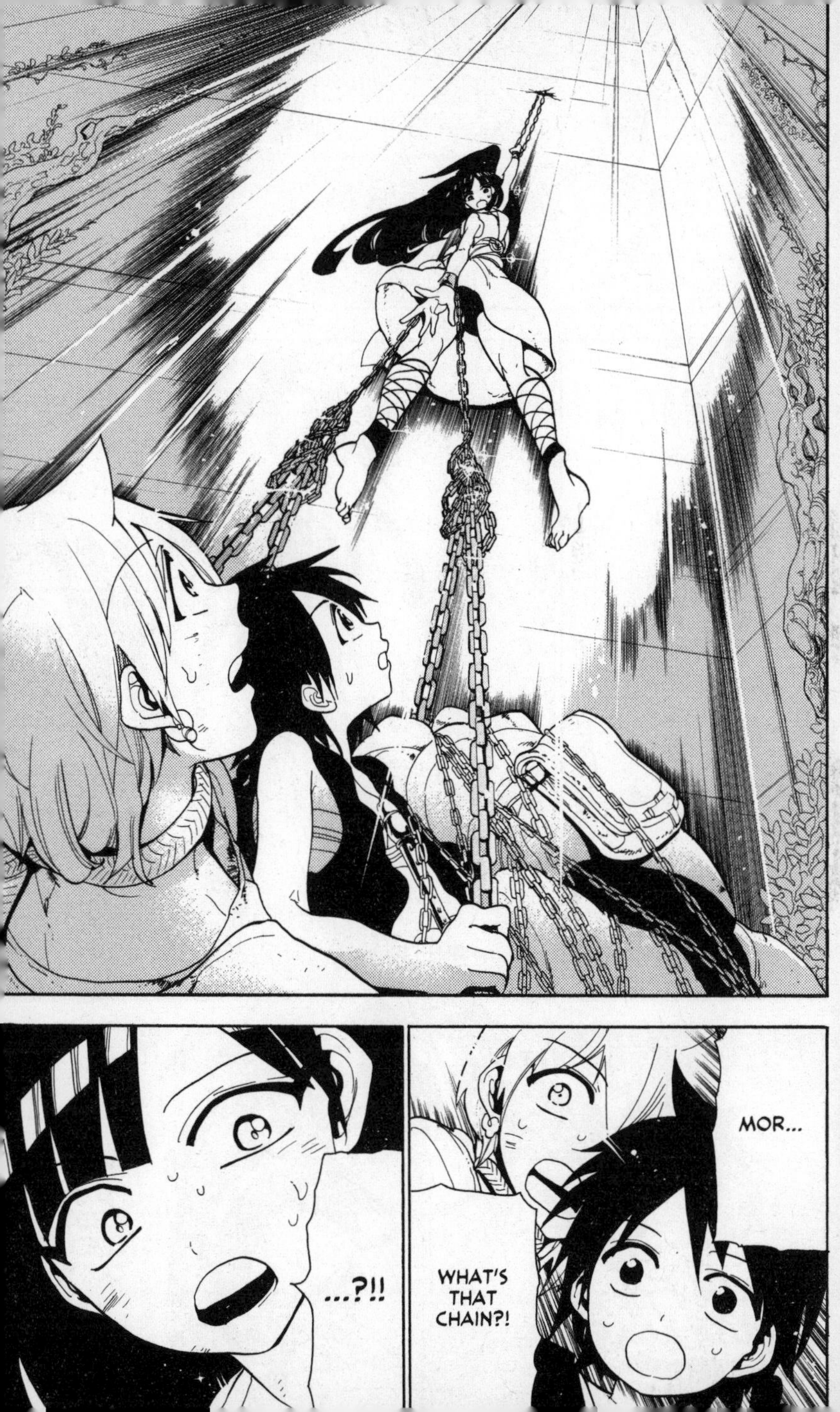
MOR...
WHAT'S THAT CHAIN?!
...?!!

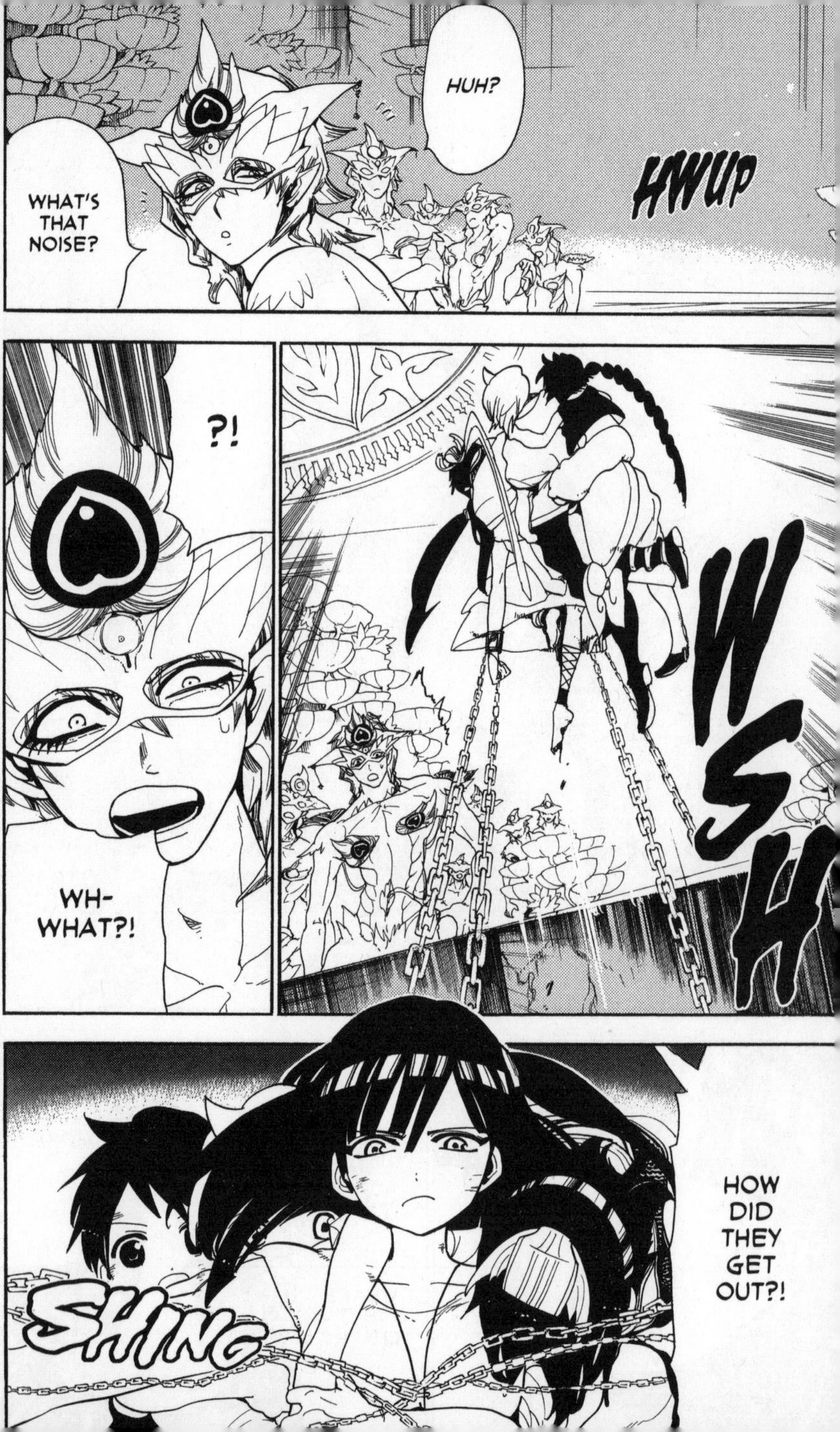

HUH?
HWUP
WHAT'S THAT NOISE?
WSH
?!
WH- WHAT?!
HOW DID THEY GET OUT?!
SHING

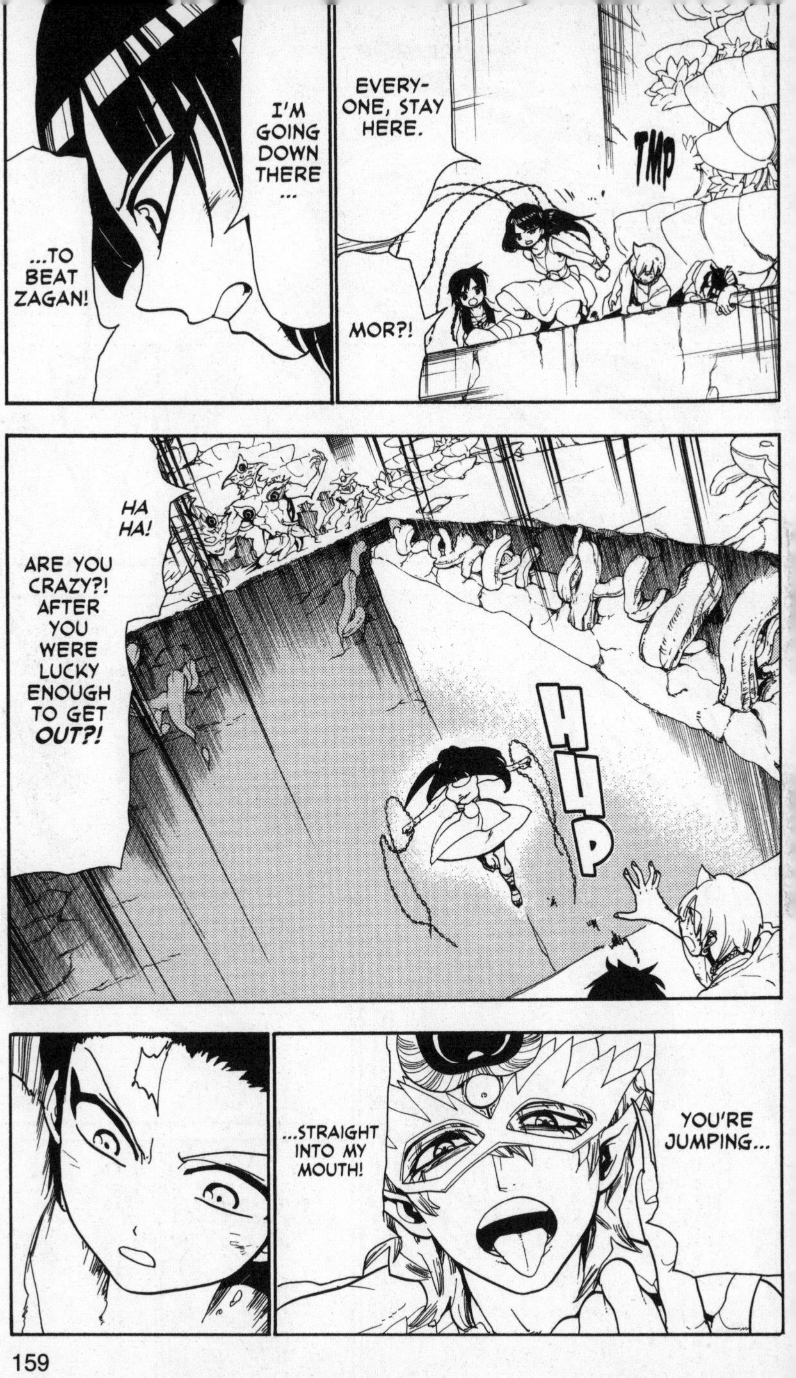

EVERY-
ONE, STAY
HERE.
TMP
MOR?!
I'M
GOING
DOWN
THERE
...
...TO
BEAT
ZAGAN!
HUP
HA
HA!
ARE YOU
CRAZY?!
AFTER
YOU
WERE
LUCKY
ENOUGH
TO GET
*OUT?!*
YOU'RE
JUMPING...
...STRAIGHT
INTO MY
MOUTH!

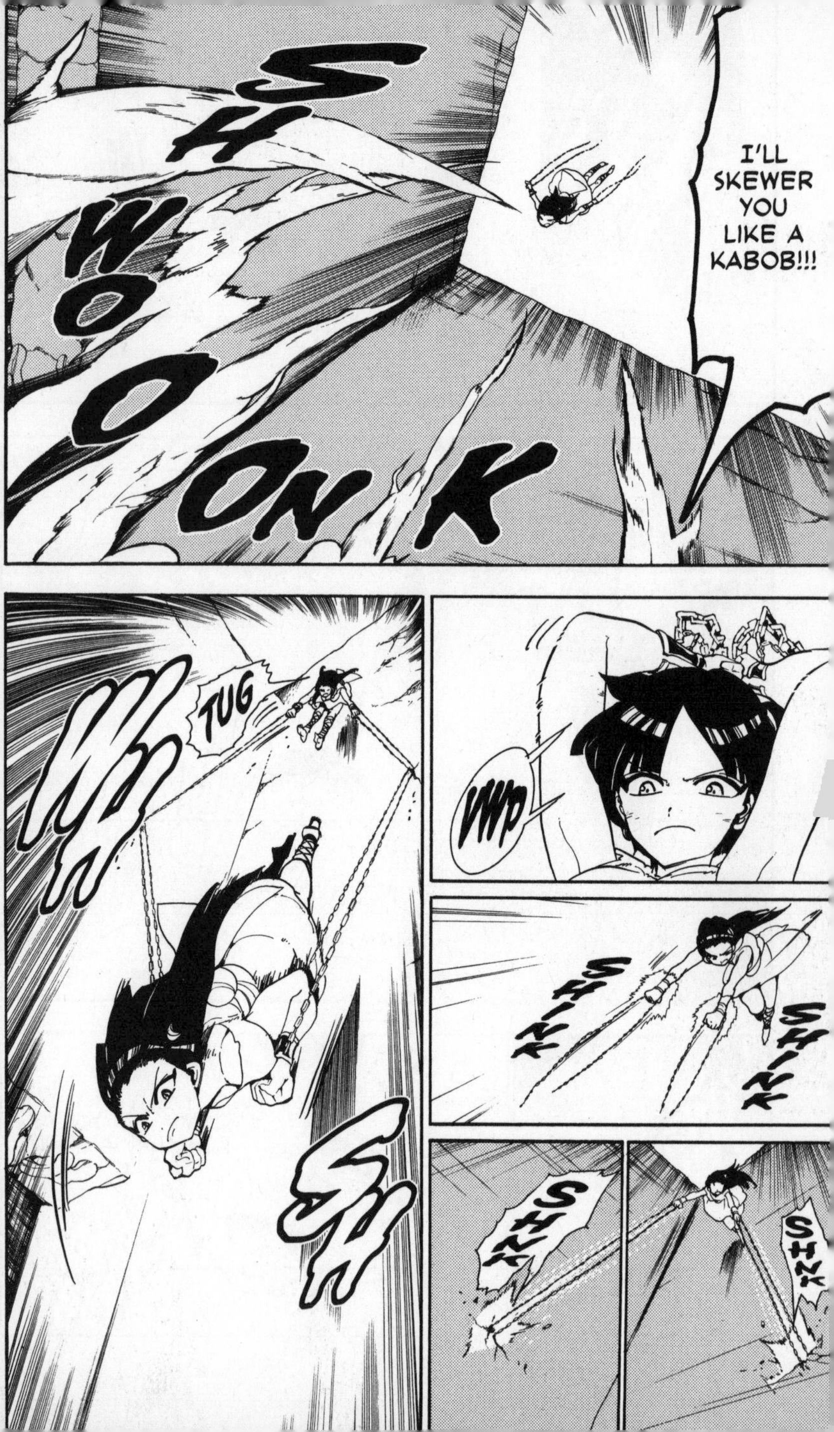
I'LL SKEWER YOU LIKE A KABOB!!!
SHWOOONK
VWP
SHINK
SHINK
SHNK
SHNK
TUG
SH

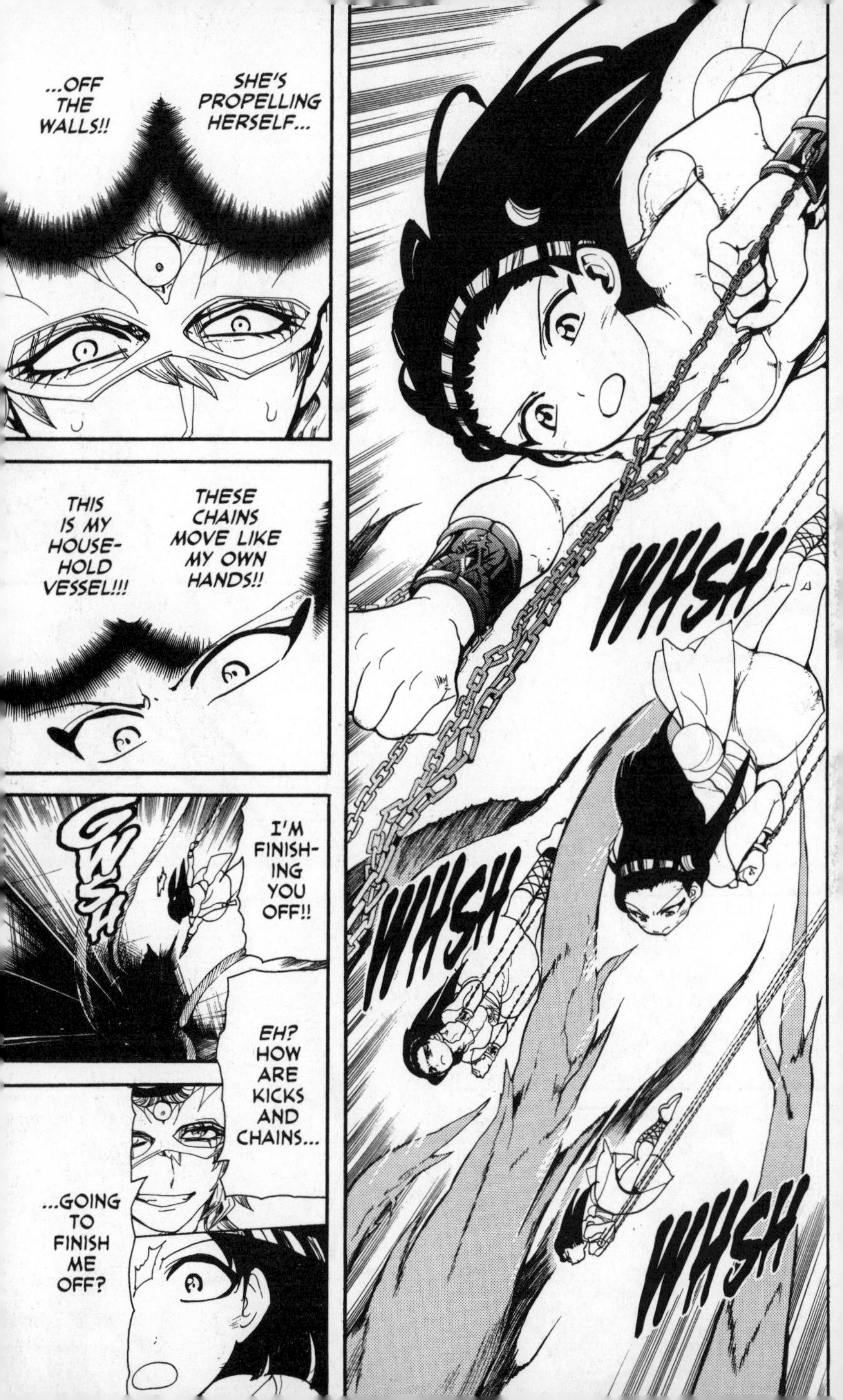
WHSH
WHSH
WHSH
SHE'S PROPELLING HERSELF...
...OFF THE WALLS!!
THESE CHAINS MOVE LIKE MY OWN HANDS!!
THIS IS MY HOUSE-HOLD VESSEL!!!
I'M FINISH-ING YOU OFF!!
GWSH
EH? HOW ARE KICKS AND CHAINS...
...GOING TO FINISH ME OFF?

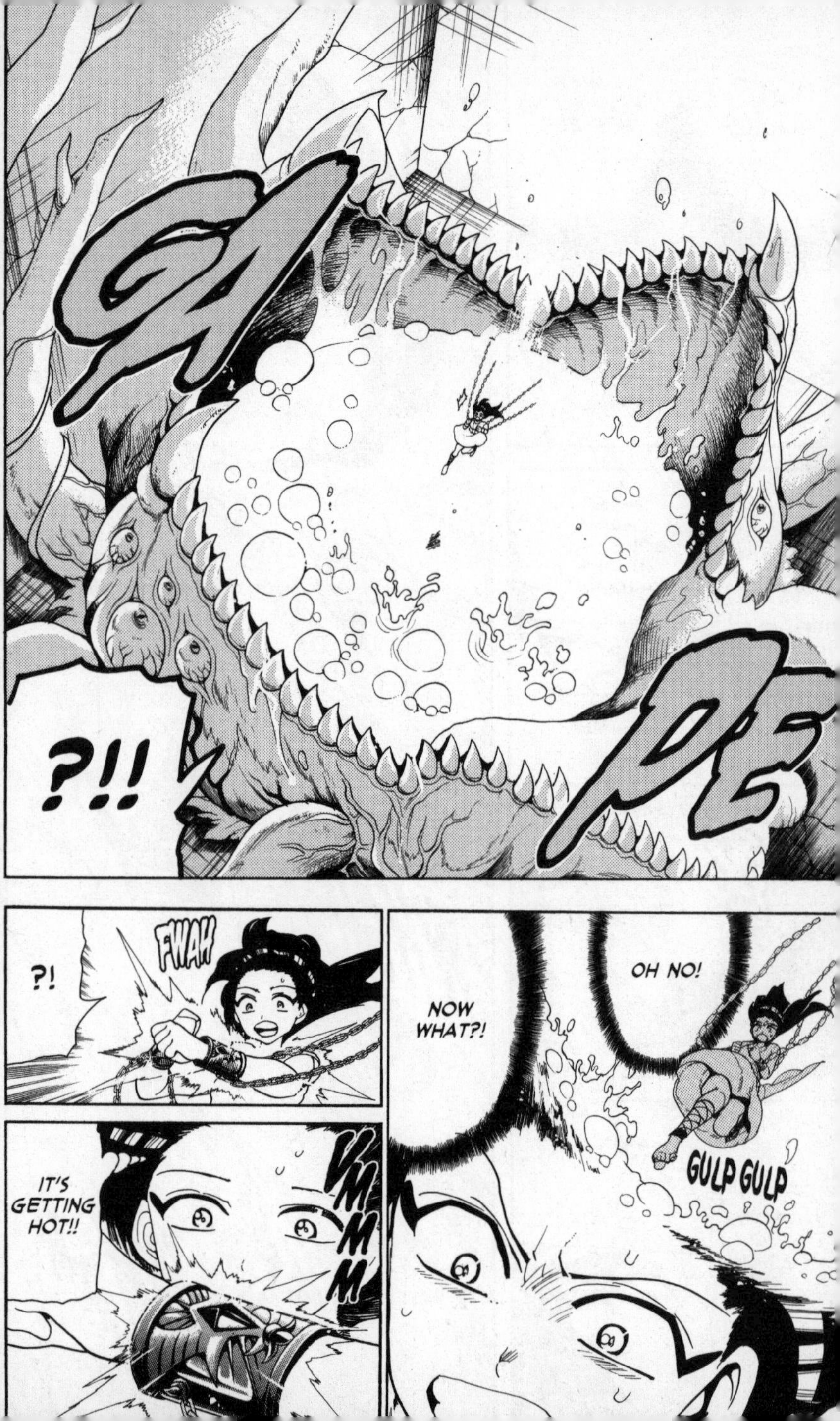
?!!
OH NO!
NOW WHAT?!
GULP GULP
FWAH
?!
IT'S GETTING HOT!!

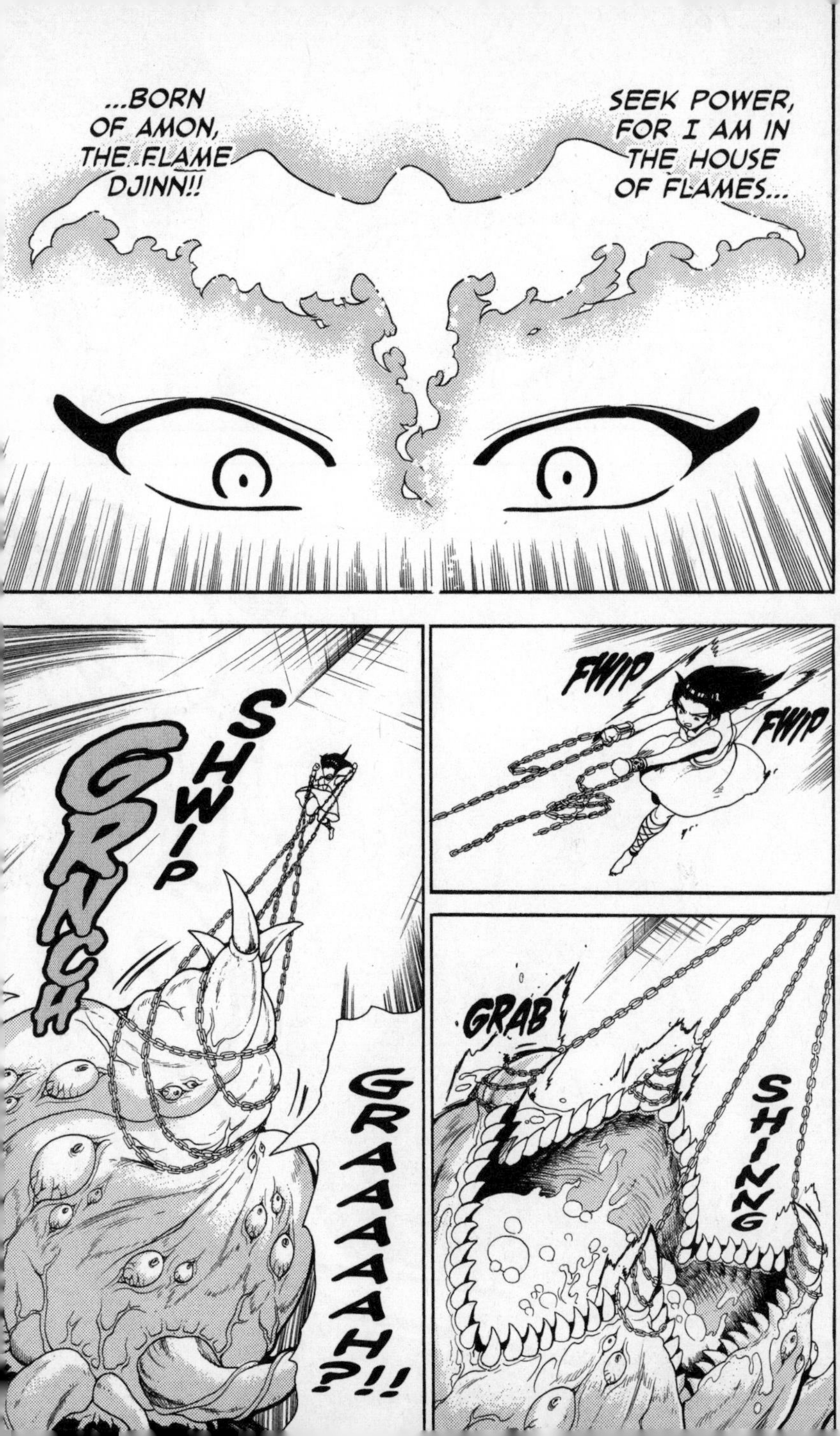
SEEK POWER, FOR I AM IN THE HOUSE OF FLAMES...
...BORN OF AMON, THE FLAME DJINN!!
FWIP
FWIP
GRAB
SHIINNG
SHWIP
GRNCH
GRAAAAAAH?!!

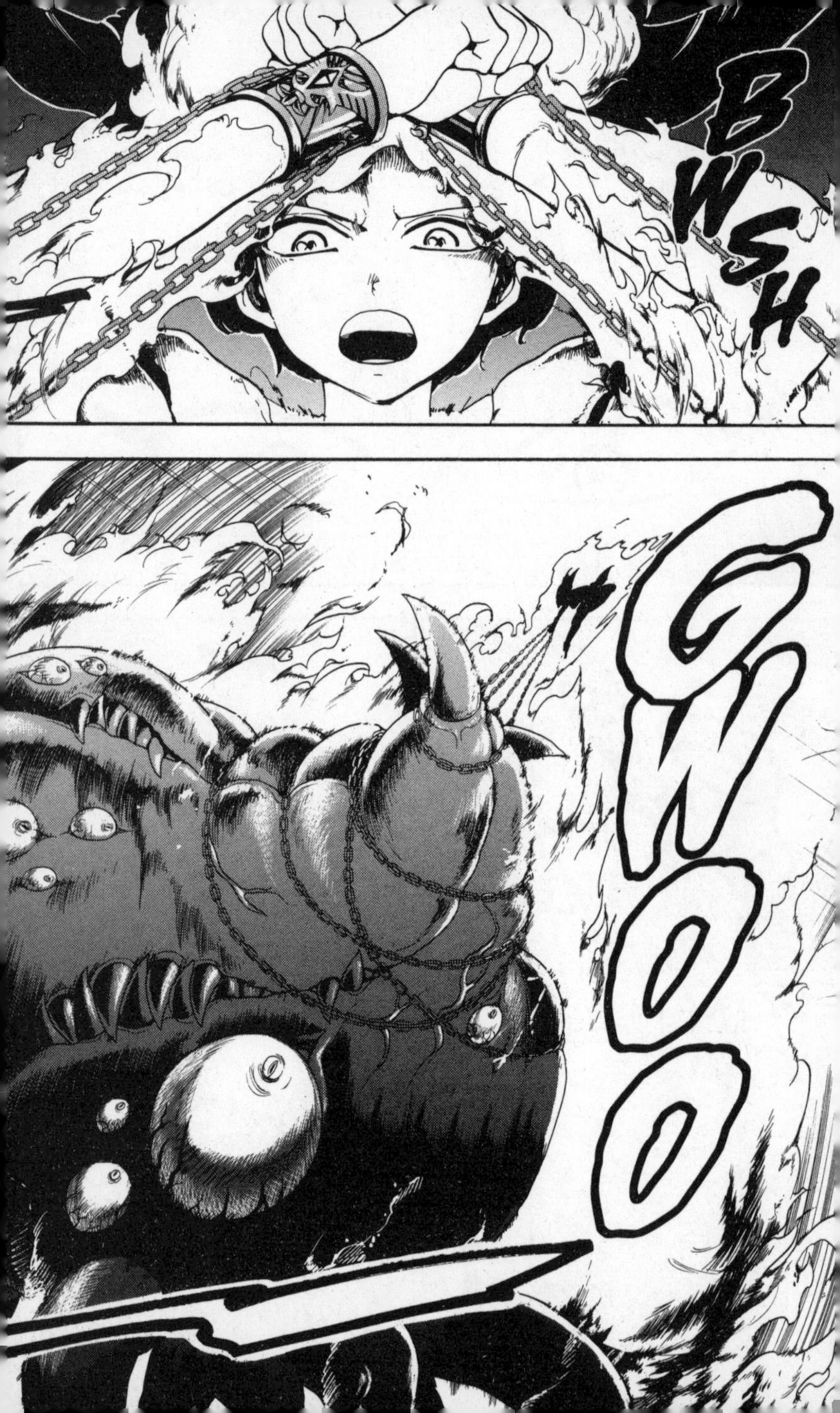
BWSH
GWOOO

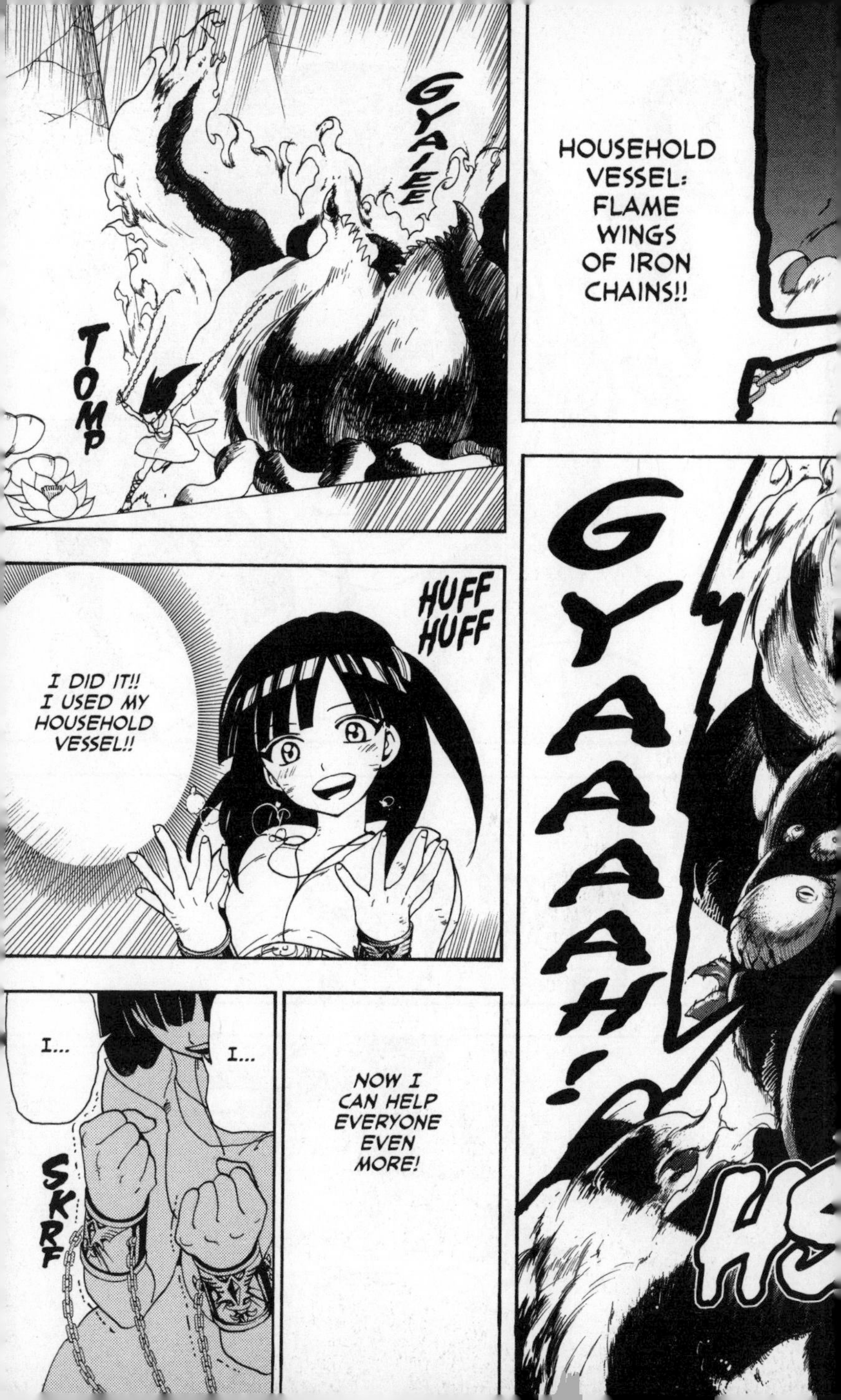
HOUSEHOLD VESSEL: FLAME WINGS OF IRON CHAINS!!
GYAAAAAH!
GYAIEE
TOMP
HUFF HUFF
I DID IT!! I USED MY HOUSEHOLD VESSEL!!
NOW I CAN HELP EVERYONE EVEN MORE!
I...
I...
SKRF

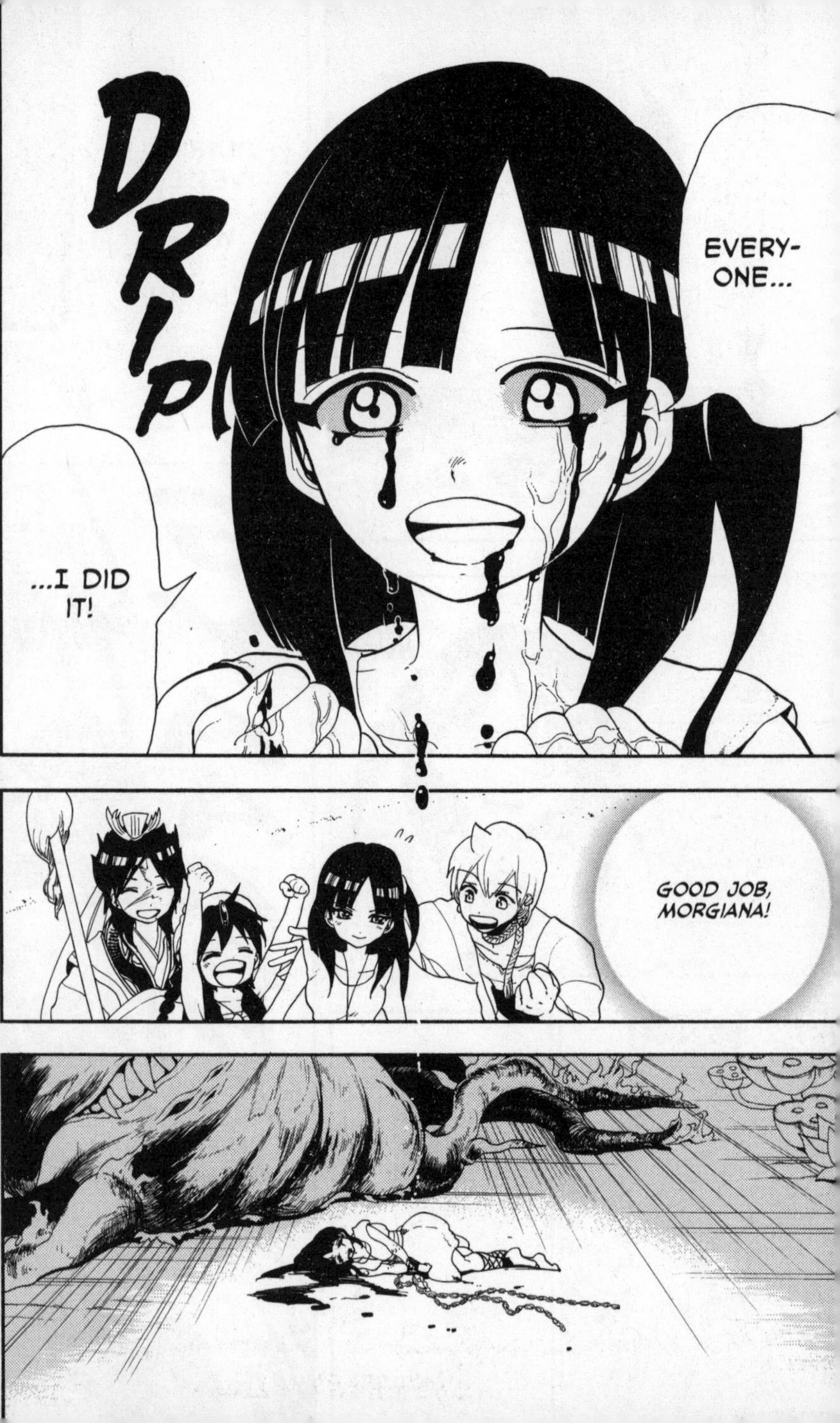
EVERY-ONE...
DRIP
...I DID IT!
GOOD JOB, MORGIANA!

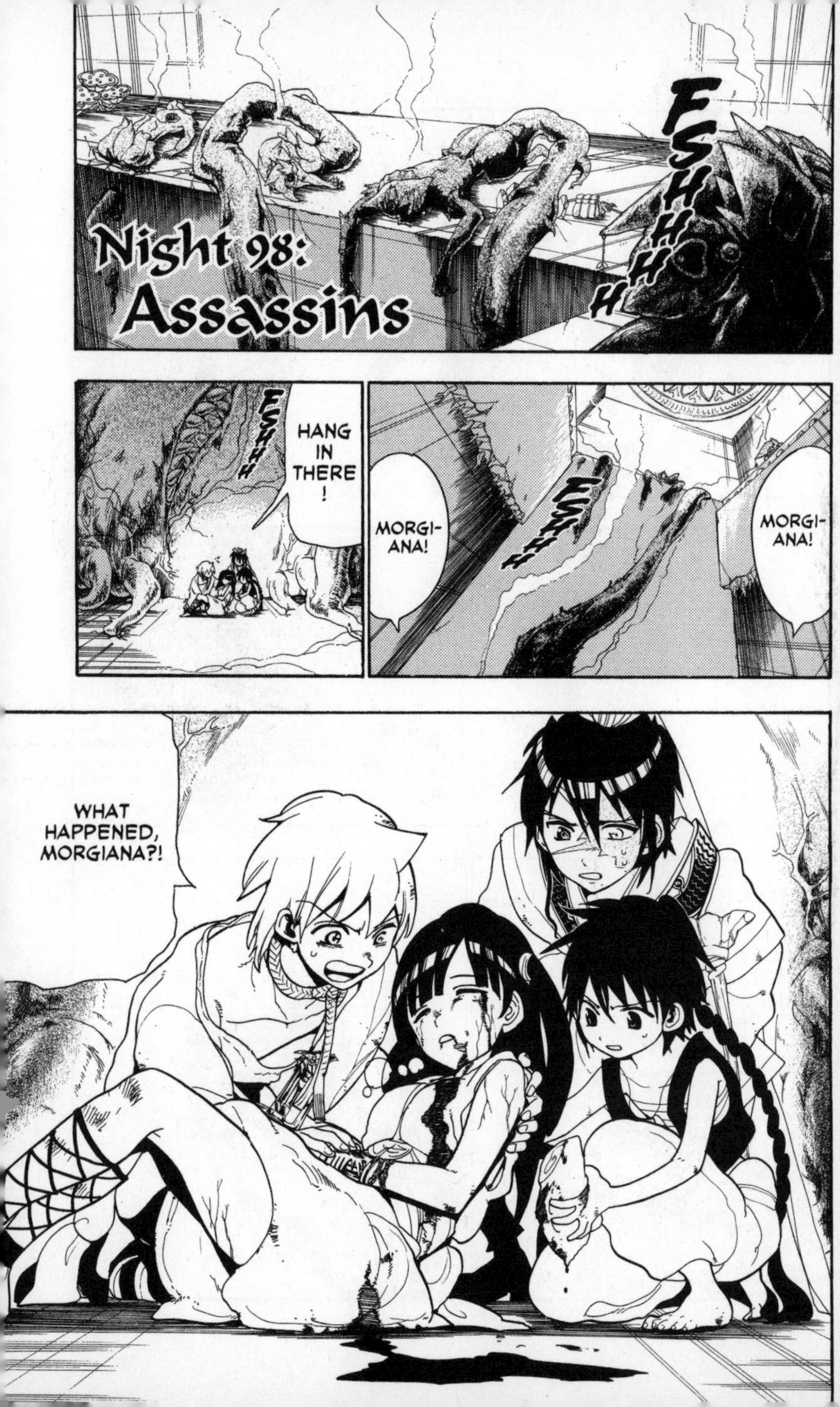
FSHHHHH
Night 98: Assassins
MORGI-ANA!
FSHHH
MORGI-ANA!
HANG IN THERE!
FSHHH
WHAT HAPPENED, MORGIANA?!

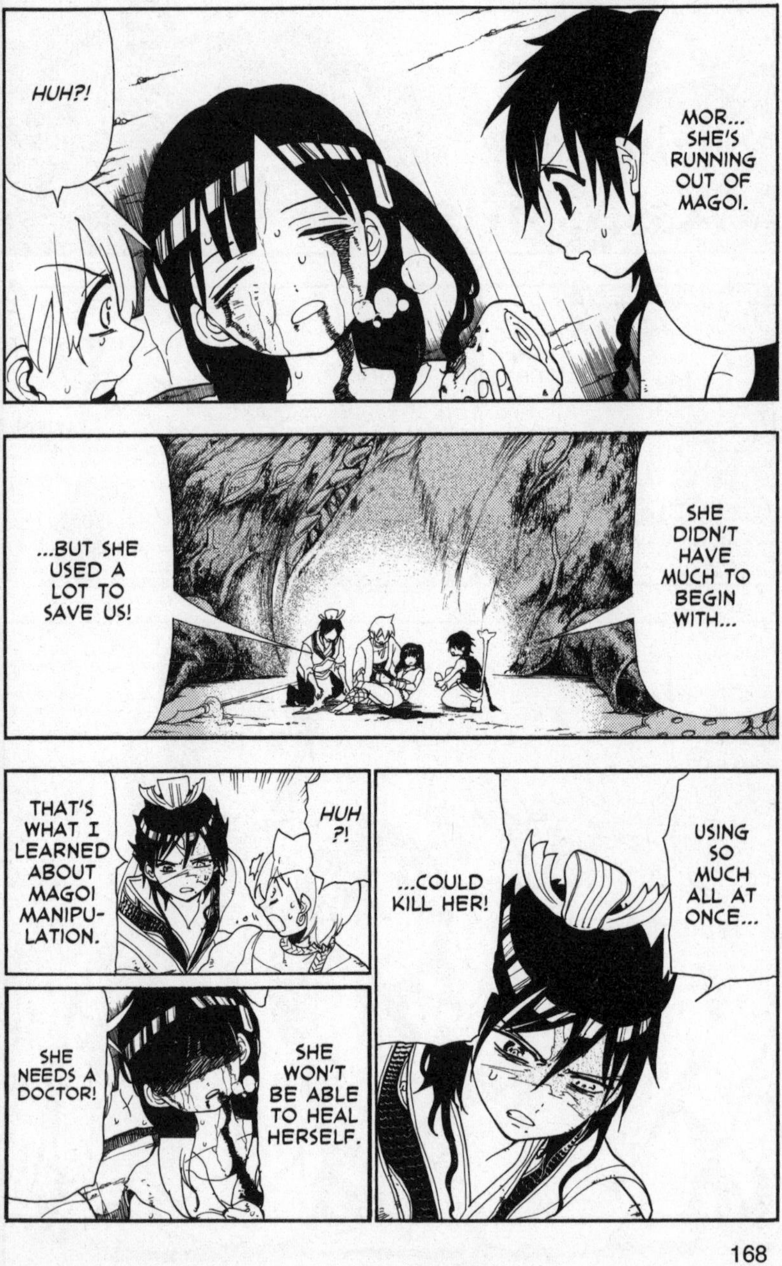
MOR... SHE'S RUNNING OUT OF MAGOI.
HUH?!
SHE DIDN'T HAVE MUCH TO BEGIN WITH...
...BUT SHE USED A LOT TO SAVE US!
USING SO MUCH ALL AT ONCE...
...COULD KILL HER!
HUH ?!
THAT'S WHAT I LEARNED ABOUT MAGOI MANIPU-LATION.
SHE WON'T BE ABLE TO HEAL HERSELF.
SHE NEEDS A DOCTOR!

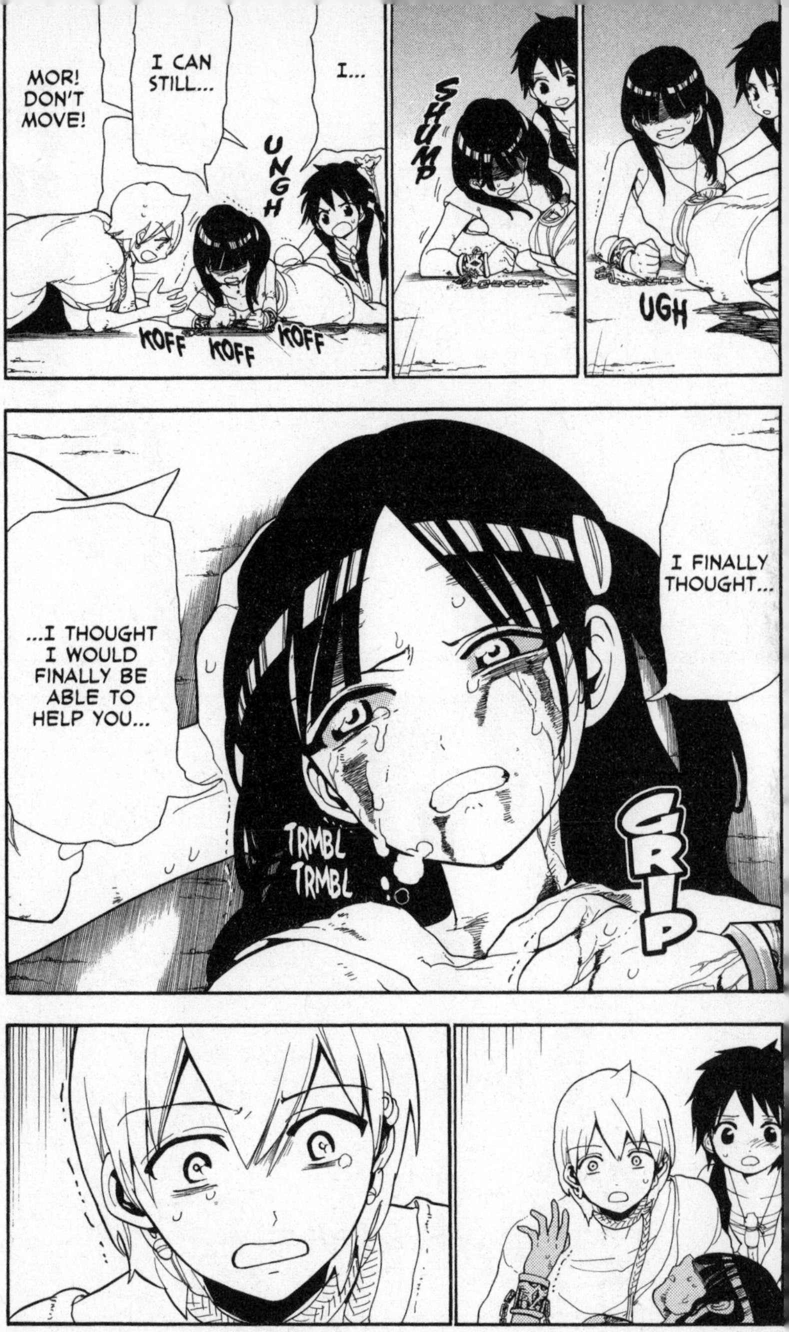
UGH
SHUMP
I...
I CAN STILL...
UNGH
MOR! DON'T MOVE!
KOFF KOFF KOFF
I FINALLY THOUGHT...
GRIP
...I THOUGHT I WOULD FINALLY BE ABLE TO HELP YOU...
TRMBL TRMBL

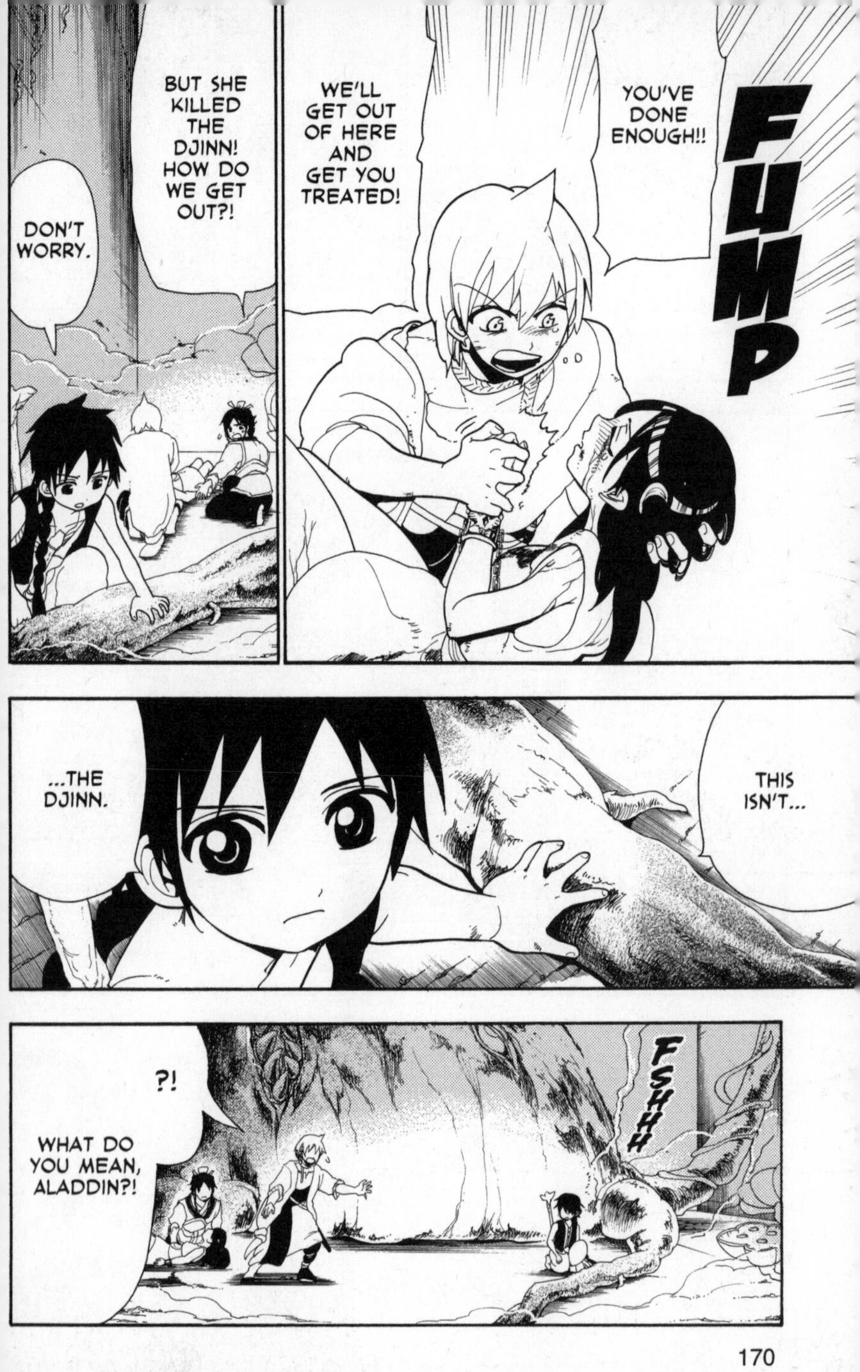
FUMP
YOU'VE DONE ENOUGH!!
WE'LL GET OUT OF HERE AND GET YOU TREATED!
BUT SHE KILLED THE DJINN! HOW DO WE GET OUT?!
DON'T WORRY.
THIS ISN'T...
...THE DJINN.
FSHHH
?!
WHAT DO YOU MEAN, ALADDIN?!

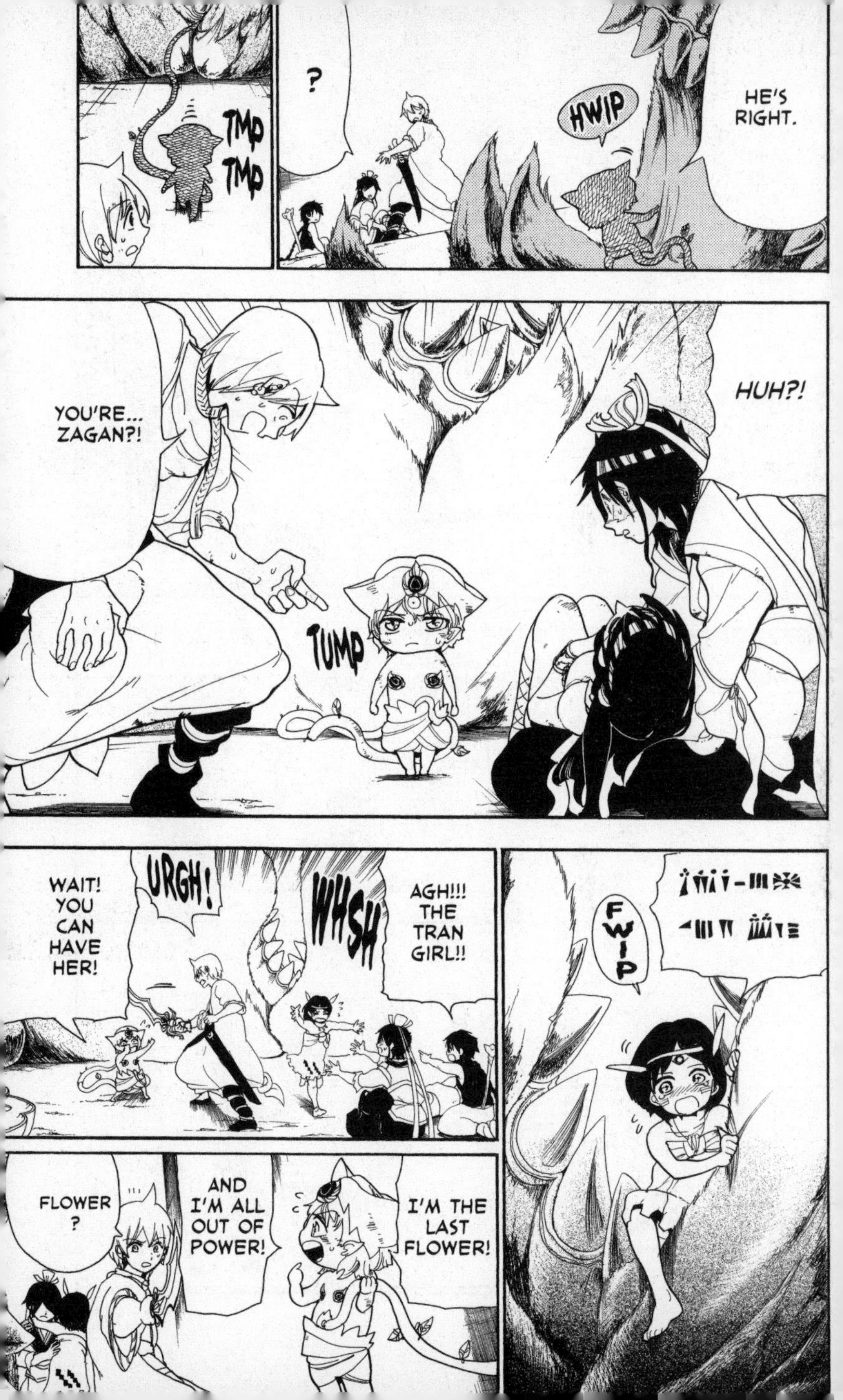
HE'S RIGHT.
HWIP
?
TMP TMP
HUH?!
YOU'RE... ZAGAN?!
TUMP
FWIP
AGH!!! THE TRAN GIRL!!
WHSH
URGH!
WAIT! YOU CAN HAVE HER!
I'M THE LAST FLOWER!
AND I'M ALL OUT OF POWER!
FLOWER?

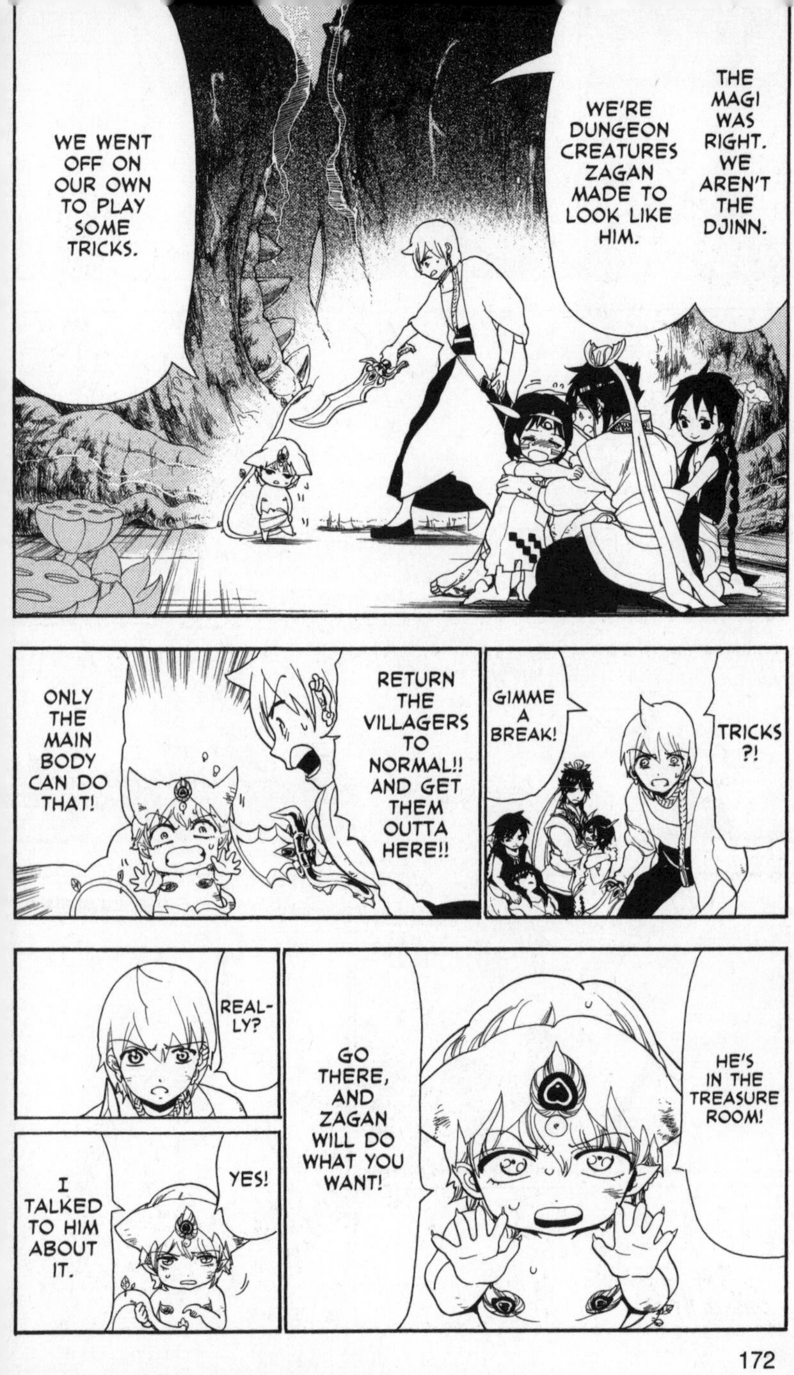
THE MAGI WAS RIGHT. WE AREN'T THE DJINN.
WE'RE DUNGEON CREATURES ZAGAN MADE TO LOOK LIKE HIM.
WE WENT OFF ON OUR OWN TO PLAY SOME TRICKS.
TRICKS?!
GIMME A BREAK!
RETURN THE VILLAGERS TO NORMAL!! AND GET THEM OUTTA HERE!!
ONLY THE MAIN BODY CAN DO THAT!
HE'S IN THE TREASURE ROOM!
GO THERE, AND ZAGAN WILL DO WHAT YOU WANT!
REAL-LY?
YES!
I TALKED TO HIM ABOUT IT.

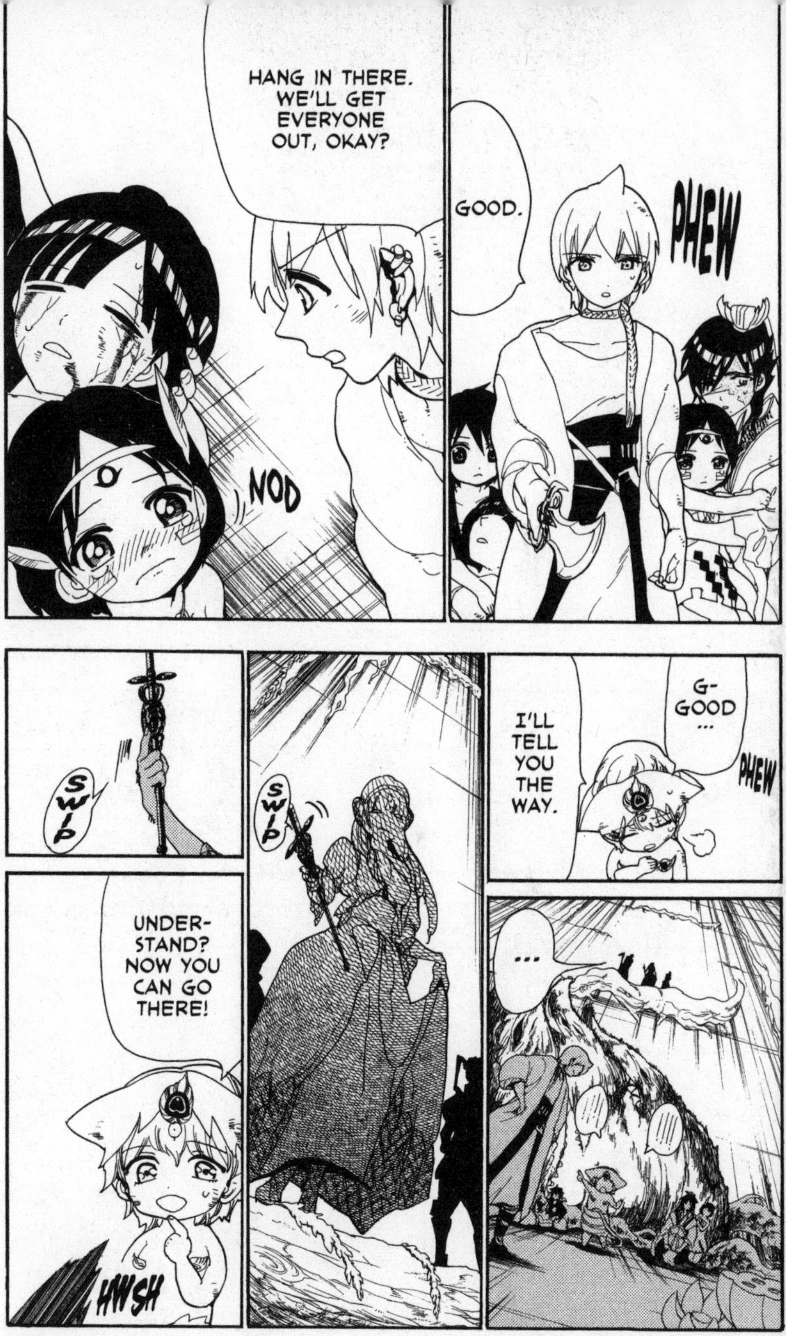
GOOD.
PHEW
HANG IN THERE. WE'LL GET EVERYONE OUT, OKAY?
NOD
G-GOOD...
I'LL TELL YOU THE WAY.
PHEW
...
SWIP
SWIP
UNDER-STAND? NOW YOU CAN GO THERE!
HWSH

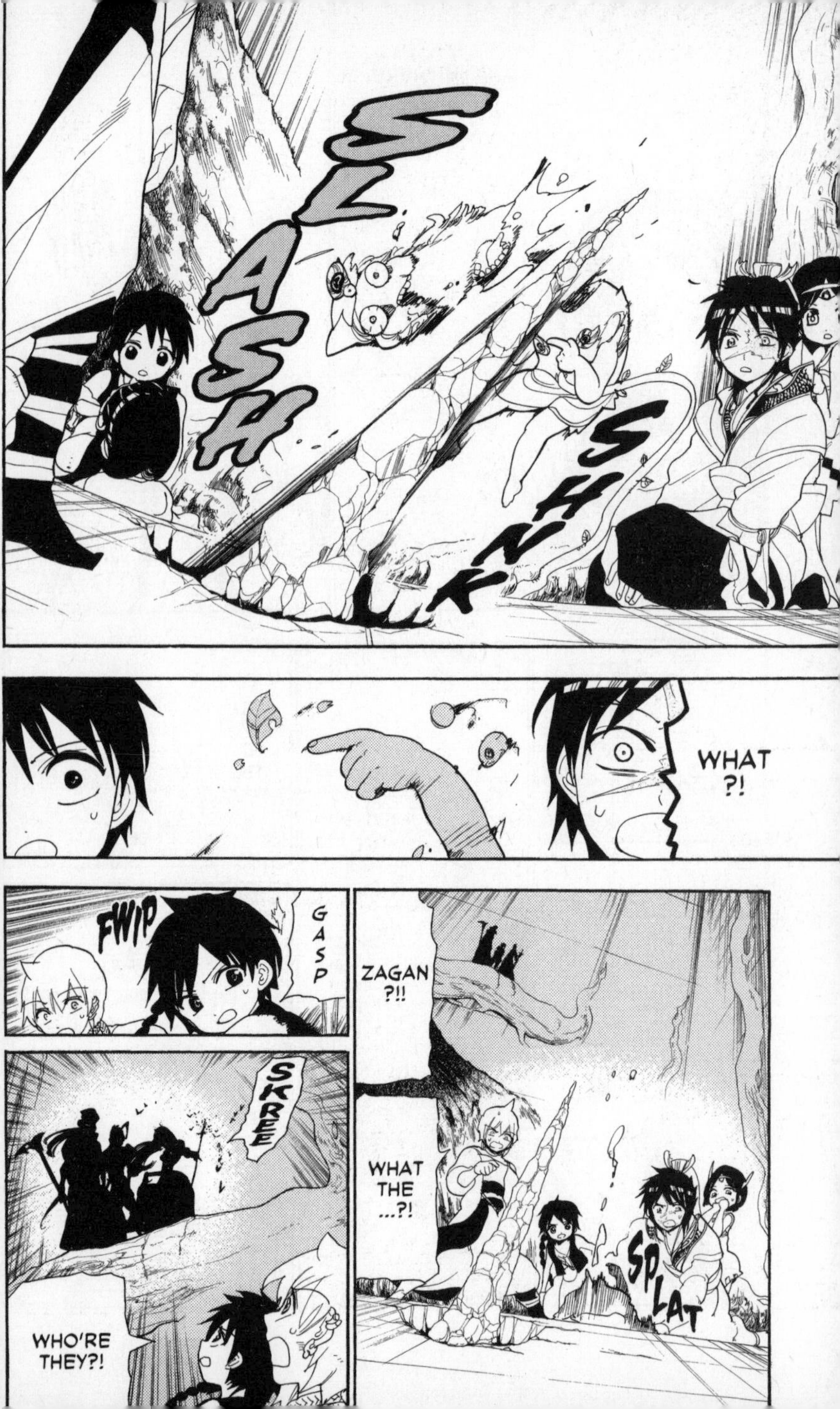
SLASH
SHINK
WHAT ?!
ZAGAN ?!!
WHAT THE ...?!
SPLAT
GASP
FWIP
SKREE
WHO'RE THEY?!

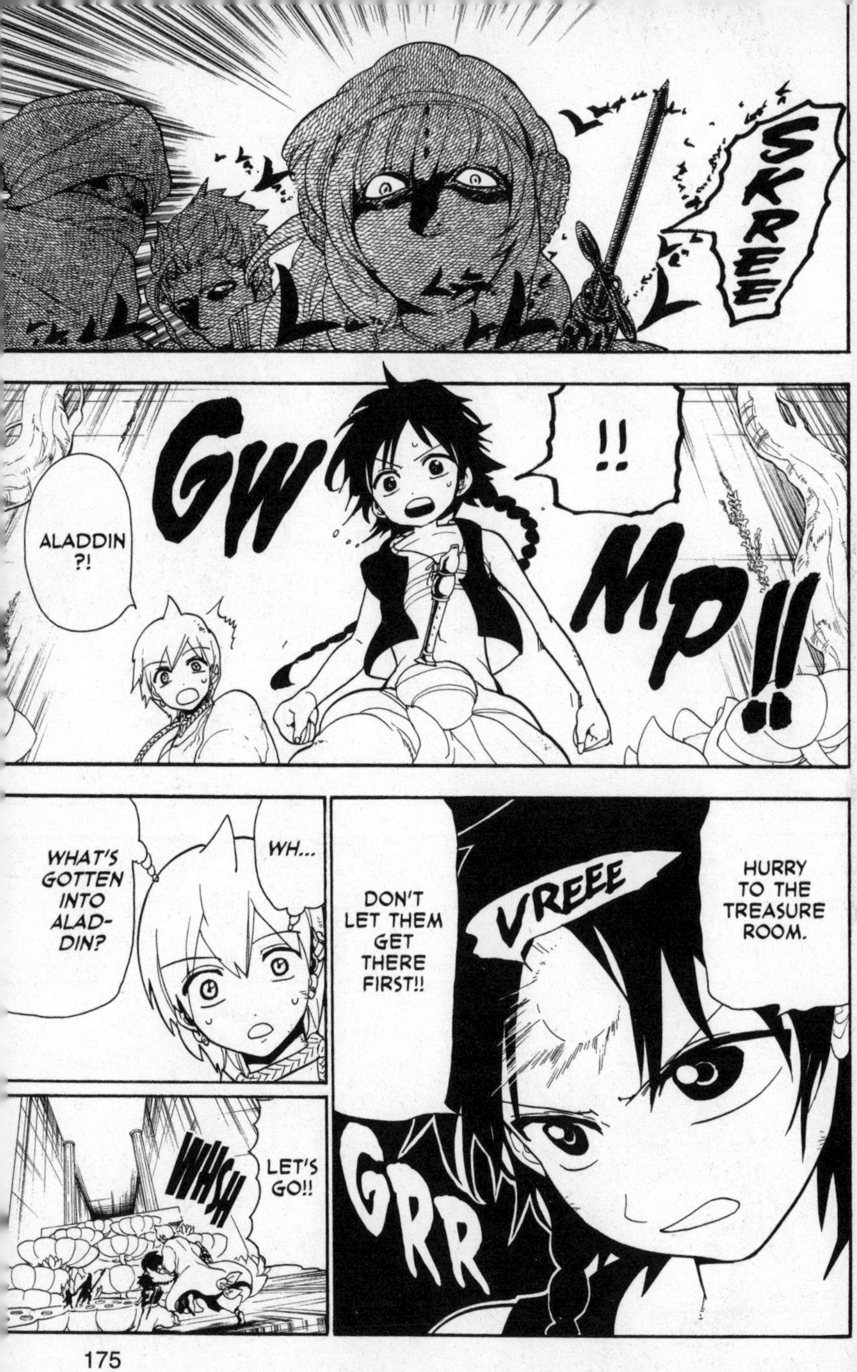
SKREE
!!
GWMP!!
ALADDIN ?!
HURRY TO THE TREASURE ROOM.
VREEE
DON'T LET THEM GET THERE FIRST!!
GRR
WH...
WHAT'S GOTTEN INTO ALAD-DIN?
LET'S GO!!
WHSH

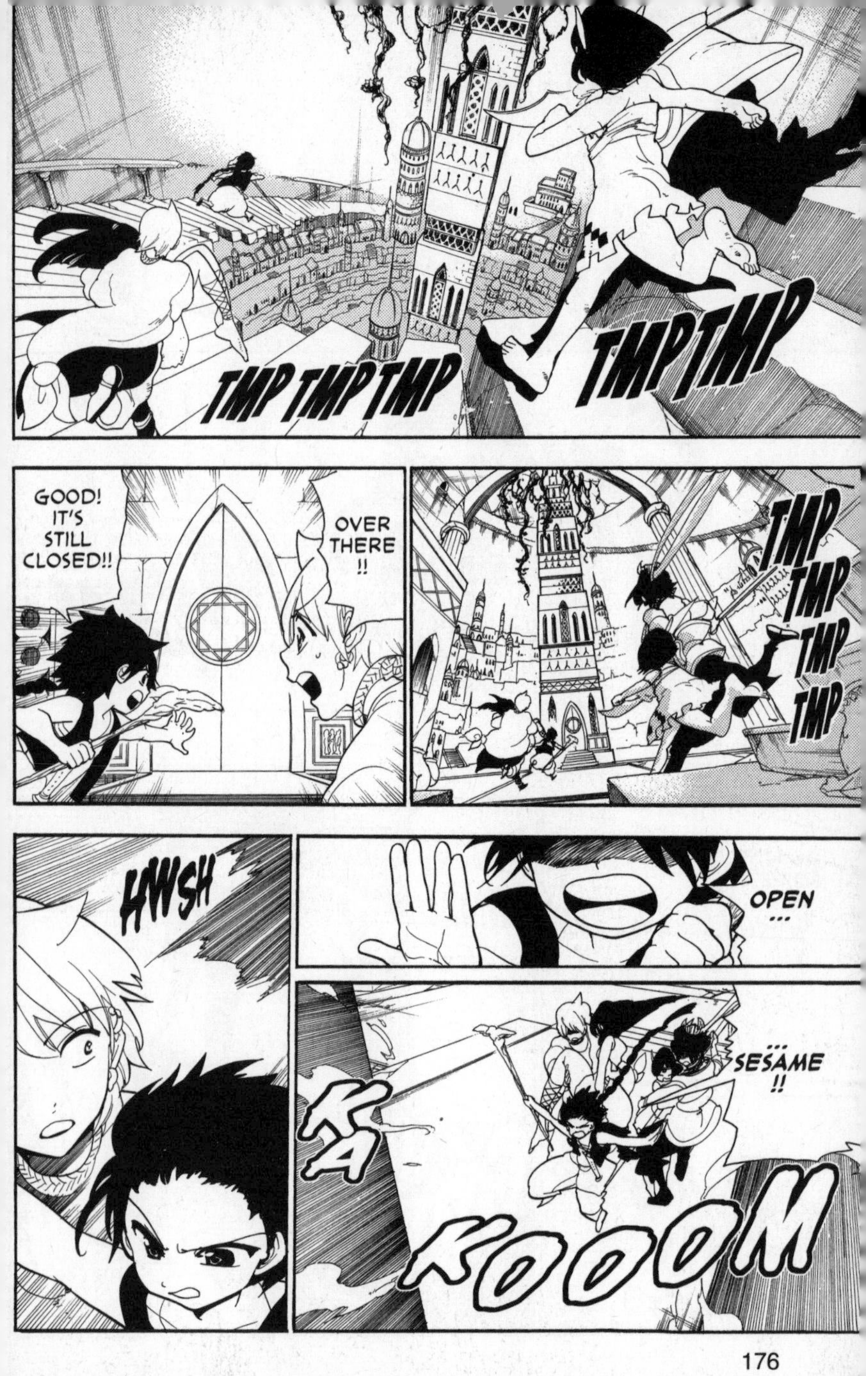
TMP TMP
TMP TMP TMP
TMP
TMP
TMP
TMP
TMP
OVER THERE !!
GOOD! IT'S STILL CLOSED!!
OPEN ...
... SESAME !!
KA
KOOOM
HWSH

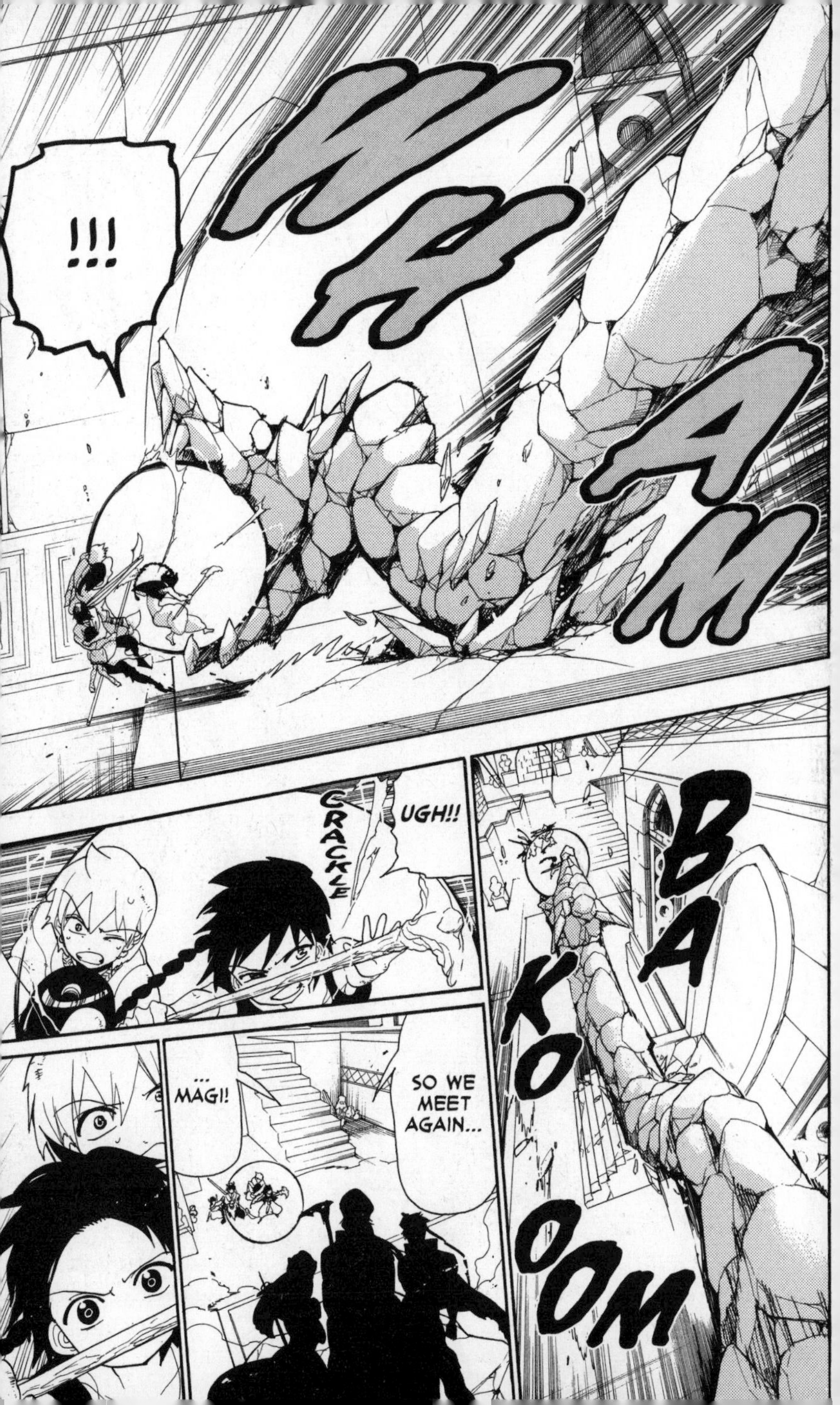
WHAM
!!!
BAKOOOM
UGH!!
CRACKLE
SO WE MEET AGAIN...
...MAGI!

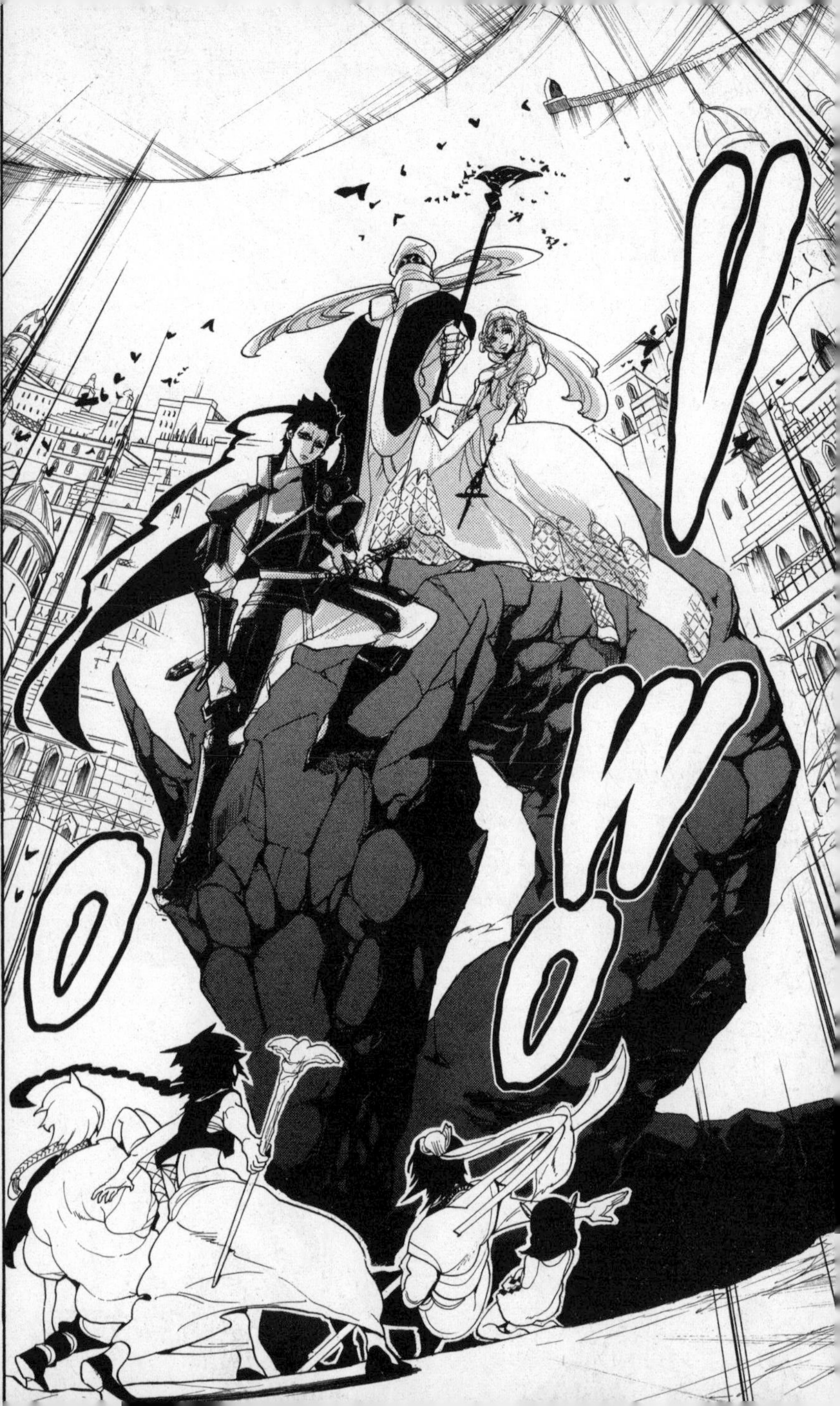
OOW!!

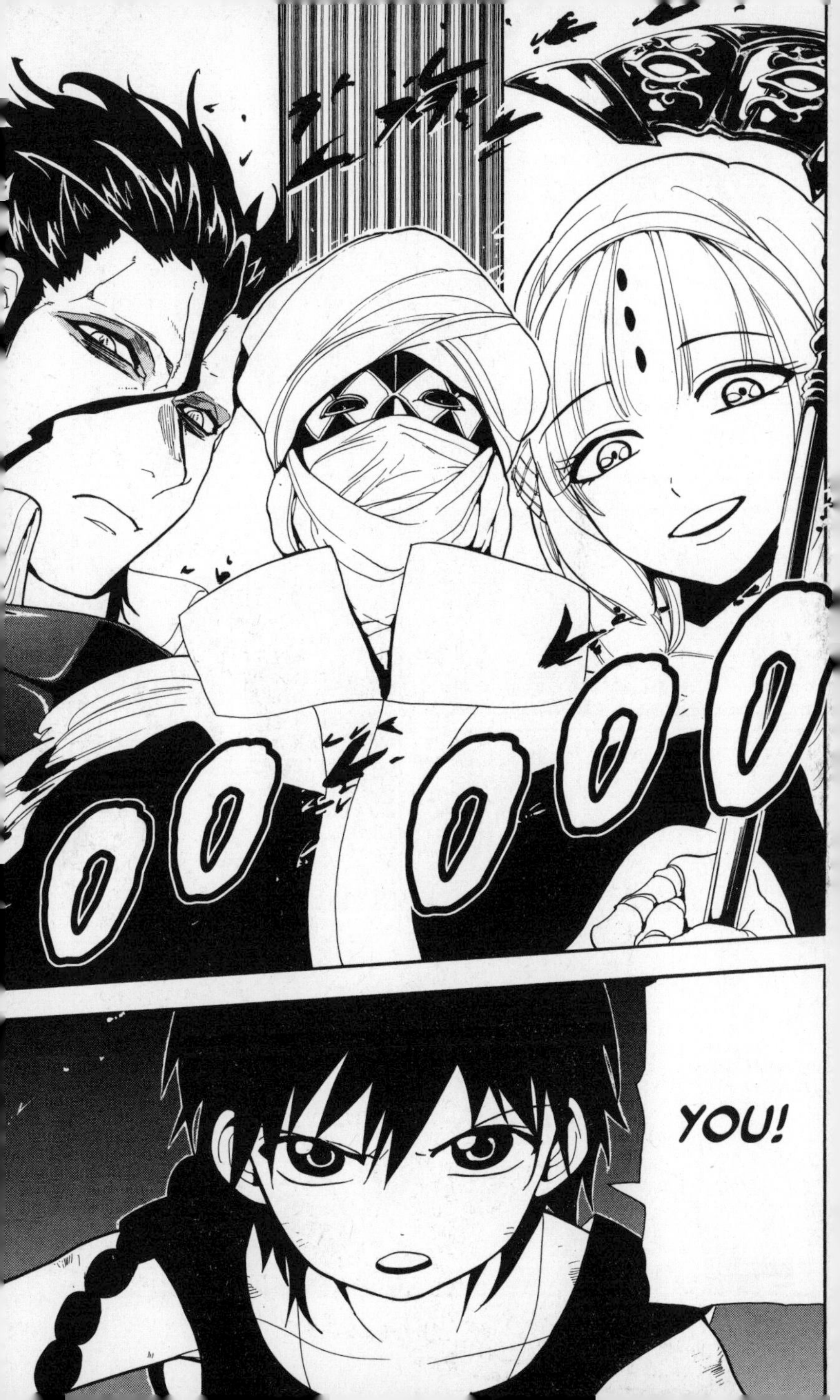
YOU!

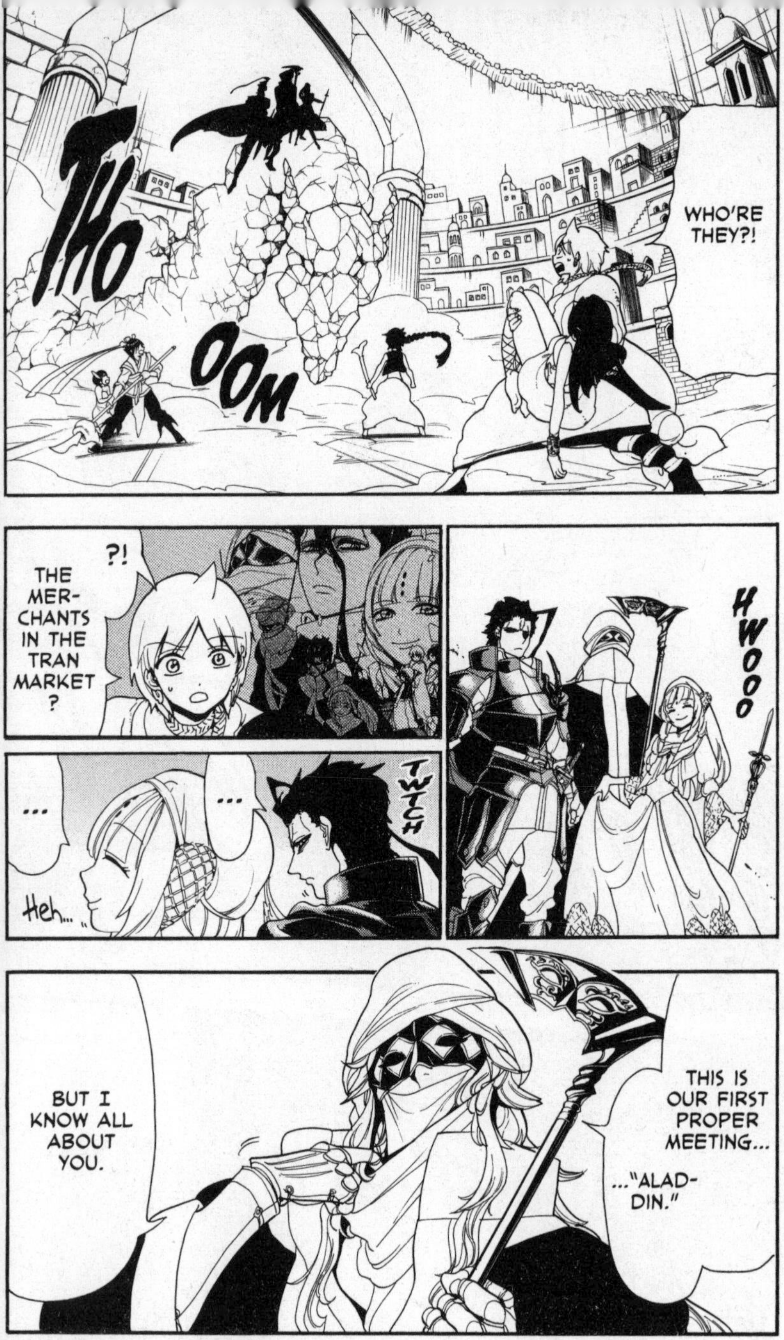
WHO'RE THEY?!
THO
OOM
HWOOO
?!
THE MER-CHANTS IN THE TRAN MARKET?
TWITCH
...
...
Heh...
THIS IS OUR FIRST PROPER MEETING...
..."ALAD-DIN."
BUT I KNOW ALL ABOUT YOU.

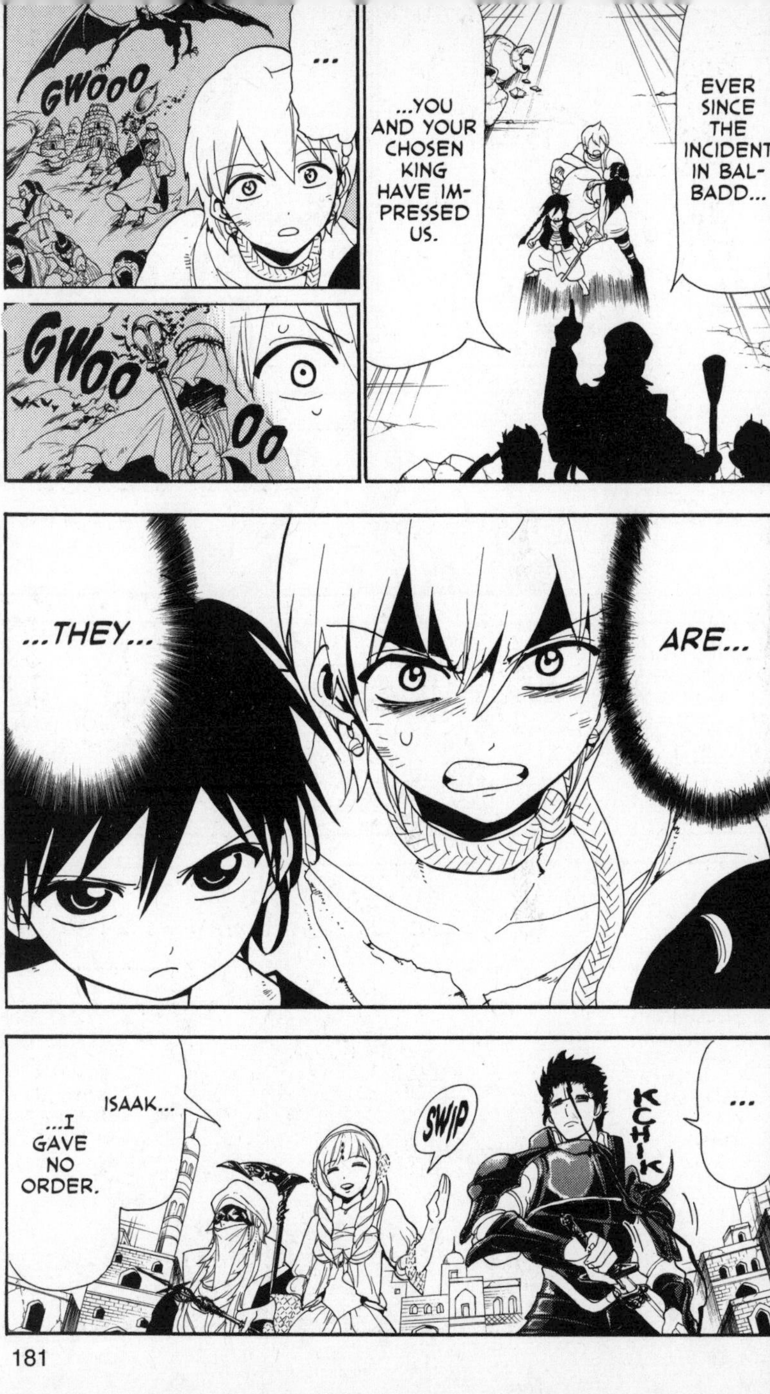
EVER SINCE THE INCIDENT IN BAL-BADD...
...YOU AND YOUR CHOSEN KING HAVE IM-PRESSED US.
...
GWOOO
GWOOO
...THEY...
ARE...
...
KCHIK
SWIP
ISAAK...
...I GAVE NO ORDER.

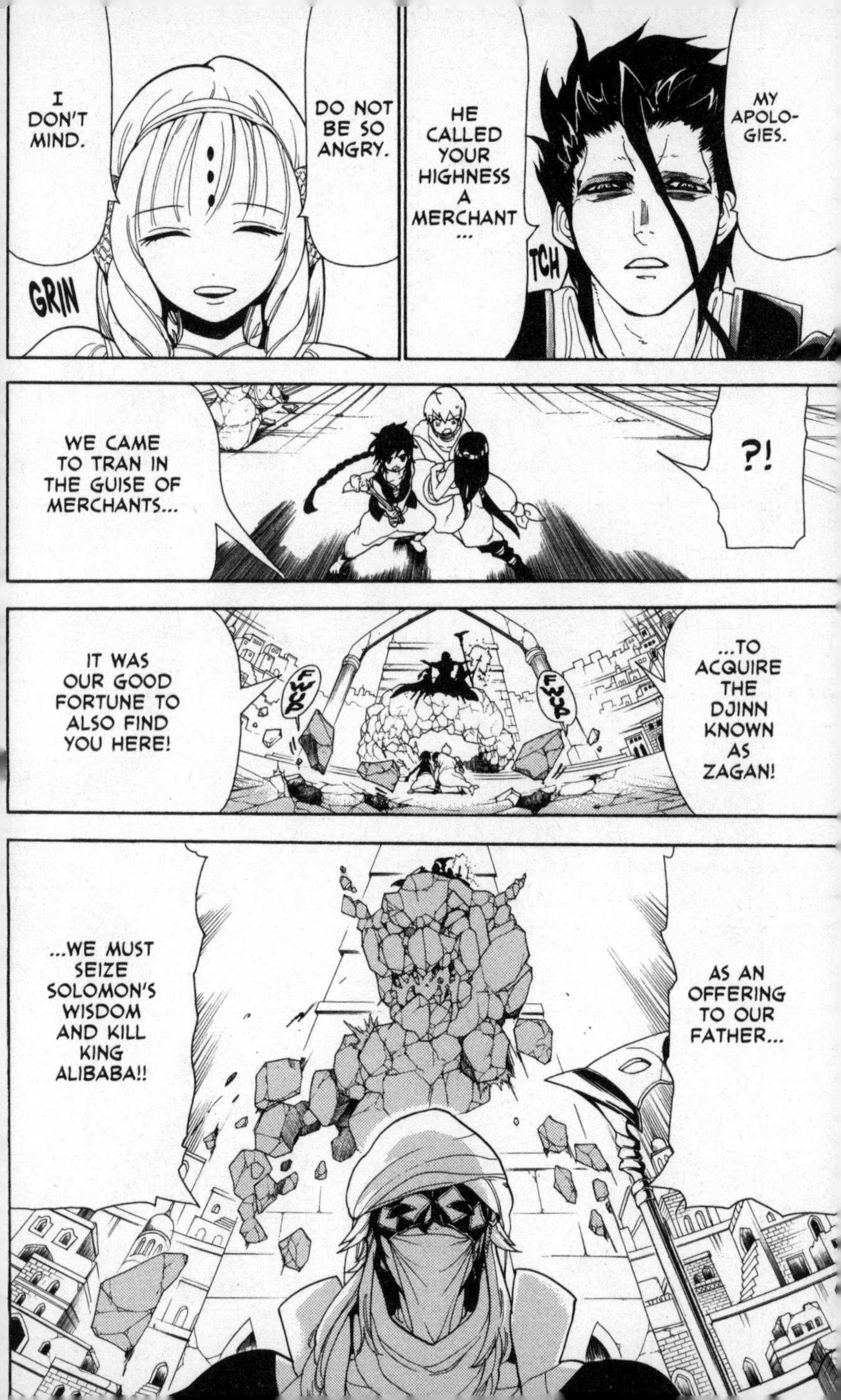
MY APOLO-GIES.
HE CALLED YOUR HIGHNESS A MERCHANT...
TCH
DO NOT BE SO ANGRY.
I DON'T MIND.
GRIN
?!
WE CAME TO TRAN IN THE GUISE OF MERCHANTS...
...TO ACQUIRE THE DJINN KNOWN AS ZAGAN!
FWUP
FWUP
IT WAS OUR GOOD FORTUNE TO ALSO FIND YOU HERE!
AS AN OFFERING TO OUR FATHER...
...WE MUST SEIZE SOLOMON'S WISDOM AND KILL KING ALIBABA!!

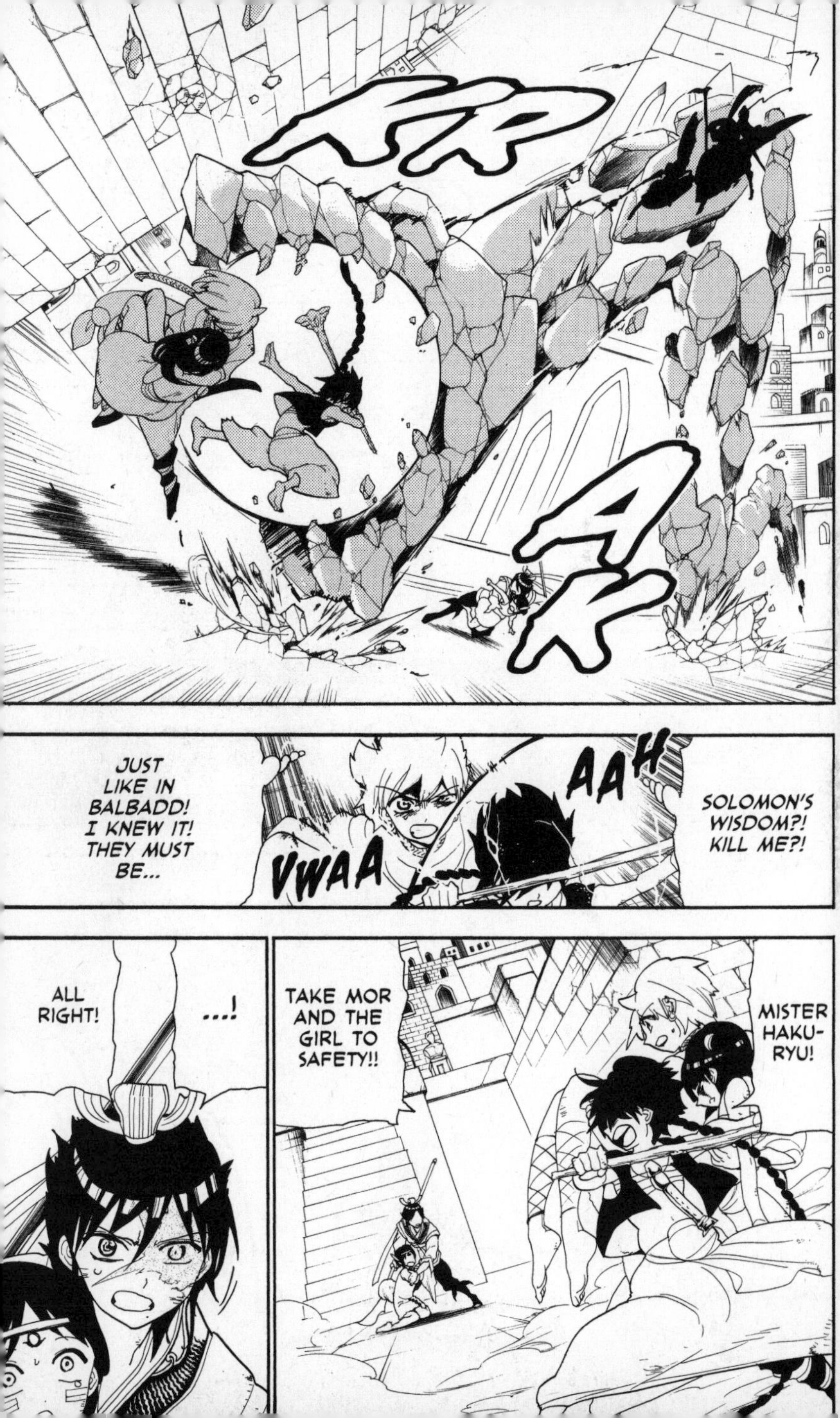
KR
AK
SOLOMON'S WISDOM?! KILL ME?!
AAH
VWAA
JUST LIKE IN BALBADD! I KNEW IT! THEY MUST BE...
MISTER HAKU-RYU!
TAKE MOR AND THE GIRL TO SAFETY!!
...!
ALL RIGHT!

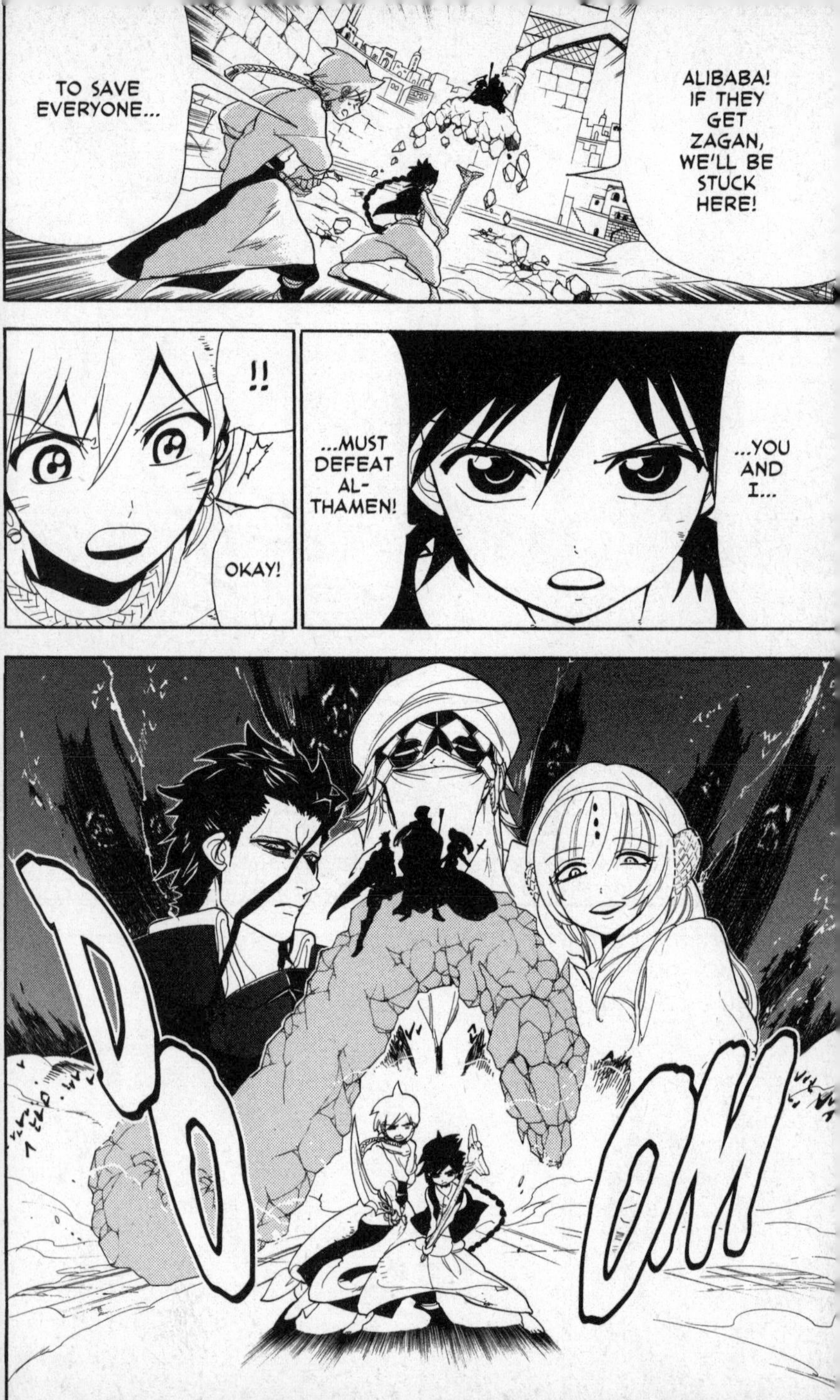
ALIBABA! IF THEY GET ZAGAN, WE'LL BE STUCK HERE!
TO SAVE EVERYONE...
...YOU AND I...
...MUST DEFEAT AL-THAMEN!
!!
OKAY!
DOOM

# MAGI
### The labyrinth of magic
**9**

# Staff

**■ Story & Art**

## Shinobu Ohtaka

**■ Regular Assistants**

### Miho Isshiki

### Akira Sugito

### Tanimoto

### Makoto Akui

### Yoshihumi Otera

**■ Editor**

### Kazuaki Ishibashi

**■ Sales & Promotion**

### Shinichirou Todaka

### Atsushi Chiku

**■ Designer**

### Yasuo Shimura + Bay Bridge Studio

# Magi Vol. 10 Bonus Manga

## Hakuryu and His Older Sister and Sometimes Seishun

HAKU-RYU REN
FOURTH PRINCE OF THE KOU EMPIRE
HAKUEI REN
FIRST PRINCESS OF THE KOU EMPIRE
SEI-SHUN RI
HAKUEI'S SERVANT

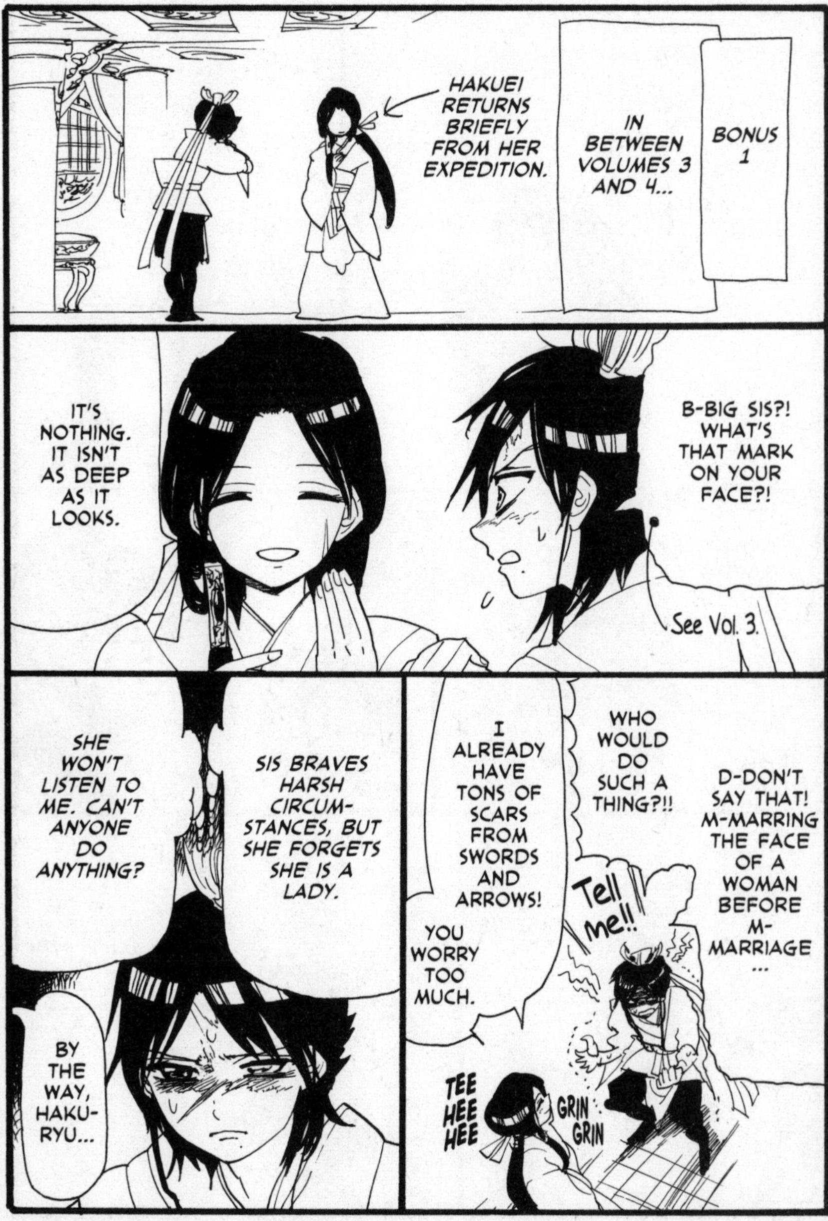
BONUS 1
IN BETWEEN VOLUMES 3 AND 4...
HAKUEI RETURNS BRIEFLY FROM HER EXPEDITION.
B-BIG SIS?! WHAT'S THAT MARK ON YOUR FACE?!
See Vol. 3.
IT'S NOTHING. IT ISN'T AS DEEP AS IT LOOKS.
D-DON'T SAY THAT! M-MARRING THE FACE OF A WOMAN BEFORE M-MARRIAGE ...
WHO WOULD DO SUCH A THING?!!
Tell me!!
I ALREADY HAVE TONS OF SCARS FROM SWORDS AND ARROWS!
YOU WORRY TOO MUCH.
GRIN GRIN
TEE HEE HEE
SIS BRAVES HARSH CIRCUM-STANCES, BUT SHE FORGETS SHE IS A LADY.
SHE WON'T LISTEN TO ME. CAN'T ANYONE DO ANYTHING?
BY THE WAY, HAKU-RYU...

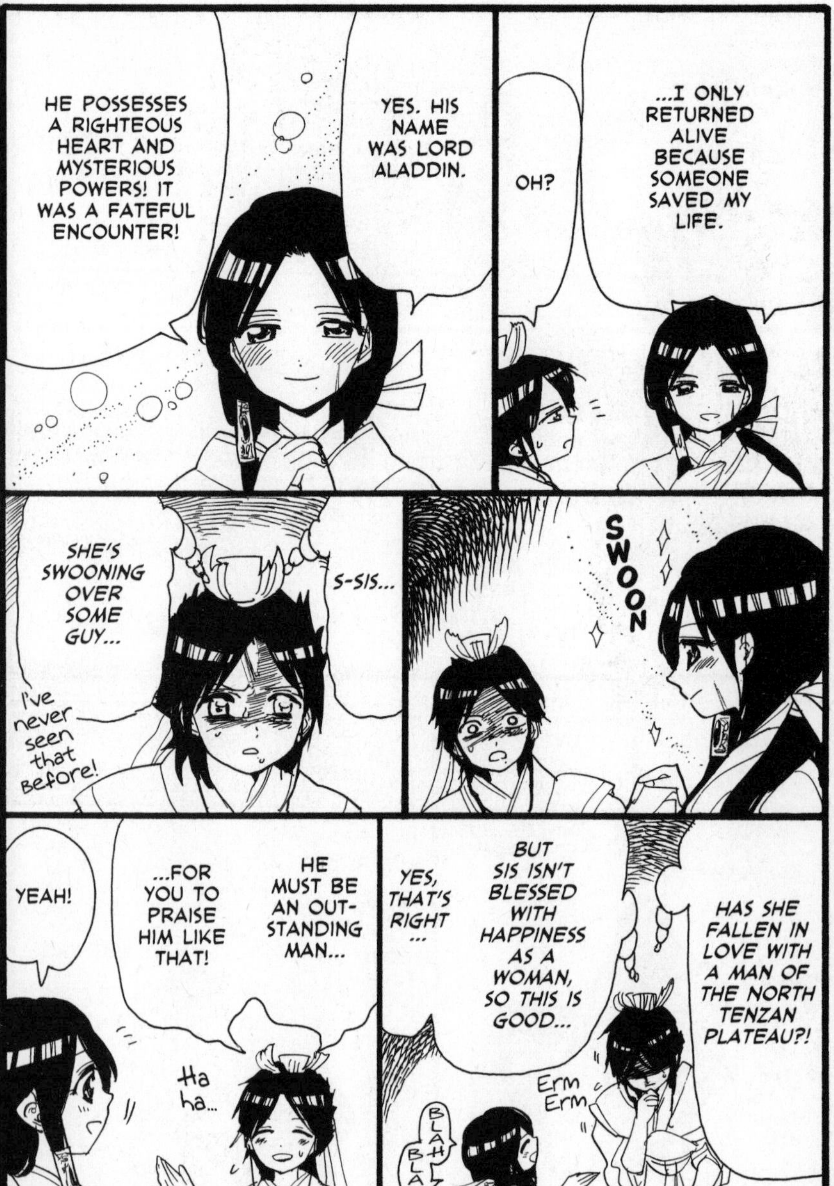
...I ONLY RETURNED ALIVE BECAUSE SOMEONE SAVED MY LIFE.
OH?
YES. HIS NAME WAS LORD ALADDIN.
HE POSSESSES A RIGHTEOUS HEART AND MYSTERIOUS POWERS! IT WAS A FATEFUL ENCOUNTER!
SWOON
S-SIS...
SHE'S SWOONING OVER SOME GUY...
I've never seen that before!
HAS SHE FALLEN IN LOVE WITH A MAN OF THE NORTH TENZAN PLATEAU?!
BUT SIS ISN'T BLESSED WITH HAPPINESS AS A WOMAN, SO THIS IS GOOD...
YES, THAT'S RIGHT...
Erm Erm
BLAH BLAH
HE MUST BE AN OUT-STANDING MAN...
...FOR YOU TO PRAISE HIM LIKE THAT!
YEAH!
Ha ha...

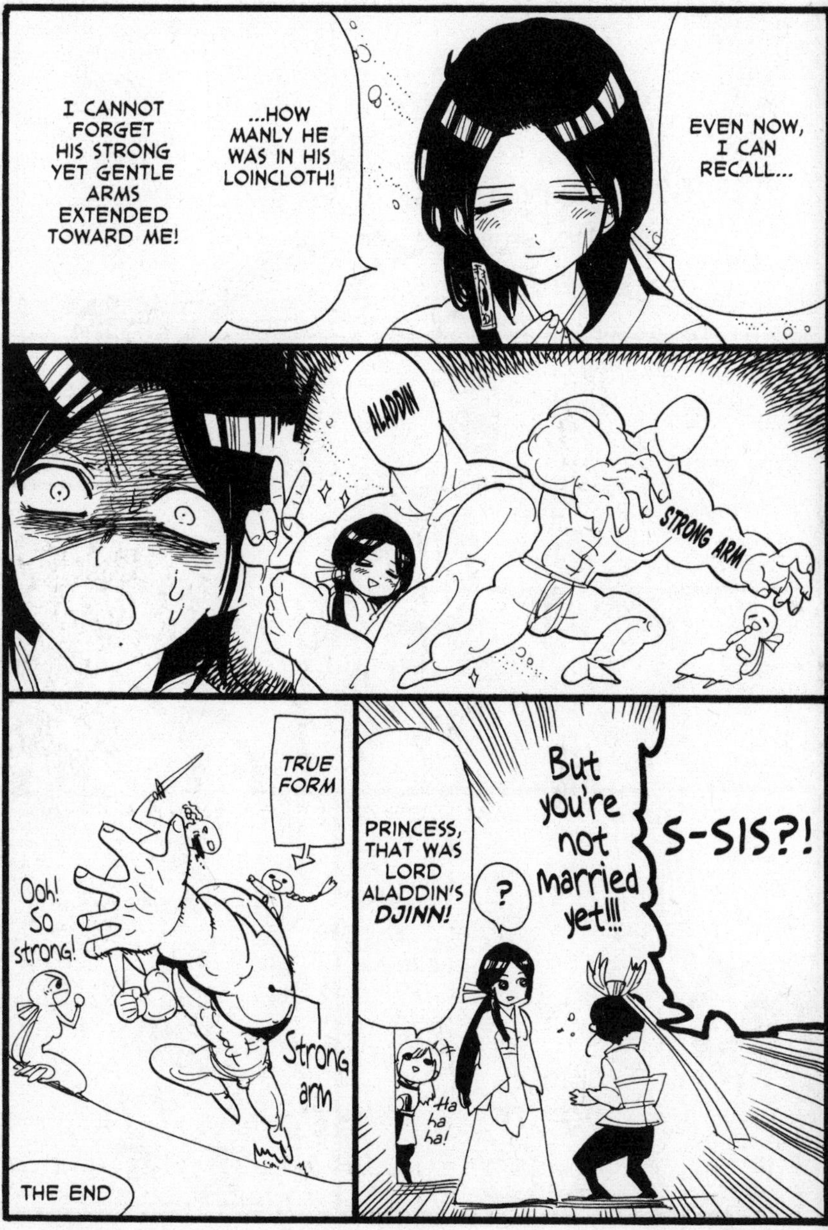
EVEN NOW, I CAN RECALL...
...HOW MANLY HE WAS IN HIS LOINCLOTH!
I CANNOT FORGET HIS STRONG YET GENTLE ARMS EXTENDED TOWARD ME!
ALADDIN
STRONG ARM
S-SIS?!
But you're not married yet!!!
?
PRINCESS, THAT WAS LORD ALADDIN'S *DJINN!*
Ha ha ha!
TRUE FORM
Ooh! So strong!
Strong arm
THE END

BONUS 2
CONTINUING HAKUEI'S VISIT HOME...
CLACK
WHACK
KLONK
BONK
!!
YOU GOT ME!
YOU'VE IMPROVED WHILE YOU WERE AWAY, PRINCE!
...
WH-WHAT'S THE MATTER?!
I DIDN'T THINK YOU HAD CHANGED...
...BUT ARE YOU SHORTER?
You're so tiny!
WHAT?!
IT'S JUST YOU SUDDENLY GREW A LOT!
BUT I'LL CATCH UP WITH YOU!
Ha ha ha!
CATCH UP...?

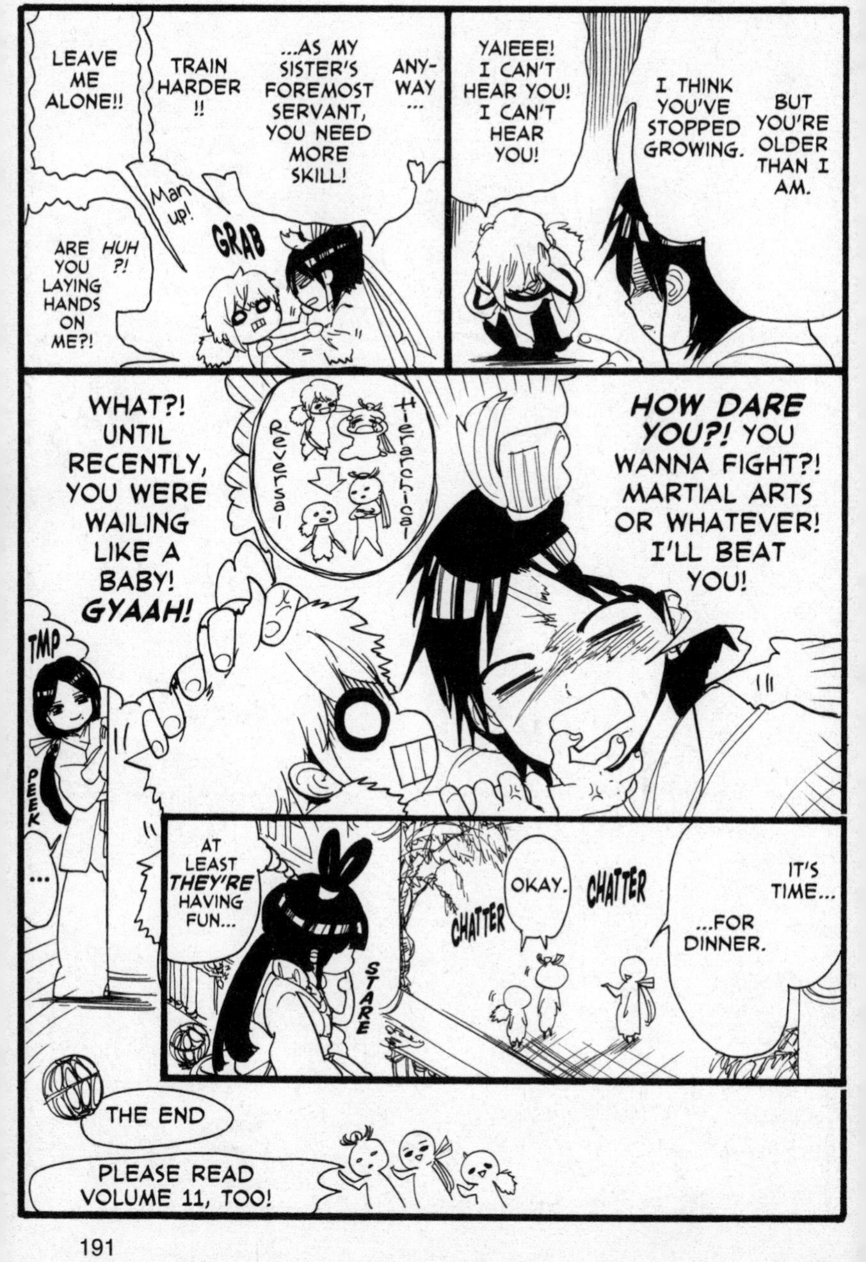
BUT YOU'RE OLDER THAN I AM.
I THINK YOU'VE STOPPED GROWING.
YAIEEE! I CAN'T HEAR YOU! I CAN'T HEAR YOU!
ANY-WAY...
...AS MY SISTER'S FOREMOST SERVANT, YOU NEED MORE SKILL!
TRAIN HARDER!!
Man up!
GRAB
LEAVE ME ALONE!!
HUH?!
ARE YOU LAYING HANDS ON ME?!
*HOW DARE YOU?!* YOU WANNA FIGHT?! MARTIAL ARTS OR WHATEVER! I'LL BEAT YOU!
Hierarchical
Reversal
WHAT?! UNTIL RECENTLY, YOU WERE WAILING LIKE A BABY! *GYAAH!*
TMP
PEEK
...
IT'S TIME...
...FOR DINNER.
CHATTER
OKAY.
CHATTER
AT LEAST *THEY'RE* HAVING FUN...
STARE
THE END
PLEASE READ VOLUME 11, TOO!

**SHINOBU OHTAKA**

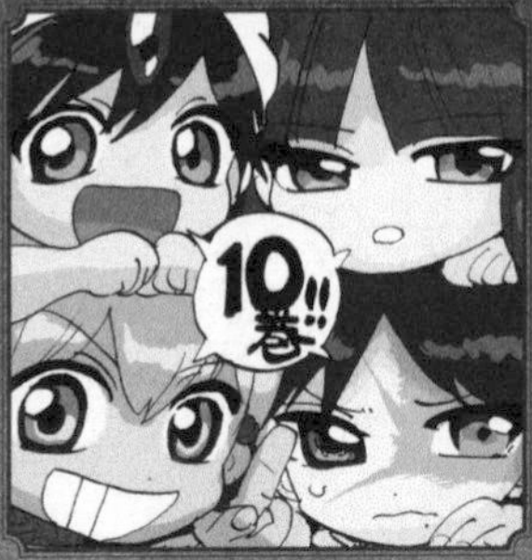
10巻!!

* Volume 10!

*Volume 10's starting!*

# MAGI

## Volume 10
### Shonen Sunday Edition

## Story and Art by
# SHINOBU OHTAKA

MAGI Vol.10
by Shinobu OHTAKA
© 2009 Shinobu OHTAKA
All rights reserved.
Original Japanese edition published by SHOGAKUKAN.
English translation rights in the United States of America, Canada, the United Kingdom,
Ireland, Australia and New Zealand arranged with SHOGAKUKAN.

Translation & English Adaptation ◆ John Werry

Touch-up Art & Lettering ◆ Stephen Dutro

Editor ◆ Mike Montesa

Printed in the U.S.A.

Published by VIZ Media, LLC
P.O. Box 77010
San Francisco, CA 94107

10 9 8 7 6 5 4 3 2 1
First printing, February 2015

**PARENTAL ADVISORY**
MAGI is rated T for Teen.
This volume contains
suggestive themes.
ratings.viz.com

WWW.SHONENSUNDAY.COM

www.viz.com

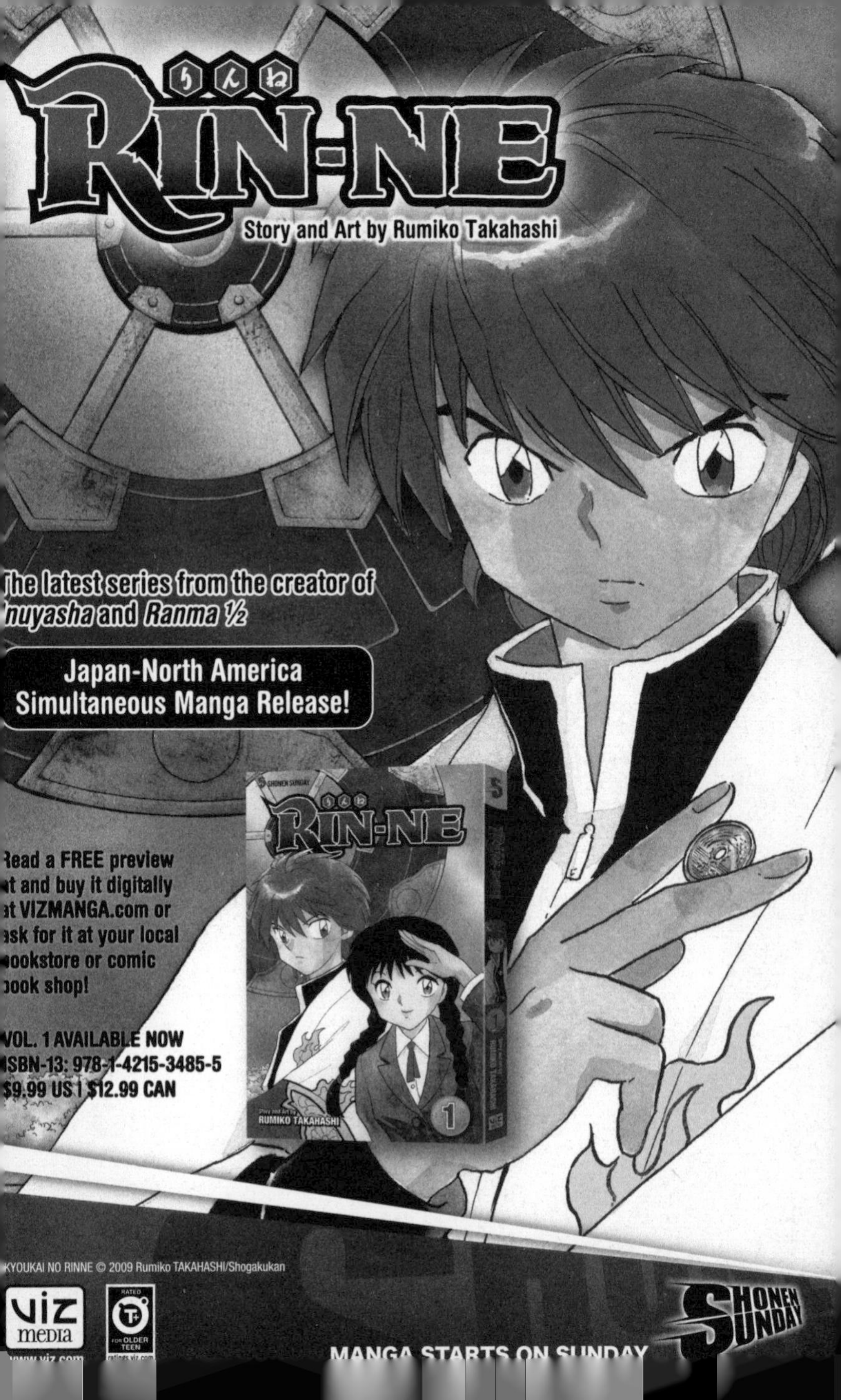

りんね
RIN-NE
Story and Art by Rumiko Takahashi
The latest series from the creator of
Inuyasha and Ranma ½
Japan-North America
Simultaneous Manga Release!
SHONEN SUNDAY
RIN-NE
Story and Art by
RUMIKO TAKAHASHI
1
Read a FREE preview
at and buy it digitally
at VIZMANGA.com or
ask for it at your local
bookstore or comic
book shop!
VOL. 1 AVAILABLE NOW
ISBN-13: 978-1-4215-3485-5
$9.99 US | $12.99 CAN
KYOUKAI NO RINNE © 2009 Rumiko TAKAHASHI/Shogakukan
viz media
RATED T+ FOR OLDER TEEN
SHONEN SUNDAY
MANGA STARTS ON SUNDAY

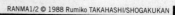

# Ranma ½ Returns!

## REMASTERED AND BETTER THAN EVER!

**One day, teenaged martial artist Ranma Saotome** went on a training mission with his father and ended up taking a dive into some cursed springs at a legendary training ground in China. Now, every time he's splashed with cold water, he changes into a girl. His father, Genma, changes into a panda! What's a half-guy, half-girl to do?

Find out what fueled the worldwide manga boom in beloved creator Rumiko Takahashi's (*Inuyasha*, *Urusei Yatsura*, *RIN-NE*) smash-hit of martial arts mayhem!

Story and Art by Rumiko Takahashi

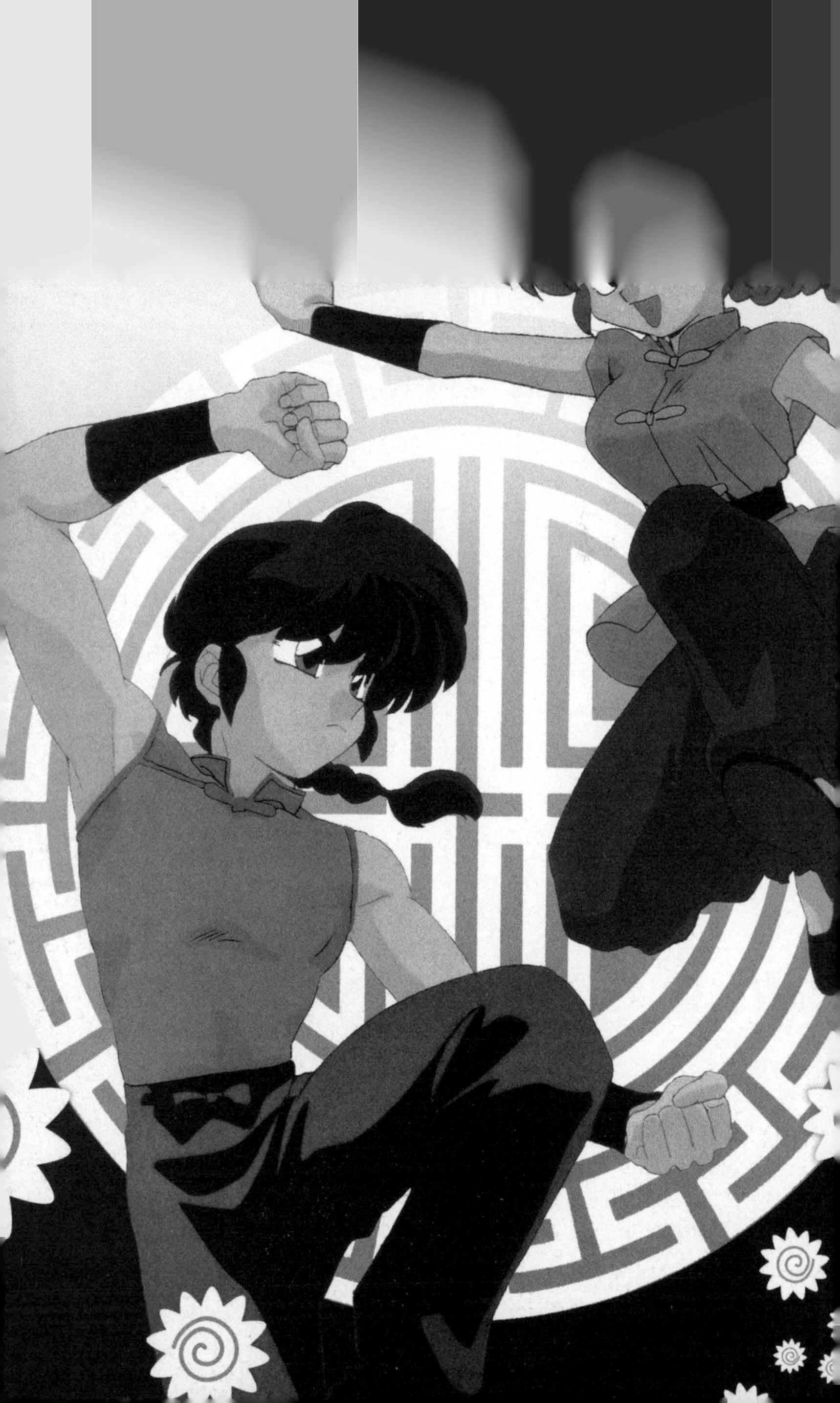

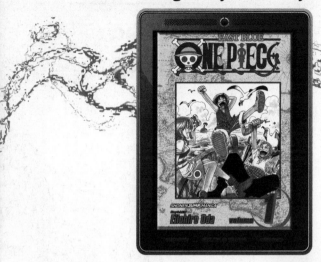

# You're reading the
# WRONG WAY

◇◇◇◇◇◇◇◇◇◇◇◇◇◇◇◇◇◇◇◇◇◇◇◇◇◇◇◇◇◇◇◇◇

**MAGI** reads from right to left, starting in the upper-right corner. Japanese is read from **right** to **left**, meaning that action, sound effects, and word-balloon order are completely reversed from English order.

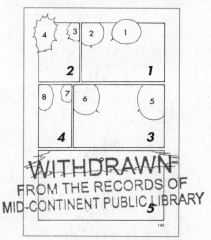